You met Althea in *Night Shift.*
Here, she meets her match....

"You could let me come home with you tonight...." Colt said with a grin.

Althea stared at him. "In your dreams, Nightshade."

He lifted a brow. Her voice hadn't been quite steady. He liked that—a whole lot. He was positive that only a privileged few had ever seen the lieutenant flustered. "Well, there's truth in that, darling. And I'm not willing to wait much longer to turn that dream into reality." He flicked a finger down her hair. "I want you, Althea, and I want you bad."

"It seems to me that you want a great many things. You want to find the missing girl, you want the men responsible caught. And—" she sipped her wine, her eyes cool and level "—you want to go to bed with me."

Colt leaned back against the counter. "That about sums it up. Now, why don't you tell me what *you* want?"

Dear Reader,

We've got a book this month that every romance reader will want to add to her personal collection, the conclusion of *New York Times* bestselling author Nora Roberts's *Night Tales*. It's called *Nightshade*, and it's also our American Hero title this month. And once you know those three facts, what else is there to say? Except—of course—don't miss it!

We've got lots more great reading for you, too. Diana Whitney's back with *Midnight Stranger*, the sequel to her popular *Still Married*, her first book for the Intimate Moments line. Carla Cassidy, a popular writer in several of our other lines— including spooky newcomer Shadows—debuts with *One of the Good Guys*. Marilyn Tracy is back with *Extreme Justice*, Elley Crain returns with *New Year's Resolution*, and new author Suzette Vann makes a promising first appearance with *His Other Mother*.

Once again, Intimate Moments is the place to be if you're looking for some of the best romantic reading to be found anywhere.

As always, enjoy!

Yours,

Leslie Wainger
Senior Editor and Editorial Coordinator

AMERICAN HERO

NIGHTSHADE

Nora
Roberts

Silhouette®
INTIMATE MOMENTS®
Published by Silhouette Books
America's Publisher of Contemporary Romance

For Dan

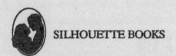 SILHOUETTE BOOKS

ISBN 0-373-07529-4

NIGHTSHADE

Copyright © 1993 by Nora Roberts

This edition published by arrangement with Harlequin Enterprises B. V.

® and TM are trademarks of Harlequin Enterprises B. V., used under
license. Trademarks indicated with ® are registered in the United States
Patent and Trademark Office, the Canadian Trade Marks Office and in
other countries.

Printed in U.S.A.

NORA ROBERTS

is one of Silhouette Books' most popular and prolific authors as well as a *New York Times* bestseller. She has contributed to every Silhouette line and several short story collections. Demand for early titles has been so great that they are being brought back as part of a special "Language of Love" collection.

Nora was the first author inducted into the Romance Writers of America's Hall of Fame and has received awards for her fiction, her creativity, her sales and her contribution to the genre. She has received lifetime achievement awards from the Romance Writers of America, Waldenbooks and *Romantic Times* magazine, and bestselling title and series awards from booksellers, readers and peers for individual titles.

Nora Roberts is a consummate storyteller. Her generous spirit, humor, creativity, willingness to take chances and commitment to her characters, her writing and, most especially, her readers, have earned her fame worldwide.

Prologue

It was a hell of a place to meet a snitch. A cold night, a dark street, with the smell of whiskey and sweat seeping through the pores of the bar door at his back. Colt drew easily on a slim cigar as he studied the spindly bag of bones who'd agreed to sell him information. Not much to look at, Colt mused—short, skinny, and ugly as homemade sin. In the garish light tossed fitfully by the neon sign behind them, his informant looked almost comical.

But there was nothing funny about the business at hand.

"You're a hard man to pin down, Billings."

"Yeah, yeah..." Billings nibbled on a grimy thumb, his gaze sweeping up and down the street. "A guy keeps healthy that way. Heard you were looking for me." He studied Colt, his eyes flying up, then away, soaring on nerves. "Man in my position has to be careful, you know? What you want to buy, it don't come cheap. And it's dangerous. I'd feel better with my cop. Generally I work through the cop, but I ain't been able to get through all day."

"I'd feel better without your cop. And I'm the one who's paying." To illustrate his point, Colt drew two fifties from his shirt pocket. He watched Billings's eyes dart toward the bills and linger greedily. Colt might be a man who'd take risks, but buying a pig in a poke wasn't his style. He held the money out of reach.

"Talk better if I had a drink." Billings jerked his head toward the doorway of the bar behind them. A woman's laugh, high and shrill, burst through the glass like a gunshot.

"You talk just fine to me." The man was a bundle of raw nerves, Colt observed. He could almost hear the thin bones rattle together as Billings shifted from foot to foot. If he didn't press his point now, the man was going to run like a rabbit. And he'd come too far and had too much at stake to lose him now. "Tell me what I need to know, then I'll buy you a drink."

"You're not from around here."

"No." Colt lifted a brow, waited. "Is that a problem?"

"Nope. Better you aren't. They get wind of you..." Billings swiped the back of his hand over his mouth. "Well, you look like you can handle yourself okay."

"I've been known to." He took one last drag before flicking the cigar away. Its single red eye gleamed in the gutter. "Information, Billings." To show good faith, Colt held out one of the bills. "Let's do business."

Even as Billings's eager fingers reached out, the frigid air was shattered by the shriek of tires on pavement.

Colt didn't have to read the terror in Billings's eyes. Adrenaline and instinct took over, with a kick as quick and hard as a mule's. He was diving for cover as the first shots rang out.

Chapter 1

Althea didn't mind being bored. After a rough day, a nice spot of tedium could be welcome, giving both mind and body a chance to recharge. She didn't really mind coming off a tough ten-hour shift after an even more grueling sixty-hour week and donning cocktail wear or slipping her tired feet into three-inch heels. She wouldn't even complain about being stuck at a banquet table in the ballroom of the Brown House while speech after droning speech muddled her head.

What she *did* mind was having her date's hand slide up her thigh under cover of the white linen table-cloth.

Men were so predictable.

She picked up her wineglass and, shifting in her seat, nuzzled her date's ear. "Jack?"

His fingers crept higher. "Mmm-hmm?"

"If you don't move your hand—say, within the next two seconds—I'm going to stab it, really, really hard, with my dessert fork. It would hurt, Jack." She sat back and sipped her wine, smiling over the rim as he arched a brow. "You wouldn't play racket ball for a month."

Jack Holmsby, eligible bachelor, feared prosecutor, and guest of honor at the Denver Bar Association Banquet, knew how to handle women. And he'd been trying to get close enough to handle this particular woman for months.

"Thea . . ." He breathed her name, gifting her with his most charming, crooked smile. "We're nearly done here. Why don't we go back to my place? We can . . ." He whispered into her ear a suggestion that was descriptive, inventive and possibly anatomically impossible.

Althea was saved from answering—and Jack was spared minor surgery—by the sound of her beeper. Several of her tablemates began shifting, checking pockets and purses. Inclining her head, she rose.

"Pardon me. I believe it's mine." She walked away with a subtle switch of hips, a long flash of leg. The compact body in the backless purple dress glinting with silver beading caused more than one head to turn. Blood pressures were elevated. Fantasies were woven.

Not unaware, but certainly unconcerned, Althea strode out of the ballroom and into the lobby, toward a bank of phones. Opening her beaded evening bag, which contained a compact, lipstick, ID, emergency cash and her nine-millimeter, she fished out a quarter and made her call.

"Grayson." While she listened, she pushed back her fall of flame-colored hair. Her eyes, a tawny shade of brown, narrowed. "I'm on my way."

She hung up, turned and watched Jack Holmsby hurry toward her. An attractive man, she thought objectively. Nicely polished on the outside. A pity he was so ordinary on the inside.

"Sorry, Jack. I have to go."

Irritation scored a deep line between his brows. He had a bottle of Napoleon brandy, a stack of apple wood and a set of white satin sheets waiting at home. "Really, Thea, can't someone else take the call?"

"No." The job came first. It always came first. "It's handy I had to meet you here, Jack. You can stay and enjoy yourself."

But he wasn't giving up that easily. He dogged her through the lobby and out into the brisk fall night. "Why don't you come by after you've finished? We can pick up where we left off."

"We haven't left off, Jack." She handed her parking stub to an attendant. "You have to start to leave off, and I have no intention of starting anything with you."

She only sighed as he slipped his arms around her. "Come on, Thea, you didn't come here tonight to eat prime rib and listen to a bunch of lawyers make endless speeches." He lowered his head and murmured against her lips, "You didn't wear a dress like that to keep me at arm's length. You wore it to make me hot. And you did."

Mild irritation became brittle and keen. "I came here tonight because I respect you as a lawyer." The quick elbow to his ribs had his breath woofing out and allowed her to step back. "And because I thought we could spend a pleasant evening together. What I wear is my business, Holmsby, but I didn't choose it so that you'd grope me under the table or make ludicrous suggestions as to how I might spend the rest of my evening.''

She wasn't shouting, but neither was she bothering to keep her voice down. Anger glinted in her voice, like ice under fog. Appalled, Jack tugged at the knot of his tie and darted glances right and left.

"For God's sake, Althea, keep it down."

"Exactly what I was going to suggest to you," she said sweetly.

Though the attendant was all eyes and ears, he politely cleared his throat. Althea turned to accept her keys. "Thank you." She offered him a smile and a generous tip. The smile had his heart skipping a beat, and he didn't glance at the bill before tucking it into his pocket. He was too busy dreaming.

"Ah...drive carefully, miss. And come back soon. Real soon."

"Thanks." She tossed her hair back, then slid gracefully behind the wheel of her reconditioned Mustang convertible. "See you in court, Counselor." Althea gunned the engine and peeled out.

Murder scenes, whether indoors or out, in an urban, suburban or pastoral setting, had one thing in common: the aura of death. As a cop with nearly ten years' experience, Althea had learned to recognize it, absorb it and file it away, while going about the precise and mechanical business of investigation.

When Althea arrived, a half block had been secured. The police photographer had finished recording the scene and was already packing up his gear. The body had been identified. That was why she was here.

Three black-and-whites sat, their lights flashing blue and their radios coughing static. Spectators—for death always drew them—were straining against the yellow police tape, greedy, Althea knew, for a glimpse of death to reaffirm that they were alive and untouched.

Because the night was cool, she grabbed the wrap she'd tossed into the back seat of her car. The emerald-green silk kept the chill off her arms and back. Flashing her badge to the rookie handling crowd control, she slipped under the barricade. She was grateful when she spotted Sweeney, a hard-bitten cop who had twice her years on the job and was in no hurry to give up his uniform.

"Lieutenant." He nodded to her, then took out a handkerchief and made a valiant attempt to clear his stuffy nose.

"What have we got here, Sweeney?"

"Drive-by." He stuffed the handkerchief back into his pocket. "Dead guy was standing in front of the bar, talking." He gestured to the shattered window of the Tick Tock. "Witnesses say a car came by, moving north, fast. Sprayed the area with bullets and kept going."

She could still smell the blood, though it was no longer fresh. "Any bystanders hit?"

"Nope. Couple of cuts from flying glass, that's all. They hit their mark." He glanced over his shoulder, and down. "He didn't have a chance, Lieutenant. Sorry."

"Yeah, me too." She stared down at the form sprawled on the stained concrete. There'd been nothing much to him to begin with, she thought. Now there was less. He'd been five-five, maybe a hundred and ten soaking wet, spindly bones and had had a face even a mother would have been hard-pressed to love.

Wild Bill Billings, part-time pimp, part-time grifter and full-time snitch.

And, damn it, he'd been hers.

"Forensics?"

"Been and gone," Sweeney confirmed. "We're ready to put him on ice."

"Then do it. Got a list of witnesses?"

"Yeah, mostly useless. It was a black car, it was a blue car. One drunk claims it was a chariot driven by flaming demons." He swore with inventive expertise, knowing Althea well enough not to worry about her taking offense.

"We'll take what we can get." She scanned the crowd—bar types, teenagers looking for action, a scattering of the homeless and—

Her antenna vibrated as she locked in on one man. Unlike the others, he wasn't goggle-eyed with either revulsion or excitement. He stood at his ease, his leather bomber jacket open to the wind, revealing a chambray shirt, a glint of silver on a chain. His rangy build made her think he'd be fast on his feet. Snug, worn jeans rode down long legs and ended at scuffed boots. Hair that might have been dark blond or brown ruffled in the breeze and curled well over his collar.

He smoked a thin cigar, his eyes scanning the scene as hers had. The light wasn't good, but she decided he looked tanned, which suited the sharply defined face. The eyes were deep-set, and the nose was long, and just shy of being narrow. The mouth was strong, the kind that looked as though it could thin into a sneer easily.

Some instinct had her dubbing him a pro before his eyes shifted and locked on hers with an impact like a bare-fisted punch.

"Who's the cowboy, Sweeney?"

"The— Oh." Sweeney's tired face creased in what might have been a smile. Damned if she hadn't called it, he thought. The guy looked as though he should be wearing a Stetson and riding a mustang. "Witness," he told her. "Victim was talking to him when he got hit."

"It that so?" She didn't look around when the coroner's team dealt with the body. There was no need to.

"He's the only one to give us a coherent account." Sweeney pulled out his pad, wet his thumb and flipped pages. "Says it was a black '91 Buick sedan, Colorado plates Able Charlie Frank. Says he missed the numbers 'cause the plate lights were out and he was a little busy diving for cover. Says the weapon sounded like an AK-47."

"Sounded like?" Interesting, she thought. She'd kept her eyes level with her witness's. "Maybe—" She broke off when she spotted her captain crossing the street. Captain Boyd Fletcher walked directly to the witness, shook his head, then grinned and enveloped the other man in the masculine equivalent of an embrace. There was a lot of back-thumping.

"Looks as though the captain's handling him for now." Althea pocketed her curiosity as she would a treat to be saved for later. "Let's finish up here, Sweeney."

Colt had watched her from the moment one long, smooth leg swung out of the door of the Mustang. A lady like that was worth watching—well worth it. He'd liked the way she moved—with an athletic and economical grace that wasted neither time nor energy. Certainly he'd liked the way she looked. Her neat, sexy little body had just enough curves to whet a man's appetite, and with all that green-and-purple silk rippling in the wind... The sunburst of hair, blowing away from a cool cameo face, brought much more interesting things to a man's mind than his grandmother's heirloom jewelry.

It was a cold night, and one look at that well-packed number had Colt thinking about heat.

It wasn't such a bad way to keep warm while he waited. He wasn't a man who waited well under the best of circumstances.

He hadn't been particularly surprised to see her flash ID to the baby-faced cop at the barricade. She carried authority beautifully on her luscious swimmer's shoulders. Idly lighting a cigar, he decided she was an assistant D.A., then realized his error when she went into conference with Sweeney.

The lady had *cop* written all over her.

Late twenties, he figured, maybe five-four without those ankle-wrecking heels, and a tidy one-ten.

They sure were making cops in interesting packages these days.

So he waited, sizing up the scene. He didn't have any feelings one way or the other about the remains of Wild Bill Billings. The man was no good to him now.

He'd dig up something, or someone, else. Colt Nightshade wasn't a man to let murder get in his way.

When he felt her watching him, he drew smoke in lazily, chuffed it out. Then he shifted his gaze until it met hers. The tightening in his gut was unexpected— it was raw and purely sexual. The one fleeting instant when his mind was wiped clean as glass was more than unexpected. It was unprecedented. Power slapped against power. She took a step toward him. He let out the breath he'd just realized he was holding.

His preoccupation made it easy for Boyd to come up behind him and catch him unawares.

"Colt! Son of a bitch!"

Colt turned, braced and ready for anything. But the flat intensity in his eyes faded into a grin that might have melted any woman within twenty paces.

"Fletch." With the easy warmth he reserved for friends, Colt returned the bear hug before stepping back to take stock. He hadn't seen Boyd in nearly ten years. It relieved him to see that so little had changed. "Still got that pretty face, don't you?"

"And you still sound like you've just ridden in off the range. God, it's good to see you. When'd you get into town?"

"Couple of days ago. I wanted to take care of some business before I got in touch."

Boyd looked past him to where the coroner's van was being loaded. "Was that your business?"

"Part of it. I appreciate you coming down like this."

"Yeah." Boyd spotted Althea, acknowledging her with an imperceptible nod. "Did you call a cop, Colt, or a friend?"

Colt looked down at the stub of his cigar, dropped it near the gutter and crushed it with his boot. "It's handy, you being both."

"Did you kill that guy?"

It was asked so matter-of-factly, that Colt grinned again. He knew Boyd wouldn't have turned a hair if he'd confessed then and there. "Nope."

Boyd nodded again. "Going to fill me in?"

"Yep."

"Why don't you wait in the car? I'll be with you in a minute."

"*Captain* Boyd Fletcher." Colt shook his head and chuckled. Though it was after midnight, he was as alert as he was relaxed, a cup of bad coffee in his hand and his scruffy boots propped on Boyd's desk. "Ain't that just something?"

"I thought you were raising horses and cattle in Wyoming."

"I do." His voice was a drawl, with the faintest whisper of a twang. "Now and again I do."

"What happened to the law degree?"

"Oh, it's around somewhere."

"And the air force?"

"I still fly. Just don't wear a uniform anymore. How long's it going to take for that pizza to get here?"

"Just long enough for it to be cold and inedible." Boyd leaned back in his chair. He was comfortable in his office. He was comfortable on the street. And, as he had been twenty years ago, in their prep school days, he was comfortable with Colt.

"You didn't get a look at the shooter?"

"Hell, Fletch, I was lucky to make the car before I was diving for cover and chewing asphalt. Not that that's going to help much. Odds are it was stolen."

"Lieutenant Grayson's tracking it. Now, why don't you tell me what you were doing with Wild Bill?"

"He contacted me. I've bee—" He broke off when Althea strolled in. She hadn't bothered to knock, and she was carrying a flat cardboard box.

"You two order pizza?" She dropped the box onto Boyd's desk, held out a hand. "Ten bucks, Fletcher."

"Althea Grayson, Colt Nightshade. Colt's an old friend." Boyd dug ten dollars out of his wallet. After folding the bill neatly and tucking it in a pocket of her purse, she set her beaded bag on a stack of files.

"Mr. Nightshade."

"Ms. Grayson."

"*Lieutenant* Grayson," she corrected. Popping up the lid on the box, she perused the contents, chose a slice. "I believe you were at my crime scene."

"Sure did look that way." He lowered his legs so that he could lean forward and take a piece himself. He caught her scent over the aroma of cooling sausage pizza. It was a whole lot more tantalizing.

"Thanks," she murmured when Boyd passed her a napkin. "I wonder what you were doing there, getting shot at with my snitch."

Colt's eyes narrowed. "Your snitch?"

"That's right." Like his hair, his eyes couldn't seem to decide what color they should be, Althea thought. They were caught somewhere between blue and green. And at the moment they were as cold as the wind whipping at the window.

"Bill told me he tried to reach his police contact off and on all day."

"I was in the field."

Colt's brow arched as he skimmed his gaze over the swirl of emerald silk. "Some field."

"Lieutenant Grayson spent all day putting the cap on a drug operation," Boyd interjected. "Now, kids, why don't we start over, and at the beginning?"

"Fine." Setting her half-eaten slice down, Althea wiped her fingers, then removed her wrap. Colt clenched his teeth to keep his tongue from falling out. Because she was turned away from him, Colt had the painful pleasure of gauging just how alluring a naked back could be when it was slim, straight and framed in purple silk.

After laying her coat over a file cabinet, Althea reclaimed her pizza and sat on the corner of Boyd's desk.

She knew just what she did to a man, Colt realized. He could see that smug, faintly amused female knowledge in her eyes. Colt had always figured every woman knew her own arsenal down to the last eyelash, but it was tough on a man when the woman was as heavily armed as this.

"Wild Bill, Mr. Nightshade..." Althea began. "What were you doing with him?"

"Talking." He knew his answer was obstinate, but at the moment he was trying to judge whether there was anything between the sexy lieutenant and his old friend. His old *married* friend, Colt mused. He was relieved, and more than a little surprised not to scent even a whiff of attraction between them.

"About?" Althea's voice was still patient, even pleasant. As if, Colt thought, she were questioning a small boy who was mentally deficient.

"The victim was Thea's snitch," Boyd reminded Colt. "If she wants the case—"

"And I do."

"Then it's hers."

To buy himself time, Colt reached for another slice of pizza. He was going to have to do something he hated, something that stuck in his craw like bad beef jerky. He was going to have to ask for help. And to get it he was going to have to share what he knew.

"It took me two days to track down Billings and get him to agree to talk to me." It had also cost him two hundred in bribes to clear the path, but he wasn't one to count the cost until the final tally. "He was nervous, didn't really want to talk unless he had his police contact with him. So I made it worth his while."

He glanced back at Althea. The lady was wiped out, he realized. The fatigue was hard to spot, but it was there—in the slight drooping of her eyelids, the faint shadows under them.

"I'm sorry you lost him, but I don't think your being there would have changed anything."

"We won't know that, will we?" She wouldn't let the regret color her voice, or her judgment. "Why did you go to so much trouble to contact Bill?"

"He used to have a girl working for him. Jade. Probably her street name."

Althea let her mind click back, nodded. "Yeah. Little blonde, babyface. She took a couple of busts for solicitation. I'll have to check, but I don't think she's worked the stroll for four or five weeks."

"That'd be about right." Colt rose to fill his cup with more of the sludge from the automatic brewer. "It would have been about that long ago that Billings got her a job. In the movies." If he was going to drink poison, he'd take it like a man, without any cream or sugar to cut the bite. Sipping, he turned back. "I ain't talking Hollywood. This was the down-and-dirty stuff, for private viewers who have the taste and the money to buy thrills. Videotapes for hard-core connoisseurs." He shrugged and sat again. "Can't say it bothers me any, if we're talking about consenting adults. Though I prefer my sex in the flesh."

"But we're not talking about you, Mr. Nightshade."

"Oh, you don't have to call me *mister*, Lieutenant. Seems cold, when we're discussing such warm topics." Smiling, he leaned back. He had yet to ruffle her feathers, and for reasons he wasn't going to take the time to explore, he wanted to ruffle them good and proper. "Well, as it happens, something spooked Jade and she lit out. I'm not one to think a hooker's got a heart of gold, but this one at least had a conscience. She sent off a letter to a Mr. and Mrs. Frank Cook." He shifted his gaze to Boyd. "Frank and Marleen Cook."

"Marleen?" Boyd's brows shot up. "Marleen and Frank?"

"The same." Colt's smile was wry. "More old friends, Lieutenant. As it happens, I was what you might call intimate friends with Mrs. Cook about a million years ago. Being a woman of sound judgment, she married Frank, settled down in Albuquerque and had herself a couple of beautiful kids."

Althea shifted, crossed her legs with a rustle of silk. The silver dangling over his shirt was a Saint Christopher medal, she noted. The patron saint of travelers. She wondered if Mr. Nightshade felt the need for spiritual protection.

"I assume this is leading somewhere other than down memory lane?"

"Oh, it's leading right back to your professional front door, Lieutenant. I just prefer the circular route now and then." He took out a cigar, running it through his long fingers before reaching for his lighter. "About a month ago, Marleen's oldest girl—that's Elizabeth. You ever meet Liz, Boyd?"

Boyd shook his head. He didn't like where this was heading. Not one bit. "Not since she was in diapers. What is she, twelve?"

"Thirteen. Just." Colt flicked his lighter on, sucked his cigar to life. Thought he knew, all too well, that the tang of smoke wouldn't cloud the bitter taste in his throat. "Pretty as a picture, like her mama. Got Marleen's hair-trigger temper, too. There was some trouble at home, the kind I imagine most families have some time or other. But Liz got her back up and took off."

"She ran away?" Althea understood the runaway's mind well. Too well.

"Tossed a few things in her backpack and took off. Needless to say, Marleen and Frank have been living in hell the past few weeks. They contacted the police, but the official route wasn't getting them very far." He blew out smoke. "No offense. Ten days ago they called me."

"Why?" Althea asked.

"Told you. We're friends."

"Do you usually track down pimps and dodge bullets for friends?"

She had a way with sarcasm, all right, Colt mused. It was one more weapon in the arsenal. "I do favors for people."

"Are you a licensed investigator?"

Pursing his lips, Colt studied the tip of his cigar. "I'm not big on licenses. I put out some feelers, had a little luck tracing her north. Then the Cooks got Jade's letter." Clamping his cigar between his teeth, he drew a folded sheet of floral stationery from his inside jacket pocket. "Save time if you read it yourself," he said, and passed it to Boyd. Althea rose, going behind Boyd's back, laying a hand on his shoulder as she read with him.

It was a curiously intimate and yet asexual gesture. One, Colt decided, that spoke of friendship and trust.

The handwriting was as girlishly fussy as the paper. But the content, Althea noted, had nothing to do with flowers and ribbons and childhood fancies.

Dear Mr. and Mrs. Cook,
I met Liz in Denver. She is a nice kid. I know she is really sorry she ran away and would come back now if she could. I would help her out, but I got to get out of town. Liz is in trouble. I would go to the cops, but I'm scared and I don't think they listen to someone like me. She is not cut out for the life, but they won't let her go. She is young and so pretty, and they are making lots of money from the movies I think. I have been in the life for five years, but some of the stuff they want us to do for the camera gives me the creeps. I think they killed one of the girls, so I am getting out before they kill me. Liz gave me your address and asked me to write and say she was sorry. She's real scared and I hope you find her okay.

Jade

P.S. They have a place up in the mountains where they do the movies. And there is an apartment on Second Avenue.

Boyd didn't give the letter back, but laid it on his desk. He had a daughter of his own. He thought of Allison, sweet, feisty and six, and had to swallow a hot ball of sick rage.

"You could have come to me with this. You *should* have come to me."

"I'm used to working alone." Colt drew on his cigar again before tamping it out. "In any case, I intended to come to you after I put a few things together. I got the name of Jade's pimp, and I wanted to shake him down."

"And now he's dead." Althea's voice was flat as she turned to stare out of Boyd's window.

"Yeah." Colt studied her profile. It wasn't just anger he felt from her. There was a lot more mixed up with it. "Word must have gotten back that I was looking for him, and that he was willing to talk to me. Leads me to think that we're dealing with well-connected slime, and slime that doesn't blink at murder."

"This is a police matter, Colt," Boyd said quietly.

"No argument." Ready to deal, he spread his hands. "It's also a personal matter. I'm going to keep digging, Fletch. There's no law against it. I'm the Cooks' representative—their lawyer, if we need a handle."

"Is that what you are?" Her emotions under control again, Althea turned back to him. "A lawyer?"

"When it suits me. I don't want to interfere with your investigation," he said to Boyd. "I want the kid back—safely back—with Marleen and Frank. I'll cooperate completely. Anything I know, you'll know. But it has to be quid pro quo. Give me a cop to work with on this, Boyd." He smiled a little—just a quirk at the corner of his mouth, as if he were amused at himself. "And you of all people know how much I hate asking for an official partner on a job. But it's Liz that matters, all that matters. You know I'm good."

He leaned forward. "You know I won't back off. Let me have your best man, and let's get these bastards."

Boyd pressed his fingers to his tired eyes. He could, of course, order Colt to back off. And he'd be wasting his breath. He could refuse to cooperate, could refuse to share any information the department unearthed. And Colt would work around him. Yes, he knew Colt was good, and he had some idea of the kind of work he'd done while in the military.

It would hardly be the first time Boyd Fletcher had bent the rules. His decision made, he gestured toward Althea.

"She's my best man."

Chapter 2

If a man had to have a partner, she might as well be easy on the eyes. In any case, Colt didn't intend to work *with* Althea so much as *through* her. She would be his conduit to the official end of the investigation. He'd keep his word—he always did, except when he didn't—and feed her whatever information he gleaned. Not that he expected her to do much with it.

There were only a handful of cops Colt respected, with Boyd topping the list. As far as Lieutenant Grayson was concerned, Colt figured she'd be decorative, marginally helpful and little else.

The badge, the bod and the sarcasm would probably be useful when it came to interviewing any possible connections.

At least he'd had a decent night's sleep—all six hours of it. He hadn't protested when Boyd insisted he check out of his hotel and check into the Fletcher household for the duration of his stay. Colt liked families—other people's, in any case—and he'd been curious about Boyd's wife.

He'd missed their wedding. Though he wasn't particularly fond of the spit and polish ceremonies called for, he would have gone. But it was a long way from Beirut to Denver, and he'd been busy with terrorists at the time.

He was delighted with Cilla. The woman hadn't turned a hair at having her husband bring home a strange man at 2:00 a.m. Bundled in a terry-cloth robe, she'd offered him the guest room, with the suggestion that if he wanted to sleep in he should put the pillow over his head. The kids apparently rose at seven to get ready for school.

He'd slept like a rock, and when he'd awakened to the sounds of shouts and clomping feet, he'd taken his hostess's advice and had caught another hour of sleep with his head buried.

Now, fortified by an excellent breakfast and three cups of first-class coffee prepared by the Fletchers' housekeeper, he was ready to roll.

His agreement with Boyd made the precinct house his first stop. He'd check in with Althea, grill her on any associates of Billings's, then go his own way.

It seemed to him that his old friend ran a tight ship. There was the usual din of ringing phones, clattering keyboards and raised voices inside the station. There were the usual scents of coffee, industrial-strength cleaners and sweaty bodies. But there was also an underlying sense of organization and purpose.

The desk sergeant had Colt's name, and he handed him a visitor's badge and directed him to Althea's office. Past the bull pen, and two doors down a narrow corridor he found her door. It was shut, so he rapped

once before pushing it open. He knew she was there
before he saw her. He scented her, as a wolf scents his
mate. Or his prey.

Gone were the bold silks, but she still looked more
the fashion plate than the cop. The tailored slacks and
jacket in smoke gray did nothing to suggest masculin-
ity. Nor did he think she chose to deny her sex, for
she'd accented the suit with a soft pink blouse and a
star-shaped jeweled lapel pin. Her mass of hair had
been trained back in some complicated braid that left
her face softly framed. Two heavy twists of gold
glinted at her ears.

The result was as neat as any maiden aunt could
want, and still had the knockout punch of frosted sex.

A lesser man might have licked his lips.

"Grayson."

"Nightshade." She gestured toward a chair. "Have
a seat."

There was only one to spare, straight-backed and
wood. Colt turned it around and straddled it. As he
did, he noted that her office was less than half the size
of Boyd's, and ruthlessly organized. File drawers were
neatly closed, papers properly stacked, pencils sharp-
ened to lethal points. There was a plant on one of the
rear corners of the desk that he was sure was meticulously watered. There were no pictures of family or
friends. The only spot of color in the small, window-
less room was a painting, an abstract in vivid blues,
greens and reds. Slashes of colors that clashed and
warred, rather than melded.

Some instinct told him it suited her down to the
ground.

"So." He folded his arms over the back of the chair and leaned forward. "You run the shooter's car through Motor Vehicles?"

"Didn't have to. It was on this morning's hot sheet." She took her copy and offered it. "Reported stolen at eleven o'clock last night. Owners had been out for dinner, came out of the restaurant and found the car gone. Dr. and Dr. Wilmer, a couple of dentists celebrating their fifth anniversary. Looks like they're clean."

"Probably." He tossed the sheet back onto her desk. He hadn't really believed he'd find a connection through the car. "Don't guess it's turned up?"

"Not yet. I've got Jade's rap sheet, if you're interested." After replacing the hot sheet in its proper place, she picked up a file. "Janice Willowby. Age twenty-two. Couple of busts for solicitation—a few charges as a juvie for more of the same. One possession arrest, also as a juvenile, when she got rousted with a couple of joints in her purse. Went through the social services route, a halfway house, counseling, then turned twenty-one and went back on the streets."

It wasn't a new story. "Have we got any family? She might head home."

"A mother in Kansas City—or she was in Kansas City as of eighteen months ago. I'm trying to track her down."

"You've been busy."

"Not all of us start our day at—" she looked down at her watch "—ten."

"I do better at night, Lieutenant." He took out a cigar.

Althea eyed it, shook her head. "Not in here, pal."

Agreeably Colt tapped the cigar back into his pocket. "Who did Billings trust, other than you?"

"I don't know that he trusted anybody." But it hurt, because she knew he had trusted somebody. He'd trusted her, and somehow she'd missed a step. And now he was dead. "We had an arrangement. I gave him money, he gave me information."

"What kind?"

"With Wild Bill, it came in a variety pack. He had his fingers in a lot of pies. Little pies, mostly." She shifted some papers on her desk, tapping the edges neatly together. "He was strictly small-time, but he had big ears, knew how to fade into the background so you forgot he was around. People talked around him, because he looked like his brain would fit in a teacup. But he was smart." Her voice changed, tipping Colt off to something she had yet to admit even to herself. She was grieving. "Smart enough to keep from crossing the line that would send him up to hard time. Smart enough to keep from stepping on the wrong toes. Until last night."

"I didn't make any secret of the fact I was looking for him, and for information he could give me. But I sure as hell didn't want him dead."

"I'm not blaming you."

"No?"

"No." She pushed away from the desk far enough to allow her to swivel the chair around and face him. "People like Bill, no matter how smart, have short life expectancies. If he'd have been able to contact me, I might have met him at the same spot you did, with the same results." She'd thought that through, carefully, ruthlessly. "I might not like your style, Nightshade, but I'm not pinning this on you."

She sat very still, he noted, no gestures, no shrugs, no restless tapping. Like the painting on the wall behind her, she communicated vibrant passion without movement.

"And just what is my style, Lieutenant?"

"You're a renegade. The kind who doesn't just refuse to play by the rules, but rejoices in breaking them." Her eyes stayed level with his, and were cool as lake water. He wondered what it would take to warm them up. "You start things, but you don't always finish them. Maybe that means you bore easily, or you just run out of energy. Either way, it doesn't say much about your dependability."

Her rundown of his personality annoyed him, but when he spoke again, his slow southwestern drawl was amused. "You figured all that out since last night?"

"I ran a make on you. The prep school where you hung out with Boyd surprised me." Her lips curved, but the eyes had yet to warm. "You don't look like the preppie type."

"My parents thought it would tame me." He grinned. "Guess not."

"Neither did Harvard, where you got your law degree—which you haven't put to much use. Parts of your military career were classified, but all in all, I got the picture." There was a dish of sugared almonds on her desk. Althea leaned over and, after careful deliberation, chose the one she wanted. "I don't work with someone I don't know."

"Me either. So why don't you fill me in on Althea Grayson?"

"I'm the cop," she said simply. "And you're not. I assume you have a recent picture of Elizabeth Cook?"

"Yeah, I got one." But he didn't reach for it. He didn't have to take this kind of bull from some glamourpuss with a badge. "Tell me, Lieutenant, just who jammed a stick up your—"

The phone cut him off, which, considering the flash in Althea's eye, might have been for the best. At least he knew how to defrost those eyes now.

"Grayson." She waited a beat, then jotted something down on a pad. "Notify Forensics. I'm on my way." She rose, tucking the pad into a snakeskin purse. "We found the car." She was frowning when she slung the bag over her shoulder. "Since Boyd wants you in, you can come along for the ride—as an observer only. Got it?"

"Oh, yeah. I got it fine."

He followed her out, then quickly moved up so that they walked side by side. The woman had the best rear view this side of the Mississippi, and Colt didn't care to be distracted.

"I didn't have much time to play catch-up with Boyd last night," he began. "I wondered how it was that you're on such . . . easy terms with your captain."

She was walking down the stairs to the garage, and she stopped, turned, aimed one razor-sharp glance.

"What?" he demanded as she assessed him silently.

"I'm trying to decide if you're insulting me and Boyd—in which case I'd have to hurt you—or if you simply phrased your question badly."

He lifted a brow. "Try the second choice."

"All right." She continued down. "We were partners for over seven years." She reached the bottom of the steps and turned sharply to the right. The flat heels of her suede half boots clicked busily on the concrete.

"When you trust someone with your life on a day-to-day basis, you'd better be on easy terms."

"Then he made captain."

"That's right." After taking out her keys, she unlocked her car. "Sorry, but the passenger seat's stuck all the way forward. I haven't had time to take it in and get it fixed."

Colt looked down at the spiffy sports car with some regret. A sexy car, sure, but with the seat in that position, he was going to have to fold himself up like an accordion and sit with his chin on his knees. "And you don't have a problem with that—Boyd's being captain?"

Althea slid in gracefully, smirking a bit as Colt grunted and arranged himself beside her. "No. Am I ambitious? Yes. Do I resent having the best cop I ever worked with as my superior? No. Do I expect to make captain myself within another five years? You bet your butt." She pushed mirrored aviator sunglasses over her eyes. "Fasten your seat belt, Nightshade." With that, she peeled out, shooting up the ramp of the garage and out onto the street.

He had to admire her driving. He had no choice, since she was behind the wheel and his life was in her hands. Easy terms? he wondered. Yeah, right. "So, you and Boyd are friends."

"That's right. Why?"

"I just wanted to establish that it wasn't all good-looking men of a certain age who put your back up." He grinned at her as she downshifted around a corner. "I like knowing it's just me. Makes me feel kind of special, you know?"

She smiled then and shot him what could have been a friendly look. It certainly was no more than friendly, and it really shouldn't have had his heart doing a slow roll in his chest. "I wouldn't say you put my back up, Nightshade. I just don't trust hotdoggers. But since we're both after the same thing here, and since Boyd's a pal on both sides, we can try to get along."

"Sounds reasonable. We've got the job and Boyd in common. Maybe we can find a couple of other things." Her radio was turned down low. Colt flicked the volume up and nodded approval at the slow, pulse-pumping blues. "There, that's one more thing. How do you feel about Mexican food?"

"I like my chili hot and my margaritas cold."

"Progress." He tried to shift in his seat, rapped his knee on the dash, and swore. "If we're going to do any more driving together, we take my four-wheel."

"We'll discuss it." She turned the music down again when she heard the police radio squawk to life.

"All units in the vicinity of Sheridan and Jewell, 511 in progress."

Althea swore as the dispatcher continued to call for assistance. "That's only a block down." She turned left and aimed a quick, dubious look at Colt. "Shots fired," she told him. "Police business, got it?"

"Sure."

"This is unit six responding," she said into the transmitter. "I'm on the scene." After squealing to a halt behind her black-and-white, she shoved open her door. "Stay in the car." With that terse order, she drew her weapon and headed for the entrance of a four-story apartment building.

She paused at the door, sucking in her breath. The minute she bolted through, she heard the blast of an-other gunshot.

One floor up, she thought. Maybe two. With her body braced and flattened against the wall, she scanned the cramped, deserted entryway, then started up. Screaming— No, she thought, crying. A child. Her mind cold, her hands steady, she swung her weapon toward the first landing, then followed it. A door opened to her left. Crouching, she aimed toward the movement and stared into the face of an elderly woman with terrified eyes.

"Police," Althea told her. "Stay inside."

The door shut. A bolt turned. Althea shifted toward the second staircase. She saw them then, the cop who was down, and the cop who was huddled over him.

"Officer." There was the snap of authority in her voice when she dropped a hand on the uninjured cop's shoulder. "What's the status here?"

"He shot Jim. He came running out with the kid and opened up."

The uniformed cop was sheet-white, she noted, as pale as his partner, who was bleeding on the stairway. She couldn't tell which of them was shaking more violently. "What's your name?"

"Harrison. Don Harrison." He was pressing a soaked handkerchief to the gaping wound low on his partner's left shoulder.

"Officer Harrison, I'm Lieutenant Grayson. Give me the situation here, and make it fast."

"Sir." He took two short, quick breaths. "Domestic dispute. Shots fired. A white male assaulted the woman in apartment 2-D. He opened fire on us and headed upstairs with a small female child as a shield."

As he finished, a woman stumbled out of the apartment above. Where she clutched her side, blood

trickled through her fingers. "He took my baby.
Charlie took my baby. Please, God..." She fell
weeping to her knees. "He's crazy. Please, God..."

"Officer Harrison." A sound on the stairs had Althea moving fast, then swearing. She should have
known Colt wouldn't stay in the car. "Get on the
horn, now," she continued. "Call for backup. Officer and civilian down. Hostage situation. Now tell me
what he was carrying."

"Looked like a .45."

"Make the call, then get in here and back me up."
She spared one look at Colt. "Make yourself useful.
Do what you can for these two."

She raced up the stairs. She could hear the baby
crying again, long terrified wails that echoed in the
narrow corridors. By the time she reached the top
floor, she heard the slam of a door. The roof, she decided. Braced on one side of the door, she turned the
knob, kicked it open and went in low.

He fired once, wildly. The bullet sang more than a
foot to her right. Althea took her stand, and faced
him.

"Police!" she shouted. "Put down your weapon!"

He stood near the edge of the roof, a big man.
Linebacker-size, she noted, his skin flushed with rage,
his eyes glazed by chemicals. That she could handle.
It was a .45 he was carrying. She could handle that, as
well. But it was the child, the little girl of perhaps two
that he was holding by one foot over the edge of the
roof, that she wasn't sure she could deal with.

"I'll drop her!" He shouted it, like a chant against
the brisk wind. "I'll do it! I'll do it! I swear to God,
I'll drop her like a stone!" He shook the child, who

continued to scream. One of her little pink tennis
shoes flew off and fell five long stories.

"You don't want to make a mistake, do you, Charlie?" Althea inched away from the door, sidestepping
slowly, her nine-millimeter aimed at the broad chest.
"Bring her back from the edge."

"I'm going to drop the little bitch." He grinned
when he said it, his teeth bared, his eyes glittering.
"She's just like her mother. Whining and crying all the
damn time. Thought they could get away from me. I
found them, didn't I? Linda's real sorry now, isn't
she? Real damn sorry now."

"Yes, she is." She had to get to the kid. There had
to be a way to get to the child. Unbidden an old, obscene memory flashed through her head. The shouting, the threats, the fear. Althea tramped on them as
she would a roach. "You hurt the little girl and it's all
over, Charlie."

"Don't tell me it's over!" Enraged, he swung the
child like a sack of laundry. Althea's heart stopped,
and so did the screaming. The little girl was merely
sobbing now, quietly, helplessly, her arms dangling
limply, her huge blue eyes fixed and glazed. "She tried
to tell me it was over. It's over, Charlie," he mim-
icked in a singsong voice. "So I knocked her around
some. God knows she deserved it, nagging me about
getting work, nagging about every damn thing. And
as soon as the kid came along, everything changed. I
got no use for bitches in my life. But *I* say when it's
over."

The wail of sirens rose up in the air. Althea sensed
movement behind her, but didn't turn. Didn't dare.
She needed the man focused on her, only on her.
"Bring the kid in and you might get away. You want

to get away, don't you, Charlie? Come on. Give her to me. You don't need her.''

"You think I'm stupid?'' His lips curled into a snarl. "You're just one more bitch.''

"I don't think you're stupid.'' She caught a movement out of the corner of her eye, and would have sworn if she'd dared. It wasn't Harrison. It was Colt, slipping like a shadow toward the man's blind side. "I don't think you'd be stupid enough to hurt the kid.'' She was closer now, five feet away. Althea knew that it might as well be fifty.

"I'm going to kill her!'' he shouted. "And I'm going to kill you, and I'm going to kill anybody who gets in my way! Nobody says it's over till I say it's over!''

It happened then, fast, like a blur at the corner of a dream. Colt lunged, wrapping one arm around the child's waist. Althea caught the flash of metal in his hand and recognized it as a .32. He might have used it, if saving the child hadn't been his priority. He pivoted back, swinging the child so that his body was her shield, and by the time he'd brought his weapon to bear it was over.

Althea watched the .45 arch from her toward Colt and the girl. And she fired. The bullet drove him back. His knees hit the low curbing at the edge of the roof. He was the one who dropped like a stone.

Althea didn't permit herself even a sigh. She holstered her weapon and strode to where Colt was cuddling the weeping child. "She okay?''

"Looks like.'' In a move so natural she would have sworn he'd spent his life doing it, he settled the girl on his hip and kissed her damp temple. "You're okay now, baby. Nobody's going to hurt you.''

"Mama." Choking on tears, she buried her face in Colt's shoulder. "Mama."

"We'll take you to your mama, honey, don't you worry." Colt still held his gun, but his other hand was busy stroking the girl's wispy blond hair. "Nice work, Lieutenant."

Althea glanced over her shoulder. Cops were already pounding up the stairs. "I've done better."

"You kept him talking so the kid had a shot, then you took him down. It doesn't get better than that." And there had been a look in her eyes, from the moment she'd started up the steps with a cop's blood on her hands. And it hadn't faded yet. A look he'd seen before, Colt mused. One he'd always termed a warrior's look.

Her eyes held his for another minute. "Let's get her out of here" was all she said.

"Fine." They started toward the door.

"Just one thing, Nightshade."

He smiled a little, certain this was the moment she'd thank him. "What's that?"

"Have you got a permit for that gun?"

He stopped, stared. Then his smile exploded into a deep, rich laugh. Charmed, the little girl looked up, sniffled, and managed a watery smile.

She didn't think about killing. Didn't permit herself. She'd killed before, and knew she would likely do so again. But she didn't think about it. She knew that if she reflected too deeply on that aspect of the job, she could freeze, or she could drink or she could grow callous. Or, worse—infinitely worse—she could grow to enjoy it.

So she filed her report and put it out of her mind. Or tried to.

She hand-carried a copy of the report to Boyd's office, laid it on his desk. His eyes flicked down to it, then back to hers. "The cop—Barkley—he's still in surgery. The woman's out of danger."

"Good. How's the kid?"

"She has an aunt in Colorado Springs. Social Services contacted her. The creep was her father. History of battering and drugs. His wife took the kid about a year ago and went to a women's shelter. Filed for divorce. She moved here about three months ago, got herself a job, started a life."

"And he found her."

"And he found her."

"Well, he won't find her again." She turned toward the door, but Boyd was up and walking around the desk. "Thea." He shut the door, cutting off most of the din from the bull pen. "Are you okay?"

"Sure. I don't see IAD hassling me on this one."

"I'm not talking about Internal Affairs." He tilted his head. "A day or two off wouldn't hurt."

"It wouldn't help, either." She lifted her shoulders, let them fall. To Boyd she could say things she could never say to anyone else. "I didn't think I'd get to her in time. I didn't get to her," she added. "Colt did. And he shouldn't have been there."

"He was there." Gently Boyd laid his hands on her shoulders. "Oh-oh, it's the supercop complex. I can see it coming. Dodging bullets, filing reports, screaming down dark alleys, selling tickets to the Policemen's Ball, ridding the world of bad guys and saving cats from the tops of trees. She can do it all."

"Shut up, Fletcher." But she smiled. "I draw the line at saving cats."

"Want to come to dinner tonight."

She rested a hand on the knob. "What's to eat?"

He shrugged, grinned. "Can't say. It's Maria's night off."

"Cilla's cooking?" She gave him a pained, sorrowful look. "I thought we were friends."

"We'll send out for tacos."

"Deal."

When she walked back into the bull pen, she spotted Colt. He had his boots up on a desk and a phone at his ear. She strolled over, sat on the corner and waited for him to finish the call.

"Paperwork done?" he asked her.

"Nightshade, I don't suppose I have to point out that this desk, this phone, this chair, are department property, and off-limits to civilians."

He grinned at her. "Nope. But go right ahead, if you want to. You look good enough to eat when you're spouting proper procedure."

"Why, your compliments just take my breath away." She knocked his feet off the desk. "The stolen car's been impounded. The lab boys are going over it, so I don't see the point in rushing to take a look."

"Got a different plan?"

"Starting with the Tick Tock, I'm going to hit a few of Wild Bill's hangouts, talk to some people."

"I'm with you."

"Don't rub it in."

When she started toward the garage, he took her arm. "My car this time, remember?"

With a shrug, she went with him out to the street. His rugged black four-wheeler had a parking ticket on

the windshield. Colt stuffed it in his pocket. "I don't
suppose I can ask you to fix this."

"No." Althea climbed in.

"That's okay. Fletch'll do it."

She slanted him a look, and what might have been
a smile, before turning to stare out of the windshield
again. "You did good with that kid today." It galled
her a bit to admit it, but it had to be done. "I don't
think she'd have made it without you."

"Us," he said. "Some people might have called it
teamwork."

She fastened her belt with a jerk of her wrist. "Some
people."

"Don't take it so hard, Thea." Whistling through
his teeth, he shoved the gearshift into first and cruised
into traffic. "Now, where were we before we were interrupted? Oh, yeah, you were telling me about yourself."

"I don't think so."

"Okay, I'll tell me about you. You're a woman who
likes structure, depends on it. No, no, it's more that
you insist on it," he said. "That's why you're so good
at your job, all that law and order."

She snorted. "You should be a psychiatrist, Nightshade. Who could have guessed a cop would prefer
law and order?"

"Don't interrupt, I'm on a roll. You're what—
twenty-seven, twenty-eight?"

"Thirty-two. You lost your roll."

"I'll pick it up again." He glanced down at her naked ring finger. "You're not married."

"Another brilliant deduction."

"You have a tendency toward sarcasm, and an affection for wearing silk and expensive perfume. Real

nice perfume, Thea, the kind that seduces a man's mind before his body gets involved.''

"Maybe you should be writing ad copy."

"There's nothing subtle about your sexuality. It's just there, in big capital letters. Now, some women would exploit it, some would disguise it. You don't do either, so I figure you've decided somewhere along the line that it's up to a man to deal with it. And that's not only smart, it's wise.''

She didn't have an answer to that, he thought. Or didn't choose to give him one.

"You don't waste time, you don't waste energy. That way, when you need either one, you've got them. There's a cop's brain inside there, so you can size up a situation fast and act on it. And I figure you can handle a man every bit as coolly as you do your gun.''

"An interesting analysis, Nightshade.''

"You didn't flinch when you took that guy out today. It bothered you, but you didn't flinch.'' He pulled up in front of the Tick Tock and turned off the ignition. "If I've got to work with somebody, with the possibility of heading into a nasty situation, I like knowing she doesn't flinch.''

"Well, gee, thanks. Now I can stop worrying that you don't approve of me.'' Her temper on the boil, she slammed out of the car.

"Finally...'' Colt reached her in a few long-legged strides and swung his arm over her shoulder. "A little heat. It's a relief to see there's some temper in there, too.''

She surprised them both by ramming an elbow into his gut. "You wouldn't be relieved if I cut it loose. Take my word for it.''

They spent the next two hours going from bar to pool hall to grubby diner. It wasn't until they tried a hole-in-the-wall called Clancy's that they made some progress.

The lights were dim, a sop to the early drinkers, who liked to forget that the sun was still up. A radio behind the bar scratched out country music that told a sad tale of cheating and empty bottles. Several of those early customers were already scattered at the bar or at tables, most of them doing their drinking steadily and solo.

The liquor was watered, and the glasses were dingy, but the whiskey came cheap and the atmosphere was conducive to getting seriously drunk.

Althea walked to the end of the bar and ordered a club soda she had no intention of sampling. Colt opted for the beer on tap. She lifted a brow.

"Had a tetanus shot recently?" She took out a twenty, but kept her finger on the corner of the bill as their drinks were served. "Wild Bill used to come in here pretty regular."

The bartender glanced down at the bill, and back at Althea. Bloodshot eyes and the map of broken capillaries over his broad face attested to the fact that he swallowed as much as he served.

Althea prompted him. "Wild Bill Billings."

"So?"

"He was a friend of mine."

"Looks like you lost a friend."

"I was in here with him a couple of times." Althea drew the twenty back a fraction. "Maybe you remember."

"My memory's real selective, but it don't have no trouble making a cop."

"Good. Then you probably figured out that Bill and I had an arrangement."

"I probably figured out the arrangement got him splattered all over the sidewalk."

"You'd have figured that one wrong. He wasn't snitching for me when he got hit, and me, I'm just the sentimental type. I want who did him, and I'm willing to pay." She shoved the bill forward. "A lot more than this."

"I don't know nothing about it." But the twenty disappeared into his pocket.

"But you might know people who know people who know something." She leaned forward, a smile in her eyes. "If you put the word out, I'd appreciate it."

He shrugged, and would have moved away, but she put a hand on his arm. "I think that twenty's worth a minute or two more. Bill had a girl named Jade. She's skipped. He had a couple others, didn't he?"

"A couple. He wasn't much of a pimp."

"Got a name?"

He took out a dirty rag and began to wipe the dirty bar. "A black-haired girl name Meena. She worked out of here sometimes. Haven't seen her lately."

"If you do, you give me a call." She took out a card and dropped it onto the bar. "You know anything about movies? Private movies, with young girls?"

He looked blank and shrugged, but not before Althea saw the flash of knowledge in his eyes. "I ain't got time for movies, and that's all you get for twenty."

"Thanks." Althea strolled out. "Give him a minute," she said under her breath to Colt. Then she peered through the dirty window. "Look at that. Funny that he'd get an urge to make a call just now."

Colt watched the bartender hurry to the wall phone, drop in a quarter. "I like your style, Lieutenant."

"Let's see how much you like it after a few hours in a cold car. We've got a stakeout tonight, Nightshade."

"I'm looking forward to it."

Chapter 3

She was right about the cold. He didn't mind it so much, not with long johns and a sheepskin jacket to ward it off. But he did mind the dragging inactivity. He'd have sworn that Althea thrived on it.

She was settled comfortably in the passenger seat, working a crossword puzzle by the dim glow of the glove-compartment light. She worked methodically, patiently, endlessly, he thought, while he tried to stave off boredom with the B. B. King retrospective on the radio.

He thought of the evening they'd both missed at the Fletchers'. Hot food, blazing fire, warm brandy. It had even occurred to him that Althea might have defrosted a bit in unofficial surroundings. It might not have helped matters to think of her that way—the ice goddess melting—but it did something for his more casual fantasies.

In his current reality, she was all cop, and emotionally as distant from him as the moon. But in the daydream, assisted by the slow blues on the radio, she was all woman—seductive as the black silk he imagined her wearing, enticing as the crackling fire he pictured burning low in a stone hearth, soft as the white fur rug they lowered themselves to.

And her taste, once his mouth sampled hers, was honeyed whiskey. Drugging, sweet, potent. Her scent tangled up with her flavor in his senses until they were one and the same. An opiate a man could drown in.

The silk slipped away, inch by seductive inch, revealing the alabaster flesh beneath. Rose-petal smooth, flawless as glass, firm and soft as water. And when she reached for him, drew him in, her lips moved against his ear in whispered invitation.

"Want more coffee?"

"Huh?" He snapped back, swiveling his head around to stare at her in the shadowed car. She held a thermos out to him. "What?"

"Coffee?" Intrigued by the look on his face, she picked up his cup herself and filled it halfway. At first glance, she would have said there was temper in his eyes, ripe and ready to rip. But she knew that look, and knew it well. This was desire, equally ripe, equally ready. "Taking a side trip, Nightshade?"

"Yeah." He accepted the cup and drank deep, wishing it was whiskey. But his lips curved, his amusement with himself and the ridiculous situation easing the discomfort in his gut. "One hell of a trip."

"Well, try to keep up with our tour, will you?" She sipped from her own cup and offered him a share of her bag of candy. "There goes another one." Efficient, she set aside her cup and picked up her camera.

She took two quick shots of the man entering the bar. He was only the second who had gone in during the past hour.

"They don't exactly do a thriving business down here, do they?"

"Most people like a little ambience with their liquor."

"Ferns and canned music?"

She set the camera aside again. "Clean glasses, for a start. I doubt we're going to see one of our moviemakers down here."

"Then why are we sitting in a cold car looking at a dive at eleven o'clock at night?"

"Because it's my job." She chose a single piece of candy, popped it into her mouth. "And because I'm waiting for something else."

It was the first he'd heard of it. "Want to clue me in?"

"No." She chose another piece and went back to her crossword puzzle.

"Okay, that tears it." He ripped the paper out of her hands. "You want to play games, Grayson? Let me tell you how I play. I get peeved when people hold out on me. I get especially peeved when I'm bored senseless while they're doing it. Then I get mean."

"Excuse me," she said, in a mild tone that was in direct contrast to the fire in her eyes. "I can hardly speak for the ball of terror in my throat."

"You want to be scared?" He moved fast, eerily so. She wouldn't have been able to evade him if she'd tried. So she submitted without any show of resistance when he grabbed her by the shoulders. "I figure I ought to be able to put the fear of God into you, Thea, and liven things up a bit for both of us."

"Back off. If you've finished your imitation of machismo, what I've been waiting for is about to walk into the bar."

"What?"

He turned his head, which presented Althea with the perfect opportunity to grab his thumb and twist it viciously. When he swore, she released him. "Meena. Wild Bill's other girl." Althea lifted her camera and took another shot. "I got her picture out of the files this afternoon. She's done time. Solicitation, running a confidence game, possession with intent to sell, disorderly behavior."

"A sweet girl, our Meena."

"*Your* Meena," Althea told him. "Since you play the big, bad type so well, you can go on in and charm Meena, get her out here so we can talk." Opening her purse, Althea took out an envelope with five crisp ten-dollar bills. "And if your charm fails, offer her fifty."

"You want me to go in and convince her I'm looking to party?"

"That's the ticket."

"Fine." He'd certainly done worse in his career than play the eager john in a seedy bar. But he shoved the envelope back into her lap. "I've got my own money."

Althea watched him cross the street, waiting until he'd disappeared inside. Then she leaned back and indulged herself for one moment by closing her eyes and letting out a long, long breath.

A dangerous man, Colt Nightshade, she thought. A deadly man. She hadn't felt simple anger when he lunged toward her and grabbed. She hadn't felt simple anything. What she'd experienced was complex, convoluted and confusing.

What she'd felt was arousal, gut-deep, red-hot, soul-searing arousal, mixed with a healthy dose of primal fear and teeth-baring fury.

It wasn't like her, she told herself as she took the time alone to gather her wits. Coming that close to losing control because a man pushed the wrong buttons—or the right ones—was uncharacteristic of her.

She pushed the buttons. That was Althea Grayson's number one hard-and-fast rule. And if Colt thought he could break that one, he was in for a big disappointment.

She'd worked too hard forming herself into what she was, laying out the stages of her life and following them. She'd come from chaos, and she'd beaten it back. Certainly it was necessary from time to time to change the pattern. She wasn't rigid. But nothing, absolutely nothing, jarred that pattern.

It was the case itself, she supposed. The child being held by strangers, almost certainly being abused.

Another pattern, she thought bitterly. All too familiar to her.

And the child that morning, she remembered. Helplessly trapped by the adults around her.

She shook that off, picked up the crumpled newspaper to fold it neatly and set it aside.

She was just tired, she told herself. The drug bust the week before had been vicious. And to tumble from that into this would have shaken anyone. What she needed was a vacation. She smiled to herself, imagining a warm white-sand beach, blue water, a tall spear of glistening hotel behind her. A big bed, room service, mud packs, and a private whirlpool.

And that was just what she was going to have when she capped this case and sent Colt Nightshade back to his cattle or his law practice or whatever the hell he called his profession.

Glancing toward the bar again, she was forced to nod in approval. Less than ten minutes had passed, and he was coming out, Meena in tow.

"Oh, a group thing?" Meena studied Althea through heavily kohled eyes. She pushed back her stiff black curls and smirked. "Well, now, honey, that's going to cost you extra."

"No problem." Gallantly Colt helped her into the back seat.

"I guess a guy like you can handle the two of us." She settled back, reeking of floral cologne.

"I don't think that'll be necessary." Althea took out her badge, flashed it.

Meena swore, shot Colt a look of intense dislike, then folded her arms. "Haven't you cops got anything better to do than roust us working girls?"

"We won't have to take you in, Meena, if you answer a few questions. Drive around a little, will you, Colt?" As he obliged, Althea turned in her seat. "Wild Bill was a friend of mine."

"Yeah, right."

"He did some favors for me. I did some for him."

"Yeah, I bet—" Meena broke off, narrowed her eyes. "You the cop he snitched for? The one he called classy." Meena relaxed a little. There was a pretty good chance she wouldn't be spending the night in lockup after all. "He said you were okay. Said you always slipped him a few without whining about it."

Althea noted Meena's greedy little smile and lifted a brow. "I'm touched. Maybe he should've said I paid when he had something worth buying. Do you know Jade?"

"Sure. She hasn't been around for a few weeks. Bill said she skipped town." Meena dug in her red vinyl purse and pulled out a cigarette. When Colt clicked on his lighter and offered the flame, she cupped her hand over his and slanted him a warm look under thickly blackened lashes. "Thanks, honey."

"How about this girl?" Colt took the snapshot of Elizabeth out of his pocket. After turning on the dome light, he offered it to Meena.

"No." She started to pass it back, then frowned. "I don't know. Maybe." While she considered, she blew out a stream of smoke, clouding the car. "Not on the stroll. Seems like maybe I saw her somewhere."

"With Bill?" Althea asked.

"Hell, no. Bill didn't deal in jailbait."

"Who does?"

Meena shifted her eyes to Colt. "Georgie Cool's got a few young ones in his stable. Nobody as fresh as this, though."

"Did Bill get you a gig, Meena? A movie gig?" Althea asked.

"Maybe he did."

"The answer's yes, or the answer's no." Althea took back the photo of Liz. "You waste my time, I don't waste my money."

"Well, hell, it don't bother me if some guy wants to take videos while I work. They paid extra for it."

"Have you got a name?"

Meena snorted in Althea's direction. "We didn't exchange business cards, sweetie."

"But you can give me a description. How many were involved. Where it went down."

"Probably." The sly look was back as Meena blew out smoke. "If I had some incentive."

"Your incentive's not to spend time in a cell with a two-hundred-pound Swede named Big Jane," Althea said mildly.

"You can't send me up. I'll scream entrapment."

"Scream all you want. With your record, the judge will just chuckle."

"Come on, Thea." Colt's drawl seemed to have thickened. "Give the lady a break. She's trying to cooperate. Aren't you, Meena?"

"Sure." Meena butted out her cigarette, licked her lips. "Sure I am."

"What she's trying to do is hose me." Althea realized she and Colt had picked up the good cop—bad cop routine without missing a beat. "And I want answers."

"She's giving them to us." He smiled at Meena in the rearview mirror. "Just take your time."

"There were three of them," Meena said, and set her cherry-red lips in a pout. "The guy running the camera, another guy sitting back in a corner. I couldn't see him. And the guy who was, like, performing with me, you know? The guy with the camera was bald. A black guy, really big—like a wrestler or something. I was there about an hour, and he never opened his mouth once."

Althea flipped open her notebook. "Did they call each other by name?"

"No." Meena thought it through, shook her head. "No. That's funny, isn't it? They didn't talk to each other at all, as I remember. The one I was working with was a little guy—except for certain vital parts." She chuckled and reached for another cigarette. "Now, *he* did some talking. Trash talk, get it? Like for the camera. Some guys like that. He was, I don't know...in his forties, maybe, skinny, had his hair pulled back in a ponytail that hit his shoulder blades. He wore this Lone Ranger mask.''

''I'm going to want you to work with a police artist,'' Althea told her.

''No way. No more cops.''

''We don't have to do it at the station.'' Althea played her trump card. ''If you give us a good enough description, one that helps us nail these film buffs, there's an extra hundred for you.''

''Okay.'' Meena brightened. ''Okay.''

Althea tapped her pencil against her pad. ''Where did you shoot?''

''Shoot? Oh, you mean the movie? Over on Second. Real nice place. It had one of them whirlpool tubs in the bathroom, and mirrors for walls.'' Meena leaned forward to brush her fingertips over Colt's shoulder. ''It was...stimulating.''

''The address?'' Althea said.

''I don't know. One of those big condo buildings on Second. Top floor, too. Like the penthouse.''

''I bet you'd recognize the building if we drove by it, wouldn't you, Meena?'' Colt's tone was all friendly encouragement, as was the smile he shot her over his shoulder.

''Yeah, sure I would.''

And she did. Minutes later she was pointing out the window. ''That place, there. See the one up top, with the big windows and the balcony thing? It was in there. Real class joint. White carpet. This really sexy bedroom, with red curtains and a big round bed. There was gold faucets in the bathroom, shaped like swans. Jeez. I woulda loved to go back.''

''You only went once?'' Colt asked her.

"Yeah. They told Billy I wasn't the right type." With a sound of disgust, she reached for yet another cigarette. "Get this. I was too old. I just had my twenty-second birthday, and those creeps tell Billy I'm too old. It really ticked me— Oh, yeah..." Suddenly inspired, she rapped Colt on the shoulder. "The kid. The one in the picture? That's where I saw her. I was leaving, but I went back 'cause I left my smokes. She was sitting in the kitchen. I didn't recognize her in the picture right off, 'cause she was all made-up when I saw her."

"Did she say anything to you?" Colt asked, struggling to keep his voice quiet and even. "Do anything?"

"No, just sat there. She looked stoned to me."

Because she sensed he needed something, Althea slid her hand across the seat and covered Colt's. His was rigid. She was surprised, but didn't protest, when he turned his hand over and gripped hers, palm to palm.

"I'm going to want to talk to you again." With her free hand, Althea reached into her purse for enough money to ensure Meena's continued cooperation. "I need a number where I can reach you."

"No sweat." Meena rattled it off while she counted her money. "I guess Billy had it right. You're square. Hey, maybe you could drop me at the Tick Tock. I think I'll go in and drink one for Wild Bill."

"We can't do anything without a warrant." Althea was repeating the statement for the third time as they stepped out of the elevator on the top floor of the building Meena had pointed out.

"You don't need a warrant to knock on a door."

"Right." With a sigh, Althea slipped a hand inside her jacket in an automatic check of her weapon. "And they're going to invite us in for coffee. If you give me a couple of hours—"

When he whirled, her jaw dropped. After the cool, matter-of-fact manner in which he'd handled everything up to this point, the raw fury on his face was staggering. "Get this, Lieutenant—I'm not waiting another two *minutes* to see if Liz is in there. And if she is, if anybody is, I'm not going to need a damn warrant."

"Look, Colt, I understand—"

"You don't understand diddley."

She opened her mouth, then shut it again, shocked that she'd been about to shout that she did understand. Oh, yes, she understood very, very well. "We'll knock," she said tightly, and strode to the door of the penthouse and did so.

"Maybe they're hard of hearing." Colt used his fist to hammer. When the summons went unanswered, he moved so fast Althea didn't have time to swear. He'd already kicked the door in.

"Good, real good, Nightshade. Subtle as a brick."

"Guess I slipped." He pulled his gun out of his boot. "And look at this, the door's open."

"Don't—" But he was already inside. Cursing Boyd and all his boyhood friends, Althea drew her weapon and went in the door behind him, instinctively covering his back. She didn't need the light Colt turned on to see that the room was empty. It had a deserted feel. There was nothing left but the carpet, and the drapes at the windows.

"Split," Colt muttered to himself as he moved quickly from room to room. "The bastards split."

Satisfied she wouldn't need it, Althea replaced her gun. "I guess we know who our friendly bartender called this afternoon. We'll see what we can get from the rental contract, the neighbors..." Yet she thought if their quarry had been this slick so far, what they got would be close to useless.

She stepped into the bathroom. It was as Meena had described, the big black whirlpool tub, the swan-shaped faucets—brass, not gold—the all-around mirrors. "You've just jeopardized the integrity of a possible crime scene, Nightshade. I hope you're satisfied."

"She could have been here," he said from behind her.

She looked over, saw their reflections trapped in the mirrored tiles. It was the expression on his face, one she hadn't expected to see there, that softened her. "We're going to find her, Colt," she said quietly. "We're going to see that she gets back home."

"Sure." He wanted to break something, anything. It took every ounce of his will not to smash his fist through the mirrors. "Every day they've got her is a day she's going to have to live with, forever." Bending, he slipped his gun back in his boot. "God, Thea, she's just a child."

"Children are tougher than most people think. They close things off when they have to. And it's going to be easier because she has family who loves her."

"Easier than what?"

Than having no one but yourself, she thought. "Just easier." She couldn't help it. She reached out, laid a hand on his cheek. "Don't let it eat at you, Colt. You'll mess up if you do."

"Yeah." He drew it back, that dangerous emotion that led to dangerous mistakes. But when she started to drop her hand and move past him, Colt snagged her wrist. "You know something?" Maybe it was only because he needed contact, but he tugged her an inch closer. "For a minute there, you were almost human."

"Really?" Their bodies were almost brushing. A bad move, she thought. But it would be cowardly to pull back. "What am I usually?"

"Perfect." He lifted his free hand—because he'd wanted to almost from the first moment he'd seen her—and tangled his fingers in her hair. "It's scary," he said. "It's the whole package—that face, the hair, the body, the mind. A man doesn't know whether to bay at the moon or whimper at your feet."

She had to tilt her head back to keep her eyes level with his. If her heart was beating a bit faster, she could ignore it. It had happened before. If she felt the little pull of curiosity, even of lust, it wasn't the first time, and it could be controlled. But what was difficult, very difficult, to channel, was the unexpected clouding of her senses. That would have to be fought.

"You don't strike me as the type to do either," she said, and smiled, a cool, tight-lipped smirk that had most men backing off babbling.

Colt wasn't most men.

"I never have been. Why don't we try something else?" He said it slowly, then moved like lightning to close his mouth over hers.

If she had protested, if she had struggled—if there had been even a token pulling back—he would have released her and counted his losses. Maybe.

But she didn't. That surprised them both.

She could have, should have. She would think later.
She could have stopped him cold with any number of
defensive or offensive moves. She would think later.
But there was such raw heat in his lips, such steely
strength in his arms, such whirling pleasure in her own
body.

Oh, yes, she would think later. Much later.

It was exactly as he'd imagined it. And he'd imagined it a lot. That tart, flamboyant flavor she carried
on her lips was the twin of the one he'd sampled in his
mind. It was as addicting as any opiate. When she
opened for him, he dived deeper and took more.

She was as small, as slim, as supple, as any man
could wish. And as strong. Her arms were locked hard
around him, and her fingers were clutching at his hair.
The low, deep sound of approval that vibrated in her
throat had his blood racing like a fast-moving river.

Murmuring her name, he spun her around, ramming her against the mirrors, covering her body with
his. His hands ran over her in a greedy sprint to take
and touch and possess. Then his fingers were jerking
at the buttons on her blouse in a desperate need to
push aside the first barrier.

He wanted her now. No, no, he needed her now, he
realized. The way a man needed sleep after a vicious
day of hard labor, the way he needed to eat after a
long, long fast.

He tore his mouth from hers to press it against her
throat, reveling in the sumptuous taste of flesh.

Half-delirious, she arched back, moaning at the
thrill of his hungry mouth on her heated skin. Without the wall for support, she knew, she would already
have sunk to the floor. And it was there, just there,
that he would take her, that they would take each

other. On the cool, hard tile, with dozens of mirrors tossing back reflections of their desperate bodies.

Here and now.

And like a thief sneaking into a darkened house, an image of Meena, and what had gone on in that apartment, crept into her mind.

What was she doing? Good Lord, what was she *doing?* she raged at herself as she levered herself away.

She was a cop, and she had been about to indulge in some wild bout of mindless sex in the middle of a crime scene.

"Stop!" Her voice was harsh with arousal and self-disgust. "I mean it, Colt. Stop. Now."

"What?" Like a diver surfacing from fathoms-deep, he shook his head, nearly swayed. Good Lord, his knees were weak. To compensate, he braced a hand on the wall as he stared down at her. He'd loosened her hair, and it spilled rich and red over her shoulders. Her eyes were more gold than brown now, huge, and seductively misted. Her mouth was full, reddened by the pressure and demand of his, and her skin was flushed a pale, lovely rose.

"You're beautiful. Impossibly beautiful." Gently he skimmed a finger down her throat. "Like some exotic flower behind glass. A man just has to break that glass and take it."

"No." She grabbed his hand to keep from losing her mind again. "This is insane, completely insane."

"Yeah." He couldn't have agreed more. "And it felt great."

"This is an investigation, Nightshade. And we're standing in what is very possibly the scene of a major crime."

He smiled and lifted her hand to nip at her fingers. Just because this was a dead end for their investigation didn't mean all activity had to come to a halt. "So, let's go someplace else."

"We are going someplace else." She shoved him away, and quickly, competently redid her blouse. "Separately." She wasn't steady, she realized. Damn him, damn her, she wasn't steady.

He felt that the safest place for his hands at the moment, was his pockets so he shoved them in. She was right, one hundred percent right, and that was the worst of it.

"You want to pretend this didn't happen?"

"I don't pretend anything." Settling on dignity, she pushed her tumbled hair back, smoothed down her rumpled jacket. "It happened, now it's done."

"Not by a long shot, Lieutenant. We're both grown-ups, and though I can only speak for myself, that kind of connection just doesn't happen every day."

"You're right." She inclined her head. "You can only speak for yourself." She made it back to the living room before he grabbed her arm and spun her around to face him.

"You want me to press the point now?" His voice was quiet, deadly quiet. "Or do you want to be straight with me?"

"All right, fine." She could be honest, because lies wouldn't work. "If I were interested in a quick, hot affair, I'd certainly give you a call. As it happens, I have other priorities at the moment."

"You've got a list, right?"

She had to take a moment to get her temper back under wraps. "Do you think that insults me?" she asked sweetly. "I happen to prefer organizing my life."

"Compartmentalizing."

She arched a brow. "Whatever. For better or worse, we have a professional relationship. I want that girl found, Colt, every bit as much as you do. I want her back with her family, eating hamburgers and worrying over her latest math test. And I want to bring down the bastards who have her. More than you could possibly understand."

"Then why don't you help me understand?"

"I'm a cop," she told him. "That's enough."

"No, it's not." There had been passion in her face, the same kind of passion he'd felt when he had her in his arms. Fierce and ragged and at the edge of control. "Not for you, or for me, either."

He let out a deep breath and rubbed the base of his neck, where most of his tension had lodged. They were both tired, he realized, tired and strung out. It wasn't the time and it wasn't the place to delve into personal reasons. He'd need to find some objectivity if he wanted to figure out Althea Grayson.

"Look, I'd apologize for back there if I was out of line. But we both know I wasn't. I'm here to get Liz back, and nothing's going to stop me. And after a taste of you, Thea, I'm going to be just as determined to have more."

"I'm not the soup du jour, Nightshade," she said wearily. "You'll only get what I give."

His grin flashed, quick and easy. "That's just the way I want it. Come on, I'll drive you home."

Saying nothing, Althea stared after him. She had the uncomfortable feeling that they hadn't resolved matters precisely as she'd wanted.

Chapter 4

Armed with a second cup of coffee, Colt stood at the edge of a whirlwind. It was obvious to him that getting three kids out of the house and onto a school bus was an event of major proportions. He could only wonder how a trio of adults could handle the orchestration on a daily basis and remain sane.

"I don't like this cereal," Bryant complained. He lifted a spoonful and, scowling, let the soggy mess plop back into his bowl. "It tastes like wet trees."

"You picked it out, because it had a whistle inside," Cilla reminded him as she slapped peanut-butter-and-jelly sandwiches together. "You eat it."

"Put a banana on it," Boyd suggested while he struggled to bundle Allison's pale, flyaway hair into something that might have passed for a braid.

"Ouch! Daddy, you're pulling!"

"Sorry. What's the capital of Nebraska?"

"Lincoln," his daughter said with a sigh. "I hate geography tests." While she pouted over it, she practiced her pliés for ballet class. "How come I have to know the stupid states and their stupid capitals, anyway?"

"Because knowledge is sacred." With his tongue caught in his teeth, Boyd fought to band the wispy braid. "And once you learn something, you never really forget it."

"Well, I can't remember the capital of Virginia."

"It's, ah..." As the sacred knowledge escaped him, Boyd swore under his breath. What the hell did he care? He lived in Colorado. One of the major problems with having kids, as he saw it, was that the parents were forced to go back to school. "It'll come to you."

"Mom, Bry's feeding Bongo his cereal." Allison sent her brother a smug, smarmy smile of the kind that only a sister can achieve.

Cilla turned in time to see her son thrusting his spoon toward their dog's eager mouth. "Bryant Fletcher, you're going to be wearing that cereal in a minute."

"But look, Mom, even Bongo won't eat it. It's crap."

"Don't say 'crap,'" Cilla told him wearily. But she noted that the big, scruffy dog, who regularly drank out of toilet bowls, had turned up his nose after one sample of soggy Rocket Crunchies. "Eat the banana, and get your coat."

"Mom!" Keenan, the youngest, scrambled into the room. He was shoeless and sockless, and was holding one grubby high-top sneaker in his hand. "I can't find my other shoe. It's not anywhere. Somebody musta stole it."

"Call a cop," Cilla muttered as she dumped the last peanut-butter-and-jelly sandwich into a lunch box.

"I'll find it, *señora.*" Maria wiped her hands on her apron.

"Bless you."

"Bad guys took it, Maria," Keenan told her, his voice low and serious. "They came in the middle of the night and swiped it. Daddy'll go out and lock them up."

"Of course he will." Equally sober, Maria took his hand to lead him toward the stairs. "Now we go look for clues, *sí?*"

"Umbrellas." Cilla turned from the counter, running a hand through her short crop of brown hair. "It's raining. Do we have umbrellas?"

"We used to have umbrellas." His hairstyling duties completed, Boyd poured himself another cup of coffee. "Somebody stole them. Probably the same gang who stole Keenan's shoe and Bryant's spelling homework. I've already put a task force on it."

"Big help you are." Cilla went to the kitchen doorway. "Maria! Umbrellas!" She turned back, tripping over the dog, swore, then grabbed three lunch boxes. "Coats," she ordered. "You've got five minutes to make the bus."

There was a mad scramble, impeded by Bongo, who decided this was the perfect time to jump on everyone in sight.

"He hates goodbyes," Boyd told Colt as he deftly collared the mutt.

"The shoe was in the closet," Maria announced as she hustled Keenan into the kitchen.

"The thieves must have hidden it there. It's too diabolical." She offered him his lunch box. "Kiss."

Keenan grinned and planted a loud smack on her lips. "I get to be the milk monitor all week."

"It's a tough job, but I know you're up to it. Bry, the banana peel goes in the trash." As she handed him his lunch box, she hooked an arm around his throat, making him giggle as she kissed him goodbye. "Allison, the capital of Virginia's Richmond. I think."

"Okay."

After everyone exchanged kisses—including, Colt noted with some amusement, Bongo—Cilla held up one hand.

"Anyone leaving their umbrella at school will be immediately executed. Scram."

They all bolted. The door slammed. Cilla closed her eyes. "Ah, another quiet morning at the Fletchers'. Colt what can I offer you? Bacon, eggs? Whiskey?"

"I'll take the first two. Reserve the last." Grinning, he took the chair Bryant had vacated. "You put on this show everyday?"

"With matinees on Saturdays." She ruffled her hair again, checked the clock on the stove. "I'd like to hang around with you guys, but I've got to get ready for work. I've got a meeting in an hour. If you find yourself at loose ends, Colt, stop by the radio station. I'll show you around."

"I might just do that."

"Maria, do you need me to pick up anything?"

"No, *señora*." She already had the bacon sizzling. *"Gracias."*

"I should be home by six." Cilla paused by the table to run a hand over her husband's shoulder. "I hear there's a big poker game here tonight."

"That's the rumor." Boyd tugged his wife down to him, and Colt saw their lips curve before they met. "You taste pretty good, O'Roarke."

"Strawberry jelly. Catch you later, Slick." She gave him one last, lingering kiss before she left him.

Colt listened to her race up the stairs. "You hit the bull's-eye, didn't you, Fletch?"

"Hmm?"

"Terrific wife, great kids. And the first time out."

"Looks that way. I guess I knew Cilla was it for me almost from the first." Remembering made him smile. "Took a little while to convince her she couldn't live without me, though."

It was tough not to envy that particular smile, Colt mused. "You and Althea, you were partners when you met Cilla, right?"

"Yeah. All three of us were working nights in those days. Thea was the first woman I'd ever partnered with. Turned out to be the best cop I'd ever partnered with, as well."

"I have to ask—you don't have to answer, but I have to ask." And how best to pose the question? Colt wondered as he picked up a fork and tapped it on the edge of the table. "You and Thea...before Cilla, there was nothing...personal?"

"There's plenty personal when you're partners, working together, sometimes around the clock." He picked up his coffee, his smile easy. "But there was nothing romantic, if that's what you're dancing around."

"It's none of my business." Colt shrugged, annoyed by just how much Boyd's answer relieved him. "I was curious."

"Curious why I didn't try to move in on a woman with her looks? Her brains? Her—what's the best word for it?" Amused by Colt's obvious discomfort, he chuckled as Maria silently served their breakfast. "Thanks, Maria. We'll call it style, for lack of something better. It's simple, Colt. I'm not going to say I didn't think about it. Could be Thea gave it a couple moments of her time, too. But we clicked as partners, we clicked as friends, and it just didn't take us down any of those other alleys." He scooped up some eggs, arched a brow. "You thinking about it?"

Colt moved his shoulders again, toyed with his bacon. "I can't say we've clicked as partners—or as friends, for that matter. But I figure we've already turned down one of those other alleys."

Boyd didn't pretend to be surprised. Anyone who said oil and water didn't mix just hadn't stirred them up enough. "There are some women who get under your skin, some that get into your head. And some who do both."

"Yeah. So what's the story on her?"

"She's a good cop, a person you can trust. Like anybody else, she's got some baggage, but she carries it well. If you want to know personal stuff, you'll have to ask her." He lifted his cup. "And she'd get the same answer from me about you."

"Has she asked?"

"Nope." Boyd sipped to hide his grin. "Now, why don't you tell me your progress in finding Liz?"

"We got a tip on the place on Second Avenue, but they'd already split." It still frustrated him. The whole bloody business frustrated him. "Figured I'd talk to the apartment manager, the neighbors. There's a wit-

ness who might be able to ID one or more of our
movie moguls.''

"That's a good start. Anything I can do to help?"

"I'll let you know. They've already had her a couple of weeks, Fletch. I'm going to get her back." He
lifted his gaze, and the quiet rage in it left no room for
doubt. "What worries me is what shape she'll be in
when I do."

"Take it one step at a time."

"That sounds like the lieutenant." Colt preferred to
take leaps, rather than steps. "I can't hook up with her
until later this afternoon. She's in court or something."

"In court?" Boyd frowned, then nodded. "Right.
The Marsten trial. Armed robbery, assault. She made
a good collar on that one. Do you want me to send a
uniform with you to Second Avenue?"

"No. I'd just as soon handle it myself."

It was good to be back on his own, Colt decided.
Working alone meant you didn't have to worry about
stepping on your partner's toes or debating strategy.
And as far as Althea was concerned, it meant he didn't
have to work overtime trying to keep himself from
thinking of her as a woman.

First he rousted the apartment manager, Nieman, a
short, balding man who obviously thought his position required him to wear a three-piece suit, a brutally
knotted tie, and an ocean of pine-scented after-shave.

"I've already given my statement to the other officer," he informed Colt through the two-inch crack
provided by the security chain on his door.

"Now you'll have to give it to me." Colt saw no
need to disabuse Nieman of the notion that he was

with the police. "Do you want me to shout my questions from out in the hall, Mr. Nieman?"

"No." Nieman shot the chain back, clearly annoyed. "Haven't I already had enough trouble? I was hardly out of my bed this morning before you people were banging on my door. Now the phone has been ringing off the hook with tenants calling, demanding to know what the police are doing sealing off the penthouse. The resulting publicity will take weeks for me to defuse."

"You got a real tough job, Mr. Nieman." Colt scanned the apartment as he entered. It wasn't as plush or as large as the empty penthouse, but it would do in a pinch. Nieman had furnished it in fussy French rococo. Colt knew his mother would have adored it.

"You can't imagine it." Resigned, Nieman gestured toward an ornately carved chair. "Tenants are such children, really. They need someone to guide them, someone to slap their hands when they break the rules. I've been a resident apartment manager for ten years, three in this building, and the stories I could tell . . ."

Because Colt was afraid he would do just that, he cut Nieman off. "Why don't you tell me about the penthouse tenants?"

"There's very little I can tell." Nieman plucked at the knees of his slacks before sitting. He crossed his legs at the ankles and revealed patterned argyle socks. "As I explained to the other detective, I never actually met them. They were only here four months."

"Don't you show the apartment to tenants, Mr. Nieman? Take their applications?"

"As a rule, certainly. In this particular case, the tenant sent references and a certified check for first and last month's rent via the mail."

"Is it usual for you to rent an apartment that way?"

"Not usual, no..." After clearing his throat, Nieman fiddled with the knot of his tie. "The letter was followed up with a phone call. Mr. Davis—the tenant—explained that he was a friend of Mr. and Mrs. Ellison. They had the penthouse before, for three years. Lovely couple, elegant taste. They moved to Boston. As he'd been acquainted with them, he had no need to view the apartment. He claimed to have attended several dinner parties and other affairs in the penthouse. He was quite anxious to have it, you see, and as his references were impeccable..."

"You checked them out?"

"Of course." Lips pursed, Nieman drew himself up. "I take my responsibilities seriously."

"What did this Davis do for a living?"

"He's an engineer with a local firm. When I contacted the firm, they had nothing but the highest regard for him."

"What firm?"

"I still have the file out." Nieman reached to the coffee table for a slim folder. "Foxx Engineering," he began, then recited the address and phone number. "Naturally, I contacted his landlord, as well. We apartment managers have a code of ethics. I was assured that Mr. Davis was an ideal tenant, quiet, responsible, tidy, and that his rent was always timely. This proved to be the case."

"But you never actually saw Mr. Davis?"

"This is a large building. There are several tenants I don't see. It's the troublemakers you meet regularly, and Mr. Davis was never any trouble."

Never any trouble, Colt thought grimly as he completed the slow process of door-to-door. He carried with him copies of the lease, the references, and Davis's letter. It was past noon, and he'd already interviewed most of the tenants who'd answered his knock. Only three of them claimed to have seen the mysterious Mr. Davis. Colt now had three markedly different descriptions to add to his file.

The police seal on the penthouse door had barred his entrance. He could have picked the lock and cut the tape, but he'd doubted he'd find anything worthwhile.

So he'd started at the top and was working his way down. He was currently canvassing the third floor, with a vicious case of frustration and the beginnings of a headache.

He knocked at 302 and felt himself being sized up through the peephole. The chain rattled, the bolt turned. Now he was being sized up, face-to-face, by an old woman with a wild mop of hair dyed an improbable orange. She had bright blue eyes that sprayed into dozens of wrinkles as she squinted to peer at him. Her Denver Broncos sweatshirt was the size of a tent, covering what Colt judged to be two hundred pounds of pure bulk. She had two chins and was working on a third.

"You're too good-looking to be selling something I don't want."

"No, ma'am." If Colt had had a hat, he'd have tipped it. "I'm not selling anything at all. The police are conducting an investigation. I'd like to ask you a few questions regarding some of your neighbors in the building."

"Are you a cop? You'd have a badge if you were."

It looked as though she were a great deal sharper than Nieman. "No, ma'am, I'm not a cop. I'm working privately."

"A detective?" The blue eyes brightened like light bulbs. "Like Sam Spade? I swear, that Humphrey Bogart was the sexiest man ever born. If I'd have been Mary Astor, I wouldn't have thought twice about some dumb bird when I could have had him."

"No, ma'am." It took Colt a moment, but he finally caught on to her reference to *The Maltese Falcon*. "I kind of went for Lauren Bacall, myself. They sure did set things humming in *The Big Sleep*."

Pleased, she let out a loud, lusty laugh. "Damned if they didn't. Well, come on in. No use standing here in the doorway."

Colt entered and immediately had to start dodging furniture and cats. The apartment was packed with both. Tables, chairs, lamps, some of them superior antiques, others yard-sale rejects, were set helter-skelter throughout the wide living room. Half a dozen cats of all descriptions were curled, draped and stretched out with equal abandon.

"I collect," she told him, then plopped herself down on a Louis XV love seat. Her girth took up three-quarters of the cushions, so Colt wisely chose a ratty armchair with a faded pattern of colonial soldiers fighting redcoats. "I'm Esther Mavis."

"Colt Nightshade." Colt took it philosophically when a lean gray cat sprang into his lap and another leapt onto a wing of the chair to sniff at his hair.

"Well, just what are we investigating, Mr. Nightshade?"

"We're doing a check on the tenant who occupied the penthouse."

"The one who just moved out?" She scratched one of her chins. "Saw a bunch of burly men carrying stuff out to a van yesterday."

So had several other people, Colt thought. No one had bothered to note whether the van had carried the name of a moving company.

"Did you notice what kind of van, Mrs. Mavis?"

"Miss," she told him. "A big one. They didn't act like any movers I ever saw."

"Oh?"

"They worked fast. Not like people who get paid by the hour. You know. Moved out some good pieces, too." Her bright eyes scanned her living room. "I like furniture. There was this Belker table I'd have liked to get my hands on. Don't know where I'd put it, but I always find room."

"Could you describe any of the movers?"

"Don't notice men unless there's something special about them." She winked slyly.

"How about Mr. Davis? Did you ever see him?"

"Can't say for sure. I don't know most of the people in the building by name. Me and my cats keep to ourselves. What did he do?"

"We're looking into it."

"Playing it close to the vest, huh? Well, Bogey would've done the same. So, he's moved out?"

"It looks that way."

"I guess I won't be able to give him his package, then."

"Package?"

"Just came yesterday. Messenger brought it, dropped it here by mistake. Davis, Mavis..." She shook her head. "People don't pay enough attention to details these days."

"I know what you mean." Colt cautiously plucked a cat from his shoulder. "What sort of a package, Miss Mavis?"

"A package package." With a few grunts and whistles, she hauled herself to her feet. "Put it back in the bedroom. Meant to take it up to him today." She moved with a kind of tanklike grace through the narrow passages between the furniture and came back with a sealed, padded bag.

"Ma'am, I'd like to take that with me. If you have a problem with that, you can call Captain Boyd Fletcher, Denver PD."

"No skin off my nose." She handed Colt the package. "Maybe when you've cracked the case, you'll come let me know what's what."

"I'll just do that." On impulse, he took out the photo of Liz. "Have you seen this girl?"

Miss Mavis looked at it, frowned over it, then shook her head. "No, not that I recollect. Is she in trouble?"

"Yes, ma'am."

"Does it have something to do with upstairs?"

"I think so."

She handed the photo back. "She's a pretty little thing. I hope you find her real soon."

"So do I."

It wasn't his usual operating procedure. Colt couldn't have said why he made the exception, why he felt he had to. Instead of opening the package and dealing with its contents immediately, he left it sealed and drove to the courthouse.

He was just in time to hear the defense's cross of Althea. She was dressed in a rust-colored suit that should have been dull. Instead, the effect was subtly powerful, with her vibrant hair twisted up off her neck and a single strand of pearls at her throat.

Colt took a seat at the back of the courtroom and watched as she competently, patiently and devastatingly ripped the defense to shreds. She never raised her voice, never stumbled over words. Anyone looking or listening, including the jury, would have judged her a cool, detached professional.

And so she was, Colt mused as he stretched out his legs and waited. Certainly no one watching her now would imagine her flaming like a rocket in a man's arms. His arms.

No one would picture this tidy, controlled woman arching and straining as a man's hands—his hands—raced over her.

But he was damned if he could forget it.

And studying her now, when she was unaware of him and completely focused on the job at hand, he began to notice other things, little things.

She was tired. He could see it in her eyes. Now and again there was the faintest whisper of impatience in her voice as she was called on to repeat herself. She shifted, crossing her legs. It was a smooth movement, economical, as always. But he sensed something else beneath it. Not nerves, he realized. Restlessness. She wanted this over with.

When the cross was complete, the judge called for a fifteen-minute recess. She winced as the gavel struck.

It was just a flicker of a movement across her face, but he caught it.

Jack Holmsby caught her arm before she could move by him. "Nice job, Thea."

"Thanks. You shouldn't have any trouble nailing him."

"I'm not worried about it." He shifted, just enough to block her path. "Listen, I'm sorry things didn't work out the other night. Why don't we give it another shot? Say, dinner tomorrow night, just you and me?"

She waited a beat, not so much amazed by his gall as fatigued by it. "Jack, do the words *no way in hell* have any meaning for you?"

He only laughed and gave her arm an intimate little squeeze. For one wild moment, she considered decking him and taking the rap for assault.

"Come on, Althea. I'd like a chance to make it up to you."

"Jack, we both know you'd like a chance to make me. And it isn't going to happen. Now let go of my arm while we're both on the same side of the law."

"There's no need to be—"

"Lieutenant?" Colt drawled out the word. He let his gaze sweep over Holmsby. "Got a minute?"

"Nightshade." It annoyed the hell out of her that he'd witnessed the little tussle. "Excuse me, Jack. I've got work to do."

She strode out of the courtroom, leaving Colt to follow. "If you've got something that's worth my time, spill it," she ordered. "I'm not real pleased with lawyers at the moment."

"Darling, I don't have any briefs with me—except the ones I'm wearing."

"You're a riot, Nightshade."

"You look like a lady who could use a laugh." He took her arm, and felt his own temper peak when she stiffened. Battling it down, he steered her toward the doors. "My car's out front. Why don't we take a ride while we catch up?"

"Fine. I walked over from the precinct. You can take me back."

"Right." He found another ticket on his windshield. Not surprising, since he'd parked in a restricted zone. He pocketed it, and climbed in. "Sorry I interrupted your mating ritual."

"Kiss my butt." She snapped her seat belt into place.

"Lieutenant, I've been dreaming of doing just that." Reaching over, he popped open the glove compartment. This time she didn't stiffen at the contact, only seemed to withdraw. "Here."

"What?" She glanced down at the bottle of aspirin.

"For your headache."

"I'm fine." It wasn't exactly a lie, she thought. What she had couldn't be termed a mere headache. It was more like a freight train highballing behind her eyes.

"I hate a martyr."

"Leave me alone." She closed her eyes and effectively cut him off.

She was far from fine. She hadn't slept. Over the years, she'd become accustomed to rolling on two or three hours a night. But last night she hadn't slept at all, and she was too proud to lay the blame where it belonged. Right at Colt's door.

She'd thought of him. And she'd berated herself. She'd run over the impossible scene in the penthouse, and she'd ached. Then she'd berated herself again. She'd tried a hot bath, a boring book, yoga, warm brandy. Nothing had done the trick.

So she'd tossed and turned, and eventually she'd crawled out of bed to roam restlessly through her apartment. And she'd watched the sun come up.

Since dawn, she'd worked. It was now slightly past one, and she'd been on the job for nearly eight hours without a break. And what made it worse, what made it next to intolerable, was that she could very well be stuck with Colt for another eight.

She opened her eyes again when he stopped with a jerk of brakes. They were parked in front of a convenience store.

"I need something," he muttered, and slammed out.

Fine, terrific, she thought, and shut her eyes again. Don't bother to ask if maybe *I* need something. Like a chain saw to slice off my head, for instance.

She heard him coming back. Odd, she mused, that she recognized the sound of his stride, the click of his boot heels, after so short a time. In defense, or simply out of obstinacy, she kept her eyes shut.

"Here." He pushed something against her hand. "Tea," he told her when she opened her eyes to stare down at the paper cup. "To wash down the aspirin." He popped the top on the bottle himself and shook out the medication. "Now take the damn pills, Althea. And eat this. You probably haven't eaten anything all day, unless it's chocolate bits or candied nuts. I've never seen a woman pick her way through a pound bag of candy the way you do."

"Sugar's loaded with energy." But she took the pills, and the tea. The package of cheese and crackers earned a frown. "Didn't they have any cupcakes?"

"You need protein."

"There's probably protein in cupcakes." The tea was too strong, and quite bitter, but it helped nonetheless. "Thanks." She sipped again, then broke down and opened the package of crackers. It was important to remember that she was responsible for her own actions, her own reactions and her own emotions. If she hadn't slept, it was her own problem. "The lab boys should have finished at the penthouse by now."

"They have. I've been there."

She muttered over a mouthful. "I'd rather you didn't go off on your own."

"I can't please everybody, so I please myself. I talked to the little weasel who manages the place. He never set eyes on the top-floor tenant."

While Althea chewed her way through the impromptu meal, he filled her in.

"I knew about Davis," she told him when he finished. "I got Nieman out of bed this morning. Already called the references. Phone disconnect on both. There is no Foxx Engineering at that address, or at any other address in Denver. Same for the apartment Davis used as a reference. Mr. and Mrs. Ellison, the former tenants, have never heard of him."

"You've been busy." Watching her, he tapped a finger on the steering wheel. "What was that you meant about not going off on your own?"

She smiled a little. The headache was backing off. "I carry a badge," she said, deadpan. "You don't."

"Your badge didn't get you into Miss Mavis's apartment."

"Should it have?"

"I think so." Darkly pleased to be one up on her, Colt reached into the back and showed Althea the package. "Messenger delivered it to the cat lady by mistake."

"Cat lady?"

"You had to be there. Uh-uh." He snatched it out of reach as she made a move toward it. "My take, darling. I'm willing to share."

Her temper spiked, then leveled off when she noticed that the package was still intact. "It's still sealed."

"Seemed fair," he said, meeting her eyes. "I figured we should open it together."

"Looks like you figured right this time. Let's have a look."

Colt reached down and drew a knife out of his boot. As he slit open the package, Althea narrowed her eyes.

"I don't think that toy's under the legal limit, champ."

"Nope," he said easily, and slid the knife back into his boot. Reaching into the package, he pulled out a videotape and a single sheet of paper.

Final edit. Okay for dupes? Heavy snows expected by weekend. Supplies good. Next drop send extra tapes and beer. Roads may be closed.

Althea held the sheet by a corner, then dug a plastic bag out of her purse. "We'll have it checked for prints. We could get lucky."

"It might tell us who. It won't tell us where." Colt slid the tape back into the bag. "Want to go to the movies?"

"Yeah." Althea set the bag on her lap, tapped it. "But I think this one calls for a private screening. I've got a VCR at home."

She also had a comfortable couch crowded with cushy pillows. Gleaming hardwood floors were accented by Navaho rugs. The art deco prints on the walls should have been at odds with the southwestern touches, but they weren't. Neither were the homey huddle of lush green plants on the curvy iron tea cart, the two goldfish swimming in a tube-shaped aquarium, or the footstool fashioned to resemble a squat, grinning gnome.

"Interesting place" was the best Colt could do.

"It does the job." She walked to a chrome-and-glass entertainment center, stepping out of her shoes on the way.

Colt decided that single gesture told him more about Althea Grayson than a dozen in-depth reports would have.

With her usual efficiency, she popped in the tape and flicked both the VCR and TV on.

There was no need to fast-forward past the FBI warning, because there wasn't one. After a five-second lag, the tape faded from gray.

And the show began.

Even for a man with Colt's experience, it was a surprise. He tucked his hands in his pockets and rocked back on his heels. It was foolish, he supposed, seeing as they were both adults, both professionals, but he felt an undeniable tug of embarrassment.

"I, ah, guess they don't believe in whetting the audience's appetite."

Althea tilted her head, studying the screen with a clinical detachment. It wasn't lovemaking. It wasn't even sex, according to her definition. It was straight porn, more pathetic than titillating.

"I've seen hotter stuff at bachelor parties."

Colt took his eyes from the screen long enough to arch a brow at her. "Oh, really?"

"Tape's surprisingly good quality. And the camera work, if you can call it that, seems pretty professional." She listened to the moans. "Sound, too." She nodded as the camera pulled back for a long shot. "Not the penthouse."

"Must be the place in the mountains. High-class rustic, from the paneling. Bed looks like a Chippendale."

"How do you know?"

"My mother's big on antiques. Look at the lamp by the bed. It's Tiffany, or a damn fine imitation. Ah, the plot thickens...."

They both watched as another woman walked into the frame. A few lines of dialogue indicated that she had come upon her lover and her best friend. The confrontation turned violent.

"I don't think that's fake blood." Althea hissed through her teeth as the first woman took a hard blow to the face. "And I don't think she was expecting that punch."

Colt swore softly as the rest of the scene unfolded. The mixture of sex and violence—violence that was focused on the women—made an ugly picture. He had to clench his fists to keep himself from slamming the television off.

It was no longer a matter of amused embarrassment. It was a matter of revulsion.

"You handling this, Nightshade?" Althea laid a hand on his arm. They both knew what he feared most—that Liz would come on-screen.

"I don't guess I'll be wanting any popcorn."

Instinctively Althea left her hand where it was and moved closer.

There was a plot of sorts, and she began to follow it. A weekend at a ski chalet, two couples who mixed and mingled in several ways. She moved beyond that, picking up the details. The furnishings. Colt had been right—they were first-class. Different camera angles showed that it was a two-story with an open loft and high beamed ceilings. Stone fireplace, hot tub.

In a few artistic shots, she saw that it was snowing lightly. She caught glimpses of screening trees and snow-capped peaks. In one outdoor scene that must have been more than uncomfortable for the actors, she noted that there was no other house or structure close by.

The tape ended without credits. And without Liz. Colt didn't know whether he was relieved or not.

"I don't think it's got much of a shot in the Oscar race." Althea kept her voice light as she rewound the tape. "You okay?"

He wasn't okay. There was a burning in his gut that needed some sort of release. "They were rough on the women," he said carefully. "Really vicious."

"Offhand, I'd say the main customers for this kind of thing would be guys who fantasize about dominance—physical and emotional."

"I don't think you can apply the word fantasy in conjunction with something like this."

"Not all fantasies are pretty," she murmured, thinking. "You know, the quality was good, but some

of the acting—and I use the term loosely—was downright pitiful. Could be they let some of their clients live
out those fantasies on film.''

"Lovely." He took one careful, cleansing breath.
"Jade's letter mentioned that she thought one of the
girls had been killed. Looks like she might have been
right."

"Sadism's a peculiar sexual tool—and one that can
often get out of hand. We might be able to make the
general area from the outside shots."

She started to eject the tape, but he whirled her
around. "How can you be so damn clinical? Didn't
that get to you? Doesn't anything?"

"Whatever does, I deal with it. Let's leave person-
alities out of this."

"No. It goes back to knowing who you're working
with. We're talking about the fact that some girl might
have been killed for the camera." There was a fury in
him that he couldn't control, and a terrible need to
vent it. "We've just seen two women slapped, shoved,
punched, and threatened with worse. I want to know
what watching that did to you."

"It made me sick," she snapped back, jerking away.
"And it made me angry. And if I'd let myself, it would
have made me sad. But all that matters, all that really
matters, is that we have our first piece of hard evidence." She snatched out the tape and replaced it in its
bag. "Now, if you want to do me a favor, you'll drop
me back at the precinct so that I can turn this over.
Then you can give me some space."

"Sure, Lieutenant." He strode to the door to yank
it open. "I'll give you all the space you need."

Chapter 5

Colt was holding three ladies. And he thought it was really too bad that the lady he wanted was sitting across the table from him, upping his bet.

"There's your twenty-five, Nightshade, and twenty-five more." Althea tossed chips into the kitty. She held her cards close to her vest, like her thoughts.

"Ah, well..." Sweeney heaved a sigh and studied the trash in his hand as if wishing alone might turn it to gold. "Too rich for my blood."

From her seat between Sweeney and a forensic pathologist named Louie, Cilla considered her pair of fives. "What do you think, Deadeye?"

Keenan, dressed for bed in a Denver Nuggets jersey, bounced on her lap. "Throw the money in."

"Easy for you to say." But her chips clattered onto the pile.

After a personal debate that included a great deal of

muttering, shifting and head shaking, Louie tossed in his chips, as well.

"I'll see your twenty-five," Colt drawled. He kept his cigar clamped between his teeth as he counted out chips. "And bump it again."

Boyd just grinned, pleased that he'd folded after the draw. The bet made the rounds again, with only Althea, Cilla and Colt remaining in.

"Three pretty queens," he announced, and laid down his cards.

Althea's eyes glinted when they met his. "Nice. But we don't have room for them in my full house." She spread her cards, revealing three eights and a pair of deuces.

"That puts my two fives to shame." Cilla sighed as Althea raked in the pot. "Okay, kid, you cost me seventy-five cents. Now you have to die." She hauled a giggling Keenan up as she rose.

"Daddy!" He spread his arms and grinned. "Help me! Don't let her do it!"

"Sorry, son." Boyd ruffled Keenan's hair and gave him a solemn kiss. "Looks like you're doomed. We're going to miss you around here."

Always ready to prolong the inevitable, Keenan hooked his arms around Colt's neck. "Save me!"

Colt kissed the waiting lips and shook his head. "Only one thing in this world scares me, partner, and that's a mama. You're on your own."

Levering in Cilla's arms, the boy made the rounds of the table. When he got to Althea, his eyes gleamed. "Okay? Can I?"

It was an old game, one she was willing to play. "For a nickel."

"I can owe you."

"You already owe me eight thousand dollars and fifteen cents."

"I get my allowance Friday."

"Okay, then." She took him onto her lap for a hug, and he sniffed her hair like a puppy. Colt saw her face soften, watched her hand slide up to stroke the tender nape of the boy's neck.

"It's good," Keenan announced, taking one last exaggerated sniff.

"Don't forget that eight thousand on Friday. Now beat it." After a kiss, she passed him back to Cilla.

"Deal me out," Cilla suggested, and, settling her son on her hip, she carried him upstairs to bed.

"A boy who can talk his way into a woman's lap's a boy to be proud of." Sweeney grinned as he gathered the cards. "My deal. Ante up."

During the next hour, Althea's pile of chips grew slowly, steadily. She enjoyed the monthly poker games that had become a routine shortly after Cilla and Boyd were married. The basic challenge of outwitting her opponents relaxed her almost as much as the domestic atmosphere that had seeped into every corner of the Fletcher home.

She was a cautious player, one who gambled only when satisfied with the odds, and who bet meticulously, thoughtfully, even then. She noted that Colt's pile multiplied, as well, but in fits and starts. He wasn't reckless, she decided. *Ruthless* was the word. Often he bumped the pot when he had nothing, or sat back and let others do the raising when he had a handful of gold.

No pattern, she mused, which she supposed was a pattern of its own.

After Sweeney won a piddling pot with a heart flush, she pushed back from the table. "Anybody want a beer?"

Everybody did. Althea strolled into the kitchen and began to pop tops. She was pouring herself a glass of wine when Colt walked in.

"Thought you could use some help."

"I can handle it."

"I don't figure there's much you can't handle." Damn, the woman was prickly, he thought. "I just thought I'd lend a hand."

Maria had prepared enough sandwiches to satisfy a hungry platoon on a long march. For lack of anything better to do Colt shifted some from platter to plate. He had to get it out, he decided. Now that they were alone and he had the opportunity, he wasn't sure how to start.

"I've got something to say about this afternoon."

"Oh?" Her tone frosty, Althea turned to the refrigerator and took out a bowl of Maria's incomparable guacamole dip.

"I'm sorry."

And nearly dropped it. "Excuse me?"

"Damn it, I'm sorry. Okay?" He hated to apologize—it meant he had made a mistake, one that mattered. "Watching that tape got to me. It made me want to smash something, someone. The closest I could come to it was ripping into you."

Because it was the last thing she would have expected, she was caught off guard. She stood with the bowl in her hand, unsure of her next move. "All right."

"I was afraid I'd see Liz," he continued, compelled to say it all. "I was afraid I wouldn't." At a loss, he picked up one of the opened beers and took a long swallow. "I'm not used to being scared like this."

There was very little he could have said, and nothing he could have done, that would have gotten through her defenses more thoroughly. Touched, and shaken, she set the bowl on the counter and opened a bag of chips.

"I know. It got to me, too. It's not supposed to, but it did." She poured the chips into the bowl, wishing there was something else she could do. Anything else. "I'm sorry things aren't moving faster, Colt."

"They haven't been standing still, either. And I've got you to thank for most of that." He lifted a hand, then dropped it. "Thea, there was something else I wanted to do this afternoon besides punching somebody. I wanted to hold you." He saw the wariness flash into her eyes, quick as a heartbeat, and had to grind down his temper. "Not jump you, Thea. Hold you. There's a difference."

"Yes, there is." She let out a long, quiet breath. There was need in his eyes. Not desire, just need. The need for contact, for comfort, for compassion. That she understood. "I guess I could have used it, too."

"I still could." It cost him to make the first move, this sort of move. But he stepped toward her and held out his arms.

It cost her, as well, to respond, to move into his arms and encircle him with her own.

And when they were close, when her cheek was resting against his shoulder and his against her hair, they both sighed. The tension drained away like water through a broken dam.

He didn't understand it, wasn't sure he could accept it, but he realized it felt right. Very simply right.

Unlike the first time he'd held her, there was no punch of lust, no molten fire in his blood. But there was a warmth, sweet and spreading and solid.

He could have held her like that, just like that, for hours.

She didn't often let herself relax so completely, not with a man, and certainly not with a man who attracted her. But this was so easy, so natural. The steady thudding of his heart lulled her. She nearly nuzzled. The urge was there—to rub her cheek against him, to close her eyes and purr. When she felt him sniffing her hair, she laughed.

"The kid's right," he murmured. "It's good."

"That's going to cost you a nickel, Nightshade."

"Put it on my tab," he told her as she lifted her head to smile at him.

Was it because she'd never looked at him quite that way that it hit him so hard? He couldn't be sure. All he knew was that she was outrageously beautiful, her hair loose and tumbling into his hands, glinting like flame in the hard kitchen light. Her eyes were smiling, deep and tawny and warm with humor. And her mouth—unpainted, curved, slightly parted. Irresistible.

He tilted his head, lowered it, waiting for her to stiffen or draw back. She did neither. Though the humor in her eyes had turned to awareness, the warmth remained. So he touched his lips to hers, gently testing, an experiment in emotions. With their eyes open, they watched each other, as if each were waiting for the other to move back, or leap forward.

When she remained pliant in his arms, he changed the angle, nipping lightly. He felt her tremble, only once, as her eyes darkened, clouded. But they remained open and on his.

She wanted to see him. Needed to. She was afraid that if she closed her eyes she might fall into whatever pit it was that yawned before her. She had to see who he was, to try to understand what there was about this one man that made him capable of turning her system to mush.

No one had done so before. And she'd been proud of her ability to resist, or to control, and smugly amused by men and women who fell under the spell of another. In falling they had suffered the torments of love. She had never been certain the joys balanced those torments.

But as he deepened the kiss, slowly, persuasively deepened it so that not only her lips, but also her mind, her heart, her body, were involved in that contact, she wondered what she had missed by never allowing surrender to mix with power.

"Althea . . ." He whispered her name as he again, teasingly, changed the angle of the kiss. "Come with me. . . ."

She understood what he was asking. He wanted her to let go, to tumble with him wherever the moment took them. To yield to him, even as he yielded to her.

To gamble, when she wasn't sure of the odds.

He closed his eyes first. The soft, drowsy warmth slid seamlessly into a numbing ache, an ache that was all pleasure. Her eyes fluttered closed on a sigh.

"Hey! How about those beers— Oops!" Boyd winced and struggled not to grin. He slipped his hands into his pockets, and had to prevent himself from whistling a tune as his old friend and his former partner jumped apart like thieves caught in a bust.

"Sorry, guys." He strolled over to gather up the beer bottles himself. It occurred to him that in all the years he'd known Althea, he'd never seen that bemused, punch-drunk look on her face. "Must be something about this kitchen," he added as he headed for the door. "Can't tell you how many times I've found myself occupied the same way in here."

The door swung shut behind him. Althea blew out a long breath.

"Oh, boy" was the best she could manage.

Colt laid a hand on her shoulder. Not for balance, he assured himself, though his legs were weak. Just to keep things nice and light. "He looked pretty damned pleased with himself didn't he?"

"He'll razz me about this," she muttered. "And he'll tell Cilla, so she can razz me, too."

"They've probably got better things to do."

"They're married," she shot back. "Married people love talking about other people's—"

"Other people's what?"

"Stuff."

The more unraveled she became, the more Colt liked it. He was positive that only a privileged few had ever seen the cool lieutenant flustered. He wanted to savor every moment of the experience. Grinning, he leaned back against the counter.

"So? If you really want to drive them crazy, you could let me come home with you tonight."

"In your dreams, Nightshade."

He lifted a brow. Her voice hadn't been quite steady. He liked that—a whole lot. "Well, there's truth in that, darling. Might as well be straight and tell you I'm not willing to wait much longer to turn that dream into reality."

She needed to calm down, needed to do something with her hands. Killing two birds with one stone, she picked up her wine and sipped. "Is that a threat?"

"Althea." There was a world of patience in his voice. That amused him. He couldn't recall ever having been patient about anything before. "We both know what just went on here can't be turned into a threat. It was nice." He flicked a finger down her hair. "If we'd been alone somewhere, it would have turned out a lot nicer." The intent flickered in his eyes too quickly for her to avoid the result. His hand fisted in her hair, held her still. "I want you, Althea, and I want you bad. You can make out of that whatever you choose."

She felt a skip of something sprint down her spine. It wasn't fear. She'd been a cop long enough to recognize fear in all its forms. And she'd lived her life her own way long enough to remain cautious. "It seems to me that you want a great many things. You want Liz back, you want the men responsible for keeping her from her parents caught and punished. You want to do those things your way, with my cooperation. And—" she sipped her wine again, her eyes cool and level "—you want to go to bed with me."

She was amazing, Colt reflected. She had to be feeling some portion of the need and the desperation he was experiencing. Yet she might have been discussing a change in the weather. "That about sums it up. Why don't you tell me what you want?"

She was afraid she knew exactly what she wanted, and it was standing almost close enough to taste. "The difference between you and me, Nightshade, is that I know you don't always get what you want. Now I'm going to pack it in. I've had a long day. You can check

with me tomorrow. We'll have the sketches from
Meena. Something might turn up when we run them."

"All right." He'd let her go—for now, he thought.
The trouble with a woman like Althea, he mused, was
that a man would always be tempted to seduce her,
and he would always crave her coming to him freely.

"Thea?"

She paused at the kitchen door, looked back.
"Yes?"

"What are we going to do about this?"

She felt a sigh building—not one of weariness, one
of longing—and choked it off. "I don't know," she
said, as truthfully as she could. "I wish I did."

By nine-thirty the following morning, Colt was
cooling his heels in Althea's office. There wasn't much
room in her cubbyhole to cool anything. Out of sheer
boredom, he flipped through some of the papers on
her desk. Reports, he noted, in that peculiar language
cops used, a language that was both concise and
florid. Vehicles proceeded in a southwesterly direction, alleged perpetrators created disturbances, ar-
resting officers apprehended suspects after responding
to 312s and 515s.

She wrote a damn good report, if you were into
such bureaucratic hogwash. Which, he decided, she
obviously was. Rules-and-Regulations Grayson, he
thought, and closed the file. Maybe his biggest problem was that he'd seen that there was a lot more to her
than the straight-arrow cop.

He'd seen her hold a gun, steady as a rock, while her
eyes were alive with fear and determination. He'd felt
her respond like glory to an impulsive and urgent em-

brace. He'd watched her cuddle a child, soften with compassion and freeze like a hailstone.

He'd seen too much, and he knew he hadn't seen nearly enough.

Liz was his priority, had to be. Yet Althea remained lodged inside him, like a bullet in the flesh. Hot, painful, and impossible to ignore.

It made him angry. It made him itchy. And when she swept into the room, it made him snarl.

"I've been waiting for the best part of a damn hour. I haven't got time for this."

"That's a shame." She dropped another file onto her desk, noting immediately that her papers had been disturbed. "Could be you're watching too much TV, Nightshade. That's the only place a cop gets to work on one case at a time."

"I'm not a cop."

"That's more than obvious. And next time you have to wait for me, keep your nose out of my papers."

"Listen, Lieutenant—" He broke off, swearing, when her phone rang.

"Grayson." She slipped into her chair as she spoke, her hand already reaching for a pencil. "Yeah. Yeah, I got it. That was quick work, Sergeant. I appreciate it. I'll be sure to do that if I get over your way. Thanks again." She broke the connection and immediately began to dial again. "Kansas City located Jade's mother," she told Colt. "She'd moved from the Kansas side to Missouri."

"Is Jade with her?"

"That's what I'm going to try to find out." As she completed the call, Althea checked her watch. "She waits tables at night. Odds are I'll catch her at home at this hour."

Before Colt could speak again, Althea shot up a hand for silence.

"Hello, I'd like to speak with Janice Willowby." A sleepy and obviously irritated voice informed her that Janice didn't live there. "Is this Mrs. Willowby? Mrs. Willowby, this is Lieutenant Grayson, Denver Police— No, ma'am, she hasn't done anything. She isn't in any trouble. We believe she might be of some help to us on a case. Have you heard from your daughter in the last few weeks?" She listened patiently as the woman denied having been in contact with Janice and irritably demanded information. "Mrs. Willowby, Janice isn't a fugitive from justice, or under any sort of suspicion. However, we are anxious to contact her." Her eyes hardened, quickly, coldly. "Excuse me? Since I'm not asking you to turn your daughter in, I don't see a reward as being applicable. If—"

Colt thrust a hand over the receiver. "Five thousand," he stated. "If she gets us Jade, and Jade leads us to Liz." He saw the spitting denial in her eyes, but held firm. "It's not up to you. The reward's private."

Althea sucked in her disgust. "Mrs. Willowby, there is a private party authorizing the sum of five thousand for information on Janice, on the condition that this then results in the satisfactory close of the investigation. Yes, I'm quite sure you can have it in cash. Oh, yes, I'm sure you will see what you can do. You can reach me twenty-four hours a day, at this number." She repeated it twice. "Collect, of course. That's Lieutenant Althea Grayson, Denver. I hope you do."

After hanging up the phone, she sat simmering. "It's no wonder girls like Jade take off and end up on the streets. She didn't give a damn about her daughter, just wanted to be sure no backlash was going to come her way. If Jade had been in any trouble, she'd have been willing to trade her for cash in the blink of an eye.''

"Not everybody has the maternal instincts of Donna Reed.''

"You're telling me.'' Because emotions would interfere with the job at hand, Althea shelved them. "Meena's been working with the police artist, and she's come up with some pretty good likenesses. One of them matches one of the stars from the production we watched yesterday.''

"Which one?''

"The guy in the red leather G-string. We're running a make through Vice to start. It'll take time.''

"I don't have time.''

She set aside the pencil, folded her hands. She wouldn't lose her temper, she promised herself. Not again. "Do you have a better way?''

"No." He turned away, then swung back. "Any prints on the car used to hit Billings?''

"Clean.''

"The penthouse?''

"No prints. Some hair fibers. They won't help us catch them, but they'll be good for tying it up in court. The lab's working on the tape, and the note. We could get lucky.''

"How about missing persons? A Jane Doe at the morgue? Jade said she thought one of the girls was killed.''

"Nothing's turned up. If they did kill someone, and she'd been in the life for a while, a missing-persons report's unlikely. I've checked all the unidentified and suspicious deaths over the last three months. Nobody fits the profile.''

"Any luck in the homeless shelters, runaway hostels, halfway houses?"

"Not yet." She hesitated, then decided it was best that they talk it through. "There's something I've been kicking around."

"Go ahead, kick it my way."

"We've got a couple of babyfaces on the force. Good cops. We can put them undercover, out on the street. See if they get a movie offer."

Colt rolled it around in his head. That, too, would take time, he mused. But at least it was a chance. "It's a tricky spot. Do you have anyone good enough to handle it?"

"I said I did. I'd do it myself—"

"No." His abrupt denial was like the lash of a whip.

Althea inclined her head and continued without a flinch. "I said, I'd do it myself, but I can't pass for a teenager. Apparently our producer prefers kids. I'll set it in motion."

"Okay. Can you get me a dupe of the tape?"

She smiled. "Evenings too dull for you?"

"Very funny. Can you?"

She thought it through. It wasn't strictly procedure, but it couldn't do any harm. "I'll check with the lab. Meanwhile, I'm going to roust the bartender at Clancy's. I'm betting he's the one who tipped off the bunch on Second Avenue. We might sweat something out of him."

"I'll go with you."

She shook her head. "I'm taking Sweeney." She smiled, fully, easily. "A big Irish cop, a bar called Clancy's. It just seems to fit."

"He's a lousy poker player."

"Yeah, but a darlin' man," she said, surprising him by slipping into a perfect Irish brogue.

"How about I go along anyway?"

"How about you wait for me to call you?" She rose, pulled a navy blazer from the back of her chair. She wore pleated slacks of the same color and texture and a paler blue blouse in a silky material. Her shoulder harness and weapon looked so natural on her, they might have been fashion accessories.

"You will call me."

"I said I would."

Because it seemed right, he laid his hands on her shoulders, and briefly rested his brow on hers. "Marleen called me this morning. I don't like to think I was giving her false hope, but I told her we were getting closer. I had to tell her that."

"Whatever eases her mind is the right thing to say." She couldn't help it. She pressed a hand briefly to his cheek in comfort, then let it drop. "Hang tough, Nightshade. We've gathered a lot of information in a short amount of time."

"Yeah." He lifted his head and slid his hands down her arms until he could link fingers with her. "I'll let you go find your intimidating Irishman. But there's one more thing." He raised their linked hands, studying the contrast of texture, tone and size. "Sooner or later, we'll be going off the clock." His gaze shifted to meet hers. "Then we'll have to deal with other things."

"Then we'll deal with them. But you may not like the way it shakes down."

He caught her chin in one hand, kissed her hard, then released her before she could do more than hiss. "Same goes. You be careful out there, Lieutenant."

"I was born careful, Nightshade." She walked away, shrugging into the blazer as she went.

Ten hours later, she parked her car in her building's garage and headed for the elevator. She was ready for a hot bath pregnant with bubbles, a glass of icy white wine, and some slow blues, heavy on the bass.

As she rode to her floor, she leaned against the back wall and shut her eyes. They hadn't gotten very far with the bartender, Leo Dorsetti. Bribes hadn't worked, and veiled threats hadn't, either. Althea didn't doubt he had connections with the pornography ring. Nor did she doubt that he was worried that the same fate might befall him that had Wild Bill.

So she needed more than a threat. She needed to dig up something on Leo Dorsetti. Something solid enough that she could drag him downtown and into interrogation.

Once she had him, she could crack him. She was damn sure of that.

She jingled her keys as she walked through the open elevator doors and into the hall. Now it was time to put the cop on hold, at least for an hour or two. Obsessing over a case usually equalled making mistakes on a case. So she'd pack it away into a corner of her mind, let it sit, let it ripen, while the woman indulged in a purely selfish evening.

She'd already unlocked the door, pushed it open, when the alarm went off in her head. She didn't question what tripped it, just whipped out her weapon. Automatically she followed standard entry procedure, checking in corners and behind the door.

Her eyes scanned the room, noting that nothing was out of place—unless she counted the Bessie Smith record currently playing on the turntable. And the scent. She took a quick whiff, identifying cooking, something spicy. It made her mouth water in response, even as her mind stayed alert.

A sound from the kitchen had her whirling in that direction, ending in the spread-legged police stance, her weapon steady in both hands.

Colt stopped in the doorway, wiping his hands on a dishcloth. Smiling, he leaned back against the jamb. "Hi there, darling. And how was your day?"

Chapter 6

Althea lowered her gun. She didn't raise her voice. The words she chose, quiet and precise, made her feelings known with more clarity than a shout could have.

When she'd finished, Colt could only shake his head in admiration. "I don't believe I've ever been cussed out with more style. Now, I'd be obliged if you'd holster that gun. Not that I figure you'd use it and risk getting blood all over your floor."

"It might be worth it." She slapped her gun back in place, but her eyes never left his. "You have the right to remain silent...." she began.

Wisely, Colt stifled a chuckle. He held up a hand. "What're you doing?"

"I'm reading you your rights before I haul your butt in for nighttime breaking and entering."

He didn't doubt she'd do it. She'd have him booked, fingerprinted and photographed without breaking stride. "I'll waive them, providing you listen to an explanation."

"It better be good." Shrugging out of her blazer, she tossed it over the back of the chair. "How did you get in here?"

"I, ah . . . Through the door?"

Her eyes narrowed. "You have the right to an attorney."

Obviously humor wasn't going to do the trick. "Okay, I'm busted." He tossed up both hands in a gesture of surrender. "I picked the lock. It's a damn good one, too. Or maybe I'm getting rusty."

"You picked the lock." She nodded, as if it were no more than she'd expected. "You carry a concealed weapon—an ASP nine-millimeter . . ."

"Good eye, Lieutenant."

"And a knife that likely exceeds the legal limit," she continued. "Now it appears you also carry lock picks."

"They come in handy." And it was something he preferred not to dwell on when she was in this sort of mood. "Now, I figured you had a rough day, and you deserved coming home to a hot meal and some cold wine. I also figured you'd be a little testy coming in and finding me here. But I have to believe you'll come around after you've had a taste of my linguine."

Maybe, she thought, maybe if she closed her eyes for a minute, it would all go away. But when she tried it, he was still there, grinning at her. "Your linguine?"

"Linguine marinara. I'd claim it was my sainted mother's recipe, but she never boiled an egg in her life. How about that wine?"

"Sure. Why the hell not?"

"That's the way." He stepped back into the kitchen. Deciding she could always kill him later, Althea followed. The aromas drifting through the air were heaven. "You like white," he said as he poured two glasses, using her best crystal. "This is a nice, full-bodied Italian that won't embarrass my sauce. Bold, but classy. See if it suits you."

She accepted the glass, allowed him to clink his against hers, then sipped. The wine tasted like liquid heaven. "Who the hell are you, Nightshade?"

"Why, I'm the answer to your prayers. Why don't we go in and sit down? You know you want to take your shoes off."

She did, but she obstinately kept them on as she walked back and lowered herself onto the couch. "Explain."

"I just did."

"If you cannot afford an attorney—"

"God, you're tough." He let out a long breath and stretched out beside her. "Okay, I have a couple of reasons. One, I know you've been putting in a lot of extra time on my business...."

"It's my—"

"Job?" he finished for her. "Maybe. But I know when someone's taking those extra steps, the kind that eat into personal time, and fixing you dinner's just a way of saying thanks."

It was a damn nice gesture, too, she thought, though she wasn't willing to say so. Yet. "You might have mentioned the idea to me earlier."

"It was an impulse. You ever have them?"

"Don't push your luck, Nightshade."

"Right. Well, to get back to the whys. There's also the fact that I haven't been able to snatch more than an hour at a time to clear this whole mess out of my head. Cooking helps me recharge. Maria wasn't likely to turn her stove over to me, so I thought of you.'' He reached out to curl a lock of her hair around his finger. ''I think of you a lot. And finally, and simply, I wanted the evening with you.''

He was getting to her. Althea wanted to believe that it was the glorious scents sneaking out of the kitchen that were weakening her. But she didn't believe it. ''So you broke into my home and invaded my privacy.''

''The only thing I poked into was your kitchen cupboards. It was tempting,'' he admitted, ''but I didn't go any farther than that.''

Frowning, Althea swirled the wine in her glass. ''I don't like your methods, Nightshade. But I think I'm going to like your linguine.''

She didn't like it. She adored it. It was difficult to harbor resentments when her palate was being so thoroughly seduced. She'd had men cook for her before, but she couldn't remember ever being so completely charmed.

Here was Colt Nightshade, very possibly armed to the teeth beneath his faded jeans and chambray shirt, serving her pasta by candlelight. Not that it was romantic, she thought. She was too smart to fall for any conventional trappings. But it was funny, and oddly sweet.

By the time she'd worked her way through one helping and was starting on a second, she'd filled him in on her progress. The lab reports were expected within twenty-four hours, the bartender at Clancy's was under surveillance, and an undercover officer was being prepped to hit the streets.

Colt filed her information away and traded it for some of his own. He'd talked to some of the local working girls that afternoon. Whether due to his charm or to the money that had changed hands, he'd learned that a girl who went by the street name Lacy hadn't been seen in any of her usual haunts for the past several weeks.

"She fits the profile," he continued, topping off Althea's wineglass. "Young, tiny. Girls said she was a brunette, but liked to wear a blond wig."

"Did she have a pimp?"

"Uh-uh. Free-lancer. I went by the rooms she'd been renting." Colt broke a piece of garlic bread in two and passed Althea half. "Talked to the land-lord—a prince of a guy. Since she'd missed a couple of weekly rent payments, he'd packed up her stuff. Pawned what was worth anything, trashed the rest."

"I'll see if anybody at Vice knows about her."

"Good. I hit some of the shelters again," he went on. "The halfway houses, showing Liz's picture around, and the police sketches." He frowned, toying with the rest of his meal. "I couldn't get anyone to ID. Had a hard enough time convincing any of the kids that they should look at the pictures. Most of the kids want to act tough, invincible, and all you see is the confusion in their eyes."

"When you're dealing with that kind of confusion, you have to be tough. Most of them come from homes that are torn apart by drugs, drinking, physical and sexual abuse. Or they got into substance abuse all on their own and don't know how to get out again." She moved her shoulders. "Either way, running seems like the best way out."

"It wasn't like that for Liz."

"No," she agreed. It was time for him to turn it off, as well, she decided. If only for a few minutes. She scraped a last bite from her plate. "You know, Nightshade, you could give up playing the adventurer and go into catering. You'd make a fortune."

He understood what she was doing, and he put some effort into accommodating her. "I prefer small, private parties."

Her gaze flicked up to his, then back to her glass. "So, if it wasn't your sainted mother who taught you to make world-class linguine, who did?"

"We had this terrific Irish cook when I was growing up. Mrs. O'Malley."

"An Irish cook who taught you Italian cuisine."

"She could make anything—from lamb stew to coq au vin. 'Colt, me boy,' she used to tell me, 'the best thing a man can do for himself is to learn to feed himself well. Depending on a woman to fill your belly's a mistake.'" The memory made him grin. "When I'd gotten into trouble, which was most of the time, she'd sit me down in the kitchen. I'd get lectures on behavior, and the proper way to debone a chicken."

"Quite a combination."

"The stuff on behavior didn't stick." He toasted her. "But I make a hell of a chicken pot pie. And when Mrs. O'Malley retired—oh, almost ten years ago now—my mother went into a dark state of depression."

Althea's lips curved on the rim of her glass. "And hired another cook."

"A French guy with a bad attitude. She loves him."

"A French chef in Wyoming."

"I live in Wyoming," he said. "They live in Houston. We get along better that way. What about your family? Are they from around here?"

"I don't have one. What about your law degree? Why haven't you done anything with it?"

"I didn't say I hadn't." He studied her for a moment. She'd certainly dropped his question like a hot coal. It was something he'd have to come back to. "I found out I wasn't suited to spending hours hunched over law books, trying to outwit justice on technicalities."

"So you went into the air force."

"It was a good way to learn how to fly."

"But you're not a pilot."

"Sometimes I am." He smiled. "Sorry, Thea, I don't fit into a slot. I've got enough money that I can do what suits me when it suits me."

That wasn't good enough. "And the military didn't suit you?"

"For a while it did. Then I had enough." He shrugged and sat back. The candlelight flickered on his face and in his eyes. "I learned some things. Just like I learned from Mrs. O'Malley, and from prep school, from Harvard, and from this old Indian horse trainer I met in Tulsa some years back. You never know when you're going to use what you've learned."

"Who taught you to pick locks?"

"You're not going to hold that against me, are you?" He leaned forward to flick a finger over her hair, and to pour more wine. "I picked it up in the service. I was in what you might call a special detachment."

"Covert operations," she said, translating. It was no surprise. "That's why so much of your record's classified."

"It's old news, should be declassified by now. But that's the way of it, isn't it? Bureaucrats like secrets almost as much as they like red tape. What I did was gather information, or plant information, maybe defuse certain volatile situations, or stir them up, depending on the orders." He drank again. "I guess we could say I started doing favors for people—only these people ran the government." His lip curled. "Or tried to."

"You don't like the system, do you?"

"I like what works." For an instant only, his eyes darkened. "I saw plenty that didn't work. So..." He shrugged, and the mood was gone. "I got out, bought myself a few horses and cows, played rancher. Looks like old habits die hard, because now I do favors for people again. Only now I have to like them first."

"Some people might say that you've had a hard time deciding what you want to do when you grow up."

"Some people might. I figure I've been doing it. What about you? What's the back story on Althea Grayson?"

"It's nothing that would sell to the movies." Relaxed, she rested her elbows on the table, running a finger around the rim of her glass until the crystal sang. "I went straight into the academy when I was eighteen. No detours."

"Why?"

"Why a cop?" She mulled over her answer. "Because I do like the system. It's not perfect, but if you keep at it, you can make it work. And the law...there are people out there who want to make it work. Too many lives get lost in the cracks. It means something when you can pull one out."

"I can't argue with that." Without thinking about it, he laid a hand over hers. "I could always see that Boyd was meant to make law and order work. Until recently, he was about the only cop I respected enough to trust."

"I think you just gave me a compliment."

"You can be sure of it. The two of you have a lot in common. A clear-sightedness, a stubborn kind of valor, a steady compassion." He smiled, toying with her fingers. "The kid we got off the roof—I went to see her, too. She had a lot to say about the pretty lady with the red hair who brought her a baby doll."

"So I did a follow-up. It's my job to—"

"Bull." Delighted with her response, he picked up her hand, kissed it. "It had nothing to do with duty, and everything to do with you. Having a soft side doesn't make you less of a cop, Thea. It just makes you a kinder one."

She knew where this was leading, but she didn't pull her hand away. "Just because I have a soft spot for kids doesn't mean I've got one for you."

"But you do," he murmured. "I get to you." Watching her, he skimmed his lips down to her wrist. The pulse there beat steady, but it also beat fast. "I'm going to keep getting to you."

"Maybe you do." She was too smart to continue to deny the obvious. "That doesn't mean anything's going to come of it. I don't sleep with every man who attracts me."

"I'm glad to hear it. Then again, you're going to do a lot more than sleep with me." He chuckled and kissed her hand again. "God, I love it when you smirk, Thea. It drives me crazy. What I was going to say was, when we get each other to bed, sleeping's not going to be a priority. So maybe you should catch some shut-eye." He rose, pulling her to her feet. "Kiss me good-night, and I'll let you get some now."

The surprise in her eyes made him grin again. He'd wait until later to pat himself on the back for his strategy.

"You thought I cooked you dinner and kept you company so I could use it as a springboard to seduction." On a windy sigh, he shook his head. "Althea, I'm wounded. Close to crushed."

She laughed, keeping a friendly hand in his. "You know, Nightshade, sometimes I almost like you. Almost."

"See, that's just a couple of short steps away from you being nuts about me." He gathered her close, and the instant twisting in his gut mocked his light tone. "If I'd bothered to make dessert, you'd be begging for me."

Amused, she tucked her tongue in her cheek. "Your loss. Everybody knows cannoli turns me into a wild woman."

"I'll sure as hell remember that." He kissed her lightly, watched her smile. And felt his heart turn over. "There must be a bakery around here where I can pick up some Italian pastries."

"Nope. You missed your shot." She brought a hand to his chest, telling herself she was going to end the interlude now, while she could still feel her legs under her. "Thanks for the pasta."

"Sure." But he continued to stare down at her, his eyes sharpening, focusing, as if he were struggling to see past the ivory skin, the delicate bones. Something was happening here, he realized. Something internal that he couldn't quite get a grip on. "You have something in your eyes."

Her nerves were dancing. "What?"

"I don't know." He spoke slowly, as if measuring each word. "Sometimes I can almost see it. When I do, it makes me wonder where you've been. Where we're going."

Her lungs were backing up. She took a careful breath to clear them. "*You* were going home."

"Yeah. In a minute. Too easy to tell you you're beautiful," he murmured, as if speaking to himself. "You hear that too much, and it's too superficial to carry any weight with you. It should be enough for me, but there's something else in there. I keep coming back to it." Still seeking, he drew her closer. "What is it about you, Althea? What is it I can't shake loose?"

"There's nothing. You're too used to looking for shadows."

"No, you've got them." Slowly he slid a hand up to cup her cheek. "And what I have is a problem."

"What problem?"

"Try this."

He lowered his mouth to hers and had every muscle in her body going lax. It wasn't demanding, it wasn't urgent. It was devastating. The kiss tumbled her deeper, deeper, bombarding her with emotions she had no defense against. His feelings were free and ripe and poured over her, into her, so that she was covered and filled and surrounded by them.

No escape, she thought, and heard her own muffled sound of despair with a dull acceptance. He'd breached a defense she had taken for granted, one she might never fully shore up again.

She could tell herself again and again that she wouldn't fall in love, that she couldn't fall in love with a man she hardly knew. But her heart was already laughing at logic.

He felt her give—not all the way, not yet, but give yet another degree of self. There was more than heat here, though, sweet heaven, there was heat. But there was a kind of discovery, as well. For Colt, it was a revelation to discover that one woman—this woman—could tangle up his mind, rip open his heart, and leave him helpless.

"I'm losing ground here." He kept his hands firm on her shoulders as he pulled back. "I'm losing it fast."

"It's too much." It was a poor response, but the best she could summon.

"You're telling me." There was tension in her shoulders again, and in his. It compelled him to step away. "I've never felt like this before. And that's no line," he said when she turned away from him.

"I know. I wish it were." She gripped the back of the chair, where her shoulder holster hung. A symbol of duty, she thought. Of control, of what she had made of herself. "Colt, I think we're both getting in deeper than we might like."

"Maybe we've been treading water long enough."

She was very much afraid that she was ready, willing, even eager, to sink. "I don't let personal business interfere with my job. If we can't keep this under control, you should consider working with someone else."

"We've been working together just fine," he said between his teeth. "Don't pull out any lame excuses because you don't want to face up to what's going on between us."

"It's the best I've got." Her knuckles had turned white on the chair. "And it's not an excuse, only a reason. You want me to say you scare me. All right. You scare me. This scares me. And I don't think you want a partner who can't focus because you make her nervous."

"Maybe I'm happier with that than with one who's so focused it's hard to tell if she's human." She wasn't going to pull away from him now. He'd be damned if he'd let her. "Don't tell me you can't work on two levels, Thea, or that you can't function as a cop when you've got a problem in your personal life."

"Maybe I just don't want to work with you."

"That's tough. You're stuck. If you want to put this on hold, I'll try to oblige you. But you're not backing off from Liz because you're afraid to let yourself feel something for me."

"I'm thinking about Liz, and what's best for her."

"How the hell would you know?" he exploded, and if it was unreasonable, he didn't give a damn. He was on the edge of falling in love with a woman who was calmly telling him she didn't want him in any area of her life. He was desperate to find a frightened girl, and the person who'd helped him make progress toward doing so was threatening to pull out. "How the hell would you know about her or anyone else? You've got yourself so wrapped up in regulations and procedure that you can't feel. No, not can't. Won't. You won't feel. You'll risk your life, but one brush with emotion and up goes the shield. Everything's so tidy for you, isn't it, Althea? There's some poor scared kid out there, but she's just another case for you, just another job.''

"*Don't* you tell me how I feel." Her control snapped as she shoved the chair aside, clattering to the floor between them. "Don't tell me what I understand. You can't possibly know what's inside me. Do you think you know Liz, or any of those girls you talked with today? You've walked into shelters and halfway houses, and you think you understand?"

Her eyes glinted, not with tears, but with a rage so sharp he could only stand and let it slice at him. "I know there are plenty of kids who need help, and not always enough help to go around."

"Oh, that's so easy." She strode across the room and back in a rare show of useless motion. "Write a check, pass a bill, make a speech. It's so effortless. You haven't a clue what it's like to be alone, to be afraid or to be caught up in that grinding machine we toss displaced kids into. I spent most of my life in that machine, so don't tell me I don't feel. I know what it's like to want out so bad you run even when there's no place to go. And I know what it's like to be yanked back, to be helpless, to be abused and trapped and miserable. I understand plenty. And I know that Liz has a family who love her, and we'll get her back to them. No matter what, we'll get her back, and she won't be caught in that cycle. So don't you tell me she's just another case, because she matters. They all matter."

She broke off, running a shaky hand through her hair. At the moment, she wasn't sure which was bigger, her embarrassment or her anger. "I'd like you to go now," she said quietly. "I'd really like you to go."

"Sit down." When she didn't respond, he walked over and pressed her into a chair. She was trembling, and the fact that he'd played a part in causing that made him feel as if he'd punched a hole in something precious and fragile. "I'm sorry. That's a record for me, apologizing to the same person twice in one day." He started to brush a hand over her hair, but stopped himself. "Do you want some water?"

"No. I just want you to leave."

"I can't do it." He lowered himself to the footstool in front of her so that their eyes were level. "Althea..."

She sat back, her eyes shut. She felt as though she'd raced to the top of a mountain and leapt off. "Nightshade, I'm not in the mood to tell you my life story, so if that's what you're waiting for, you know where the door is."

"That'll keep." He took a chance and reached for her hand. It was steady now, he noted, but cold. "Let's try something else. What we've got here are two separate problems. Finding Liz is number one. She's an innocent, a victim, and she needs help. I could find her on my own, but that would take too long. Every day that goes by... Well, too many days have gone by already. I need you to work with me, because you can cut through channels it would take me twice as long to circumvent. And because I trust you to put everything you've got into getting her home."

"All right." She kept her eyes closed, willing the tension away. "We'll find her. If not tomorrow, the next day. But we'll find her."

"Second problem." He looked down at their hands, studying the way the second hand on her watch ticked off the time. "I think...ah, and since this is a new area for me, I want to qualify it by saying that it's only an opinion..."

"Nightshade." She opened her eyes again, and there was a ghost of a smile in them. "I swear you sound just like a lawyer."

He winced, shifted. "I don't think you should insult a man who's about to tell you he's pretty sure he's in love with you." She jolted. He'd have bet the farm that he could pull a gun and she wouldn't flinch. But mention love and she jumped six inches off the chair. "Don't panic," he continued while she searched for her voice. "I said 'I think.' That leaves us with a safe area to play with."

"Sounds more like a mine field to me." Because she was afraid it might start shaking again, she drew her hand away from his. "I think it would be wise, under the circumstances, to table that for the time being."

"Now who sounds like a lawyer?" He grinned, not at all sure why it seemed so appropriate to laugh at himself. "Darling, you think it puts the fear of God into you? Picture what it does to me. I only brought it up because I'm hoping that'll make it easier to deal with. For all I know, it's just a touch of the flu or something."

"That would be good." She choked back a laugh, terrified it would sound giddy. "Get plenty of rest, drink fluids."

"I'll give that a try." He leaned forward, not displeased to see the wariness in her eyes or the bracing of her shoulders. "But if it's not the flu, or some other bug, I'm going to do something about it. Whatever that might be can wait until we've settled the first problem. Until we do, I won't bring up love, or all the stuff that generally follows along after it—you know, like marriage and family and a two-car garage.''

For the first time since he'd known her, he saw her totally at a loss. Her eyes were huge, and her mouth was slack. He would have sworn that if he tapped her, she'd keel over like a sapling in a storm.

''Guess it's just as well I don't, since talking about them in the abstract sense seems to have put you in a coma.''

''I...'' She managed to close her mouth, swallow, then speak. ''I think you've lost your mind.''

''Me, too.'' Lord knew why he felt so cheerful about it. ''So for now let's concentrate on digging up those bad guys. Deal?''

''And if I agree, you're not going to sneak in any of that other stuff?''

His smile spread slowly. ''Are you willing to take my word on it?''

''No.'' She steadied herself and smiled back. ''But I'm willing to bet I can deflect anything you toss out.''

''I'll take that bet.'' He held out a hand. ''Partner.'' They shook, solemnly. ''Now, why don't we—''

The phone interrupted what Althea was sure would have been an unprofessional suggestion. She slipped by Colt and picked up the extension in the kitchen.

It gave him a moment to think about what he'd started. To smile. To think about how he'd like to finish it. Before he'd wound his fantasy up, she was striding back. She righted the chair, snagged her shoulder harness.

''Our friend Leo, the bartender? We just busted him for selling coke out of his back room.'' The warrior look was back on her face as she shrugged into the harness. "They're bringing him in for interrogation."

"I'm right behind you."

"Behind me is just where you'll stay, Nightshade," she said as she slipped into her blazer. "If Boyd clears it, you can observe through the glass, but that's the best deal you'll get."

He chafed at the restraint. "Let me sit in. I'll keep my mouth shut."

"Don't make me laugh." She grabbed her purse on the way to the door. "Take it or leave it—partner."

He swore at her, and slammed the door behind him. "I'll take it."

Chapter 7

Colt's initial frustration at being stuck behind the two-way glass faded as he watched Althea work. Her patient, detail-by-detail interrogation had a style all its own. It surprised Colt to label that style not only meticulous, but relentless, as well.

She never allowed Leo to draw her off track, never betrayed any reaction to his sarcasm, and never—not even when Leo tried abusive language and veiled threats—raised her voice.

She played poker the same way, he remembered. Coolly, methodically, without a flicker of emotion until it was time to cash in her chips. But Colt was beginning to see through the aloof shell into the woman behind it.

Certainly he'd been able to surprise many varied emotions from the self-contained lieutenant. Passion, anger, sympathy, even speechless shock. He had a feeling he'd only scratched the surface. There was a wealth of emotions beneath that tidy, professional and undeniably stunning veneer. He intended to keep digging until he unearthed them all.

"Long night." Boyd came up behind him bearing two mugs of steaming coffee.

"I've had longer." Colt accepted the mug, sipped. "This stuff's strong enough to do the tango." He winced and drank again. "Does the captain usually come in for a routine interrogation?"

"The captain does when he has a personal interest." Fletcher watched Althea a moment, noting that she sat, serene and unruffled, as Leo jerkily lit one cigarette from the butt of another. "Is she getting anything?"

With some effort, Colt restrained an urge to beat against the glass just to prove he could do something. "He's still tap dancing."

"He'll wear out long before she does."

"I've already figured that out for myself." They both lapsed into silence as Leo snarled out a particularly foul insult and Althea responded by asking if he'd like to repeat that statement for the record. "She doesn't ruffle," Colt commented. "Fletch, have you ever seen the way a cat'll sit outside a mouse hole?" He flicked a glance at Boyd, then looked back through the glass. "That cat just sits there, hardly blinking, maybe for hours. Inside the hole, the mouse starts to go crazy. He can smell that cat, see those eyes staring in at him. After a while, I guess, the mouse circuits in his brain overload, and he makes a break for it. The cat just whips out one paw, and it's over."

Colt sipped more coffee, nodded at the glass. "That's one gorgeous cat."

"You've gotten to know her pretty well in a short amount of time."

"Oh, I've got a ways to go yet. All those layers," he murmured, almost to himself. "Can't say I've ever run into a woman who had me just as interested in peeling the layers of her psyche as peeling off her clothes."

The image had Boyd scowling into his coffee. Althea was a grown woman, he reminded himself, and more than able to take care of herself. Boyd remembered he'd been amused to find Colt and his former partner in a clinch in his kitchen. But the idea of it going further, of his friends leaping into the kind of quick, physical relationship that could leave them both battered at the finish, disturbed him.

Particularly when he thought of Colt's talent with women. It was a talent they both had, and both of them had enjoyed the benefits of that talent over the years. But they weren't discussing just any woman this time. This was Althea.

"You know," Boyd began, feeling his way with the care of a blind man in a maze, "Thea's special. She can handle pretty much anything that comes her way."

"And does," Colt added.

"Yeah, and does. But that's not to say that she doesn't have her vulnerabilities. I wouldn't want to see her hurt. I wouldn't like that at all."

Mildly surprised, Colt lifted a brow. "A warning? Sounds like the same kind you gave me about your sister Natalie about a million years ago."

"Comes to the same thing. Thea's family."

"And you think I could hurt her."

Boyd let out a weary breath. He wasn't enjoying this conversation. "I'm saying, if you did, I'd have to bruise several of your vital organs. I'd be sorry, but I'd have to do it."

Colt acknowledged that with a thoughtful nod. "Who won the last time we went at it?"

Despite his discomfort, Boyd grinned. "I think it was a draw."

"Yeah, that's how I remember it. It was over a woman then, too, wasn't it?"

"Cheryl Anne Madigan." This time Boyd's sigh was nostalgic.

"Little blonde?"

"Nope, tall brunette. Big . . . blue eyes."

"Right." Colt laughed, shook his head. "I wonder whatever happened to pretty Cheryl Anne."

They fell into a comfortable silence for a moment, reminiscing. Through the speakers they could hear Althea's calm, relentless questioning.

"Althea's a long way from Cheryl Anne Madigan," Colt murmured. "I wouldn't want to hurt her, but I can't promise it won't happen. The thing is, Fletch, for the first time I've run into a woman who matters enough to hurt me back." Colt took another bracing sip. "I think I'm in love with her."

Boyd choked and was forced to set down his mug before he dumped the contents all over his shirt. He waited a beat, tapped a hand against his ear as if to clear it. "You want to say that again? I don't think I caught it."

"You heard me," Colt muttered. Leave it to a friend, he thought, to humiliate you at an emotionally vulnerable moment. "I got almost the same reaction from her when I told her."

"You told her?" Boyd struggled to keep one ear on the interrogation while he absorbed this new and fascinating information. "What did she say?"

"Not much of anything."

The frustration in Colt's voice tickled Boyd so much, he had to bite the tip of his tongue to keep from grinning. "Well, at least she didn't laugh in your face."

"She didn't seem to think it was very funny." Colt blew out a breath and wished Boyd had thought to lace the coffee with a good dose of brandy. "She just sat there, going pale, kind of gaping at me."

"That's a good sign." Boyd patted Colt's shoulder comfortingly. "It's real hard to throw her off that way."

"I figured it was best if it was out, you know? It would give us both time to decide what to do about it." He smiled through the glass at Althea, who continued to sit, cool and unruffled, while Leo gulped down water with a trembling hand. "Though I've pretty much figured out what I'm going to do about it."

"Which is?"

"Well, unless I wake up some morning real soon and realize I've had some sort of brain seizure, I'm going to marry her."

"Marry her?" Boyd rocked back on his heels and chuckled. "You and Thea? Lord, wait until I tell Cilla."

The murderous look Colt aimed at him only made Boyd's grin widen.

"I can't thank you enough for your support here, Fletch."

FREE BOOKS!

FREE GIFTS!

PLAY THE "LUCKY 7" SLOT MACHINE GAME!

AND YOU COULD GET FREE BOOKS <u>PLUS</u> A FREE VICTORIAN PICTURE FRAME!

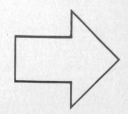

NO COST! NO OBLIGATION TO BUY!
NO PURCHASE NECESSARY!

PLAY "LUCKY 7"
AND GET AS MANY AS FIVE FREE GIFTS . .

HOW TO PLAY:

1. With a coin, carefully scratch off the silver box at the right. This makes you eligible to receive two or more free books, and possibly another gift, depending on what is revealed beneath the scratch-off area.

2. Send back this card and you'll receive brand-new Silhouette Intimate Moments® novels. These books have a cover price of $3.50 each, but they are yours to keep absolutely free.

3. There's no catch. You're under no obligation to buy anything. We charge nothing—ZERO—for your first shipment. And you don't have to make any minimum number of purchases—not even one!

4. The fact is thousands of readers enjoy receiving books by mail from the Silhouette Reader Service™ months before they're available in stores. They like the convenience of home delivery and they love our discount prices!

5. We hope that after receiving your free books you'll want to remain a subscriber. But the choice is yours—to continue or cancel, anytime at all! So why not take us up on our invitation, with no risk of any kind. You'll be glad you did!

This lovely Victorian pewter-finish miniature is perfect for displaying a treasured photograph. And it's yours FREE as added thanks for giving our Reader Service a try!

PLAY "LUCKY 7"

**Just scratch off the silver box with a coin.
Then check below to see which gifts you get.**

YES! I have scratched off the silver box. Please send me all the gifts for which I qualify. I understand I am under no obligation to purchase any books, as explained on the back and on the opposite page.

245 CIS AK9Z
(U-SIL-IM-11/93)

NAME

ADDRESS   APT.

CITY   STATE   ZIP

7	7	7	**WORTH FOUR FREE BOOKS PLUS A FREE VICTORIAN PICTURE FRAME**
🍒	🍒	🍒	**WORTH THREE FREE BOOKS PLUS A FREE VICTORIAN PICTURE FRAME**
●	●	●	**WORTH THREE FREE BOOKS**
🔔	🔔	🍒	**WORTH TWO FREE BOOKS**

Offer limited to one per household and not valid to current Silhouette Intimate Moments® subscribers. All orders subject to approval.

© 1990 HARLEQUIN ENTERPRISES LIMITED   **PRINTED IN U.S.A.**

THE SILHOUETTE READER SERVICE™: HERE'S HOW IT WORKS

Accepting free books places you under no obligation to buy anything. You may keep the books and gift and return the shipping statement marked "cancel." If you do not cancel, about a month later we will send you 6 additional novels, and bill you just $2.71 each plus 25¢ delivery and applicable sales tax, if any.* That's the complete price and — compared to cover prices of $3.50 each — quite a bargain! You may cancel at any time, but if you choose to continue, every month we'll send you 6 more books, which you may either purchase at the discount price ... or return at our expense and cancel your subscription.

*Terms and prices subject to change without notice. Sales tax applicable in N.Y.

Boyd gamely swallowed another chuckle, but he couldn't defeat the grin. "Oh, you've got it, pal. All the way. It's just that I never thought I'd be using the word *marriage* in the same sentence with *Colt Night-shade*. Or *Althea Grayson,* for that matter. Believe me, I'm with you all the way."

Inside the interrogation room, Althea continued to wear down her quarry. She scented his fear, and used it ruthlessly.

"You know, Leo, a little cooperation would go a long way."

"Sure, a long way to seeing me greased like Wild Bill."

Althea inclined her head. "As much as it pains me to offer it, you'd have protection."

"Right." Leo snorted out smoke. "You think I want cops on my butt twenty-four hours a day? You think it would work if I did?"

"Maybe not." She used her disinterest as another tool, slowing down the pace of the interview until Leo was squirming in his chair. "But, then again, no co-operation, no shield. You go out of here naked, Leo."

"I'll take my chances."

"That's fine. You'll make bail on the drug charges—probably deal them down so you won't do any time to speak of. But it's funny how word spreads on the street, don't you think?" She let that thought simmer in his brain. "Interested parties already know you've been tagged, Leo. And when you walk out, they won't be real sure about what you might have spilled while you were inside."

"I didn't tell you anything. I don't know any-thing."

"That's too bad. Because it might work against you, this ignorance. You see, we're closing in, and those same interested parties might wonder if you helped out." Casually she opened a file and revealed the police sketches. "They might wonder if I got the descriptions of these suspects from you."

"I didn't give you anything." Sweat popped out on Leo's forehead as he stared at the sketches. "I never seen those guys before."

"Well, that may be. But I'd have to say—if the subject came up—that I talked with you. A long time. And that I have detailed sketches of suspects. You know, Leo," she added, leaning toward him, "some people add two and two and get five. Happens all the time."

"That ain't legal." He moistened his lips. "It's blackmail."

"Don't hurt my feelings. You want me to be your friend, Leo." She nudged the sketches toward him. "You see, it's all a matter of attitude, and whether or not I care if you walk out of here and end up a smear on the sidewalk. Can't say I do at the moment." She smiled, chilling him. "Now, if you were my friend, I'd do everything I could to make sure you lived a long and happy life. Maybe not in Denver, maybe someplace new. You know, Leo, a change of scene can work wonders. Change your name, change your life."

Something flickered in his eyes. She knew it was doubt. "You talking witness protection program?"

"I could be. But if I'm going to ask for something that big, I have to be able to prime the pump." When he hesitated, she sighed. "You better choose sides, pal. Remember Wild Bill? All he did was meet a guy. They might have been talking about the Broncos' chances for the Superbowl. Nobody gave him the benefit of the doubt. They just iced him."

The fear was back, running in the sweat down his temples. "I get immunity. And you drop the drug charges."

"Leo, Leo..." Althea shook her head. "A smart man like you knows how life works. You give me something, if it's good enough, I give you something back. It's the American way."

He licked his lips again, lit yet another cigarette. "Maybe I've seen these two before."

"These two?" Althea tapped the sketches, and then, like Colt's cat, she pounced. "Tell me."

It was 2:00 a.m. before she was finished. She'd questioned Leo, listened to his long, rambling story, made notes, made him backtrack, repeat, expand. Then she'd called in a police stenographer and had Leo go over the same ground again, making an official statement for the tape.

She was energized as she strode back to her office. She had names now, names to run through the computer. She had threads—thin threads, perhaps, but threads nonetheless, tying an organization together.

Much of what Leo had told her was speculation and gossip. But Althea knew that a viable investigation could be built on less.

Peeling off her jacket, she sat at her desk and booted up her computer. She was peering at the screen when Colt walked in and stuck a cup under her nose.

"Thanks." She sipped, winced and spared him a glance. "What is this? It tastes like a meadow."

"Herbal tea," he told her. "You've had enough coffee."

"Nightshade, you're not going to spoil our relationship by thinking you have to take care of me, are you?" She set the cup aside and went back to the screen.

"You're wired, Lieutenant."

"I know how much I can take before the system overloads. Aren't you the one who keeps saying time's what we don't have?"

"Yeah." From his position behind her chair, he lowered his hands to her shoulders and began to rub. "You did a hell of a job with Leo," he said before she could shrug his hands off. "If I ever decide to go back to law, I'd hate to have you take on one of my clients."

"More compliments." His fingers were magic, easing without weakening, soothing without softening. "I didn't get as much as I wanted, but I think I got all he had."

"He's small-time," Colt agreed. "Passing a little business to the big boys, taking his commission."

"He doesn't know the main player. I'm sure he was telling the truth about that. But he ID'd the two Meena described. Remember the cameraman she'd told us about—the big African-American? Look." She gestured toward the screen. "Matthew Dean Scott, alias Dean Miller, alias Tidal Wave Dean."

"Catchy."

"He played some semipro football about ten years ago. Made a career out of unnecessary roughness. He broke an opposing quarterback's leg."

"These things happen."

"After the game."

"Ah, a poor sport. What else have we got on him?"

"I'll tell you what else *I've* got on him," she said, but she couldn't resist leaning back against his massaging hands. "He was fired for breaking training—having a woman in his room."

"Boys will be boys."

"This particular woman was tied up and screaming her lungs out. They dealt it down from rape to assault, but Scott's football days were over. After that, we've got him on a couple more assaults, indecent exposure, drunk and disorderly, petty larceny, lewd behavior." She punched another button on the keyboard. "That was up to four years ago. After that, nothing."

"You figure he turned over a new leaf? Became a pillar of the community?"

"Sure, just like I believe men read girlie magazines because of the erudite articles."

"That's what motivates me." Grinning, he leaned down to kiss the top of her head.

"I bet. We've got a similar history on contestant number two," she continued. "Harry Kline, a small-time actor from New York whose rap sheet includes drunk and disorderly, possession, sexual assault, several DWIs. He drifted into porno films about eight years ago, and was, incredibly enough, fired from several jobs because of his violent and erratic behavior. He headed west, got a few similar gigs in California, then was arrested for raping one of his costars. The defense pleaded it down and, due to the victim's line of work, made it all go away. The victim's only justice came from the fact that Harry was finished in film—blue or otherwise. Nobody even partially legit would touch him. That was five years ago. There's been nothing on him since."

"Once again, one would think our friends either became solid citizens or died in their sleep."

"Or found a handy hole to hide in. Leo claimed that he was first approached—by Kline—two, maybe three years ago. He knows it was at least two. Kline wanted women, young women who were interested in making private films. Citing free enterprise, Leo obliged him and took his commission. The number he was given to contact Kline is out of service. I'll run it through the phone company to see if it was the penthouse or another location."

"He never saw the other man, the one Meena said sat off in the corner?"

"No. His only contacts were Scott and Kline. Apparently Scott would drop in for a few drinks and brag about how good he was with a camera, and how much money he was pulling in."

"And about the girls," Colt said under his breath. The fingers rubbing Althea's shoulders went rigid. "How he and his friends had— How did he put it? The pick of the litter?"

"Don't think about it." Instinctively she lifted a hand to cover his. "Don't, Colt. You'll mess up if you do. We're a big step closer to finding her. That's what you have to concentrate on."

"I am." He turned away and paced to the far wall. "I'm also concentrating on the fact that if I find out either of those slime touched Liz, I'm going to kill them." He turned back, his eyes blank. "You won't stop me, Thea."

"Yes, I will." She rose and went to him to take both of his fisted hands in hers. "Because I understand how much you'll want to. And that if you do, it won't change what happened. It won't help Liz. But we'll cross that bridge after we find her." She gave his hands a hard squeeze. "Don't go renegade on me now, Nightshade. I'm just starting to like working with you."

He pulled himself back, let himself look down at her. Though her eyes were shadowed and her cheeks were pale with fatigue, he could feel energy vibrating from her. She was offering him something. Compassion—with restrictions, of course. And hope, without any. The viciousness of his anger faded into the very human need for the comfort of contact.

"Althea . . ." His hands relaxed. "Let me hold you, will you?" She hesitated, her brow lifting in surprise. He could only smile. "You know, I'm beginning to read you pretty well. You're worried about your professional image, snuggling up against a guy in your office." Sighing, he brushed a hand through her hair. "Lieutenant, it's almost three in the morning. There's nobody here to see. And I really need to hold you."

Once again she let instinct rule, and she moved into his arms. Every time, she mused as she settled her head in the curve of his neck, every time they stood like this, they fitted perfectly. And each time it was easier to admit it.

"Feel better?" she asked, and felt him move his head against her hair.

"Yeah. He didn't know anything about Lacy, the girl who's missing?"

"No." Without thinking, she stroked his back, soothing muscles there as he had soothed hers. "And when I mentioned the possibility of murder, he was genuinely shaken. He wasn't faking that. That's why I'm certain he gave us everything he had."

"The house in the mountains." Colt let his eyes close. "He couldn't give us much."

"West or maybe north of Boulder, near a lake." She moved her shoulders. "It's a little better than we had before. We'll narrow it down, Colt."

"I feel like I'm not putting the pieces together."

"We're putting the pieces we have together," she told him. "And you're feeling that way because you're tired. Go home." She eased back so that she could look up at him. "Get some sleep. We'll start fresh in the morning."

"I'd rather go home with you."

Amused, exasperated, she could only shake her head. "Don't you ever quit?"

"I didn't say I expected to, only that I'd rather." Lifting his hands, he framed her face, stroking his thumbs over her cheekbones, then back to her temples. "I want time with you, Althea. Time when there isn't so much on my mind, or on yours. Time to be with you, and time to figure out what it is about you, just you, that makes me start thinking of long-term, permanent basis."

Instantly wary, she backed out of his arms. "Don't start that now, Nightshade."

Instantly relaxed, he grinned. "That sure does make you nervous. I never knew anyone so spooked by the thought of marriage—unless it was me. Makes me wonder why—and whether I should just sweep you right off your feet and find out the reasons after I've got a ring on your finger. Or—" he moved toward her, backing her against the desk "—if I should take things real slow, real easy, sliding you into the *I do*'s so slick that you wouldn't know you were hitched until it was over and done."

"Either way, you're being ridiculous." There was something lodged in her throat. Althea recognized it as nerves, and bitterly resented it. Feigning indifference, she picked up the tea and sipped. Now it tasted like cold flowers. "It's late," she said. "You go ahead. I can requisition a unit and drive myself home."

"I'll take you." He caught her chin in his hand and waited until her eyes were level with his. "And I mean that, Thea. Any way I can get you. But you're right— it's late. And I owe you."

"You don't—" Her denial ended on a moan when his mouth swooped down to cover hers.

She tasted frustration in the kiss, a jagged need that was barely restrained. And most difficult of all to resist, she tasted the sweetness of affection, like a thin, soothing balm over the pulsing heat.

"Colt." Even as she murmured his name against his mouth, she knew she was losing. Her arms had already lifted to wrap around him, to bring him closer, to accept and to demand.

Her body betrayed her. Or was it her heart? She could no longer tell the two apart, as the needs of one so closely matched the needs of the other. Her fingers dug deep into his shoulders as she struggled to regain her balance. Then they went lax as she allowed herself one moment of madness.

It was Colt who drew back—for himself, and for her. She'd become more important than the satisfactions of the moment. "I owe you," he said again, carefully spacing the words as he stared down into her eyes. "If I didn't, I wouldn't let you go tonight. I don't think I could. I'll drive you home." He picked up her jacket, offered it to her. "Then I'm probably going to spend the rest of the night wondering what it would have been like if I'd just locked that door there and let nature take its course."

Shaken, she draped her jacket over her shoulders before walking to the door. But she'd been damned if she'd be outdone or outmaneuvered. She paused and sent one slow smile over her shoulder. "I'll tell you what it would have been like, Nightshade. It would have been like nothing you've ever experienced. And when I'm ready—if I'm ever ready—I'll prove it."

Stunned by the punch of that single cool smile, he watched her saunter off. Letting out a long breath, he pressed a hand to the knot in his gut. Sweet God, he thought, this was the woman for him. The only woman for him. And damned if *he* wasn't ready to prove it.

With four hours' sleep, two cups of black coffee and a cherry Danish under her belt, Althea was ready to roll. By 9:00 a.m., she was at her desk, putting through a call to the telephone company with an official request for a check on the number she'd gotten from Leo. By 9:15, she had a name and address, and the information that the customer had cancelled the service only forty-eight hours before.

Though she didn't expect to find anything, she was putting in a request for a search warrant when Colt walked in.

"You don't let moss grow under your feet, do you?"

Althea hung up the phone. "I don't let anything grow under my feet. I've got a line on the number from Leo. The customer canceled the service. I imagine we'll find the place cleaned out, but I can pick up a search warrant within the hour."

"That's what I love about you, Lieutenant—no wasted moves." He eased a hip down on her desk— and was delighted to discover she smelled as good as she looked. "How'd you sleep?"

She slanted a look up at him. Direct challenge. "Like a rock. You?"

"Never better. I woke up this morning with a whole new perspective. Can you be ready to roll by noon?"

"Roll where?"

"This idea I had. I ran it by Boyd, and he—" He scowled down at her shrilling phone. "How many times a day does that ring?"

"Often enough." She plucked up the receiver. "Grayson. Yes, this is Lieutenant Althea Grayson." Her head snapped up. "Jade." With a nod for Colt, Althea covered the receiver. "Line two," she whispered. "And keep your mouth shut." She continued to listen as Colt shot from the room to pick up an extension. "Yes, we have been looking for you. I appreciate you calling in. Can you tell me where you are?"

"I'd rather not." Jade's voice was thin, jumping with nerves. "I only called because I don't want any trouble. I'm getting a job and everything. A straight job. If there's trouble with the cops, I'll lose it."

"You're not in any trouble. I contacted your mother because you can be of some help on a case I'm investigating." Althea swiveled her chair to the right so that she could see Colt through the doorway. "Jade, you remember Liz, don't you? The girl whose parents you wrote?"

"I . . . I guess. Maybe."

"It took a lot of courage to write that letter, and to get out of the situation you'd found yourself in. Liz's parents are very grateful to you."

"She was a nice kid. Didn't really know the score, you know? She wanted out." Jade paused, and Althea heard the sound of a scraping match, a deep intake of breath. "Listen, there was nothing I could do for her. We only had a couple of minutes alone once or twice. She slipped me the address, asked me if I'd write her folks. Like I said, she was a nice kid in a bad spot."

"Then help me find her. Tell me where they've got her."

"I don't know. Man, I really don't. They took a couple of us up in the mountains a few times. Really out there, you know. Wilderness stuff. They had this really classy cabin, though. First-rate, with a Jacuzzi, and a big stone fireplace, and this big-screen TV."

"Which way did you go out of Denver? Can you remember that?"

"Well, yeah, sort of. It was like Route 36, toward Boulder, but we just kept going on it forever. Then we took this other little road for a while. Not a highway. One of those two-lane winding jobs."

"Do you remember going by any towns? Anything that sticks out in your mind?"

"Boulder. After that there wasn't much."

"Did you go up in the morning, afternoon, night?"

"The first time it was in the morning. We got a really early start."

"After Boulder, was the sun in front of you, or behind?"

"Oh, I get it. Ah . . . I guess it was kind of behind us."

Althea continued to press for details, about the location, the routine, descriptions of the people Jade had seen. As a witness, Jade proved vague but cooperative. Still, Althea had no problem recognizing Scott and Kline from Jade's descriptions. There was again a mention of a man who stayed in the background, keeping to the shadows, watching.

"He was creepy, you know?" Jade continued. "Like a spider, just hanging there. The job paid good, so I went back a couple of times. Three hundred for one day, and a fifty-dollar bonus if they needed you for two. I . . . You know you just can't make that kind of money on the street."

"I know. But you stopped going."

"Yeah, because sometimes they got really rough. I had bruises all over me, and one of the guys even spilt my lip while we were doing this scene. I got scared, because it didn't seem like they were acting. It seemed like they wanted to hurt you. I told Wild Bill, and he said how I shouldn't go back. And that he wasn't going to send any more girls. He said he was going to do some checking into it, and if it was bad, he was going to talk to his cop. I knew that was you, so that's why I called back when I got the message. Bill thinks you're okay."

Wearily Althea rubbed a hand over her brow. She didn't tell Jade that she should be using the past tense as far as Wild Bill was concerned. She didn't have the heart. "Jade, you said something in your letter about thinking they'd killed one of the girls."

"I guess I did." Her voice quavered, weakened. "Listen, I'm not going to testify or anything. I'm not going back there."

"I can't promise anything, only that I'll try to keep you out of it. Tell me why you think they killed one of the girls."

"I told you how they could get rough. And it wasn't no playacting, either. The last time I was up, they really hurt me. That's when I decided I wasn't going back. But Lacy, that's a girl I hung with some, she said how she could handle it, and how the money was too good to pass up. She went up again, but she never came back. I never saw her again."

She paused, another match scraped. "It's not like I can prove anything. It's just... She left all her stuff in her room, 'cause I checked. Lacy was real fond of her things. She had this collection of glass animals. Real pretty, crystal, like. She wouldn't have left them behind. She'd have come back for them, if she could. So I thought she was dead, or they were keeping her up there, like with Liz. And I figured I better split before they tried something with me."

"Can you give me Lacy's full name, Jade? Any other information about her?"

"She was just Lacy. That's all I knew. But she was okay."

"All right. You've been a lot of help. Why don't you give me a number where I can contact you?"

"I don't want to. Look, I've told you all I know. I want out of it. I told you, I'm starting over out here."

Althea didn't press. It was a simple matter to get the number from the phone company. "If you think of anything else, no matter how insignificant it seems, will you call me back?"

"I guess. Look, I really hope you get the kid out of there, and give those creeps what they deserve."

"We will. Thanks."

"Okay. Say hi to Wild Bill."

Before Althea could think of a reply, Jade broke the connection. When she looked up, Colt was standing in her doorway. His eyes held that blank, dangerous look again.

"You can get her back here. Material witness."

"Yeah, I could." Althea dialed the phone again. She'd get the number now. Keep it for backup. "But I won't." She held up a hand for silence before Colt could speak, and made the official request to the operator.

"A 212 area code," Colt noted as Althea scribbled on her pad. "You can get the NYPD to pick her up."

"No," she said simply, then slipped the pad into her purse and rose.

"Why the hell not?" Colt grabbed her arm as she reached for her coat. "If you can get that much out of her on the phone, you'd get that much more face-to-face."

"It's because I got that much out of her." Resentful of his interference, she jerked away. "She gave me everything she had, just for the asking. No threats, no promises, no maneuvering. I asked, she answered. I don't betray trusts, Nightshade. If I need her to drop the hammer on these bastards, then I'll use her. But not until then, and not if there's another way. And not," she added deliberately, "without her consent. Is that clear?"

"Yeah." He scrubbed his hands over his face. "Yeah, it's clear. And you're right. So, you want to pick up that warrant, check that other address?"

"Yes. Do you intend to tag along?"

"You bet. We should have just enough time to finish that before we take off."

She stopped in the doorway. "Take off?"

"That's right, Lieutenant. You and I are taking a little trip. I'll tell you all about it on the way."

Chapter 8

"I think we've all lost our minds." Althea gripped her seat as the nose of the Cessna rose into the soft autumn sky.

Comfortable at the controls, Colt spared her a glance. "Come on, tough stuff, don't you like planes?"

"Sure I like planes." A tricky patch of cross-currents sent the Cessna rocking. "But I like them with flight attendants."

"There's stuff in the galley. Once we level off, you can serve yourself."

That wasn't precisely what she'd meant, but Althea said nothing, just watched the land tilt away. She enjoyed flying, really. It was just that she had a routine. She would strap in, adjust her headset to the music of her choice, open a book and zone out for the length of the flight.

She didn't like to think of all the gauges over which she had no control.

"I still think this is a waste of time."

"Boyd didn't argue," Colt pointed out. "Look, Thea, we know the general location of the cabin. I studied that damn tape until my eyes bugged out. I'll recognize it when I see it, and plenty of the surrounding landmarks. This is worth a shot."

"Maybe" was all she'd give him.

"Think about it." Colt banked the plane and set his course. "They know the heat's on. That's why they pulled out of the penthouse. They're going to be wondering where that tape ended up, and if they try to contact Leo, they won't find him, since you've got him stashed in a safe house."

"So they'll stay out of Denver," she agreed. The engines were an irritating roar in her ears. "They might even pull up stakes and move on."

"That's just what I'm afraid of." Colt's mouth thinned as they left Denver behind. "What happens to Liz if they do? None of the options have a happy ending."

"No." That, and Boyd's approval, had convinced her to go with Colt. "No, they don't."

"I have to think they'd stick to the cabin for the time being. Even if they figure we know it exists, they wouldn't think we'd know its location. They don't know about Jade."

"I'll give you that, Nightshade. But it seems to me that you're relying on blind luck to guide you there."

"I've been lucky before. Better?" he asked when the plane leveled. "It's pretty up here, don't you think?"

There was snow on the peaks to the north, and there were broad, flat valleys between the ridges. They were cruising low enough that she could make out cars along the highway, communities that were little huddles of houses, and the deep, thick green of the forest to the west.

"It has its points." A thought erupted in her mind, making her swivel her head in his direction. "Do you have a pilot's license, Nightshade?"

He glanced over, stared, then nearly collapsed with laughter. "Lord, I'm crazy about you, Lieutenant. Do you want one of those big blowout weddings or the small, intimate kind?"

"You're crazy, period," she muttered, and shifted deliberately to stare out through the windscreen. She'd check on his license when they got back to Denver. "And you said you weren't going to bring up that kind of thing."

"I lied." He said it cheerfully. Despite the worry that never quite dissipated, he didn't think he'd ever felt better in his life. "I've got a problem with that. A woman like you could probably cure me of it."

"Try a psychiatrist."

"Thea, we're going to make a hell of a pair. Wait until my family gets a load of you."

"I'm not meeting your family." She attributed the sudden hollowness in her stomach to another spot of turbulence.

"Well, you're probably right about that—at least until we're ready to walk down the aisle. My mother tends to manage everything, but you can handle her. My father likes spit and polish, which means the two of you would get along like bacon and eggs. A regulation type, that's the admiral."

"Admiral?" she repeated, despite her vow to remain stubbornly silent.

"Navy man. Broke his heart when I joined the air force." Colt shrugged. "That's probably why I did it. Then I have this aunt . . . Well, better you should meet them for yourself."

"I'm not meeting your family," she said again, annoyed that the statement sounded more petulant than firm. She unstrapped herself and marched back into the tiny galley, rooting about until she found a can of nuts and a bottle of mineral water. Curiosity had her opening the small refrigerated compartment and studying a tin of caviar and a bottle of Beaujolais. "Whose plane is this?"

"Some friend of Boyd's. A weekend jockey who likes to take women up."

Her answer to that was a grunt as she came back to take her seat. "Must be Frank the lecher. He's been after me to fly the sexy skies for years." She chose a cashew.

"Oh, yeah? Not your type?"

"He's so obvious. But then, men tend to be."

"I'll have to remind myself to be subtle. You going to share those?"

She offered the can. "Is that Boulder?"

"Yep. I'm going to track northwest from here, circle around some. Boyd tells me he has a cabin up here."

"Yes. Lots of people do. They like to escape from the city on weekends and tramp through the snow."

"Not your speed?"

"I don't see any purpose for snow unless you're skiing. And the main purpose of skiing, as far as I'm concerned, is coming back to a lodge and having hot buttered rum in front of a fire."

"Ah, you're the adventurous type."

"I live for adventure. Actually, Boyd's place does have a nice view," she admitted. "And the kids get a big kick out of it."

"So you've been there."

"A few times. I like it better in late spring, early summer, when there isn't much chance of the roads being closed." She glanced down at the patchy snow in the foothills. "I hate the thought of being stuck."

"It might have its advantages."

"Not for me." She was silent for a time, watching hills and trees take over from city and suburbs. "It is pretty," she conceded. "Especially from up here. Like a segment on public television."

He grinned at that. "Nature at a distance? I thought city girls always yearned for a country retreat."

"Not this city girl. I'd rather—" There was a violent bump that sent nuts flying and had Althea grabbing for a handhold. "What the hell was that?"

Narrow-eyed, Colt studied his gauges while he fought to bring the nose of the plane back up. "I don't know."

"You don't know? What do you mean, you don't know? You're supposed to know!"

"Shh!" He tilted his head to listen hard to the engines. "We're losing pressure," he said, with the icy calm that had kept him alive in war-torn jungles, in deserts and in skies alive with flak.

Once she understood that the trouble was serious, Althea responded in kind. "What do we do?"

"I'm going to have to set her down."

Althea looked down, studying the thick trees and rocky hills fatalistically. "Where?"

"According to the map, there's a valley a few degrees east." Colt adjusted the course, fighting the wheel as he jiggled switches. "Watch for it," he ordered, then flipped on his radio. "Boulder tower, this is Baker Able John three."

"There." Althea pointed to what looked to be a very narrow spit of flat land between jagged peaks. Colt nodded, and continued to inform the tower of his situation.

"Hang on," he told her. "It's going to be a little rough."

She braced herself, refusing to look away as the land rushed up to meet them. "I heard you were good, Nightshade."

"You're about to find out." He cut speed, adjusting for the drag of currents as he finessed the plane toward the narrow valley.

Like threading a needle, Althea thought. Then she sucked in her breath at the first vicious thud of wheels on land. They bounced, teetered, shook, then rolled to a gentle halt.

"You okay?" Colt asked instantly.

"Yeah." She let out a breath. Her stomach was inside out, but apart from that she thought she was all in one piece. "Yeah, I'm fine. You?"

"Dandy." He reached out, grabbed her face in both of his hands and dragged her, straining against her seat belt, close enough to kiss. "By damn, Lieutenant," he said, and kissed her again, hard. "You never flinched. Let's elope."

"Can it." When a woman was used to level emotions, it was difficult to know what to do when she had the urge to laugh and scream simultaneously. She shoved him away. "You want to let me out of this thing? I could use some solid ground under my feet."

"Sure." He released the door, even helped her alight. "I'm going to radio in our position," he told her.

"Fine." Althea took a deep gulp of fresh, cold air and tried out her legs. Not too wobbly, she discovered, pleased. All in all, she'd handled her first—and hopefully last—forced landing rather well. She had to give Colt credit, she mused as she looked around. He'd chosen his spot, and he'd made it work.

She didn't get down on her knees and kiss the ground, but she was grateful to feel it under her. As an added bonus, the view was magnificent. They were cupped between mountain and forest, sheltered from the wind, low enough to look up at the snow cascading down from the rocky peaks without being inconvenienced by it.

There was a good clean scent to the air, a clear blue sky overhead, and a bracing chill that stirred the blood. With any luck, a rescue could be accomplished within the hour, so she could afford to enjoy the scenery without being overwhelmed by the solitude.

She was feeling in tune with the world when she heard Colt clamber out of the cockpit. She even smiled at him.

"So, when are they coming to get us?"

"Who?"

"Them. Rescue people. You know, those selfless heroes who get people out of tricky situations such as this."

"Oh, them. They're not." He dropped a tool chest on the ground, then went back inside for a short set of wooden steps.

"Excuse me?" Althea managed when she found her voice. She knew it was an illusion, but the mountains suddenly seemed to loom larger. "Did you say no one's coming to get us? Isn't the radio working?"

"Works fine." Colt climbed on the steps and uncovered the engine. He'd already stuck a rag in the back pocket of his jeans. "I told them I'd see if I could do the repairs on-site and keep in contact."

"You told them—" She moved fast, before either of them understood her intention. Her first swing caught him in the kidneys and had him tumbling off the steps. "You *idiot!* What do you mean, you'll do the repairs?" She swung again, but he dodged, more baffled than annoyed. "This isn't a Ford broken down on the highway, Nightshade. We haven't got a damn flat tire."

"No," he said carefully, braced and ready for her next move. "I think it's the carburetor."

"You think it's—" Her breath whistled out through her teeth, and her eyes narrowed. "That's it. I'm going to kill you with my bare hands."

She launched herself at him. Colt made a split-second decision, pivoted, and let her momentum carry them both to the ground. It only took him another second to realize the lady was no slouch at hand-to-hand. He took one on the chin that snapped his teeth together. It looked like it was time to get serious.

He scissored his legs around her and managed, after a short, grunting tussle, to roll her onto her back. "Hold on, will you? Somebody's going to get hurt!"

"You're damn right."

Since reason wouldn't work, he used his weight, levering himself over her as he cuffed her wrists with his hands. She bucked twice, then went still. They both knew she was only biding her time until she found an opening.

"Listen." He gave himself another moment to catch his breath, then spoke directly into her ear. "It was the most logical alternative."

"That's bull."

"Let me explain. If you still disagree afterward, we'll go for two falls out of three. Okay?" When she didn't respond, Colt set his teeth. "I want your word you won't take another punch at me until I finish."

It was a pity he couldn't see her expression at that moment. "Fine," Althea said tightly. Cautious, Colt eased back until he could watch her face. He was halfway into a sitting position when she brought her knee solidly into his crotch.

He didn't have the breath to curse her as he rolled into a ball.

"That wasn't a punch," she pointed out. She took the time to smooth back her hair, brush down her parka, before she rose. "Okay, Nightshade, let's hear it."

He only lifted a hand, made a couple of woofing noises, and waited for the stars to fade from behind his eyes. "You may have endangered our bloodline, Thea." He got creakily to his knees, breathing shallowly. "You fight dirty."

"It's the only way to fight. Spill it."

As his strength returned, he shot her a killing look. "I owe you. I owe you big. We're not injured," he ground out. "At least I wasn't until you started on me. The plane's undamaged. If you'll take a look around, you'll see that there isn't room to land another plane safely. They could send a copter, lift us out, but for what? Odds are, if I make a few minor adjustments I can fly us out.''

Maybe it made sense, Althea thought. Maybe. But it didn't alter one simple fact. "You should have consulted me. I'm here, too, Nightshade. You had no right to make that decision on your own."

"My mistake." He turned to walk—limp—back to the steps. "I figured you were the logical type and, being a public servant, wouldn't want to see other public servants pulled out for an unnecessary rescue. And, damn it, Liz might be over that ridge." With a violent clatter, he pulled a wrench from the toolbox. "I'm not going back without her."

Oh, he would have to push that button, Althea thought as she turned away to stare into the deep green of the neighboring forest. He would have to let her hear that terrible worry in his voice, see the fire of it in his eyes.

He would have to be perfectly and completely right.

Pride was the hardest of all pills to swallow. Making the effort, she turned back and walked to stand beside the steps. "I'm sorry. I shouldn't have lost my temper."

His response was a grunt.

"Does it still hurt?"

He looked back down at her then, with a gleam in his eyes that would have made lesser women grovel. "Only when I breathe."

She smiled and patted his leg. "Try to think about something else. Do you want me to hand you tools or something?"

His eyes only narrowed further, until they were thin blue slits. "Do you know the difference between a ratchet and a torque wrench?"

"No." She tossed her hair back. "Why should I? I have a perfectly competent mechanic to look after my car."

"And if you break down on the highway?"

She sent him a pitying look. "What do you think?"

He ground his teeth and went back to the carburetor. "If I made a comment like that, you'd call it sexist."

She grinned behind his back, but when she spoke, her voice was sober. "Why is calling a tow truck sexist? I think there's some instant coffee in the galley," she continued. "I'll make some."

"It isn't smart to use the battery," he muttered. "We'll make do with soft drinks."

"No problem."

When she returned twenty minutes later, Colt was cursing the engine. "This friend of Boyd's should be shot for taking such haphazard care of his equipment."

"Are you going to fix it or not?"

"Yeah, I'm going to fix it." He found several interesting names to call a bolt he was fighting to loosen. "It's just going to take a little longer than I expected." Prepared for some pithy comment, he glanced down. She merely stood there patiently, the breeze ruffling her hair. "What's that?" he asked, nodding down at her hands.

"I think it's called a sandwich." She held up the bread and cheese for his inspection. "Not much of one, but I thought you might be hungry."

"Yeah, I am." The gesture mollified him somewhat. He lifted his hands and showed her palms and fingers streaked with grease. "I'm a little handicapped."

"Okay. Bend over." When he obeyed, she brought the bread to his mouth. They watched each other over it as he took a bite.

"Thanks."

"You're welcome. I found a beer." She pulled the bottle out of her pocket and tipped it back. "We'll share." Then she held it to his lips.

"Now I know I love you."

"Just eat." She fed him more of the sandwich. "Do you have any idea how much longer it's going to take you to get us airborne?"

"Yeah." And because he did, he made sure he got his full share of the beer and the sandwich before he told her. "It'll be an hour, maybe two."

She blinked. "Two hours? We'll have run out of daylight by then. You don't plan to fly this out of here in the dark?"

"No, I don't." Though he remained braced for a sneak attack, he went back to the engine. "It'll be safer to wait until morning."

"Until morning," she repeated, staring at his back. "And just what are we supposed to do until morning?"

"Pitch a tent, for starters. There's one in the cabin, in the overhead. I guess old Frank likes to take his ladies camping."

"That's great. Just great. You're telling me we have to sleep out here?"

"We could sleep in the plane," he pointed out. "But it wouldn't be as comfortable, or as warm, as stretching out in a tent beside a fire." He began to whistle as he worked. He'd said he owed her one. He hadn't realized he'd be able to pay her back so soon, or so well. "I don't suppose you know how to start a campfire."

"No, I don't know how to start a damn campfire."

"Weren't you ever a Girl Scout?"

She made a sound like steam escaping a funnel. "No. Were you?"

"Can't say I was—but I was friendly with a few of them. Well, you go on and gather up some twigs, darling. I'll talk you through your first merit badge."

"I am not going to gather twigs."

"Okay, but it's going to get cold once that sun goes down. A fire keeps the chill—and other things— away."

"I'm not—". She broke off, looked uneasily around. "What other things?"

"Oh, you know. Deer, elk ... wildcats ..."

"Wildcats." Her hand went automatically to her shoulder rig. "There aren't any wildcats around here."

He lifted his head and glanced around as if considering. "Well, it might be too early in the year yet. But they do start coming down from the higher elevations near winter. Of course, if you want to wait until I've finished here, I'll get a fire going. May be dark by then, though."

He was doing it on purpose. She was sure of it. But then again ... She cast another look around, toward the forest, where the shadows were lengthening. "I'll get the damn wood," she muttered, and stomped off toward the trees. After she checked her weapon.

He watched her, smiling. "We're going to do just fine together," he said to himself. "Just fine."

Following Colt's instructions, Althea managed to start a respectable fire within a circle of stones. She didn't like it, but she did it. Then, because he claimed to be deeply involved in the final repairs to the plane, she was forced to rig the tent.

It was a lightweight bubble that Colt declared would nearly erect itself. After twenty minutes of struggle and swearing, she had it up. A narrow-eyed study showed her that it would shelter the two of them—as long as they slept hip to hip.

She was still staring at it, ignoring the chill of the dusk, when she heard the engine spring to life.

"Good as new," Colt shouted, then shut off the engines. "I have to clean up," he told her. He leapt out of the cabin, holding a jug of water. He used it sparingly, along with a can of degreaser from the toolbox. "Nice job," he said, nodding toward the tent.

"Thanks a bunch."

"There are blankets in the plane. We'll do well enough." Still crouched, he drew in a deep breath, tasting smoke and pine and good, crisp air. "Nothing quite like camping out in the hills."

She shoved her hands into her pockets. "I'll have to take your word for it."

He finished scrubbing his hands with a rag before he rose. "Don't tell me you've never done any camping."

"All right, I won't tell you."

"What do you do for a vacation?"

She arched a brow. "I go to a hotel," she said precisely. "Where they have room service, hot and cold running water and cable TV."

"You don't know what you're missing."

"I suppose I'm about to find out." She shivered once, sighed. "I could use a drink."

* * *

In addition to the Beaujolais, they feasted on rich, sharp cheese, caviar and thin crackers spread with a delicate pâté.

All in all, Althea decided, it could have been worse.

"Not like any camp meal I ever had," Colt commented as he scooped more caviar onto a cracker. "I thought I'd have to go kill us a rabbit."

"Please, not while I'm eating." Althea sipped more wine and found herself oddly relaxed. The fire did indeed keep the chill away. And it was soothing to watch it flicker and hiss. Overhead, countless stars wheeled and winked, stabbing the cloudless black sky. A quarter-moon silvered the trees and lent a glow to the snow capping the peaks that circled them.

She'd stopped jerking every time an owl hooted.

"Pretty country." Colt lit an after-dinner cigar. "I never spent much time here before."

Neither had she, Althea realized, though she'd lived in Denver for a dozen years. "I like the city," she said, more to herself than Colt. She picked up a stick to stir the fire, not because it needed it, but because it was fun to watch the sparks fly.

"Why?"

"I guess because it's crowded. Because you can find anything you want. And because I feel useful there."

"And that's important to you, feeling useful."

"Yeah, it's important."

He watched the way the flames cast shadow and light over her face, highlighting her eyes, sharpening her cheekbones, softening her skin. "It was rough on you, growing up."

"It's over." When he took her hand, she neither re- sisted nor responded. "I don't talk about it," she said flatly. "Ever."

"All right." He could wait. "We'll talk about something else." He brought her hand to his lips, and felt a response, just a slight flexing, then relaxing, of her fingers. "I guess you never told stories around the campfire."

She smiled. "I guess not."

"I could probably think of one—just to pass the time. Lie or truth?"

She started to laugh, but then she shot to her feet, whipping out her weapon. Colt's reaction was light- ning-fast. In an instant he was beside her, shoving her back, his own gun slapped from his boot into his palm.

"What?" he demanded, his eyes narrowed and searching every shadow.

"Did you hear that? There's something out there."

He cocked an ear, while she instinctively shifted to guard his back. After a moment of throbbing silence, he heard a faint rustling, then the far-off cry of a coy- ote. The plaintive call had Althea's blood drumming.

Colt swore, but at least he didn't laugh. "Ani- mals," he told her, bending to replace his gun.

"What kind?" Her eyes were still scanning the pe- rimeter, wary, watchful.

"Small ones," he assured her. "Badgers, rabbits." He laid a hand over the ones that gripped her weapon. "Nothing you have to put a hole in, Deadeye."

She wasn't convinced. The coyote called again, and an owl hooted in counterpoint. "What about those wildcats?"

He started to respond, thought better of it, and tucked his tongue in his cheek. "Well, now, darling, they aren't likely to come too close to the fire."

Frowning, she replaced her weapon. "Maybe we should have a bigger fire."

"It's big enough." He turned her toward him, running his hands up and down her arms. "I don't think I've ever seen you so spooked."

"I don't like being this exposed. There's too much here, out here." And the sterling truth was that she would rather face a hopped-up junkie in a dark alley than one small, furry creature with fangs. "Don't grin at me, damn it!"

"Was I grinning?" He ran his tongue around his teeth and struggled to look sober. "It looks like you're going to have to trust me to get you through this."

"Oh, am I?"

He tightened his grip when she started to back away. The look in his eyes changed so quickly, from amusement to desire, that it took her breath away. "There's just you and me, Althea."

She let the clogged air slowly out of her lungs. "It looks like."

"I don't figure I have to tell you again how I feel about you. Or how much I want you."

"No." Tension flooded into her when he brushed his lips over her temple. And heat, a frightening spear of it, stabbed up her spine.

"I can make you forget where you are." He trailed his lips down to her jawline and nibbled up the other side. "If you'll let me."

"You'd have to be damn good for that."

He laughed, because there had been a challenge in the statement, even though her breath had caught on the words. "It's a long time until morning. I'm betting I can convince you before sunrise."

Why was she resisting something she wanted so terribly? Hadn't she told herself long ago never again to let fear cloud her desires? And hadn't she learned to sate those desires without penalty?

She could do so now, with him, and erase this grinding ache.

"All right, Nightshade." Fearlessly she linked her arms around his neck, met his eyes straight on. "I'll take that bet."

His hand fisted in her hair, dragged her head back. For one long, humming moment, they stared at each other. Then he plundered.

Her mouth was hot and honeyed under his, as demanding as hunger, as wild as the night. He plunged into the kiss, using tongue and teeth, knowing he could gorge himself on her and never be filled. So he took more, relentlessly savaging her mouth while she met demand with demand and power with power.

It was like the first time, she realized giddily. The first time he'd dragged her to him and made her taste what he had to offer. Like some fatal drug, the taste had her pulses pounding, her blood swimming fast and her mind spinning away from reason.

She wondered how she had expected to come away whole. And then she forgot to care.

She no longer wanted to be safe, to be in control. Now, here, with him, she wanted only to feel, to experience everything that had once seemed impossible, or at least unwise. And if she sacrificed survival, so be it.

Driven by greed, she tore at his coat, desperate to feel the hard, solid body beneath. He didn't have to be stronger than she, but if he was, she would accept the vulnerability that came with being a woman. And the power that raced alongside it.

She was like a volcano ready to erupt, and she wanted nothing more than to be joined with him when the tremors came.

She was stripping him of his sanity, layer by layer. Those wild lips, those frantic hands. On an oath that was almost a prayer, he half carried, half dragged her toward the tent, feeling like some primeval hunter flinging his chosen mate into his cave.

They tumbled into the small shelter together, a tangle of limbs, a tangle of needs. He yanked her coat down her shoulders, fighting for breath as he raced greedy kisses down her throat.

He felt the vibration of her groan against his lips as he fought her shoulder rig, tearing aside that symbol of control and violence, knowing he was losing control, overwhelmed by a violence of feelings that he couldn't suppress.

He wanted her naked and straining. And screaming.

Her breath caught in gasps as she tugged, pulled, ripped, at his clothes. The firelight glowed orange through the thin material of the tent, and she could see his eyes, the dark, dangerous purpose in them. She reveled in it, in the panicked excitement that racked her body where he groped and possessed. He would ravage her tonight, she knew. And be ravaged in turn.

Levering himself back, he dragged her sweater up and over her head and tossed it aside. She wore lace beneath, a snow-white fancy that in a saner place, in a saner time, would have aroused him by its blatant femininity. He might have toyed with the straps, skimmed his fingers over her subtle peaks. Now he only ripped it apart in one jerky move to free her breasts for his greedy mouth.

The flavor of that warm, scented flesh hit his system like a blow. And her response, the lovely arching of her body against his, the long, throaty moan, the quick, helpless quiver, drove him toward a summit of pleasure he had never dreamed of.

He feasted.

A whimper caught in her throat. She dug her nails into the naked flesh of his shoulders, needing to drive him on, terrified of where he was taking her. She clutched at him for balance, moved under him in sinuous invitation, arching once more as he peeled her slacks away, skimming those impossibly clever fingers down her thighs.

The triangle of lace that shielded her tore jaggedly. Once again his mouth feasted.

Her cry of stunned release rippled through his blood. She shot up like a rocket, exploding, imploding, feeling herself scatter and burn. But where the release should have peaked and leveled, he gave her no respite. She clutched at the blanket while he battered her system with sensations that had no name, no form.

When he rose over her, every muscle trembling, he found her eyes open and on his. He watched her face, filled himself with it even as he buried himself inside her in one desperate stroke. Her eyes glazed, closed. His own vision grayed before he buried his face in her hair.

His body took over, matching the fast, furious rhythm of her hips. They rode each other like fury, greedy children gorging themselves on forbidden fruit.

Her final cry of dark pleasure echoed through the air seconds before his own.

Strength sapped, he collapsed onto her, gulping in air as he felt her tremble beneath him from the aftershocks.

"Who won?" he managed after a moment.

She hadn't thought it possible to laugh at such a time, but a chuckle rumbled into her throat. "Let's call it a draw."

"Good enough for me." He thought about lifting himself off her, but was afraid he might shatter if he tried to move. "Plenty good enough. I'm going to kiss you in a minute," he murmured, "but first I have to drum up the strength."

"I can wait." Althea let her eyes close again, and savored the closeness. His body continued to radiate heat, and his heart was far from steady. She stroked her hand down his back for the simple pleasure of the contact, frowning a bit when her fingers ran over a raised scar. "What's this?"

"Hmm?" He stirred himself, surprised that he'd nearly fallen asleep on top of her. "Desert Storm."

She hadn't realized he'd been there. It occurred to her that there was quite a bit about him that lay in shadows. "I thought you'd retired before that went down."

"I had. I agreed to do a little job—sort of a side job."

"A favor."

"You could call it that. Caught a little flak—nothing to worry about." He tilted his head, nuzzling. "You have the most gorgeous shoulders. Have I mentioned that?"

"No. Do you still do favors for the government?"

"Only if they ask nicely." He grunted and rolled so that he could shift her on top of him. "Better?"

"Mmm...." She rested her cheek on his chest. "But I think we might freeze to death."

"Not if we keep active." He grinned when she lifted her head to look down at him. "Survival methods, Lieutenant."

"Of course." Her lips curved into a smile. "I have to say, Nightshade, I like your methods."

"That so?" Gently he combed his fingers through her hair, tested its weight with his hand.

"That's very so. How soon do we have to add wood to that fire?"

"Oh, we've got a little while yet."

"Then we shouldn't waste time, should we?" Still smiling, she lowered her mouth to his.

"Nope." He felt himself hardening again inside her, and prepared to let her take the lead. As his lips curved against hers, he was struck by a stab of love so sharp it stole his breath. He clutched her close, held on. "I know it's a tired line, Thea, but it's never been like this for me before. Not with anyone."

That frightened her, and what frightened her more than the words was the flush of warmth they brought to her. "You talk too much."

"Thea..."

But she shook her head and rose up, taking him deep inside her, tantalizing his body so that the need for words slipped away.

Chapter 9

Colt awakened quickly. An old habit. He registered his surroundings—the pale light of dawn creeping into the tent, the rough blanket and hard ground beneath his back, and the soft, slender woman curled on top of him. It made him smile, remembering the way she'd rolled over him during the night, seeking a place more comfortable than the unyielding floor of the valley.

At the time, they'd both been too exhausted to do more than cuddle up and sleep. Now the sun had brought a reminder of the outside world, and their duties in it. Still, he took a moment to enjoy the lazy intimacy, and to imagine other times, other places, where it would once again be only the two of them.

Gently he tugged the blanket over her bare shoulder and let his fingers trail down over her hair where it lay pooled across her cheek and throat.

She shifted, her eyes opening and locking on his.

"Good reflexes, Lieutenant."

She ran her tongue over her teeth, letting her mind and body adjust to the situation. "I guess it's morning."

"Right the first time. Sleep okay?"

"I've slept better." Every muscle in her body ached, but she figured a couple of aspirin and some exercise would handle that. "You?"

"Like a baby," he said. "Some of us are used to roughing it."

She only lifted a brow, then rolled off him. "Some of us want coffee." The moment she left his warmth, the chill stung her skin. Shivering, she groped for her sweater.

"Hey." Before she could bundle up in the sweater, he grabbed her around the waist and hauled her to him. "You forgot something." His hand slid up her back to cup her head as his mouth met hers.

Her body went fluid, sweetly so, and her lips parted in invitation. She could feel herself melting into him, and wondered at it. All through the night they had come together, again and again, each time like lightning, with flashes of greed. But this was softer, steadier, stronger, like a candle that remained alight long after a raging fire had burned itself out.

"You sure are nice to wake up to, Althea."

She wanted to burrow into him, to grab hold and hang on as though her life depended on it. Instead, she flicked a finger down the stubble on his chin. "You're not so bad, Nightshade."

She moved away quickly, a little too quickly, to give herself the time and space to settle. Because he was beginning to read her very well, he smiled.

"You know, once we're married, we should get ourselves one of those king-size beds, so we'll have plenty of room to roll around and get tangled up."

She tugged the sweater on. When her head emerged, her eyes were cool. "Who's making the coffee?"

He nodded thoughtfully. "That is something we'll have to decide. Keeping those little routines straight helps a marriage run smooth."

She bit back a laugh and reached for her slacks. "You owe me some underwear."

He watched her pull the slacks up her long, smooth legs. "Buying it for you is going to be pure pleasure." He shrugged into his shirt while Althea hunted for her socks. Knowing the value of timing, he waited until she'd found them both. "Darling, I've been thinking...."

She answered with a grunt as she tugged on her shoes.

"How do you feel about getting hitched on New Year's Eve? Kind of romantic, starting out the next year as husband and wife."

This time she hissed out her breath. "I'll make the damn coffee," she muttered, and crawled out of the tent.

Colt gave her retreating bottom a friendly pat and chuckled to himself. She was coming around, he decided. She just didn't know it yet.

By the time Althea got the fire started again, she'd had more than enough of the great outdoors. Maybe it was beautiful, she thought as she rummaged through the small supply of pots they'd found on the plane. Maybe it was even magnificent, with its rugged, snow-capped peaks and densely forested slopes. But it was also cold, and hard and deserted.

They had a handful of nuts between them, and not a restaurant in sight.

Too impatient to wait until it boiled, she heated water until it was hot to the touch, then dumped in a generous amount of instant coffee. The scent was enough to make her drool.

"Now that's a pretty sight." Colt stood just outside the tent, watching her. "A beautiful woman bending over a campfire. And you do have a nice way of bending, Thea."

"Stuff it, Nightshade."

He strolled to her grinning. "Cranky before your coffee, darling?"

She knocked aside the hand he'd lifted to toy with her hair. He was charming her again, and it was just going to have to stop. "Here's breakfast." She shoved the can of nuts at him. "You can pour your own coffee."

Obligingly he crouched down and poured the mixture into two tin mugs. "Nice day," he said conversationally. "Low wind, good visibility."

"Yeah, great." She accepted the mug he offered. "God, I'd kill for a toothbrush."

"Can't help you there." He sampled the coffee, grimaced. It was mud, he decided, but at least it packed a punch. "Don't you worry, we'll be back in civilization before much longer. You can brush your teeth, have yourself a nice hot bubble bath, go to the hairdresser."

She started to smile—it was the bubble bath that did it—but then she whipped her head up and scowled. "Leave my hair out of this." Setting the mug down, she knelt and began to rummage through her purse. Once she found her brush, she sat cross-legged on the ground, her back to Colt, and began to drag it through her tangled hair.

"Here now." He sat behind her, snuggling her back into the vee of his legs. "Let me do that."

"I can do it myself."

"Yeah, but you're about to brush yourself bald." After a short tussle, he snatched the brush away. "You should take more care with this," he murmured, gently working out the tangles. "It's the most beautiful head of hair I've ever seen. Up close like this, I can see a hundred different shades of red and gold and russet."

"It's just hair." But if Althea had a point of vanity, Colt was stroking it now. And it felt wonderful. She couldn't resist a sigh as he brushed and lifted, caressed and smoothed. They might be in the middle of nowhere, but for that moment Althea felt as though she were in the lap of luxury.

"Look," Colt whispered against her ear. "At three o'clock."

Responding instinctively to the direction, Althea turned her head. There, just at the verge of the forest, stood a deer. No, not a deer, she realized. Surely no deer could be so huge. His shoulders were nearly as high as a man, and massive. His head was lifted, scenting the air, with his high crown of antlers spearing upward.

"It's, ah . . ."

"Wapiti," Colt murmured, wrapping his arms companionably around her waist. "American elk. That's one beautiful bull."

"Big. Big is what he is."

"Close to seven hundred pounds, by the look of him. There, he's caught our scent."

Althea felt her heart jolt when the elk turned his great head and looked at her. He seemed both arrogant and wise as he studied the humans who were trespassing on his territory.

And suddenly there was an aching in her throat, a response to beauty, a trembling deep inside, a kind of wonder. For a moment the three of them remained poised, measuring each other. A lark called, a searingly beautiful cascade of notes.

The elk turned, vanished into the shadowed trees.

"I guess he didn't want coffee and cashews," Althea said quietly. She couldn't say why she was moved. She only knew that she was, deeply. Relaxed against Colt, cradled in his arms, she was completely and inexplicably content.

"Can't say I blame him." Colt rubbed his cheek against her hair. "It's a hell of a way to start the day."

"Yeah." She turned, impulsively winding an arm around his neck, pressing her lips to his. "This is better."

"Much better," he agreed, sinking in when she deepened the kiss. He nuzzled, and was amused when she laughed and shoved his unshaven face away from the tender curve of her throat. "Once we're back in Denver, I want you to remind me where we left off."

"I might do that." With some regret, she drew away. "We'd better—what do you call it? Break camp? And, by the way," she added, shrugging into her shoulder rig, "you owe me more than new lingerie—you owe me breakfast."

"Put it on my tab."

* * *

Twenty minutes later, they were strapped into the cockpit. Colt checked his gauges while Althea applied blusher to her cheekbones.

"We ain't going to a party," he commented.

"I may not be able to brush my teeth," she said, and crunched down on a mint she'd found in her purse. "I may not be able to take a shower. But, by damn, I haven't lost all sense of propriety."

"I like your cheeks pale." He started the engines. "Kind of fragile."

After one narrow-eyed stare, she deliberately added more blusher. "Just fly, Nightshade."

"Yes, sir, Lieutenant."

He didn't see the point in telling her it would be a tricky takeoff. While she was occupied braiding her hair, he maneuvered the plane into the best position for taxiing. After touching a finger to the medal that rested under his shirt, he let her rip.

They jolted, bounced, shuddered and finally lifted, degree by degree. Colt fought the crosscurrents, dipping one wing, leveling off, nosing upward. Finally they cleared the ridge and shot over the tops of the trees.

"Not too shabby, Nightshade." Althea flipped her braid behind her back. When he glanced over, he saw the awareness in her eyes. The hands that were currently uncapping a tube of mascara were rock-steady, but she knew. He should have realized she would know.

"Boyd was right, Thea. You're a hell of a partner."

"Just try to hold this thing steady for a few minutes, will you?" Smiling to herself, she angled her purse mirror and began to do her lashes. "So, what's the plan?"

"Same as before. We circle this area. Look for cabins. The one we want has a sloped drive."

"That certainly narrows things down."

"Shut up. It's also a two-story with a covered wraparound deck and a trio of windows on the front, facing west. The sun was going down in one scene in the video," he explained. "According to the other information we have, there's a lake somewhere in the general area. I also saw fir and spruce, which gives us the elevation. The cabin was whitewashed logs. It shouldn't be that hard to spot."

He might be right about that, but Althea knew there was something else that needed to be said. "She might not be there, Colt."

"We're going to find out." He banked the plane and headed west.

Because she could see the worry come into his eyes, Althea changed tacks. "Tell me, what rank were you in the air force?"

"Major." He drummed up a smile. "Looks like I outrank you."

"You're retired," she reminded him. "I bet you looked swell in uniform."

"I wouldn't mind seeing you in dress blues. Look."

Following his direction, she spotted a cabin below. It was a three-level structure fashioned from redwood. She noted two others, separated from each other by lines of trees.

"None of them fit."

"No," he agreed. "But we'll find the one that does."

They continued to search, with Althea peering through binoculars. Hideaways were snuggled here and there, most of them seemingly unoccupied. A few had smoke puffing out of a chimney and trucks or four-wheel-drive vehicles parked outside.

Once she saw a man in a bright red shirt splitting wood. She spotted a herd of elk grazing in a frosty meadow, and the flash of White-tail deer.

"There's nothing," she said at length. "Unless we want to do a documentary on— Wait." A glint of white caught her attention, then was lost. "Circle around. Four o'clock." She continued to scan, searching the snow-dusted ridges.

And there it was, two stories of whitewashed logs, a trio of windows facing west, the deck. At the end of the sloping gravel drive sat a muscular-looking truck. As further proof of habitation, smoke was spiraling out of the chimney.

"That could be it."

"I'm betting it is." Colt circled once, then veered off.

"I might take that bet." She unhooked the radio mike. "Give me the position. I'll call it in, get a surveillance team up here so we can go back and talk a judge into issuing a warrant."

Colt gave her the coordinates. "Go ahead and call it in. But I'm not waiting for a piece of paper."

"What the hell do you think you can do?"

His eyes flashed to hers, then away. "I'm setting the plane down, and I'm going in."

"No," she said, "you're not."

"You do what you have to." He angled for the meadow where Althea had spotted the grazing elk.

"There's a good chance she's in there. I'm not leaving her."

"What are you going to do?" she demanded, too incensed to noticed the perilous descent. "Break in, guns blazing? That's movie stuff, Nightshade. Not only is it illegal, but it puts the hostage in jeopardy."

"You've got a better idea?" He braced himself. They were going to slide once the wheels hit. He hoped to God they didn't roll.

"We'll get a team up here with surveillance equipment. We figure out who owns the cabin, get the paperwork pushed through."

"Then we break in? No thanks. You said you'd been skiing, right?"

"What?"

"You're about to do it in a plane. Hold on."

She jerked her head around, gaped through the windscreen as the glittering meadow hurled toward them. She had time for an oath—a vicious one—but then she lost her breath at the impact.

They hit, and went sliding. Snow spewed up the side of the plane, splattering the windows. Althea watched almost philosophically as they hurtled toward a wall of trees. Then the plane spun in two wicked circles before coming to a grinding stop.

"You maniac!" She took deep breaths, fighting back the worst of her temper. She would have let it loose, but there wasn't enough room to maneuver in the cabin. And when she murdered him she wanted to do it right.

"I landed a plane in the Aleutians once, when the radar was down. It was a lot worse than this."

"What does that prove?" she demanded.

"That I'm still a hell of a pilot?"

"Grow up!" she shouted. "This isn't fantasyland. We're closing in on suspected kidnappers, suspected murderers, and there's very possibly an innocent kid caught in the middle. We're going to do this right, Nightshade."

With one jerk, he unstrapped himself, then grabbed both her hands at the wrists. "You listen to me." She would have winced at the way his fingers dug into her flesh, but the fury in his eyes stopped her. "I know what's real, Althea. I've seen enough reality in my life—the waste of it, and the cruelty of it. I know that girl. I held her when she was a baby, and I'm not leaving her welfare up to paperwork and procedure."

"Colt—"

"Forget it." He shoved her hands aside, jerked back. "I'm not asking for your help, because I'm trying to respect your ideas of rules and regulations. But I'm going after her, Thea, and I'm going now."

"Wait." She held up a hand, then dragged it through her hair. "Let me think a minute."

"You think too damn much." But when he started to rise, she shoved a fist into his chest.

"I said wait." Then she tipped her head back, closed her eyes and thought it through.

"How far is it to the cabin?" she asked after a moment. "Half a mile?"

"More like three-quarters."

"The roads leading in were all plowed."

"Yeah." Impatience shimmered around him. "So?"

"It would have been handier if I could have been stuck in a snowdrift. But a breakdown's good enough."

"What are you talking about?"

"I'm talking about working together." She opened her eyes, pinned him with them. "You don't like the way I work, I don't like the way you work. So we're going to have to find a middle ground. I'm calling this in, arranging to have the local police back us up, and I'm going to have them get word to Boyd. See if he can get some paperwork started."

"I told you—"

"I don't care what you told me," she said calmly. "This is how it's going down. We can't go bursting in there. Number one, we might be wrong about the cabin. Number two," she said, cutting him off again, "it puts Liz in increased jeopardy if they're holding her there. And number three, without probable cause, without proper procedure, these bastards might wiggle out, and I want them put away. Now, you listen . . ."

He didn't like it. It didn't matter how much sense it made or how good a plan she'd devised. But during the long trek to the cabin she defused whatever arguments he voiced with calm, simple logic.

She was going in.

"What makes you think they'll let you inside just because you ask?"

She tilted her head, slanted a look up from under her lashes. "I haven't wasted any on you, Nightshade, but I have a tremendous amount of charm at my disposal." She lengthened her stride to match his. "What do you think most men will do when a helpless woman comes knocking, begging for help because she's lost, her car's broken down and—" she gave a delicate shiver and turned her voice into a purr "—and it's so awfully cold outside."

He swore and watched his breath puff away in smoke. "What if they offer to drive you back to your car and fix it?"

"Well, I'll be terribly grateful. And I'll stall them long enough to do what needs to be done."

"And if they get rough?"

"Then you and I will have to kick butt, won't we?"

He couldn't help but look forward to that. And yet... "I still think I should go in with you."

"They're not going to be sympathetic if the little woman has a big strong man with her." Sarcasm dripped in the chilly air. "With any luck, the local boys will be here before things get nasty." She paused, judging the distance. "We're close enough. One of them might be out for a morning stroll. We don't want to be spotted together."

Colt shoved his fists into his pockets, then made them relax. She was right—more, she was good. He pulled his hands out, grabbed her shoulders and hauled her close. "Watch your step, Lieutenant."

She kissed him, hard. "Same goes."

She turned, walked away with long, ground-eating strides. He wanted to tell her to stop, to tell her he loved her. Instead, he headed over the rough ground toward the rear of the cabin. This wasn't the time to throw her any emotional curves. He'd save them for later.

Blocking everything from his mind, he sprinted through the hard-crusted snow, keeping low.

Althea moved fast. She wanted to be out of breath and a little teary-eyed when she reached the cabin. Once she came into view of the windows, she switched to a stumbling run, pantomiming relief. She all but fell against the door, calling and banging.

She recognized Kline when he opened it. He wore baggy gray sweats, and his bleary eyes were squinting against the smoke from the cigarette tucked into the corner of his mouth. He smelled of tobacco and stale whiskey.

"Oh, thank God!" Althea slumped against the doorjamb. "Thank God! I was afraid I'd never find anyone. I feel like I've been walking forever."

Kline sized her up. She was one sweet-looking babe, he decided, but he wasn't big on surprises. "What do you want?"

"My car..." She pressed a fluttering hand to her heart. "It broke down—it must be a mile from here, at least. I was coming to visit some friends. I don't know, maybe I made a wrong turn." She shuddered, wrapped her parka closer around her. "Is it all right if I come in? I'm so cold."

"There ain't nobody up around here. No other cabins near here."

She closed her eyes. "I knew I must have turned wrong somewhere. Everything starts to look the same. I left Englewood before sunup—wanted to start my vacation first thing." Staring up at him, wide-eyed, she managed a weak smile. "Some vacation so far. Look, can I just use the phone, call my friends so they can come get me?"

"I guess." The broad was harmless, Kline decided. And a pleasure to look at.

"Oh, a fire..." With a moan of relief, Althea dashed toward it. "I didn't know I could be so cold." While she rubbed her hands together, she beamed over her shoulder at Kline. "I can't thank you enough for helping me out."

"No problem." He pulled the dangling cigarette from his mouth. "We don't get much traffic up here."

"I can see why." She shifted her gaze to the windows. "Still, it is lovely. And this place!" She circled, looking dazzled. "It's just fabulous. I guess if you were all cozied up by the fire with a bottle of wine, you wouldn't mind sitting out a blizzard or two."

His lips curled. "I like to cozy up with something other than a bottle."

Althea fluttered her lashes, lowered them modestly. "It certainly is romantic, Mr—?"

"Kline. You can call me Harry."

"All right, Harry. I'm Rose," she said, giving him her middle name in case he'd recognized the name of Wild Bill's cop. She offered her hand. "It's a real pleasure. I think you've saved my life."

"What the hell's going on down there?"

Althea glanced up to the loft and saw a tall, wiry man with an untended shock of blond hair. She tagged him as the second male actor in the video.

"Got us an unexpected guest, Donner," Kline called up. "Car broke down."

"Well, hell . . ." Donner blinked his eyes clear and took a good look. "You're out early, sweetie."

"I'm on vacation," she said, and flashed him a smile.

"Isn't that nice?" Donner started downstairs, preening, Althea noticed, like a rooster in a henhouse. "Why don't you fix the lady a cup of coffee, Kline?"

"Tidal Wave's already in the kitchen. It's his turn."

"Fine." Donner sent what was meant to be an intimate smile toward Althea. "Tell him to pour another cup for the lady."

"Why don't you—"

"Oh, I would *love* a cup of coffee," Althea said, turning her big brown eyes on Kline. "I'm just frozen."

"Sure." He shrugged, shot Donner a look that made Althea think of one male dog warning off a competitor, then strode off.

How many more of the organization were in the cabin? she wondered. Or was it just the three of them?

"I was just telling Harry how beautiful your house is." She wandered the living room, dropping her purse onto a table. "Do you live here year-round?"

"No, we just use it now and again."

"It's so much bigger than it looks from outside."

"It does the job." He moved closer as Althea sat on the arm of a chair. "Maybe you'd like to hang out here for your vacation."

She laughed, making no objection when he brushed a finger through her hair. "Oh, but my friends are expecting me. Still, I do have two weeks..." She laughed again, low and throaty. "Tell me, what do you guys do around here for fun?"

"You'd be surprised." Donner laid a hand on her thigh.

"I don't surprise easily."

"Back off." Kline came back in with a mug of black coffee. "Here you are, Rose."

"Thanks." She sniffed deeply, curling her shoulders in for effect. "I feel warm and toasty already."

"Why don't you take off your coat?" Donner put a hand to her collar, but she shifted, smiling.

"As soon as my insides defrost a little more." She'd taken the precaution of removing her shoulder rig, but she preferred more camouflage, as her weapon was snug at the small of her back. "Are the two of you brothers?" she asked conversationally.

Kline snorted. "Not hardly. You could say we're partners."

"Oh, really? What kind of business are you in?"

"Communications," Donner stated, flashing white teeth.

"That's fascinating. You sure have a lot of equipment." She glanced toward the big-screen TV, the state-of-the-art VCR and stereo. "I love watching movies on long winter nights. Maybe we can get together sometime and..." She let her words trail off, alerted by a movement at the back of the loft. Glancing up, she saw the girl.

Her hair was tousled, and her eyes were unbearably tired. She'd lost weight, Althea thought, but she recognized Liz from the snapshot Colt had shown her.

"Why, hello there," she said, and smiled.

"Get back in your room," Kline snapped. "Now."

Liz moistened her lips. She was wearing tattered jeans and a bright blue sweater that was tattered at the cuffs. "I wanted some breakfast." Her voice was quiet, Althea noted, but not cowed.

"You'll get it." He glanced back at Althea, satisfied that she was smiling with friendly disinterest. "Now get on back to your room until I call you."

Liz hesitated, long enough to aim one cold glare at him. That warmed Althea's heart. The kid wasn't beaten yet, Althea noted as Liz turned and walked to the door behind her. It shut with a slam.

"Kids," Kline muttered, and lit another cigarette.

"Yeah." Althea smiled sympathetically. "Is she your sister?"

Kline choked on the smoke, but then he grinned. "Right. Yeah, she's my sister. So, you wanted to use the phone?"

"Oh, yes." Setting the mug of coffee aside, Althea rose. "I appreciate it. My friends'll be getting worried about me soon."

"There it is." He gestured. "Help yourself."

"Thanks." But when she picked up the receiver, there was no dial tone. "Gee, I think it's dead."

Kline swore and strode over, pulling a thin L-shaped tool from his pocket. "Forgot. I, ah, lock it up at night, so the kid can't use it. She was making all these long-distance calls and running up the bill. You know how girls are."

"Yes." Althea smiled. "I do." When she heard the dial tone, she punched in the number for the local police. "Fran," she said merrily, addressing the dispatcher as they had arranged. "You won't believe what happened. I got lost, my car broke down. If it hadn't been for these terrific guys, I don't know what I'd have done." She laughed, hoping Colt was making his move. "I do *not* always get lost. I hope Bob's up to coming for me."

While Althea chatted with the police dispatcher, Colt shimmied up a pole to the second floor. With his binoculars, he'd seen everything he needed to see through the expansive glass of the cabin. Althea was holding her own, and Liz was on the second floor.

They'd agreed that if the opportunity presented itself, he would get her out of the house. Out of harm's way. He might have preferred a direct route—straight through Kline and the other jerk in the living room, and on into the big guy doing kitchen duty.

But Liz's safety came first. Once he got her out, he'd be coming back.

With a grunt, he swung himself onto the narrow overhang and clutched at the window ledge. He saw Liz lying on a rumpled bed, her body turned away and curled up protectively. His first urge was to throw up the window and leap inside. Afraid he might frighten her into crying out, he tapped gently on the glass.

She shifted. When he tapped again, she turned wearily over, unfocused eyes gazing into the sunlight. Then she blinked and cautiously pushed herself up from the bed. Hurriedly Colt put a finger to his lips, signaling silence. But it didn't stop the tears. They poured out of her eyes as she rushed to the window.

"Colt!" She shook the window, then laid her cheek against the glass and wept. "I want to go home! Please, please, I want to go home!"

He could barely hear her through the glass. Afraid their voices would carry, he tapped again, waiting until she turned her head to look at him.

"Open the window, baby." He mouthed it carefully, but she only shook her head.

"Nailed shut." Her breath hitched, and she rubbed her fists against her eyes. "They nailed it shut."

"Okay, okay. Look at me. Look." He used hand signals to focus her attention. "A pillow. Get a pillow."

A dim spark glowed in her eyes. He'd seen it before, that cautious return of hope. She moved fast, doing as he instructed.

"Hold it against the glass. Hold it steady, and turn your head. Turn your head away, baby."

He used his elbow to smash the glass, satisfied that the pillow muffled most of the noise. When he'd broken enough to ease his body through, he nudged the pillow aside and swung inside.

She was immediately in his arms, clinging, sobbing. He picked her up, cradled her like a baby. "Shh... Liz. It's going to be all right now. I'm going to take you home."

"I'm sorry. I'm so sorry."

"Don't worry about it. Don't worry about anything." He drew back to look into her eyes. She looked so thin, he thought, so pale. And he had a lot more to ask of her. "Honey, you're going to have to be tough for a little while longer. We're going to get you out, and we have to move fast. Do you have a coat? Shoes?"

She shook her head. "They took them. They took everything so I couldn't run away. I tried, Colt, I swear I did, but—"

"It's all right." He pressed her face to his shoulder again, recognizing bubbling hysteria. "You're not going to think about it now. You're just going to do exactly what I tell you. Okay?"

"Okay. Can we go now? Right now?"

"Right now. Let's wrap you in this blanket." He dragged it off the bed with one hand and did his best to bundle it around her. "Now we're going to have to take a little fall. But if you hang on to me, and stay real loose, real relaxed, it's going to be fine." He carried her to the window, careful to cover her face against the cold and the jagged teeth of broken glass. "If you want to scream, you scream in your head, but not out loud. That's important."

"I won't scream." With her heart hammering, she pressed hard against his chest. "Please, just take me home. I want Mom."

"She wants you, too. So does your old man." He kept talking in the same low, soothing tone as he inched toward the edge. "We're going to call them as soon as we get out of here." He said a quick prayer and jumped.

He knew how to fall, off a building, down stairs, out of a plane. Without the child, he would simply have tucked and rolled. With her, he swiveled his body to take the brunt of the impact, so that he would land on his back and cushion her.

The impact stole his breath, wrenched his shoulder, but he was up almost as soon as he landed, with Liz still cradled against his chest. He sprinted toward the road and was halfway there when he heard the first shot.

Chapter 10

Althea drew out her conversation with the police dispatcher, pausing in her own chatter to take in the information that her backup's E.T.A. was ten minutes. She sincerely hoped Colt had managed to get Liz away from the cabin, but either way, it looked like it was going to go down as smooth as silk.

"Thanks, Fran. I'm looking forward to seeing you and Bob, too. Just let me get some idea of where I am from Harry. I don't have a clue." Beaming a new smile in Harry's direction, Althea cupped a hand over the phone. "Do you have, like, an address or something? Bob's going to come pick me up and take a look at my car."

"No problem." He glanced over as Tidal Wave came in from the kitchen. "Hope you made enough breakfast for our guest," Harry told him. "She's had a rough morning."

"Yeah, there's enough." Tidal Wave turned his hard brown eyes on Althea, narrowed them. "Hey! What the hell is this?"

"Try for some manners," Donner suggested. "There's a lady present."

"Lady, hell! That's a cop. That's Wild Bill's cop."

He made his lunge, but Althea was ready. She'd seen the recognition in his eyes and had already reached for her weapon. There wasn't time to think or to worry about the other two men, as two hundred and sixty pounds of muscle and bulk rammed her.

Her first shot veered wide as she went flying, slamming against an antique table. A collection of snuff bottles crashed, spewing shards of amethyst and aquamarine. She saw stars. Through them, she saw her opponent bearing down on her like a freight train.

Pure instinct had her rolling to the left to avoid a blow. Tidal Wave was big, but she was quick. Althea scrambled to her knees and gripped her weapon in both hands.

This time her shot was true. She had only an instant to note the spread of blood on his white T-shirt before she leapt to her feet.

Donner was heading for the door, and Kline was swearing as he dragged open a drawer. She saw the glint of chrome.

"Freeze!"

Her order had Donner throwing up his hands and turning into a statue, but Kline whipped out the gun.

"Do it and die," she told him, stepping back so that she could keep both Kline and Donner in sight. "Drop it, Harry, or you're going to be staining the carpet like your friend there."

"Son of a bitch." Teeth set, he tossed the weapon down.

"Good choice. Now, on the floor, facedown, hands behind your head. You, too, Romeo," she told Donner. While they obeyed, she picked up Kline's gun. "You two should know better than to invite a stranger into the house."

Lord, she hurt, Althea realized now that her adrenaline was leveling off. From the top of her head to the soles of her feet, she was one huge ache. She hoped Tidal Wave's flying tackle hadn't dislodged anything vital.

She caught the thin wail of a siren in the distance. "Looks like old Fran told the troops to come in. Now, in case you don't get the picture, I'm the law, and you're under arrest."

Althea was calmly reading her prisoners their rights when Colt burst in, a gun in one hand, a knife in the other. By her calculations, it had been roughly three minutes since she'd fired the first shot. The man moved fast.

She spared him a glance, then finished the procedure. "Cover these idiots, will you, Nightshade?" she asked as she picked up the dangling receiver. "Officer Mooney? Yes, this is Lieutenant Grayson. We'll need an ambulance out here. I have a suspect down with a chest wound. No, the situation's under control. Thank you. You were a big help."

She hung up and looked back at Colt. "Liz?"

"She's okay. I told her to wait by the road for the cops. I heard the shots." His hands were steady. He could be grateful for that. But his insides were jelly. "I figured they'd made you."

"You figured right. That one." She jerked her head toward Tidal Wave. "He must have seen me with Wild Bill. Why don't you go find us a towel? We'd better try to stop that bleeding."

"The hell with that!" The fury came so suddenly, and so violently, that the two men on the floor quaked. "Your head's cut."

"Yeah?" She touched her fingers to the throbbing ache at her right temple, then studied her blood-smeared fingers in disgust. "Hell. That better not need stitches. I really hate stitches."

"Which one of them hit you?" Colt scanned the three men with icy eyes. "Which one?"

"The one I shot. The one who's currently bleeding to death. Now get me a towel, and we'll see if we can have him live long enough to go to trial." When he didn't respond, she stepped between him and the wounded man. Colt's intentions were clear as crystal. "Don't pull this crap on me, Nightshade. I'm not a damsel in distress, and white knights annoy the hell out of me. Got it?"

"Yeah." He sucked in his breath. There were too many emotions ripping through him. None of them could change the situation. "Yeah, I got it, Lieutenant."

He turned away to do as she'd asked. After all, he thought, she could handle the situation. She could handle anything.

It wasn't until they were in the plane again that he began to calm. He had to at least pretend to be calm for Liz's sake. She'd clung to him, begging him not to send her back with the police, to stay with her. So he'd agreed to fly back with Liz in the copilot's seat and Althea in the jump seat behind.

Looking lost in his coat, Liz stared through the windscreen. No matter how Colt had tried to bundle her up, she continued to shiver. When they leveled off, heading east, the tears began to flow. They fell fast, hot, down her cheeks. Her shoulders shook violently, but she made no sound. No sound at all.

"Come on, baby." Helpless, Colt reached out to take her hand. "Everything's all right now. Nobody's going to hurt you now."

But the silent tears continued.

Saying nothing, Althea rose. She came forward, calmly unstrapped Liz. Communicating by touch, Althea urged Liz to shift, then took her place in the chair. Then she gathered the girl on her lap, cradled her head on her shoulder. Enfolded her grief.

"Don't hold back," she murmured.

Almost at once, Liz's sobs echoed through the cabin. The pain in them cut at Althea's heart as she rocked the girl and held her close. Devastated by the weeping, Colt lifted a hand to brush it down Liz's tangled hair. But she only curled closer to Althea at the touch.

He dropped his hand and concentrated on the sky.

It was Althea's gentle insistence that convinced Liz it would be wise to go to the hospital first. She wanted to go home, she said over and over again. And over and over again, Althea patiently reminded Liz that her parents were already on their way to Denver.

"I know it's hard." Althea kept her arm tight around Liz's shoulders. "And I know it's scary, but the doctor needs to check you out."

"I don't want him to touch me."

"I know." How well she knew. "But he's a she." Althea smiled, rubbing her hand down Liz's arm. "She won't hurt you."

"It'll be over real quick," Colt assured her. He fought to keep his easy smile in place. What he wanted to do was scream. Kick something. Kill someone.

"Okay." Liz glanced warily toward the examining room again. "Please..." She pressed her lips together and looked pleadingly at Althea.

"Would you like me to go in with you? Stay with you?" At Liz's nod, she drew the girl closer. "Sure, no problem. Colt, why don't you go find a soft-drink machine, maybe a candy bar?" She smiled down at Liz. "I could sure use some chocolate. How about you?"

"Yeah." Liz drew in a shaky breath. "I guess."

"We'll be back in a few minutes," Althea told Colt. He could read nothing in her eyes. Feeling useless, he strode down the corridor.

Inside the examining room, Althea helped Liz exchange her tattered clothes for a hospital gown. She noted the bruises on the girl's flesh, but made no comment. They would need an official statement from Liz, but it could wait a little longer.

"This is Dr. Mailer," she explained as the young doctor with the soft eyes approached the table.

"Hello, Liz." Dr. Mailer didn't offer her hand, or touch her patient in any way. She specialized in trauma patients, and she understood the terrors of rape victims. "I'm going to need to ask you some questions, and to run some tests. If there's anything you want to ask me, you go ahead. And if you want me to stop, to wait a while, you just say so. Okay?"

"All right." Liz lay back and focused on the ceiling. But her hand remained tight around Althea's.

Althea had requested Dr. Mailer because she knew the woman's reputation. As the examination progressed, she was more than satisfied that it was well deserved. The doctor was gentle, kind and efficient. It seemed she instinctively knew when to stop, to give Liz a chance to regroup, and when to continue.

"We're all done." Dr. Mailer stripped off her gloves and smiled. "I just want you to rest in here for a little while, and I'm going to have a prescription for you before you leave."

"I don't have to stay here, do I?"

"No." Dr. Mailer closed a hand over Liz's. "You did fine. When your parents get here, we'll talk again. Why don't I see about getting you something to eat?"

As she left, Dr. Mailer sent Althea a look that clearly stated that they, too, would talk later.

"You did do fine," Althea said, helping Liz to sit up. "Do you want me to go see if Colt found that candy bar? I don't imagine that's the sort of food Dr. Mailer had in mind, so we'll have to sneak it while we can."

"I don't want to be alone here."

"Okay." Althea took her brush from her purse and began to untangle Liz's hair. "Let me know if I'm pulling."

"When I saw you downstairs—at the cabin—I thought you were another of the women they brought up. That it was going to happen again." Liz squeezed her eyes shut. Tears spilled through her lashes. "That they were going to make me do those things again."

"I'm sorry. There wasn't any way to let you know I was there to help you."

"And when I saw Colt at the window, I thought it was a dream. I kept dreaming somebody would come, but no one did. I was afraid Mom and Dad just didn't care."

"Honey, your parents have been trying to find you all along." She tipped Liz's chin upward. "They've been so worried. That's why they sent Colt. And I can tell you he loves you, too. You can't imagine the stuff he's bullied me in to doing so he could find you."

Liz tried to smile, but it quivered and fell. "But they don't know about— Maybe they won't love me after they find out . . . everything."

"No." Althea's fingers firmed on Liz's chin. "It'll upset them, and it will hurt them, and it'll be hard, really hard, for them. That's because they do love you. Nothing that happened is going to change that."

"I—I can't do anything but cry."

"Then that's all you have to do, for now."

Liz swiped a shaky hand across her cheeks. "It was my fault I ran away."

"It was your fault you ran away," Althea agreed. "That's all that was your fault."

Liz jerked her head away. The tears gushed out again as she stared at the tiles on the floor. "You don't understand how it feels. You don't know what it's like. How awful it is. How humiliating."

"You're wrong." Gently, firmly, Althea cupped Liz's face again, lifting it until their eyes met. "I do understand. I understand exactly."

"You?" Air shuddered out between Liz's lips. "It happened to you?"

"When I was just about your age. And I felt as though someone had carved something out of me that I'd never get back again. I thought I'd never get clean again, be whole again. Be me again. And I cried for a long, long time, because there didn't seem to be anything else I could do.''

Liz accepted the tissue Althea pressed into her hand. "I kept telling myself it wasn't me. It wasn't really me. But I was so scared. It's over. Colt keeps saying it's over now, but it hurts."

"I know." Althea cradled Liz in her arms again. "It hurts more than anything else can, and it's going to hurt for a while. But you're not alone. You have to keep remembering you're not alone. You have your family, your friends. You have Colt. And you can talk to me whenever you need to."

Liz sniffled, rested her cheek against Althea's heart. "What did you do? After. What did you do?"

"I survived," Althea murmured, staring blankly over Liz's head. "And so will you."

Colt stood in the doorway of the examining room, his arms piled high with cans of soda and candy bars. If he'd felt useless before, he now felt unbearably helpless.

There was no place for him here, no way for him to intrude on this woman pain. His first and only reaction was rage. But where to channel it? He turned away to dump the cans and candy onto a table in the waiting room. If he couldn't comfort either of them, couldn't stop what had already happened, then what could he do?

He scrubbed his hands over his face and tried to clear his mind. Even as he dropped them, he saw Liz's parents dashing from the elevator.

This, at least, he could do. He strode to meet them.

Inside the examining room, Althea finished tidying Liz's hair. "Do you want to get dressed?"

Liz managed what passed for a smile. "I don't ever want to put those clothes on again."

"Good point. Well, maybe I can scrounge up—" She turned at a flurry of movement in the doorway. She saw a pale woman and a haggard man, both with red-rimmed eyes.

"Oh, baby! Oh, Liz!" The woman raced forward first, with the man right on her heels.

"Mom!" Liz was sobbing again even as she threw open her arms. "Mom!"

Althea stepped aside as parents and child were reunited, with tears and desperate embraces. When she spotted Colt in the doorway, she moved to him. "You'd better stay with them. I'll tell Dr. Mailer they're here before I go."

"Where are you going?"

She slid her purse back on her shoulder. "To file my report."

She did just that before she went home to indulge in that long, steamy bath. She soaked until her body was numb. Giving in to exhaustion, both physical and emotional, she fell into bed naked and slept dreamlessly until the battering on her door awoke her.

Groggy, she fumbled for her robe, belting it as she walked to the door. She scowled at Colt through the peephole, then yanked the door open.

"Give me one good reason why I shouldn't book you for disturbing the peace. My peace."

He held out a flat, square box. "I brought you pizza."

She blew out a breath, then drew one in—as well as the rich scent of cheese and spice. "That might get you off. I guess you want to come in with it."

"That was the idea."

"Well, come on, then." With that dubious invitation, she walked away to fetch plates and napkins. "How's Liz holding up?"

"Surprisingly well. Marleen and Frank are as solid as they come."

"They'll have to be." She came back to set the plates on the table. "I hope they understand they're all going to need counseling."

"They've already talked to Dr. Mailer about it. She's going to help them find a good therapist back home." Trying to choose his words properly, he took his time sliding pizza onto the plates. "The first thing I want to do is thank you. And don't brush me off, Thea. I'd really like to get this out."

"All right, then." She sat, picked up a slice. "Get it out."

"I'm not just talking about the official cooperation, the way you helped me find her and get her out. I owe you big for that, but that's professional. You got anything to drink with this?"

"There's some burgundy in the kitchen."

"I'll get it," he said as she started to rise.

Althea shrugged and went back to eating. "Suit yourself." She was working on her second slice when Colt came back with a bottle and two glasses. "I guess I was too tired to realize I was starving."

"Then I don't have to apologize for waking you up." He filled both glasses, but didn't drink. "The other thing I have to thank you for is the way you were with Liz. I figured getting her out was enough—play-

ing that white knight you said irritates you so much."
He looked up, met her eyes. There was a new understanding in them, and a weariness she hadn't seen before. "It wasn't. Telling her it was all right, that it was
over—that wasn't enough, either. She needed you."

"She needed a woman."

"You are that. I know it's a lot to expect—over and
above, so to speak—but she asked about you a couple of times after you left." He toyed with the stem of
his glass. "They're going to be staying in town at least
for another day, until Dr. Mailer has some of the results in. I was hoping you could talk to Liz again."

"You don't have to ask me that, Colt." She reached
out for his hand. "I got involved, too."

"So did I, Thea." He turned their joined hands
over, brought them to his lips. "I'm in love with you.
Big-time. No, don't pull away from me." He tightened his grip before she could. "I've never said that to
another woman. I used alternate terms." He smiled a
little. "I'm crazy about you, you're special to me, that
kind of thing. But I never used *love,* not until you."

She believed him. What was more frightening, she
wanted to believe him. Tread carefully, she reminded
herself. One step at a time. "Listen, Colt, the two of
us have been on a roller coaster since we met—and
that's only been a short while. Things, emotions, get
blown out of proportion on roller coasters. Why don't
we slow this down some?"

He could feel her nerves jittering, but he couldn't be
amused by them this time. "I had to accept that I
couldn't change what had happened to Liz. That was
hard. I can't change what I feel for you. Accepting
that's easy."

"I'm not sure what you want from me, Colt, and I don't think I can give it to you."

"Because of what happened to you before. Because of what I heard you telling Liz in the examining room."

She withdrew instantly and completely. "That was between Liz and me," she said coldly. "And it's none of your business."

It was exactly the reaction he'd expected, the one he'd prepared for. "We both know that's not true. But we'll talk about it when you're ready." Knowing the value of keeping an opponent off balance, he picked up his wine. "You know they're giving Scott a fifty-fifty chance of making it."

"I know." She watched him warily. "I called the hospital before I went to bed. Boyd's handling the interrogation of Kline and Donner for now."

"Can't wait to get at them, can you?"

"No." She smiled again. "I can't."

"You know, I heard those shots, and it stopped my heart." Feeling more relaxed, he bit into his pizza. "I come tearing back, ready to kick butt, crash through the door like the cavalry, and what do I see?" He shook his head and tapped her glass with his. "There you are, blood running down your face..." He paused to touch a gentle finger to the bandage at her temple. "A gun in each hand. There's a three-hundred-pound hulk bleeding at your feet, and two others facedown with their hands behind their heads. You're just standing there, looking like Diana after the hunt, and reciting Miranda. I have to say, I felt pretty superfluous."

"You did okay, Nightshade." She let out a small, defeated breath. "And I guess you deserve to know that I was awfully glad to see you. You looked like Jim Bowie at the Alamo.''

"He lost."

She gave in and leaned forward to kiss him. "You didn't."

"We didn't," he corrected, pleased that her mouth had been soft, relaxed and friendly. "I brought you a present."

"Oh, yeah?" Because the dangerous moment seemed to have passed, her lips curved and she kissed him again. "Gimme."

He reached behind himself for his coat, dug into the pocket. Taking out a small paper bag, he tossed it into her lap.

"Aw, and you wrapped it so nice." Chuckling, she dipped into the bag. And pulled out a lacy bra and panties, in sheer midnight blue. Her chuckle turned into a rich appreciative laugh.

"I pay my debts," he informed her. "Since I figured you probably had a supply of the white kind, I picked out something a little different." He reached over to feel the silk and lace. "Maybe you'll try them on."

"Eventually." But she knew what she wanted now. What she needed now. And she rose to take it. She combed her fingers through his hair, tugging so that his face lifted and his mouth met hers. "Maybe you'll come to bed with me."

"Absolutely." He skimmed his hands up her hips, keeping his mouth joined to hers as he stood to gather her close. "I thought you'd never ask."

"I didn't want the pizza to get cold."

He slipped a finger down the center of her body to toy with the belt of her robe. "Still hungry?"

She tugged his shirt out of his jeans. "Now that you mention it." Then she laughed as he swung her up into his arms. "What's this for?"

"I decided to sweep you off your feet. For now." He started toward the bedroom, deciding she was in for another surprise.

The spread was turned back, but the plain white sheets were barely disturbed from her nap. Colt laid her down, following her onto the bed as he skimmed light, teasing kisses over her face.

Her fingers were busy undoing his buttons. She knew what it would be like, and was prepared—eager—for the storm and the fire and the fast flood of sensations. When her hands pushed away cotton and encountered warm, firm flesh, she gave a low, satisfied moan.

He continued to kiss her, nibbling, nuzzling, as she hastily stripped off his clothes. There was a frantic energy burning in her that promised the wild, the frenzied. Each time desire stabbed through him, he absorbed the shock and kept his pace easy.

Eager, edgy, Althea turned her mouth to his and arched against him. "I want you."

He hadn't realized that three breathy words could make the blood swim in his head. But it would be too easy to take what she offered, too easy to lose what she held back. "I know. I can taste it."

He dipped his mouth to hers again, drawing out the kiss with such trembling tenderness that she groaned again. The hand that had been fisted tight against his bare shoulder went lax.

"And I want you," he murmured, levering back to stare down at her. "All of you." Fascinated, he drew his fingers through her hair, spreading it out until it lay flaming against the white sheet. Then he lowered his head again, gently, so gently, to kiss the bandage at her temple.

Emotion curled inside her like a spiked fist. "Colt—"

"Shh . . . I just want to look."

And look he did, while he traced her face with a fingertip, rubbed her lower lip with his thumb, then trailed it down to her jawline, skimmed over the pulse that fluttered in her throat.

"The sun's going down," he said quietly. "The light does incredible things to your face, your eyes. Just now they're gold, with darker, brandy-colored specks sprinkled through them. I've never seen eyes like yours. You look like a painting." He brushed his thumb over her collarbone. "But I can touch you, feel you tremble, know you're real."

She lifted a hand, wanting to drag him back to her, to make the ache go away. "I don't need words."

"Sure you do." He smiled a little, turning his face into her palm. "Maybe I haven't found the right ones, but you need them." He started to press his lips to her wrist, and then he noticed the faint smudge of bruises. And remembered.

His brows drew together when he straddled her and took both of her hands. He examined her wrists carefully before looking down at her again. "I did this."

Sweet God, she thought, there had to be a way to stop this terrible trembling. "It doesn't matter. You were upset. Make love with me."

"I don't like knowing I hurt you in anger, or that I'm liable to do it again eventually." Very carefully, he touched his lips to each of her wrists, and felt her pulse scramble. "You make it too easy to forget how soft you are, Althea." The sleeves of her robe slithered down her arms as he skimmed his lips to her elbow. "How small. How incredibly perfect you are. I'll have to show you."

He cupped a hand under her head, lifting her so that her hair tumbled back, her face tilted up. Then his mouth was on hers again, savoring a deep, dreamy kiss that left her weak. He felt her give, felt yet another layer dissolve. Her arms linked around his neck; her muscles quivered.

What was he doing to her? She only knew she couldn't think, couldn't resist. She'd been prepared for need, and he'd given her tenderness. What defense could there be against passion wrapped so softly in sweetness? His mouth was gentle, enchanting her even as it seduced.

She wanted to tell him that seduction was unnecessary, but, oh, it felt glorious to surrender to the secrets he unearthed with that quietly devastating mouth and those slow, easy hands.

The last rays of the sun slanted across her eyes as he eased her back so that he could trail his lips down her throat. She heard the whisper of her robe as he slipped it down to bare her shoulder, to free it for lazy, open-mouthed kisses and the moist trail of his tongue.

He could feel it the instant she let herself go. The warmth of triumph surged through him as her hands, as gentle as his, began to caress. He resisted the urge to quicken his pace, and let his hands explore her, over the robe, under it, then over again, as her body melted like warm wax.

All the while, he watched her face, aroused by each flicker of emotion, lured by the way her breath would catch, then rush through her lips at his touch. He could have sworn he felt her float as he slipped the robe away.

Then her eyes opened, dark and heavy. He understood that, though she had surrendered, she would not be passive. Her hands were as thorough as his, seeking, touching, possessing, with that unbearable tenderness.

Until he was as seduced as she.

Soft, breathy moans. Quiet secrets told in murmurs. Long, lingering caresses. The sunlight faded to dusk, and dusk to that deepening of night. There was need, but no frantic rush to sate it. There was pleasure, and the dreamy desire to prolong it.

Indulgence. Tonight there was only indulgence.

He touched, she trembled. She tasted, he shuddered.

When at last he slipped into her, she smiled and gathered him close. The rhythm they set was patient, loving, and as true as music. They climbed together, steadily, beautifully, until his gasp echoed hers. And then they floated back to earth.

She lay a long time in silence, dazed by what had happened. He had given her something, and she had given freely in return. It couldn't be taken back. She wondered what steps could be taken to protect herself now that she had fallen in love.

For the first time. For the only time.

Perhaps it would pass. A part of her cringed at the thought of losing what she'd just found. No matter how firmly she reminded herself that her life was precisely the way she wanted it, she couldn't bring herself to think too deeply about what it would be like without him.

And yet she had no choice. He would leave. And she would survive.

"You're thinking again." He rolled onto his back, hooking an arm around her to gather her close. "I can almost hear your brain humming." Outrageously content, he kissed her hair, closed his eyes. "Tell me the first thing that pops into your mind."

"What? I don't—"

"No, no, don't analyze. This is a test. The first thing, Thea. Now."

"I was wondering when you were going back," she heard herself say. "To Wyoming."

"Ah." He smiled—smugly. "I like knowing I'm the first thing on your mind."

"Don't get cocky, Nightshade."

"Okay. I haven't made any firm plans. I have some loose ends to tie up first."

"Such as?"

"You, for starters. We haven't set the date."

"Colt..."

He grinned again. Maybe it was wishful thinking, but he thought he'd heard exasperation in her tone instead of annoyance. "I'm still shooting for New Year's Eve—I guess I've gotten sentimental—but we've got time to hash that out. Then there's the fact that I haven't finished what I came here to do."

That brought her head up. "What do you mean? You found Liz."

"It's not enough." His eyes glowed in the shadows. "We don't have the head man. It's not finished until we do."

"That's for me and the department to worry about. Personal vendettas have no place here."

"I didn't say it was a vendetta." Though it was. "I intend to finish this, Althea. I'd like to keep working with you on this."

"And if I say no?"

He twirled her hair around his finger. "I'll do my best to change your mind. Maybe you haven't noticed, but I can be tenacious."

"I've noticed," she muttered. But there was a part of her that glowed at the idea that their partnership wasn't at an end. "I suppose I can give you a few more days."

"Good." He shifted her so that he could run a hand down her side to her hips. "Does the deal include a few more nights?"

"I suppose it could." Her smile flashed wickedly. "If you make it worth my while."

"Oh, I will." He lowered his head. "That's a promise."

Chapter 11

With the scream still tearing at her throat, Althea shot up in bed. Blind with terror and rage, she fought the arms that wound around her, struggling wildly against the hold while she sucked in the air to scream again. She could feel his hands on her, feel them groping at her, hot, hurtful. But this time...God, please, this time...

"Althea." Colt shook her, hard, forcing his voice to remain calm and firm, though his heart was hammering against his ribs in fast, hard blows. "Althea, wake up. You're dreaming. Pull out of it."

She clawed her way through the slippery edges of the dream, still fighting him, still dragging in air. Reality was a dim light through the murky depths of the nightmare. With a final burst of effort, she grasped at it, and at Colt.

"Okay, okay..." Still shaken by the sound of the scream that had awakened him, he rocked her, hold-

ing her close to warm her body, which was chill with
clammy sweat. "Okay, baby. Just hold on to me."

"Oh, God..." Her breath came out in a long, shaky
sob as she buried her face against his shoulder. Her
hands fisted impotently at his back. "Oh, God... Oh,
God..."

"It's okay now." He continued to stroke and
soothe, growing concerned when her hold on him increased. "I'm right here. You were dreaming, that's
all. You were only dreaming."

She'd fought her way out of the dream, but the fear
had come back with her, and it was too huge to allow
for shame. So she clung, shivering, trying to absorb
some portion of the strength she felt in him.

"Just give me a minute. I'll be all right in a minute." The shaking would stop, she told herself. The
tears would dry. The fear would ebb. "I'm sorry." But
it wasn't stopping. Instinctively she turned her face
into his throat for comfort. "God, I'm sorry."

"Just relax." She was quivering like a bird, he
thought, and she felt as frail as one. "Do you want me
to turn on the light?"

"No." She pressed her lips together, hoping to stop
the trembling in her voice. She didn't want the light.
Didn't want him to see her until she'd managed to
compose herself. "No. Let me get some water. I'll be
fine."

"I'll get it." He brushed the hair from her face, and
was shaken all over again to find it wet with tears. "I'll
be right back."

She brought her knees up close to her chest when he
left her. Control, she ordered herself, but dropped her
head onto her knees. While she listened to water
striking glass, watched the splinter of light spill

through the crack around the bathroom door, she took long, even breaths.

"Sorry, Nightshade," she said when he came back with the water. "I guess I woke you up."

"I guess you did." Her voice was steadier, he noted. But her hands weren't. He cupped his around hers and lifted the glass to her lips. "Must have been a bad one."

The water eased her dry throat. "Must have been. Thanks." She pushed the glass back into his hands, embarrassed that she couldn't hold it herself.

Colt set the glass on the night table before easing down on the bed beside her. "Tell me."

She moved her shoulders dismissively. "Chalk it up to a rough day and pizza."

Very firmly, very gently, he took her face in his hands. The light he'd left on in the bathroom sent out a dim glow. In it he could see how pale she was.

"No. I'm not going to brush this off, Thea. You're not going to brush me off. You were screaming." She tried to turn her head away, but he wouldn't permit it. "You're still shaking. I can be every bit as stubborn as you, and right now I think I have the advantage."

"I had a nightmare." She wanted to snap at him, but couldn't find the strength. "People have nightmares."

"How often do you have this one?"

"Never." She lifted a weary hand and dragged it through her hair. "Not in years. I don't know what brought it on."

He thought he did. And unless he was very much mistaken, he thought she did, as well. "Do you have a shirt, a nightgown or something? You're cold."

"I'll get one."

"Just tell me where." Her quick, annoyed sigh did quite a bit toward easing his mind.

"Top drawer of the dresser. Left-hand side."

He rose, and opening the drawer grabbed the first thing that came to hand. Before he tugged it over her head, he examined the oversize man's undershirt. "Nice lingerie you have, Lieutenant."

"It does the job."

He smoothed it down over her, tucked pillows behind her, as fussy as a mother with a colicky infant.

She scowled at him. "I don't like being pampered."

"You'll live through it."

When he was satisfied he'd made her as comfortable as possible, he tugged on his jeans. They were going to talk, he decided, and sat beside her again. Whether she wanted to or not. He took her hand, waited until they were eye-to-eye.

"The nightmare. It was about when you were raped, wasn't it?" Her fingers went rigid in his. "I told you I heard you talking to Liz."

She ordered her fingers to relax, willed them to, but they remained stiff and cold. "It was a long time ago. It doesn't apply now."

"It does when it wakes you up screaming. It brought it all back," he continued quietly. "What happened to Liz, seeing her through it."

"All right. So what?"

"Trust me, Althea." He said it quietly, his eyes on hers. "Let me help."

"It hurts," she heard herself say. Then she shut her eyes. It was the first time she had admitted that to anyone. "Not all the time. Not even most of the time. It just sneaks up now and then and slices at you."

"I want to understand." He brought her hand to his lips. When she didn't pull away, he left it there. "Talk, talk to me."

She didn't know where to begin. It seemed safest to start at the beginning. Letting her head rest against the pillows, she closed her eyes again.

"My father drank, and when he drank, he got drunk, and when he got drunk, he got mean. He had big hands." She curled hers into fists, then relaxed them. "He used them on my mother, on me. My earliest memory is of those hands, the anger in them that I couldn't understand, and couldn't fight. I don't remember him very well. He tangled with somebody meaner one night and ended up dead. I was six."

She opened her eyes again, realizing that keeping them closed was just another way of hiding. "Once he was gone, my mother decided to take up where he'd left off—in the bottle. She didn't hit it as hard as he did, but she was more consistent."

He could only wonder how the people she'd described could have created anything as beautiful or as true as the woman beside him. "Did you have anyone else?"

"I had grandparents, on my mother's side. I don't know where they lived. I never met them. They hadn't had anything to do with her since she'd run off with my father."

"But did they know about you?"

"If they did, they didn't care."

He said nothing, trying to comprehend it. But he couldn't, simply couldn't understand family not caring. "Okay. What did you do?"

"When you're a child, you do nothing," she said flatly. "You're at the mercy of adults, and the reality is, a great many adults have no mercy." She paused a moment to pick up the threads of the story. "When I was about eight, she went out—she went out a lot—but this time she didn't come home. A couple of days later, a neighbor called Social Services. They scooped me up into the system."

She reached for the water again. This time her hands didn't shake. "It's a long, typical story."

"I want to hear it."

"They placed me in a foster home." She sipped her water. There wasn't any point in telling him how frightened, how lost, she'd been. The facts were enough. "It was okay. Decent. Then they found her, slapped her wrists a couple of times, told her to clean up her act, and gave me back."

"Why in the hell did they do that?"

"Things were different back then. The court believed the best place for a kid was with her mother. Anyway, she didn't stay dry for long, and the cycle started all over again. I ran away a few times, they dragged me back. More foster homes. They don't leave you in any one too long, especially when you're recalcitrant. And I'd developed my own mean streak by that time."

"Small wonder."

"I bounced around in the system. Social workers, court hearings, school counselors. All overburdened. My mother hooked up with another guy and finally took off for good. Mexico, I think. In any case, she didn't come back. I was twelve, thirteen. I hated not being able to say where I wanted to go, where I wanted to be. I took off every chance I got. So they labeled me a j.d.—juvenile delinquent—and they put me in a girls' home, which was one step up from reform school." Her lips twisted into a dry smile. "That put the fear of God into me. It was rough, as close to prison as I ever want to be. So I straightened up, put on my best behavior. Eventually they placed me in foster care again."

She drained the glass and set it aside. She knew her hands wouldn't be steady for long. "I was scared that if I didn't make it work this time, they'd put me back until I was eighteen. So I took a real shot at it. They were a nice couple, naive, maybe, but nice, good intentions. They wanted to do something to right society's ills. She was PTA president, and they went to protest rallies against nuclear power plants. They talked about adopting a Vietnamese orphan. I guess I smirked at them behind their backs sometimes, but I really liked them. They were kind to me."

She took a moment, and he said nothing, waiting for her to build to the next stage. "They gave me boundaries, good ones, and they treated me fairly. There was one drawback. They had a son. He was seventeen, captain of the football team, homecoming king, A student. The apple of their eye. A real company man."

"Company man?"

"You know, the kind who's all slick and polished on the outside, he's got a terrific rap, lots of charm, lots of angles. And underneath, he's slime. You can't get to the slime because you keep slipping on all that polish, but it's there." Her eyes glinted at the memory. "I could see it. I hated the way he looked at me when they weren't watching." Her breath was coming quicker now, but her voice was still controlled. "Like I was a piece of meat he was sizing up, getting ready to grill. They couldn't see it. All they saw was this perfect child who never gave them a moment's grief. And one night, when they were out, he came home from a date. God.''

When she covered her face with her hands, Colt gathered her close. "It's all right, Thea. That's enough."

"No." She shook her head violently, pushed back. She'd gone this far. She'd finish it. "He was angry. I suppose his girl hadn't surrendered to his many charms. He came into my room. When I told him to get out, he just laughed and reminded me it was his house, and that I was only there because his parents felt sorry for me. Of course, he was right."

"No. No, he wasn't."

"He was right about that," Althea said. "Not about the rest, but about that. And he unzipped his pants. I ran for the door, but he threw me back on the bed. I hit my head pretty hard on the wall. I remember being dizzy for a minute, and hearing him telling me that he knew girls like me usually charged for it, but that I should be flattered that he was going to give me a thrill. He got on the bed. I slapped him, I swore at him. He backhanded me, and pinned me. And I started to scream. I kept screaming and screaming while he raped me. When he was finished, I wasn't screaming anymore. I was just crying. He got off the bed, and zipped up his pants. He warned me that if I told anyone he'd deny it. And who were they going to believe, someone like him, or someone like me? He was blood, so there was no contest. And he could always get five of his buddies to say that I'd been willing with all of them. Then they'd just put me back in the home.

"So I didn't say anything, because there was nothing to say and no one to say it to. He raped me twice more over the next month, before I got the nerve to run away again. Of course, they caught me. Maybe I'd wanted them to that time. I stayed in the home until I was eighteen. And when I got out, I knew no one was ever going to have that kind of control over me again. No one was ever going to make me feel like I was nothing ever again."

Unsure what to do, Colt reached up tentatively to brush a tear from her cheek. "You made your life into something, Althea."

"I made it into mine." She let out a breath, then briskly rubbed the tears from her cheeks. "I don't like to dwell on before, Colt."

"But it's there."

"It's there," she agreed. "Trying to make it go away only brings it closer to the surface. I learned that, too. Once you accept it's simply a part of what makes you what you are, it doesn't become as vital. It didn't make me hate men, it didn't make me hate myself. It did make me understand what it is to be a victim."

He wanted to gather her close, but was afraid she might not want to be touched. "I wish I could make the hurt go away."

"Old scars," she murmured. "They only ache at odd moments." She sensed his withdrawal, and felt the ache spread. "I'm the same person I was before I told you. The trouble is, after people hear a story like that, they change."

"I haven't changed." He started to touch her, drew back. "Damn it, Thea, I don't know what to say to you. What to do for you." Rising, he paced away from the bed. "I could make you some tea."

She nearly laughed. "Nightshade's cure-all? No thanks."

"What do you want?" he demanded. "Just tell me."

"Why don't you tell me what you want?"

"What I want." He strode to the window, whirled back. "I want to go back to when you were fifteen and kick that bastard's face in. I want to hurt him a hundred times worse than he hurt you. Then I want to go back further and break your father's legs, and I want to kick your mother's butt while I'm at it."

"Well, you can't," she said coolly. "Pick something else."

"I want to hold you!" he shouted, jamming his fists into his pockets. "And I'm afraid to touch you!"

"I don't want your tea, and I don't want your sympathy. So if that's all you have to offer, you might as well leave."

"Is that what you want?"

"What I want is to be accepted for who and what I am. Not to be tiptoed around like an invalid because I survived rape and abuse."

He started to snap back at her, then stopped himself. He wasn't thinking of her, he realized, but of his own rage, his own impotence, his own pain. Slowly he walked back to the bed and sat beside her. Her eyes were still wet; he could see them gleaming against the shadows. He slipped his arms around her, gently drew her close until her head rested on his shoulder.

"I'm not going anywhere," he murmured. "Okay?"

She sighed, settled. "Okay."

Althea awakened at sunrise with a dull headache. She knew instantly that Colt was no longer beside her.

Wearily she rolled onto her back and rubbed her swollen eyes.

What had she expected? she asked herself. No man would be comfortable around a woman after hearing a story like the one she'd told him. And why in God's name had she dumped out her past that way? How could she have trusted him with pieces of herself that she'd never given anyone before?

Even Boyd, the person she considered her closest friend, knew only about the foster homes. As for the rest, she'd buried it—until last night.

She didn't doubt that her tie to Liz had unlocked the door and let the nightmare back in. But she should have been able to handle it, to hold back, to safeguard her privacy. The fact that she hadn't could mean only one thing.

Indulging in a sigh, Althea pushed herself up and rested her brow on her knees.

She was in love with Colt. Ridiculous as it was, she had to face the truth. And, just as she'd always suspected, love made you stupid, vulnerable and unhappy.

There ought to be a pill, she mused. A serum she could take. Like an antidote for snakebite.

The sound of footsteps had her whipping her head up. Her eyes widened when Colt came to the doorway carrying a tray.

He had a split second to read her reaction before she closed it off. She'd thought he'd taken a hike, he realized grimly. He was going to have to show the lady that he was sticking, no matter how hard she tried to shake him off.

"Morning, Lieutenant. I figured you'd planned on a full day."

"You figured right." Cautious, she watched as he crossed to the bed, waited until he'd set the tray at her feet. "What's the occasion?" she asked, gesturing toward the plates of French toast.

"I owe you a breakfast. Remember?"

"Yeah." Her gaze shifted from the plates to his face. Love still made her feel stupid, it still made her feel vulnerable, but it no longer made her unhappy. "You're a regular whiz in the kitchen."

"We all have our talents." He sat cross-legged on the other side of the tray and dug in. "I figure—" he chewed, swallowed "—after we're married, I can handle the meals, you can handle the laundry."

She ignored the quick sprint of panic and sampled her first bite. "You ought to see someone about this obsessive fantasy life of yours, Nightshade."

"My mother's dying to meet you." He grinned when Althea's fork clattered against her plate. "She and Dad send their best."

"You—" Words failed her.

"She and my father know Liz. I called to relieve their minds, and I told them about you." Smiling, he brushed her hair back from her shoulders. He hadn't known a woman could look so sexy in a man's undershirt. "She's for a spring wedding—you know, all that June-bride stuff. But I told her I wasn't waiting that long."

"You're out of your mind."

"Maybe." His grin faded. "But I'm in yours, Thea. I'm in there real good, and I'm not getting out."

He was right about that, but it didn't change the bottom line. She was not walking down the aisle and saying 'I do.' That was that.

"Listen, Colt." Try reason, she thought. "I'm very fond of you, but—"

"You're what?" His mouth quirked again. "You're what of me?"

"Fond," she spit out, infuriated by the gleam of good humor in his eyes.

"Euphemisms." Affectionately he patted her hand, shook his head. "You disappoint me, I had you pegged as a straight shooter."

Forget reason. "Just shut up and let me eat."

He obliged her, because it gave him time to think, and to study her. She was still a bit pale, he mused. And her eyes were swollen from the bout of tears during the night. But she wouldn't let herself be fragile. He had to admire her unceasing supply of strength. She didn't want sympathy, he remembered, she wanted understanding. She would just have to learn to accept both from him.

She'd accepted his comfort the night before. Whether she knew it or not, she'd already come to rely on him. He wasn't about to let her down.

"How's the coffee?"

"Good." And because it was, because the meal he'd prepared had already conquered her headache, she relented. "Thanks."

"My pleasure." He leaned forward, touched his mouth to hers. "I don't suppose I could interest you in an after-breakfast tussle."

She smiled now, fully, easily. "I'll have to take a rain check." But she spread a hand over his chest and kissed him again. Her fingers closed over his medal. "Why do you wear this?"

"My grandmother gave it to me. She said that when a man was determined not to settle down in one place, he should have someone looking out for him. It's worked pretty well so far." He set the tray on the floor, then scooped Althea into his arms.

"Nightshade, I said—"

"I know, I know." He hitched her up more comfortably. "But I had this idea that if we had that tussle in the shower, we could stay pretty much on schedule."

She laughed, nipped at his shoulder. "I'm a firm believer in time management."

She had more than a full day to fit into twenty-four hours. There was a mountain of paperwork waiting for her, and she needed to talk to Boyd about his interrogation of Donner and Kline before she met with them herself. She wanted, for personal, as well as professional, reasons, to interview Liz again.

She sat down and began efficiently chipping away at the mountain.

Cilla knocked on the open door. "Excuse me, Lieutenant. Got a minute?"

"For the captain's wife," she said, smiling and gesturing Cilla inside, "I've got a minute and a half. What are you doing down here?"

"Boyd filled me in." Cilla leaned down, peered close and, as a woman would, saw through the meticulously applied cosmetics to the signs of a difficult night. "Are you all right?"

"I'm fine. I have decided that anyone who camps out on purpose needs immediate psychiatric help, but it was an experience."

"You should try it with three kids."

"No," Althea said definitely. "No, I shouldn't."

With a laugh, Cilla rested a hip against the edge of the desk. "I'm so glad you and Colt found the girl. How's she doing?"

"It'll be rough for a while, but she'll come through."

"Those creeps should be—" Cilla's eyes flashed, but she cut herself off. "I didn't come here to talk cop, I came to talk turkey."

"Oh?"

"As in Thanksgiving. Don't give me that look." Cilla angled her chin, readying for battle. "Every year you've got some excuse for not coming to Thanksgiving dinner, and this time I'm not buying it."

"Cilla, you know I appreciate the offer."

"The hell with that. You're family. We want you." Even as Althea was shaking her head, Cilla was plowing on. "Deb and Gage are coming. You haven't seen them in a year."

Althea thought of Cilla's younger sister, Deborah, and her husband. She would like to see Deb again. They'd gotten close while Deborah was in Denver finishing up college. And Gage Guthrie. Althea pursed her lips as she thought of him. She genuinely liked Deborah's husband, and a blind man could have seen that he adored his wife. But there was something about him—something Althea couldn't put her finger on. Not a bad thing, she thought now, not a worrying thing. But something.

"Taking a side trip?" Cilla asked.

"Sorry." Althea snapped back and fiddled with the papers on her desk. "You know I'd love to see them again, Cilla, but—"

"They're bringing Adrianna." Cilla's secret weapon was her sister's baby girl, whom Althea had seen only in snapshots and videotapes. "You and I both know what a sucker you are for babies."

"You want to keep that down?" Althea stated with an uneasy glance toward the bull pen. "I've got a reputation to uphold around here." She sighed and leaned back in her chair. "You know I want to see them, all of them. And since I'm sure they'll be here through the holiday weekend, I will. We'll shoot for Saturday."

"Thanksgiving dinner." Cilla dusted her hands together as she straightened. "You're coming this year, if I have to tell Boyd to make it an order. I'm having my family. My whole family."

"Cilla—"

"That's it." Cilla folded her arms. "I'm taking this to the captain."

"You're in luck," Boyd said as he came to the door. "The captain happens to be available. And he's brought you a present." He stepped aside.

"Natalie!" With a whoop of pleasure, Cilla threw her arms around her sister-in-law and squeezed. "I thought you were in New York."

"I was." Natalie's dark green eyes sparkled with laughter as she drew Cilla back to kiss her. "I had to fly in for a few days, and I figured I'd make this my first stop. I didn't know I'd hit the jackpot. You look great."

"You look phenomenal, as always." It was perfectly true. The tall, willow-slim woman with the sleek blond hair and the conservatively cut suit would always turn heads. "The kids are going to be thrilled."

"I can't wait to get my hands on them." She turned, held out both hands. "Thea. I can't believe I'm lucky enough to get all three of you at once."

"It's really good to see you." With their hands still linked, Althea pressed her cheek to Natalie's. In the years Althea had been Boyd's partner, she and his younger sister had become fast friends. "How are your parents?"

"Terrific. They send love to everyone." In an old habit, she glanced around Althea's office, let out a sigh. "Thea, can't you at least get a space with a window?"

"I like this one. Less distractions."

"I'm calling Maria as soon as I get to the station," Cilla announced. "She'll whip up something special for tonight. You're coming, Thea."

"Wouldn't miss it."

"What is this?" Colt demanded as he tried to squeeze into the room. "A conference? Thea, you're going to have to get a bigger—" He broke off, stared. "Nat?"

Her stunned expression mirrored his. "Colt?"

His grin split his face. "Son of a gun." He elbowed past Boyd to grab Natalie in a hug that lifted her feet from the floor. "I'll be damned. Pretty Natalie. What's it been? Six years?"

"Seven." She kissed him full on the mouth. "We ran into each other in San Francisco."

"At the Giants game, right. You look better than ever."

"I am better than ever. Why don't we have a drink later, and catch up?"

"Now, that's..." He fumbled to a halt when he glanced at Althea. She was sitting on the edge of her desk, watching their reunion with an expression of mild curiosity and polite interest. When he realized his arm was still around Natalie's waist, he dropped it quickly to his side. "Actually, I, ah..."

How was a man supposed to talk to an old female friend when the woman he loved was studying him as if he were something smeared on a glass slide?

Natalie caught the look that passed between Althea and Colt. Surprise came first, then a chuckle she disguised by clearing her throat. Well, well, she thought, what an interesting stew she'd dropped into. She couldn't resist stirring the pot.

"Colt and I go way back," she said to Althea. "I had a terrible crush on him when I was a teenager." She smiled wickedly up at Colt. "I've been waiting for years for him to take advantage of it."

"Really?" Althea tapped a finger to her lips. "He doesn't strike me as being slow off the mark. A little dense, maybe, but not slow."

"You're right about that. Cute, too, isn't he?" She winked at Althea.

"In an overt sort of way," Althea agreed, enjoying Colt's discomfort. "Why don't you and I have that drink later, Natalie? It sounds as though you and I have quite a bit to chat about."

"It certainly does."

"I don't think this is the place to set up social engagements." Well aware that he was outnumbered and outgunned, Colt stuck his hands into his pockets. "Althea looks busy."

"Oh, I've got a minute or two. What are you doing in town, Natalie?"

"Business. Always nice when you can mix it with pleasure. I have an emergency meeting in an hour with the board of directors on one of Boyd's and my downtown units. Owning real estate is a full-time job.

Without proper management, it can be a huge headache,'' she explained.

"You don't happen to own one on Second Avenue, do you?" Althea asked.

"Mmm, no. Is one up for sale?" A gleam came into her eyes, and then she laughed. "It's a weakness," she explained. "There's something about owning property, even with all the problems that come with it."

"What's the trouble now?" Boyd asked, trying to work up some interest.

"The manager decided to up all the rents and keep the difference." Natalie said, her eyes hardening in startling contrast to her soft, lovely face. "I hate being duped."

"Pride," Boyd said, and tapped a finger on her nose. "You hate making a mistake."

"I didn't make a mistake." Her chin angled upward. "The man's résumé was outstanding." When Boyd continued to grin, she wrinkled her nose at him. "The problem is, you have to give a manager autonomy. You can't be everywhere at once. I remember one manager we had who was running a floating crap game in an empty apartment. He kept it rented under a fake name," she continued, nearly amused now. "He'd even filled out an application, complete with faked references. He made enough profit off the games to afford the overhead, so the rent came in like clockwork. I'd never have found out if someone hadn't tipped the cops and they raided the place. It turned out he'd done the same thing twice before."

"Good Lord," Althea said, looking stunned.

"Oh, it wasn't that bad," Natalie went on. "Actually, it was pretty exciting stuff. I just— What is it?" she demanded when Althea sprang to her feet.

"Let's move." Colt was already headed out the door.

Althea grabbed her coat and sprinted after him. "Boyd, run a make on—"

"Nieman," he called out. "I got it. You want backup?"

"I'll let you know."

When the room emptied, Natalie threw up her hands and stared at Cilla. "What brought that on?"

"Cops." Cilla shrugged. That said it all.

Chapter 12

"I can't believe we let that slip by us." Colt slammed the door to the Jeep and peeled away from the curb. This time he didn't bother to remove the parking ticket under the windshield wiper.

"We're going on a hunch," Althea reminded him. "We could very well get slapped down."

"You don't think so."

She shut her eyes a moment, letting the pieces fall into place. "It fits," she said grimly. "Not one single tenant could swear they'd ever seen this Mr. Davis. He was the man who wasn't there—maybe because he never was."

"And who would have had access to the penthouse? Who could have faked references—references that didn't have to exist? Who could have slipped through the building virtually unnoticed, because he was always there?"

"Nieman."

"I told you he was a weasel," Colt said between his teeth.

She was forced to agree, but cautiously. "Don't get ahead of yourself, Nightshade. We're doing some follow-up questioning. That's all."

"I'm getting answers," he shot back. "That's all."

"Don't make me pull rank on you, Colt." She said it quietly, calming him. "We're going in there to ask questions. We may be able to shake him into slipping up. We may very well have to walk out without him. But now we have a place to start digging."

They'd dig, all right, Colt thought. Deep enough to bury Nieman. "I'll follow your lead," he said. For now. He pulled up at a red light, drumming his fingers impatiently on the wheel. "I'd like to, ah . . . explain about Nat."

"Explain what?"

"That we aren't—weren't. Ever," he said savagely. "Got it?"

"Really?" She'd laugh about this later, she was sure. Once there weren't so many other things on her mind. Still, she wasn't so preoccupied that she'd blow a chance to bait him. "Why not? She's beautiful, she's fun, she's smart. Looks like you fell down on that one, Nightshade."

"It wasn't that I didn't . . . I mean, I thought about it. Started to—" He swore, revved the engine when the light turned. "She was Boyd's sister, all right? Before I knew it, she was like my sister, too, so I couldn't . . . think about her that way."

She sent him a long, curious look. "Why are you apologizing?"

"I'm not." His voice took on a vicious edge, because he realized he was doing just that. "I'm explaining. Though God knows why I'd bother. You think what you want."

"All right. I think you're overreacting to a situation in typical, and predictable, male fashion." The look he speared at her should have sliced to the bone. She merely smiled. "I don't hold it against you. Any more than I would hold it against you if you and Natalie *had* been involved. The past is just that. I know that better than anyone."

"I guess you do." He jammed the gearshift into fourth, then reached out to cover her hand with his. "But we weren't involved."

"I'd have to say that was your loss, pal. She's terrific."

"So are you."

She smiled at him. "Yeah, I am."

Colt steered to the curb, parking carelessly in a loading zone. He waited while Althea called in their location. "Ready?"

"I'm always ready." She stepped out of the car. "I want to play this light," she told Colt. "Just follow-up questions. We've got nothing on him. Nothing. If we push too hard, we'll lose our chance. If we're right about this—"

"We are right. I can feel it."

So could she. She nodded. "Then I want him. For Liz. For Wild Bill." And for herself, she realized. To help her close the door this ordeal had opened again.

They walked in together and approached Nieman's apartment. Althea sent Colt one last warning look, then knocked.

"Yes, yes..." Nieman's voice came through the door. "What is it?"

"Lieutenant Grayson, Mr. Nieman." She held her shield up to the peephole. "Denver PD. We need a few minutes of your time."

He pulled open the door to the width of the security chain. His eyes darted from Althea's face to Colt's and back again. "Can't this wait? I'm busy."

"I'm afraid not. It shouldn't take long, Mr. Nieman. Just routine."

"Oh, very well." With a definite lack of grace, he yanked off the chain. "Come in, then."

When she did, Althea noted the packing boxes set on the carpet. Many were filled with shredded paper. For Althea, they were as damning as a smoking gun.

"As you can see, you've caught me at a bad time."

"Yes, I can see that. Are you moving, Mr. Nieman?"

"Do you think I would stay here, work here, after this—this scandal?" Obviously insulted, he tugged on his tightly knotted tie. "I think not. Police, reporters, badgering tenants. I haven't had a moment's peace since this began."

"I'm sure it's been a trial for you," Colt stated. He wanted to get his hands on that tie. Nieman would hang nicely from it.

"It certainly has. Well, I suppose you must sit." Nieman waved a hand toward chairs. "But I really can't spare much time. I've a great deal of packing left to do. I don't trust the movers to do it," he added. "Clumsy, always breaking things."

"You've had a lot of experience with moving?" This from Althea as she sat and took out her pad and pencil.

"Naturally. As I've explained before, I travel. I enjoy my work." He smiled by tightening his lips over his teeth. "But I find it tedious to remain in one place for too long. Landlords are always looking for a responsible, experienced manager."

"I'm sure they are." She tapped her pencil against the pad. "The owners of this building . . ." She began to flip pages.

"Johnston and Croy, Inc."

"Yes." She nodded when she found the notation. "They were quite upset when they were told about the activities in the penthouse."

"I should say." Nieman hitched up the knees of his trousers and sat. "They're a respectable company. Quite successful in the West and Southwest. Of course, they blame me. That's to be expected."

"Because you didn't do a personal interview with the tenant?" Althea prompted.

"The bottom line in real estate, Lieutenant, is regular monthly rentals and low turnover. I provided that."

"You also provided the scene of the crime."

"I can hardly be held responsible for the conduct of my tenants."

It was time, Althea decided, to take a risk. A calculated one. "And you never entered the premises? Never checked on it?"

"Why would I? I had no reason to bother Mr. Davis or go into the penthouse."

"You never went in while Mr. Davis was in residence?" Althea asked.

"I've just said I didn't."

She frowned, flipped more pages. "How would you explain your fingerprints?"

Something flickered in Nieman's eyes, then was gone. "I don't know what you mean."

She was reaching, but she pressed a bit further. "I wondered how you would explain it if I told you that your fingerprints were found inside the penthouse—since you claim never to have entered the premises."

"I don't see..." He was scrambling now. "Oh, yes, I remember now. A few days before... before the incident... the smoke alarm in the penthouse went off. Naturally, I used my passkey to investigate when no one answered my knock."

"You had a fire?" Colt asked.

"No, no, simply a defective smoke detector. It was so minor an incident, I quite forgot it."

"Perhaps you've forgotten something else," Althea said politely. "Perhaps you forgot to tell us about a cabin, west of Boulder. Do you manage that property, as well?"

"I don't know what you're talking about. I don't manage any property but this."

"Then you just use it for recreation," Althea continued. "With Mr. Donner, Mr. Kline and Mr. Scott."

"I have no knowledge of a cabin," Nieman said stiffly, but a line of sweat had popped out above his top lip. "Nor do I know any people by those names. Now you'll have to excuse me."

"Mr. Scott isn't quite up to visitors," Althea told him, and remained seated. "But we can go downtown

and see Kline and Donner. That might refresh your
memory."

"I'm not going anywhere with you." Nieman rose
then. "I've answered all your questions in a reasonable and patient manner. If you persist in this harass-
ment, I'll have to call my attorney."

"Feel free." Althea gestured toward the phone. "He
can meet us at the station. In the meantime, I'd like
you to think back to where you were on the night of
October 25. You could use an alibi."

"Whatever for?"

"Murder."

"That's preposterous." He drew a handkerchief out
of his breast pocket to wipe his face. "You can't come
in here and accuse me this way."

"I'm not accusing you, Mr. Nieman. I'm asking for
your whereabouts on October 25, between the hours
of 9:00 and 11:00 p.m. You might also tell your lawyer that we'll be questioning you about a missing
woman known as Lacy, and about the abduction of
Elizabeth Cook, who is currently in protective custody. Liz is a very bright and observant girl, isn't she,
Nightshade?"

"Yeah." She was amazing, Colt thought. Absolutely amazing. She was cracking Nieman into pieces
with nothing but innuendo. "Between Liz and the
sketches, the D.A. has plenty to work with."

"I don't believe we mentioned the sketches to Mr.
Nieman." Althea closed her notebook. "Or the fact
that both Kline and Donner were thoroughly interro-
gated yesterday. Of course, Scott is still critical, so
we'll have to wait for his corroboration."

Nieman's face went pasty. "They're lying. I'm a respectable man. I have credentials." His voice cracked. "You can't prove anything on the word of some two-bit actors."

"I don't believe we mentioned Kline and Donner were actors, did we, Nightshade?"

"No." He could have kissed her. "No, we didn't."

"You must be psychic, Nieman," Althea stated. "Why don't we go to the station and see what else you can come up with?"

"I know my rights." Nieman's eyes glittered with rage as he felt the trap creaking shut. "I'm not going anywhere with you."

"I'll have to insist." Althea rose. "Go ahead and call your lawyer, Nieman, but you're coming in for questioning. Now."

"No woman's going to tell me what to do." Nieman lunged, and though Althea was braced, even eager, Colt stepped between them and merely used one hand to shove Nieman back onto the couch.

"Assaulting an officer," he said mildly. "I guess we'll take him in on that. It should give you enough time to get a search warrant."

"More than enough," she agreed. She took out her cuffs.

"Ah, Lieutenant..." Colt watched as she competently secured Nieman's skinny wrists. "They didn't find prints upstairs, did they?"

"I never said they did." She tossed her hair back. "I simply asked what he'd say *if* I said they were found."

"I was wrong," he decided. "I do like your style."

"Thanks." Satisfied, she smiled. "I wonder what we might find in all these neatly packed boxes."

* * *

They found more than enough. Tapes, snapshots, even a detailed journal in Nieman's own hand. It painstakingly recorded all his activities, all his thoughts, all his hatred for women. It described how the woman named Lacy had been murdered, and how her body had been buried behind the cabin.

By that afternoon, he had been booked on enough charges to keep him away from society for a lifetime.

"A little anticlimactic," Colt commented as he followed Althea into her office, where she would type up her report. "He was so revolting, I couldn't even drum up the energy to kill him."

"Lucky for you." She sat, booted up her machine. "Listen, if it's any consolation, I believe he was telling the truth about not touching Liz himself. I'm betting the psychiatric profile bears it out. Impotence, accompanied by rage against women and voyeuristic tendencies."

"Yeah, he just likes to watch." His fury came and went. Althea had been right about not being able to change what had been.

"And to make piles of money from his hobby," she added. "Once he rounded up his cameraman and a couple of sleazy actors, he went into the business of pandering to others with his peculiar tastes. Got to give him credit. He kept a very precise set of books on his porn business. Kept him in antiques and silk ties."

"He won't need either one in a cell." He rested his hands on her shoulders. "You did good, Thea. Real good."

"I usually do." She glanced over her shoulder to study him. Now all she had to do was figure out what to do about Colt. "Listen, Nightshade, I really want to get this paperwork moving, and then I need some downtime. Okay?"

"Sure. I hear there's going to be some spread at the Fletchers' tonight. Are you up for it?"

"You bet. Why don't I meet you there?"

"All right." He leaned down to press his lips to her hair. "I love you, Thea."

She waited until he left, shutting her door behind him. *I know,* she thought, *I love you, too.*

She went to see Liz. It helped to be able to give the girl and her family some sort of resolution. Colt had beaten her to it, had already come and gone. But Althea sensed that Liz needed to hear it from her, as well.

"We'll never be able to repay you." Marleen stood with her arm around Liz as if she couldn't bear not to touch her daughter. "I don't have the words to tell you how grateful we are."

"I—" She'd almost said she'd just been doing her job. It was the truth, but it wasn't all of it. "Just take care of each other," she said instead.

"We're going to spend a lot more time doing just that." Marleen pressed her cheek against Liz's. "We're going home tomorrow."

"We're going into family counseling," Liz told Althea. "And I—I'm going to join a rape victims' support group. I'm a little scared."

"It's all right to be scared."

Nodding, Liz looked at her mother. "Mom, can I— I just want to talk to Lieutenant Grayson for a minute."

"Sure." Marleen clung for a final moment. "I'll just go down to the lobby, help your father when he gets back with that ice cream."

"Thanks." Liz waited until her mother left the room. "Dad doesn't know how to talk about what happened to me yet. It's awful hard on him."

"He loves you. Give him time."

"He cried." Liz's own eyes filled with tears. "I never saw him cry before. I thought he was too busy with work and stuff to care. I was stupid to run away." Once she'd blurted it out, she exhaled deeply. "I didn't think they understood me, or what I wanted. Now I see how bad I hurt them. It won't ever be exactly the same again, will it?"

"No, Liz, it won't. But if you help each other through it, it can be better."

"I hope so. I still feel so empty inside. Like a part of me's not there anymore."

"You'll fill it with something else. You can't let this block off your feelings for other people. It can make you strong, Liz, but you don't want it to make you hard."

"Colt said—" She sniffled and reached for the box of tissues her mother had left on the coffee table. "He said whenever I felt like I couldn't make it, I should think of you."

Althea stared. "Of me?"

"Because you'd had something horrible happen to you, and you'd used it to make yourself beautiful. Inside and out. That you hadn't just survived, you'd triumphed." She gave a watery smile. "And I could, too. It was funny to hear him talk that way. I guess he must like you a lot."

"I like him, too." And she did, Althea realized. It wasn't a weakness to love someone, not when you could admire and respect him at the same time. Not when he saw exactly what you were, and loved you back.

"Colt's the best," Liz stated. "He never lets you down, you know? No matter what."

"I think I do."

"I was wondering . . . I know the counseling's important, and everything, but I wonder if I could just call you sometimes. When I—when I don't think I can get through it."

"I hope you will." Althea rose to go over and sit beside Liz. She opened her arms. "You call when you're feeling bad. And when you're feeling good. We all need somebody who understands us."

Fifteen minutes later, Althea left the Cooks to their ice cream and their privacy. She decided she had a lot of thinking to do. She'd always known where her life was going. Now that it had taken this sudden and dramatic detour, she needed to get her bearings again.

But Colt was waiting for her in the lobby.

"Hey, Lieutenant." He tipped her head back and kissed her lightly.

"What are you doing here? Marleen said you'd been by already."

"I went with Frank. He needed to talk."

She touched a hand to his cheek. "You're a good friend, Nightshade."

"It's the only kind of friend there is." She smiled, because she knew he meant it. "Want a lift?"

"I've got my car." But when they walked outside together, she discovered she didn't want that downtime alone after all. "Look, do you want to take a walk or something? I'm wired."

"Sure." He draped an arm casually over her shoulder. "You can help me scope out some of the shop windows. My mother has a birthday next week."

Resistance surged instantly—a knee-jerk response. "I'm no good at picking out presents for people I don't know."

"You'll get to know her." He strolled to the corner and turned left, heading toward a row of downtown shops. He glanced in one window at an elegant display of fine china and crystal. "Hey, you're not the type who, like, registers a pattern and that stuff, are you? You know, for wedding presents?"

"Get a grip." She moved past him so that he had to lengthen his stride to catch up.

"What about a trousseau? Do women still do that?"

"I haven't any idea, or any interest."

"It's not that I mind the T-shirt you wore in bed last night. I was just thinking that something a little more...no, a little less, would be nice for the honeymoon. Where do you want to go?"

"Are you going to cut this out?"

"No."

With an impatient breath, she turned and stared at the next window. "That's a nice sweater." She pointed to a rich blue cowl-neck on a mannequin. "Maybe she'd go for cashmere."

"Maybe." He nodded. "Fine. Let's go get it."

"See, that's your problem." Althea whirled around, hands on hips. "You don't give anything enough thought. You look at one thing, and boom—that's it."

"When it's the right thing, why look around?" He smiled and tugged on her hair. "I know what works for me when I see it. Come on." He took her hand and pulled her into the shop. "The blue sweater in the window?" he said to the clerk. "Have you got it in a size . . ." He measured in the air with his hands.

"Ten?" the clerk guessed. "Certainly, sir. Just one moment."

"You didn't ask how much it cost," Althea pointed out.

"When something's right, cost is irrelevant." He turned to smile at her. "You're going to keep me in line. I appreciate that. I tend to let details slip."

"There's news." She stepped away to poke through a rack of silk blouses.

He was careless, Althea reminded herself. He was impulsive and rash and quick on the draw. All the things she was not. She preferred order, routine, meticulous calculation. She had to be crazy to think they could mesh.

She turned her head, watching him as he waited for the clerk to ring up the sweater and gift-wrap it.

But they did mesh, she realized. Everything about him fitted her like a glove. The hair wasn't really blond or brown and was never quite disciplined. The eyes, caught somewhere between blue and green, that could stop her heart with one look. His recklessness. His dependability.

His total and unconditional understanding.

"Problem?" he asked when he caught her staring.

"No."

"Would you like a pink bow, sir, or blue?"

"Pink," he said, without glancing back. "Do you have any wedding dresses in here?"

"Not formal ones, no, sir." But the clerk's eyes lit up at the prospect of another sale. "We do have some very elegant tea gowns and cocktail suits that would be perfect for a wedding."

"It should be something festive," he decided, and the humor was back in his eyes. "For New Year's Eve."

Althea straightened her shoulders, turned on her heel to face him. "Get this, Nightshade. I am not marrying you on New Year's Eve."

"Okay, okay. Pick another date."

"Thanksgiving," she told him, and had the pleasure of watching his mouth fall open as he dropped the box the clerk had handed him.

"What?"

"I said Thanksgiving. Take it or leave it." She tossed her hair back and strode out the door.

"Wait! Damn!" He started after her, kicked the gift box halfway across the room. The clerk called after him as he scooped it up on the run.

"Sir, the dresses?"

"Later." He swung through the door and caught up with Althea halfway down the block. "Did you say you'd marry me on Thanksgiving?"

"I hate repeating myself, Nightshade. If you can't keep up, that's your problem. Now, if you've finished your shopping, I'm going back to work."

"Just one damn minute." Exasperated, he stuffed the box under his arm, crushing the bow. It freed his hands to snag her by the shoulders. "What made you change your mind?"

"It must have been your smooth, subtle approach," she said dryly. Lord, she was enjoying this, she realized. Deep-down enjoying it. "Keep manhandling me, pal, and I'll haul you in."

He shook his head, as if to realign his thoughts. "You're going to marry me?"

She arched a brow. "Ain't no flies on you."

"On Thanksgiving. *This* Thanksgiving. The one that's coming up in a few weeks?"

"Getting cold feet already?" she began, then found her mouth much too occupied for words. It was a heady kiss, filled with promises and joy. "Do you know the penalty for kissing a police officer on a public street?" she asked when she could speak again.

"I'll risk it."

"Good." She dragged his mouth back to hers. Pedestrians wound around them as they clung. "You're going to get life for this, Nightshade."

"I'm counting on it." Carefully he drew her back so that he could see her face. "Why Thanksgiving?"

"Because I'd like to have a family to celebrate it with. Cilla's always bugging me to join them, but I...I couldn't."

"Why?"

"Is this an interrogation or an engagement?" she demanded.

"Both, but this is the last one. Why are you going to marry me?"

"Because you nagged me until I broke down. And I felt sorry for you, because you seemed so set on it. Besides, I love you, and I've kind of gotten used to you, so—"

"Hold on. Say that again."

"I said I've kind of gotten used to you."

Grinning, he kissed the tip of her nose. "Not that part. The part right before that."

"Where I felt sorry for you?"

"Uh-uh. After that."

"Oh, the I-love-you part."

"That's the one. Say it again."

"Okay." She took a deep breath. "I love you." And let it out. "It's tougher to say it all by itself that way."

"You'll get used to it."

"I think you're right."

He laughed and crushed her against him. "I'm betting on it."

Epilogue

"I think I need to consider this again."

Althea stood in front of the full-length mirror in Cilla's bedroom, staring at her own reflection. There was a woman inside the mirror, she noted dispassionately. A pale woman with a tumble of red hair. She looked elegant in a slim ivory suit trimmed with lace and accented with tiny pearl buttons that ran the length of the snugly fitted jacket.

But her eyes were too big, too wide, and too fearful.

"I really don't think this is going to work."

"You look fabulous," Deborah assured her. "Perfect."

"I wasn't talking about the dress." She pressed a hand to her queasy stomach. "I meant the wedding."

"Don't start." Cilla tugged at the line of Althea's ivory silk jacket. "You're fidgeting again."

"Of course I'm fidgeting." For lack of anything better to do, Althea reached up to make sure the pearl drops at her ears were secure. Colt's mother had given them to her, she remembered, and felt a trickle of warmth at the memory. Something to be handed down, his mother had said, as they had been from Colt's grandmother to her.

Then she'd cried a little, and kissed Althea's cheek and welcomed her to the family.

Family, Althea thought on a fresh wave of panic. What did she know about family?

"I'm about to commit myself for life to a man I've known a matter of weeks," she muttered to the woman in the mirror. "I should *be* committed."

"You love him, don't you?" Deborah asked.

"What does that have to do with it?"

Laughing, Deborah took Althea's restless hand in hers. "Only everything. I didn't know Gage very long, either." And had known the depths of his secrets for an even shorter time. "But I loved him, and I knew. I've seen the way you look at Colt, Thea. You know, too."

"Lawyers," Althea complained to Cilla. "They always turn things around on you."

"She's great, isn't she?" Pride burst through as Cilla gave her sister a hard squeeze. "The best prosecutor east of the Mississippi."

"When you're right, you're right," Deborah returned with a grin. "Now, let's take a look at the matron of honor." She tilted her head to examine her sister. "You look wonderful, Cilla."

"So do you." Cilla brushed a hand through her sister's dark hair. "Marriage and motherhood agree with you."

"If you two will finish up your admiration hour, I'm having a nervous breakdown over here." Althea sat down on the bed, squeezed her eyes shut. "I could make a run for it out the back."

"He'd catch you," Cilla decided.

"Not if I had a really good head start. Maybe if I—" A knock on the door interrupted her. "If that's Nightshade, I am not going to talk to him."

"Of course not," Deborah agreed. "Bad luck." She opened the door to her husband and daughter. That was good luck, she thought as she smiled at Gage. The very best luck of all.

"Sorry to break in on the prep work, but we've got some restless people downstairs."

"If those kids have touched that wedding cake . . ." Cilla began.

"Boyd saved it," Gage assured her. Barely. With the baby tucked in one arm, he slipped the other around his wife. "Colt's wearing a path in the den carpet."

"So he's nervous," Althea shot back. "He should be. Look what he's gotten us into. Boy, would I like to be a fly on the wall down there."

Gage grinned, winked at Deborah. "It has its advantages." He nuzzled his infant daughter when she began to fuss.

"I'll take her, Gage." Deborah gathered Adrianna into her arms. "You go help Boyd calm down the groom. We're nearly ready."

"Who said?" Althea twisted her hands together.

Cilla brushed Gage out of the room, closed the door. It was time for the big guns. "Coward," she said softly.

"Now, just a minute..."

"You're afraid to walk downstairs and make a public commitment to the man you love. That's pathetic."

Catching on, Deborah soothed the baby, and played the game. "Now, Cilla, don't be so harsh. If she's changed her mind—"

"She hasn't. She just can't make it up. And Colt's doing everything to make her happy. He's selling his ranch, buying land out here."

Althea got to her feet. "That's unfair."

"It certainly is." Deborah ranged herself beside Althea, and bit the inside of her lip to keep from grinning. "I'd think you'd be a little more understanding, Cilla. This is an important decision."

"Then she should make it instead of hiding up here like some vestal virgin about to be sacrificed."

Althea's chin jutted out. "I'm not hiding. Deb, go out and tell them to start the damn music. I'm coming down."

"All right, Thea. If you're sure." Deborah patted her arm, winked at her sister, and hurried out.

"Well, come on." Althea stormed to the door. "Let's get going."

"Fine." Cilla sauntered past her, then started down the steps.

Althea was nearly to the bottom before she realized she'd been conned. The two sisters had pulled off the good cop–bad cop routine like pros.

Now her stomach jumped. There were flowers everywhere, banks of color and scent. There was music, soft, romantic. She saw Colt's mother leaning heavily against his father and smiling bravely through a mist of tears. She saw Natalie beaming and dabbing at her eyes. Deborah, her lashes wet, cradling Adrianna.

There was Boyd, reaching out to take Cilla's hand, kissing her damp cheek before looking back at Althea to give her an encouraging wink.

Althea came to a dead stop. If people cried at weddings, she deduced, there had to be a good reason.

Then she looked toward the fireplace, and saw nothing but Colt.

And he saw nothing but her.

Her legs stopped wobbling. She crossed to him, carrying a single white rose, and her heart.

"Good to see you, Lieutenant," he murmured as he took her hand.

"Good to see you, too, Nightshade." She felt the warmth from the fire that glowed beside them, the warmth from him. She smiled as he brought her hand to his lips, and her fingers were steady.

"Happy Thanksgiving."

"Same goes." She brought their joined hands to her lips in turn. Maybe she didn't know about family, but she'd learn. They'd learn. "I love you, very much."

"Same goes. Ready for this?"

"I am now."

As the fire crackled, they faced each other and the life they'd make together.

* * * * *

HE'S AN

AMERICAN HERO

He's a cop, a fire fighter or even just a fearless drifter who gets the job done when ordinary men have given up. And you'll find one American Hero every month, only in Intimate Moments—created by some of your favorite authors. Look at what we've lined up for the last months of 1993:

October: GABLE'S LADY by Linda Turner—With a ranch to save and a teenage sister to protect, Gable Rawlings already has a handful of trouble...until hotheaded Josey O'Brian makes it an armful....

November: NIGHTSHADE by Nora Roberts—Murder and a runaway's disappearance force Colt Nightshade and Lt. Althea Grayson into an uneasy alliance....

December: LOST WARRIORS by Rachel Lee—With one war behind him, Medevac pilot Billy Joe Yuma still has the strength to fight off the affections of the one woman he can never have....

AMERICAN HEROES: Men who give all they've got for their country, their work—the women they love.

IMHERO6

Take 4 bestselling love stories FREE

Plus get a FREE surprise gift!

What a year for romance!

Silhouette has five fabulous romance collections coming your way in 1993. Written by popular Silhouette authors, each story is a sensuous tale of love and life—as only Silhouette can give you!

Three bachelors are footloose and fancy-free...until now.
(March)

Heartwarming stories that celebrate the joy of motherhood.
(May)

Put some sizzle into your summer reading with three of Silhouette's hottest authors.
(June)

Take a walk on the dark side of love—with tales just perfect for those misty autumn nights.
(October)

Share in the joy of yuletide romance with four award-winning Silhouette authors.
(November)

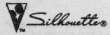

A romance for all seasons—it's always time for romance with Silhouette!

INTIMATE MOMENTS®
Silhouette.

Southern Alberta—wide open ranching country
marked by rolling rangelands and roiling passions.
That's where the McCall family make their home.
You can meet Tanner, the first of the McCalls, in
BEYOND ALL REASON, (IM #536), the premiere book in

JUDITH DUNCAN's

WIDE
OPEN
SPACES

miniseries beginning in December 1993.

Scarred by a cruel childhood and narrow-minded
neighbors, Tanner McCall had resigned himself to a
lonely life on the Circle S Ranch. But when Kate Quinn,
a woman with two sons and a big secret, hired on,
Tanner discovered newfound needs and a woman
worthy of his trust.

In months to come, join more of the McCalls as
they search for love while working Alberta's
WIDE OPEN SPACES—only in
Silhouette Intimate Moments

To Mom and Papa, my intelligent and talented parents,
who taught me to embrace life and always encouraged me
to pursue my dreams.

Acknowledgments

In writing this book, I was reminded of those who have shaped my life and brought me personal happiness and professional success. Executive producer Ken Corday has always made *Days* more than just a workplace, but a family; I thank him and casting director Fran Bascom for making me part of such an amazing show. My *Days* family (cast and crew) has taught me so much, especially Deidre Hall, who from my first day on the set has been my mentor and my friend; and my favorite co-star Bryan Dattilo, who doesn't know how truly talented he is. With *Days* has come an incredible group of NBC executives whose support has led to more opportunities than I could have ever imagined.

Many people are fortunate to have even one strong support system; I've been blessed with several. A special thanks to my family—the Sweeneys, Gleasons, and Sanovs—especially Mom and Papa; my brothers, Ryan and Sten, who always encouraged me to soar but kept me grounded; my cousin Christy, the sister I never had; and Aunt Jane, whose wisdom, style, and friendship have always been invaluable to me.

Growing up, I aspired to have a circle of friends for life and I'm lucky to have found them: My best friend Carrie, with whom I share a brain, not to mention everything else in our lives; and Stephanie, Lauren, Shari and Ari are always with me, whether by phone or e-mail, in traffic or on a red carpet. *"I love us!"*

This book could not have been written without the advice, guidance, and support of my literary agent, Jane Dystel; my co-writer Richard Trubo, who trans-

formed my stories into what I hope you'll find to be an interesting book; my publicist of eleven years, Charles Riley; and my editor (and *Days* fan), John Scognamiglio, who offered so many good suggestions to keep the book accurate and on target.

Saving the most important for last, my husband, Dave, has filled my life with love, laughter, understanding, and encouragement.

Like sands through the hourglass, I thank all of you for the days of my life . . . so far!

Chapter 1

"Like sands through the hourglass, so are the days of our lives . . ."

Sound familiar?

I've been serenaded by that opening mantra of *Days of Our Lives* for more than ten years now—and loving every minute of it. Since that January morning in 1993 when I walked onto the set of *Days* for the first time, I've taken a wonderful ride that is as exciting today as it was a decade ago.

For more than a third of my life, the Midwestern town of Salem has been home, and let me tell you, it's never been dull. Because you're reading this book, you're probably a *Days* fan, and perhaps even a fan of my amazing character, Sami Brady. I've been so lucky to play someone like her who millions of viewers love—or, to be more accurate, often love to hate.

Admit it—there are probably dozens of Sami moments that are indelibly imprinted in your own mind. She has survived a brutal rape, struggled with bulimia, given birth to a beautiful son, spent some

terrifying moments on death row, kidnapped and tried to sell her own baby sister on the black market, was stranded at the altar (how many times now?), fought repeatedly and viciously with her mother (and just about everyone else in Salem!), lied about her son's paternity, and slept with her older sister's fiancé. All in a day's work! Yet through it all, Sami's still standing, still scheming, still devious and dangerous, and still winning the hearts, minds (and, let's face it) the animosity of the six million fans who watch the show each week and seem barely able to survive without their daily fix of *Days*. As the NBC Web site recently said, "Alison Sweeney has become pretty good at playing bad."[1]

I know what it's like to be a *Days of Our Lives* "addict." Before I joined the show, I was already happily hooked on *Days*. I had started watching the show during the summer vacation before the ninth grade, and once I returned to school in the fall, I set up the VCR each morning and taped every episode without fail. When I'd watch the show, it was the perfect way for me to "chill out" after school. The day-to-day turmoil in Salem provided the perfect escape from my own real-life dramas at school. *Days* was (and is) absolutely habit-forming.

So when I was chosen to play Sami in 1993, at the age of sixteen, I felt like the luckiest girl in the world. And in many ways, I still do. The writers of *Days* have created a character that you can't stop thinking about or trying to figure out. Even if some viewers don't want to admit it, many of them relate

1. You might be wondering why I refer to Sami in the third person throughout this book. Sami is a huge part of my life, and I love playing her. But Sami is her own person, and she and I are not one in the same. If you know her through the show, you'll understand why I keep her separate in my own mind.

to her, even though she certainly isn't the most angelic character on daytime television.

(NBC)

While some *Days* watchers are absolutely baffled by Sami, others love her and are proud of being a "Sami-Fan." I am well known for surfing the Web and stopping by to visit and post at Sami-friendly

sites. Still, hardly a week goes by when someone doesn't ask me skeptically, "Do you *really* like playing Sami?" In fact, I love Sami. Okay, she does the kinds of unbelievably crazy things that are so outrageous. But admit it, she behaves the way that most of us have wanted to at one time or another, but never had the nerve.

Sami's saving grace is that her behavior—the good, the bad, and the ugly—comes from a genuine place. It's a product of her love for the people in her life, her own insecurities, and her unwavering determination to go after what she wants. You have to respect that about Sami. She's definitely someone who millions of people identify with and even secretly admire, even when her mean streak is creating havoc throughout Salem.

Okay, I admit it—there are moments now and then when Sami even makes my own skin crawl. At times, I even wonder what it would be like to play a heroine who warms people's hearts and souls. I may look like someone with "girl-next-door wholesomeness" (as *TV Guide* once described me), but I certainly don't play one on TV! So I get plenty of letters and e-mails from fans who need to get things about Sami off their chest. Almost to a person, there's very little holding back.

But that's what makes playing Sami so interesting. She's a character who everyone has an opinion about—and I think I've heard all of them from fans who stop me on the street or interrupt me between bites at restaurants. Some offer warm hugs, telling me how much they adore Sami. Occasionally, however, they'll give me a good tongue-lashing, or (in one unforgettable moment) swing a purse at me in disgust over Sami's eccentric behavior. Viewers have told me that they've actually thrown things at

the TV screen when Sami becomes more than they can bear. The most common refrain: "Sami's a real bitch!"

Through it all, I still love portraying Sami. I think she's so much fun. At the same time, I adore every one of my fans, whether they love Sami or hate her. This book is for them and for you.

A Show Business Tale

In this book, you'll read my story. It is not only an account of my ten-plus years at the Burbank studio where *Days of Our Lives* is taped. It is also about my life offscreen—the good fortune that I've had and also how I've navigated over both the ordinary and extraordinary speed bumps that can derail you if you're not careful. Of course, from the outside looking in, it may seem as though I've had it all. Since my midteens, I've starred on one of TV's most popular daytime soaps, I'm living out my lifelong dream of being a successful actress, and both fans and critics have been generous with their compliments about my acting. *Time* magazine once called *Days of Our Lives* the "most daring drama" on daytime television, and Sami and I have been right in the middle of it for more than a decade. No complaints at all! In fact, sometimes I can't believe it! ☺

At the same time, as I've moved from my own adolescence into adulthood, my life and my problems have been no different than those of so many other girls and young women. Problems with friends. Concerns about weight. Balancing work and play. Being pulled in every possible direction, and not always the right ones. Discovering my inner self, ex-

ploring my beliefs, and shaping my values. Along
the way, there has often been a disconnect between
the storybook image of a TV actress and what the
real world dishes out. Yes, I've been lucky to have a
wonderful show business career and a so-called
glamorous life. But guess what? Most of my life is
just like the lives of millions of other girls and
women—confronting insecurities, coping with shyness, dealing with everyday anxieties, at times preoccupied with the way I look, and (of course)
obsessing about the number on the bathroom scale.
For better or worse, I've done it all in the public
eye, where the smallest piece of gossip can make
its way into the tabloids and ruin your day.

As I write this book, I still feel young, and like
I'm just starting out in some ways. At the same time,
I know that I'm somewhat of a "veteran" on a network soap. I've done the math, and I've been on
Days for more than a third of my life. And, if I'm
still there at age thirty, it'll be exactly half of my
life! But I still think of myself as a kid, and if you
had seen my best friend and me at a recent Bon
Jovi concert, you would have thought we were
fourteen-year-old groupies. I can giggle and gossip
with the best of 'em, and I never want to take myself too seriously or feel as though I can't do youth-
ful things (like visiting Disney-land—the "happiest
place on earth").

Of course, it has been interesting growing up in
L.A., which may be a little crazier than finding your
way into adulthood in many other parts of the country. But I think most of the societal pressures and
standards aren't that different, no matter where
you call home. How well I remember high school,
where it always seemed that other girls had the
perfect bodies and the perfect lives—perhaps be-

cause they were on the cheerleading squad or dated the cutest guys in the class. Sounds a little shallow and superficial, right? But those are the kinds of things that are important when you're a teenager. Years later as an adult, when you look back with a little perspective and maturity, you can see that no one's life is perfect. Everyone has challenges, and the issues that once seemed so important often become insignificant.

Hollywood's Weighting Game

In Hollywood, many of life's pressures become exaggerated, and they can become suffocating if you let them. Take weight, for example. That's right, that scary scale can affect your mood for the whole day or week or. . . . In a high-profile industry like show business, you can't escape the fact that most young actresses have waiflike bodies and wrist-sized waists, and have never met a diet they didn't like. I've met most of those same diets, too, and have been taken hostage by a few! But let me tell you, I've never felt much affection for any of them. Of course, America devours diets and the hottest new diet book on the block with infinite enthusiasm (do the names Atkins, Sears, and Ornish ring a bell?), and for as long as I can remember, I was often consumed with my weight, even though I was never terribly heavy. In high school, during those times when I tipped the scales at a little more than I'd like, I might find myself overcome with doubts that I just wasn't pretty enough or that I wasn't going to be attractive to boys (welcome to adolescent anxiety!).

On my home turf—Hollywood—dieting has been taken to another level. For many actresses, it has become an obsession that borders on the maniacal. I won't say that I've never bought into this "Honey, I Shrunk the Actress" mindset. In fact, for many years, even though I was never obese, I tried fitting into a culture that reveres lean, angular bodies in women, and for a long time I really became fixated on my weight. In this book, I'll tell you about my struggles—how I became one of the sweating masses crowding into trendy health clubs in L.A. . . . how I went on a dozen or more absolutely crazy diets . . . how I ate only fruit . . . tried not eating after 5 P.M. . . . ordered meals that were prepared by nutritionists and delivered to my door. But nothing worked very long. Absolutely nothing.

Sounds insane, doesn't it? It really was a sad and pathetic way to live, diet after diet, year after year. Frankly, I get exhausted just thinking about it. Yet more than once, casting directors told me that I didn't get a particular role—perhaps for a "Movie of the Week"—because "you're just too fat for the part." Ouch! Yep, they really can be that brutally honest!

But here's the real tragedy: After a while, I began believing them. I absolutely hated myself when I glared at the scale and it glared back at me with unwelcome news. There were even a few times when I felt such despair that I wanted to throw up my hands and say, "Forget Holly-wood! Maybe I'll do something else with my life. I don't need this agony." There were desperate moments when I just wanted to stop at Krispy Kreme on the way home from the studio and curl up in bed with a dozen doughnuts instead of the next day's script. But as you'll read,

"giving up" on my weight or anything else just isn't who I am.

Turning Points

Before we go on, let me make this clear: This certainly isn't a diet book. As I tell my own story, I'm *not* going to advise you on what to eat and when to eat it. Far from it. A nutritionist or dietician can handle that much better than I can. But I hope you'll find some inspiration when you read about my own turning points, finally overcoming the struggles with an issue that got too much of my attention for much too long. Whether you live in California or Canada, New York or New Mexico, we all watch the same television shows and read the same fashion magazines, which leave most women thinking that we shouldn't have eaten that yummy slice of cheesecake the night before or allowed our jogging shoes to collect dust in the closet. *US Weekly, Women's World,* VH1, *Entertainment Tonight* and *E! Entertainment* have documented my own dieting efforts. Even so, diets no longer dominate my life 24/7. And with a more relaxed attitude, my excess weight really has disappeared and certainly isn't the issue it once was.

But still, let's be honest: Wherever I go, people are *always* talking about losing weight. It's been over five years since I went through my own significant weight loss, but still I can hear their words echoing through my mind—"How many calories is that?" . . . "No, thanks, that food isn't on my diet." . . . "Does this outfit make me look fat?" . . .

Then there's my favorite, sometimes said with tongue in cheek: "Don't you absolutely *hate* her—she can eat anything she wants."

It's an insane way to live!

Fortunately, as I'll describe in these pages, a lot of my actress-friends and I have developed a much healthier outlook, recognizing just how ridiculous the weight game can be. We're very clear that the attention on our waistlines and the bathroom scale can be curses for Hollywood actresses and women everywhere. But I'm also clear about another thing: Since I had my first Kodak moment on a TV commercial when I was just five years old, acting has been my dream. I'm good at it. I'm certainly passionate about it. It's what I know and what I love. So I've made a conscious decision to remain strong, fight back, and try to stay above the fray and the need to fit the stereotypical mold of the perfect actress with the perfect figure.

Yes, I've waged a lot of internal psychological warfare over the years, and I've tried shifting the focus away from the scale and more toward leading a happy, healthy, fulfilling life. Of course, I still watch what I eat, and I'm always weighing my options when I'm reading a menu or shopping in the supermarket. But as you'll read in this book, I'm not the fanatic I used to be. I know that my body type will never allow me to look like the next Kate Moss or any other supermodel, for that matter.

But here's the amazing part of this story: The producers of *Days of Our Lives* have never made an issue of my weight. I'm so lucky to work for people who are so supportive. Whether I've been a little overweight or just right, they have only been interested in creating a great character who fans love—or hate! It really hasn't mattered what I weigh.

Sami's Longevity

Years ago, when I joined the cast of *Days of Our Lives,* I never could have imagined that I'd be sitting here, over a decade later, having gone through adolescence and young adulthood in the public eye and still having the privilege of playing Sami. So many soap characters come and go quicker than you can strike the delete button on a scriptwriter's computer. Characters are done in by diseases, laid to rest by jealous lovers—or they sometimes just "go upstairs" and are never heard from again. But somehow Sami has survived every transgression and every misstep—and she's had plenty of them. When I won a fan-voted Emmy award in 2002, do you remember the category? It was "America's Favorite Villain," of course. The award was custom-made for Sami!

Sure, Sami may never be the girl who guys dream of bringing home to mom. But many fans have looked beyond her character flaws—and beyond Sami herself—and have turned me into their sounding board and perhaps even role model. Every week, I receive hundreds of letters and e-mails, some from fans who just want to give Sami or me a piece of their mind. But others ask for my advice on "girl concerns" that are important in their lives. Why me? Here's what I think: Every afternoon on *Days,* I come into their living rooms, and many of them feel that I'm part of their family (no kidding!). They confide in me. They describe their own relationships with parents and friends, husbands and boyfriends. They recount their personal stories of dating, marriage, and sex . . . and of weight gain and weight loss. They even sometimes say, "Ali, I don't

know why I'm writing to you—I really don't know you—but I feel like I can talk to you more honestly than to most other people in my life."

Later in this book, I'll include some of the letters and e-mails I've received from fans. Many of them are quite remarkable and very touching. When fans have written to me about confronting their insecurities, seeing themselves in a new way, and building their own self-confidence—and they give some of the credit to me because of inspirational things I've said in the media—they've motivated me to write this book, to tell my story, to share my experiences on *Days*, and I hope, to infuse them (and you) with some additional encouragement to be courageous, to be bold, and to follow your dreams.

When I respond to fan mail, I often tell viewers that while my life may seem glamorous, I'm really just like them. I haven't escaped any of the pressures and anxieties experienced by virtually every girl or woman. No matter where you live or what your life circumstances are, I'm convinced that all of us should strive for happiness by enjoying old friendships and creating new ones, embracing our families, and nurturing the love in our lives. I hope you'll search for who you really are, and accept yourself with all of your good qualities as well as your shortcomings. Set meaningful goals and work hard to reach them.

Of course, in this book you won't catch me claiming that I have all the answers. But like Sami, I've learned a lot and I go after what I want. Whether it's setting my sights on an acting role or learning to play racquetball with my husband, Dave, my expectations have always been high. I enjoy challenges and doing some out-of-the-box thinking about goals

and how to reach them. That's where the fun of living can be.

Like so many actors, I'm following my dreams and my heart. I've never been the kind of person to sit at home, waiting for the phone to ring or for the world to come to me. I go after what I want—and I hope I'll inspire you to do the same! I keep my eyes open to everything the world has to offer, and I try to make things happen, developing my talents and working to excel at every opportunity.

At the same time, I've also become better at finding balance in my life. As Dave and my girlfriends will tell you, I take time just to hang out "away from the office." I try not to spread myself too thin. A life without balance isn't genuine, and I'm enjoying life more as I become older.

Navigating Through the Book

So turn the page and let's get started. I hope you'll enjoy reading about my experiences—all the rewards, all the challenges—as well as life on the set of *Days of Our Lives*. I'll tell you about the other actors on the show . . . recollections of my most memorable scenes . . . and everything you always wanted to know about Sami. At the same time, even though my own profession may be different than yours, I think you'll find a lot in these pages that will remind you of times in your own life. Growing up, I've yearned for friends, ached to have love in my life, felt overwhelmed at times by the pressures and stresses, and struggled with the scale. Welcome to Life 101!

- -

After reading my story, you might be inspired by the journey that I've taken. I may light a fire that encourages you to follow your own dreams. More than anything, I want you to enjoy this book, and through my story, find yourself motivated to live in rhythm with the person you are and want to become.

Chapter 2

(Author's personal collection)

Salem's Future Hellraiser!

In some ways, playing Samantha Jean Brady is like wearing an old comfy pair of jeans that I can put on anytime, anywhere, knowing that they'll fit perfectly. After more than a decade, I know Sami so well that sometimes I think I know what she's going to do and say, even without looking at the script.

When the producers of *Days of Our Lives* hired me in 1992, they told me that I was the perfect fit to play Sami. There had been previous incarnations of the character, played by five different child actors (from Ronit Aronoff to Christina Wagoner),

(Jon McKee)

dating back to 1984. But now the producers and writers had decided to bring Sami back as a teenager. What a wonderful opportunity for the actress who would get the part!

When my agent told me about the auditions, I was skeptical about my chances. After all, I know what the odds are in this industry. You may know that dozens and sometimes even hundreds of actors often try out for a single part. You've probably heard about the "cattle calls." The stories are true. So it's smart not to get your hopes up too high.

At the time, I certainly didn't fit the stereotype of the typical underweight, undersized, undernourished actress. See, I was a little overweight (especially by Hollywood standards)—maybe by about ten to fifteen pounds at the most. It was nothing to be particularly concerned about—unless you're

an actress. If you think America is obsessed with its waistlines, just try show business on for size. This is a community and a profession where the anthem seems to be that you can never be too slender.

Fortunately, however, the producers of *Days* had something else in mind when casting Sami. Of course, Sami is Marlena Evans' (Deidre Hall's) daughter and Carrie's (Christie Clark's) younger sister, and the soap's writers already had a story line in the works for their new addition to the cast. They were considering a story line where Sami would battle bulimia, the bingeing-purging eating disorder that affects millions of Americans, mostly adolescent girls and young women. As a result, the producers were thinking outside the box when searching for the next Sami. They weren't necessarily seeking a razor-thin actress who looked like she had never craved a Godiva chocolate or never had a weakness for French pastry. (As one magazine noted when describing the search for an actress to play Sami, "Most soaps would have cast a glammy, reed-thin sexpot in such a conspicuous role.") Later, I found out that their "job description" for Sami was simple yet demanding—a young actress who could carry her own weight (so to speak) with the rest of the cast. Everything else was secondary.

Yet when I first heard that *Days* was casting Sami, I was baffled. After all, I was already a big fan of the show, and at the time, Marlena didn't have a sixteen-year-old daughter on the show, or at least I had never seen her. So what the heck was this audition all about?

Well, when I got the script for the tryout, the mystery was solved. Here's what I learned: The very young Sami was being aged, and she was

about to reemerge as a key character on the show. What a cool idea! I couldn't have been more excited. I *really* wanted this part.

The Tryout

I was a bundle of nervous energy leading up to the audition. When the day finally arrived—a Monday afternoon after school—I drove to the interview, which was with Fran Bascom, *Days'* casting director. Fran, who is still in charge of casting for *Days*, is a great lady, and I was really anxious about meeting her. But she was so nice that, almost right away, I felt much more comfortable. As for the reading itself, I certainly did my best but wasn't really sure how well (or how poorly) I had done.

As I was walking out the door, Fran stopped me in my tracks and pulled me aside. "Ali," she said, "you did a great job."

A great job?! Wow! Believe me, you don't usually hear that kind of positive feedback at an audition. It just doesn't happen. Usually, it's just an emotionless "thank you" or something equally vague so that you leave having no idea whether they hated you or loved you. Normally, you have to wait a few days, and you don't hear back directly, but rather through your agent or manager.

"Look," Fran continued, "we're holding the screen test on Wednesday. Ali, I want you to come back on Wednesday. Can you make it?"

Was she kidding or what?! I couldn't believe Fran was telling me this right then and there. She seemed to have instantly made a decision that I

might be right for the part. I was so excited—and absolutely stunned.

"Definitely," I told her, desperately clinging to my composure. "I'll be there."

On the way home, I was so ecstatic—but so nervous—that I could barely think. Homework would have to wait. So would everything else except learning my lines for Wednesday's screen test.

I couldn't believe this was really happening.

I called my friend Mary that night. She was also a fan of *Days*, and I told her what had happened. We were both screaming and freaking out over the phone (I'm sure our parents—not to mention the neighbors—thought we had completely flipped out!). For the moment at least, I was on cloud nine!

The Screen Test

Then I had to think about the screen test.

I went to school on Tuesday and Wednesday, but I can't tell you much of anything that happened there. I spent every free moment reading and re-reading the script that would be used in the screen test. For forty-eight hours, butterflies fluttered in my stomach. I can assure you that I didn't sleep much on Monday and Tuesday nights. How could I, with my mind running wild with images of everything that might happen during the screen test—and what it would be like if I actually got the part?!

One really important way for me to prepare for the screen test was to schedule an appointment with my acting coach. I am a firm believer in coaches, and I still take acting classes today (I'll write more

about this later). Having another eye to read the material and scrutinize my performance helped me lock down the character and also gave me the confidence to do my best in front of the cameras.

I carried the "sides"—which is what they call the audition scene—around with me everywhere. I'd sneak it out during chemistry (I was terrible at chemistry anyway) and review the notes I'd made during my coaching session. I swear, those were the longest two days of my life, waiting for that screen test!

At 3:30 on Wednesday afternoon, I arrived at the NBC studios in Burbank. I was so nervous. And so excited. I knew my lines but didn't know how much my nerves might affect my performance. I also knew that I had plenty of competition: At the studio, four other actresses were there, all of us being screen-tested for the part of Sami.

After I had my makeup applied, a stage manager told me to wait in an empty dressing room until my name was called. So I sat and waited. And waited. 4 o'clock. 4:30. 5:00. 5:30. More nervous. More excited. More waiting.

Finally, at 6 P.M., the stage manager called me and the other actresses to the set we'd be using, right next to the one for *Days.* The soap had just finished taping for the day, and the director was finally ready for our screen test. After talking to us for a few moments, he walked all of us through the scene, telling us where we'd be standing and how we'd be moving when we spoke our lines.[2]

Then Patrick Muldoon (ex-Austin) and Christie Clark (ex-Carrie) walked in. Just seeing them almost

---

2. This process is known as dry-blocking. "Blocking" is the technical term for the physical moves the director gives you during a scene, and "dry" because it's just the actors and the directors—no cameras.

took my breath away, and ratcheted up my nervousness a notch or two. What a thrill to meet them, not to mention to do a scene with each of them! I was so embarrassed to meet Patrick in particular—I had such a crush on him from watching the show. I blushed to the tips of my ears, and even the thick makeup couldn't hide it. In fact, Joe, one of our stage managers, still teases me about it today!

The other girls and I had the amazing experience of rehearsing our scenes with Patrick and Christie, and I somehow got through it. Then Joe told us to go back to the dressing rooms for some more waiting until it was finally our time before the cameras. All the actresses auditioning for the role were given separate "call times" and different rooms, so I never got a chance to talk to any of them. It was such an awkward situation, to know they were competing against me, but still needing someone to share the experience with. All the waiting was killing me (of course since then, I've grown very accustomed to waiting—it's practically in the job description).

I wouldn't have guessed I could become so tense and so starstruck at the same time, but I managed it when I spotted Lisa Rinna and a few other actors on the show. I was too embarrassed to introduce myself or say anything to them, but I do remember thinking how incredible it would be to work on the same show with them. For some reason, I still didn't expect to get the part, but it was so exciting for me just to be there, to spend time on the set, and to see some of *Days'* cast members. I had to pinch myself and wonder, "Could this really be happening to me?"

So, you're asking, how did the screen test go? Funny, but I really thought I might have blown it.

Big time. The cameras were almost ready to start rolling for my scene with Patrick. That's when the stage manager said to me, "Don't forget to close the door behind you after you enter the scene."

Close the door? That wasn't in the script!

I suddenly started to become unglued. What if I forgot to close the door? Or what if I didn't close it just right? What if the door slammed? Could it cost me the job? Don't mess this up, Ali.

Patrick sensed that I was starting to melt down.

"Don't worry about the door," he told me gently. "It's not a big deal."

I managed a smile. Patrick's words were very comforting. He was so reassuring and the pressure lifted a little. I felt back in control. And, guess what? I *did* close the door. It *didn't* slam. And, of course, I got the part!

Waiting for the News

After Wednesday's screen test, I returned to school for the rest of the week, sitting on pins and needles waiting for word from the studio. They seemed like the longest days of my life.

On Friday, my agent finally got a call from the producers saying that I'd been hired. My agent contacted my mom, who immediately called my high school. Minutes later, when my classmates and I were filing out of my geometry class, one of the office assistants met me at the classroom door and handed me a note.

"From your mom," it read. "You got it!!"

Yes, there were two exclamation points at the end of the note. I felt like adding a thousand more.

My reaction? I was almost delirious. I screamed. I literally jumped for joy. I almost couldn't control myself. (Hey, I was 16 years old!)

So just how good was I on that screen test? Obviously, good enough to get the part. But let me put it in perspective: A few years ago some of the *Days* cast got together in my dressing room and we watched the videotapes of all of our screen tests, which Austin Peck (who played Austin Reed after Patrick Muldoon) had tracked down in the *Days* video library. Oh, my goodness! We were so bad!! Every one of us! We roared with laughter watching those tapes. Bryan Dattilo (Lucas) got some ribbing over the short gym shorts he wore on his videotape. I laughed so hard over how my bouncy walk had my "Jan Brady" hair swinging all over the place. We teased Austin about how different his voice sounded . . . well, the list goes on and on. Julianne Morris (ex-Greta), Arianne Zuker (Nicole) and I couldn't get over the now-out-of-fashion clothes that we wore with pride in the early '90s. It's not one of those videos that you want to share with the world.

But here's the good news: We were able to laugh at ourselves because we had grown so much as actors since we had auditioned for *Days*. That's one of the blessings of working on a soap. You're acting all the time, one day after another, with new opportunities to refine your acting abilities and develop your talent. Here's the way I think about it: As a soap actor, you know that even if you're unhappy with your performance in today's episode, you always have tomorrow to make things better (even though today's episode might continue to bug you for a while!). Because you're acting so much and so often, you're always growing and al-

ways learning something new about yourself and
the craft of acting. When you look around you and
recognize how talented the cast and crew are, you
realize everyone there is at the top of his or her
profession, and they all have something to teach
you if you're willing to learn. Not only that, but
your character is developing and changing as well,
which continuously presents you with new acting
challenges and demands. And the twists and turns
in Sami's life have never allowed me to become
blasé about playing her.

Into the Fire

On January 6, 1993, I began my new life as a cast
member of *Days of Our Lives.* What a day!

If you thought I was nervous for the screen test,
you should have seen me on that first day of playing Sami. I was absolutely petrified. Shortly after I
arrived at NBC, I got a tour of the set, and was introduced to the cast. Everyone—and I do mean
everyone—was so friendly and supportive, to my
great relief. I don't know why I was anticipating
anything else, but being the new kid on the block,
I just wasn't sure if I'd fit in and how I'd be accepted.

Well, those fears were certainly unfounded. The
cast embraced me, and everyone behind the
scenes—from the makeup people to the stage
crew—couldn't have been any nicer. In no time at
all, I felt like part of the family. But still, do you
know what worried me the most? In the first few
days, I was scared stiff that I'd accidentally call the

actors by their characters' names. (Can you imagine me introducing myself to Matt Ashford, and calling him "Jack"?) Those are the kinds of embarrassing scenarios that created some sleepless nights.

During that first week, I got my feet wet in a few scenes, but without a lot of dialogue. In fact, Sami was introduced slowly to the TV audience, and (as you might expect of Sami) in a most peculiar way. In fact, in the viewers' first glimpse of her, she was lurking around Salem, shrouded in a dark hat and coat. She made a phone call . . . but did not utter a word. I didn't even have to put on makeup for those scenes, since there was only a shot of my arm, or a camera angle from behind my shoulder, keeping me concealed in shadows. From the start, Sami was a mysterious character. Millions of *Days'* fans must have been asking themselves, "Who is this person and what is she doing in Salem?"

On the third day, Sami turned up at her parents' home. She peered under the doormat, but didn't find a house key there. So she removed her hat, pulled a bobby pin from her long, blonde hair, and used the bobby pin to break into her parents' house. Sami's father, Roman (played by Wayne Northrop at the time), heard the commotion that Sami was creating, and grabbed his gun. He snuck around the side of his house, confronted Sami in the shadows, pointed his gun at her and shouted, "Don't move."

Sami froze. After a few tense moments, I spoke my first words on *Days*:

"Daddy, don't shoot me!"

Fortunately, Roman didn't fire the gun. If he had, my career on *Days* may have ended right then and there.

A Little Help from My Friends

Ironically, in my first few months of playing Sami, she gave no hint of becoming the sassy (and, let's face it, sometimes obnoxious) character that she turned out to be. In fact, in those early days, Sami was a sweet, "good girl," and Marlena (played by Deidre Hall) and Sami had a close, loving relationship. But I've had to remind die-hard fans about Sami's innocent beginning many times—*how could they forget?* I ask myself! ☺ As it turns out, the writers of *Days* had originally created Sami as an innocent, naïve girl who may have felt a little inferior to her peers. Before long, however, she began to create chaos throughout Salem, one show after another, one year after the next. Early on, one of the

(Lesley Bohm)

prop guys and I would sometimes joke that there were two kinds of people in Salem—those who were given the key to the city, and the others who were given a bobby pin to pick any lock that got in their way; as Sami proved in that first week, she was definitely gifted with bobby pins!

From the beginning, I was lucky to be surrounded by actors on the set of *Days* who were not only talented, but were always generous with their advice and guidance. I learned so much just by watching the seasoned cast working around me. What a wonderful experience to be in scenes with actresses like Deidre (Marlena), who is not only brilliant at what she does, but has always been willing to offer suggestions and words of wisdom. It's amazing how quickly you can learn in that kind of environment. From the start, working with Deidre has given me an incredible opportunity to grow as an actress.

Looking back, I was actually a little hesitant at first to ask questions of someone of the stature of Deidre, who created the role of Marlena in 1976 (she once described her role on *Days* as "my longest-lived relationship"). But then I figured, "Which would be more embarrassing—to ask Deidre a foolish question, or to make a foolish mistake with the cameras rolling?" The answer to that one was obvious, so I asked again and again—and she couldn't have been nicer (and always has been!). I think Deidre could see that I was interested and eager to learn. So she was always receptive, always helpful, and definitely someone I knew I could turn to. She'd offer advice ("Why not try saying it this way?"), or give me an open-ended invitation to grill her with any question I had ("If you feel you don't get anything, just ask.").

It may seem silly, but when you're a teenager and new to the show, you're afraid of what you don't know. On *Days*, however, there were always people to turn to for advice. And as far as Deidre goes, I've always loved acting in scenes with her, even when our characters were fighting. She has always made it easy.

A Juggling Act

When I joined the cast of *Days*, I found myself with more challenges than just adapting to the demands of playing Sami Brady. Along with this wonderful opportunity to chase my dream of an acting career, at age 16 I still needed to make school my first priority. Both goals were worth pursuing. My challenge was to create room for both school and acting in my life.

At the beginning, I figured that I'd work one day a week on *Days*, maybe less. My contract stipulated a commitment of at least half a day a week on the show, and I didn't expect to be doing much more. After all, I had been a fan of *Days*, and I had noticed that the child actors weren't on it very often, particularly during the school year. But the producers caught me by surprise. In no time, I learned that the scriptwriters had big plans for Sami. Almost from the start, she was a key player in the story lines of *Days*, requiring me to adapt to a three-day-a-week schedule. Fortunately, my schoolwork wasn't a casualty of the increased demands on my time—and I loved the challenge of juggling the two.

I was so fortunate that my own high school—a private school in the L.A. area—couldn't have been

more accommodating. My teachers were thoroughly understanding and supportive of my career, and they made every effort to make sure I didn't fall behind. If I needed help after school, the teachers were always there. If I had questions, they patiently answered every one of them.

On the set of *Days*, the producers were just as supportive of my academics. They provided me with a teacher (by law, they have to do so, allowing minors to spend at least three hours a day on school-work while on the set). They even hired a special tutor to help me with my chemistry homework because (yes, let's face it) chemistry was not my strong suit.

At the time, the *Days'* daily schedule was very demanding for both the actors and the crew. Although our timetable has changed since then, the entire cast arrived at the studio sometime between 6 and 8 A.M. (ugh!) to prepare for what's called a "dry block" through the script, which I explained a little at the bottom of page 20. ("Blocking" is the physical movement in a scene—and when Sami decides to turn away from Lucas and move over to the table in the corner, that's called a "cross"; so in "dry blocking," the director will tell me that on a specific line, I am supposed to "cross" stage left. Is this making sense?)

At 8 A.M., we'd "camera block" the entire show, which means that the actors act out the scenes one by one so the cameramen and the rest of the crew know exactly where we'll be positioned during taping later in the day. The cameramen have to know where we're standing, and on which spoken lines we'll move, and the audio department needs to know where we'll be standing when we speak, so they can be sure to hear us! This rehearsal or "run

through" of the day's entire show lasted until lunch-
time.

After a meal break (which was also time to apply
our makeup, touch up our hair, and change into
our wardrobe), we'd move into a dress rehearsal of
the show, and then wait for notes from the producers, which might include suggestions for script
changes for the final taping. By 3 o'clock, the taping would begin, which might take three or more
hours from beginning to end. It was a very long,
very full day—but it was not over yet. I'd head
home for an evening of homework—and learning
my lines for the next show.

This schedule was so rigorous that it could wear
you out if you didn't pace yourself. Imagine being
on the set from early morning 'til night, squeezing
in at least three hours of academic work somewhere
during the day, and then catching up on any remaining schoolwork at home. I don't know how it
all worked out, but it did. The studio teacher was
always nearby, ready to work with me in-between
rehearsals and during any other free moments
during the day.

But as exhausting as my life may have seemed, I
really think school itself had prepared me for it.
Think back to your own middle school and high
school years, when you'd attend classes for a full
day and then spend hours doing homework at
night. That kind of schedule can run you ragged,
too, even without trying to squeeze in a day of acting. So it never really felt like an impossible transition from full-time student to full-time student/
actor—except, that is, for one added source of
anxiety that often disrupted my nighttime sleep. I
began having nightmares—the kind of nightmares
where you awaken startled and a bit panicky. The

dream was always the same: I'd sleep through my alarm, wake up late, and rush to the studio, disheveled and scared to death that I had kept everyone else waiting. It was a terrifying dream, and ever since, I've always been petrified of being late to the set. The morning "calls" or reporting times were so early that oversleeping seemed like a real possibility (or in my case, perhaps a likelihood!). Even today, if I "sleep in" until 8 A.M. on a day off, I still wake up a bit stunned and disoriented, convinced that I'm late for work until I can figure out where I am and what day it is.

Except for minor inconveniences like that, my career on *Days of Our Lives* has been a wonderful part of my life, and the cast and crew have become very important to me. Even so, I knew that acting was "in my blood" for years before Sami Brady entered my life. In the next chapter, I'll take you back to my earliest moments in front of the cameras.

Chapter
3

How long have I known that I wanted to be an actress?

Just about forever.

I think I might have been born with a passion for performing. I'm a native of Los Angeles, and I grew up in a musical household (my mom is a concert and studio musician who filled our home with classical music every day). I took the obligatory violin lessons and studied the violin seriously for eight years before I realized that my real love was acting—and I guess my mom realized it, too.

With my mother's support, I auditioned for and landed roles in many TV commercials. The first one was for Kodak film when I was just four years old. But if you're thinking that my talent was immediately recognizable to the world in that first acting experience—well, not exactly. I didn't have any lines to memorize, and frankly, the weather didn't exactly make it a magical experience. Al-

(Author's personal collection)

Daddy's Little Girl

(Author's personal collection)

Virtuoso in training!

though the ad depicted a winter scene, it was shot under a scorching 103-degree sun in L.A. But not to let sizzling weather interfere with the winter fun, the undaunted ad agency shipped in a truckload of snow to create a Hollywood version of a snow bank. Bundled up in a little red snowsuit, I climbed aboard a sled with my on-screen dad, and on the director's command of "Action," we rode down the slope while photos were being snapped of us (Kodak photos, I'm sure!). It was an all-day shoot, and as one take followed the next, the temperature became ever more blistering. But the show must go on, right? The prop guys worked overtime, frantically hauling in fresh snow to reinforce the man-made "mountain" that was melting under us. It was *very* hot, and the snowsuit sure didn't help! In fact, I almost passed out from heat exhaustion!

Despite the boiling sun, despite the snowsuit, and despite what others might call a nightmare day, I do remember this: I *really* had fun. I absolutely loved making that commercial. I somehow knew even then that acting would be something I'd do for the rest of my life. There wasn't a doubt. Some people are just lucky to be born knowing what they want and having the drive to pursue it. I guess I'm one of them.

A Word from Our Sponsor . . .

In the next few years, I took some commercial acting classes and went on a lot of auditions. By the time I was ten years old, I had appeared in about sixty TV ads. Some were as challenging as the hours on the snow slopes under a red-hot California sun;

(Author's personal collection)

Wasn't I cute?!

others were a breeze. Let me tell you about a few of my more interesting experiences.

When I was about six years old, I appeared in a McDonald's commercial. In it, four other girls and I were sitting in a McDonald's restaurant, eating French fries and giggling. Not too demanding, right? Well, at least not until the director ordered one take after another after another—requiring us to eat one handful of French fries after the next. You can imagine what happened. I was almost sick to my stomach by the end of the shoot. Now believe me, I think McDonald's has the best fries around. But I ate so many of them that I was feeling pretty ill that night at home. I don't think I

had another French fry for about a year after that!
Can you blame me?

Then there was a memorable commercial for
Chewy Chips Ahoy. I was eight years old, and it was
a two-day shoot, filmed by a lake more than two
hours out of L.A. My "call time" was something
crazy like 5 A.M., and I remember my mom having
to wake me up at 2 in the morning to make sure
we got there on time. I had only one line in the commercial, but there were a lot of different scenes—
one of me eating cookies at a picnic, another of
me eating cookies with my on-camera mom somewhere else in the park, and so on. You get the picture. Plenty of scenes. Plenty of cookies. If I had a
cookie craving at the beginning of the day, it was
gone by early afternoon.

When I was asked to appear in a second Chewy
Chips Ahoy commercial, I guess I had forgotten
just how demanding it can be to devour cookies
virtually nonstop for a day or two. We did fifty
takes of that second commercial—yes, fifty—each
one requiring that I take a few bites of a Chewy
Chips Ahoy cookie. This time, however, the director must have had visions of stomachaches sabo-
taging his commercial. So, he insisted, "Instead of
swallowing the cookies, as soon as I yell 'cut' spit
them into a bucket."

You've got to be kidding! At first, I resisted. But
the prop guy kept warning me, "You'll wish you
had." It didn't take me long to realize that he was
right. I probably ate only five cookies that day—
and spit out 45 more! Fortunately, the bucket never
appeared in the commercial itself. It was pretty disgusting.

Nabisco promotes their cookies with the phrase
"Ooey gooey warm 'n chewy." At the time, I'm not

sure if I would have described it quite that way. They are delicious cookies—however, after hours of eating (and spitting out) cookies, I must have worked myself into a sugar frenzy that took a week or two to wear off!

The message, my friends, is that even a dream job like eating cookies may require biting off more than you can chew. The same goes with feasting on ice cream cones all day long. In one commercial, three little girls and I were supposed to walk through the park, licking ice cream cones. Sounds great so far. But it also happened to be a very hot day, and the director knew the ice cream wouldn't survive a single take, much less a day's worth of shooting. So he ordered the ice cream back into the freezer, and replaced it with "mashed potato cones," with the mashed potatoes dyed green! Sounds delicious, doesn't it? It wasn't exactly a child's *crème de la crème* dessert. But I made the best of it. As it turned out, we taped about forty takes, licking green mashed potatoes and pretending to enjoy every morsel. Now that's acting!

Child Acting 101

I'm so lucky to have always had an amazing and supportive family. From the earliest days, they encouraged my interest in acting without pushing me in one direction or another. My mom was always there to drive me to auditions, but she certainly didn't fit the stereotype of the pushy stage mom. She let me take the lead, and she always said that if I didn't want to go on auditions anymore, all I had to do was say so. With all that driving my

mom had to do, going to and from auditions across town every other day, she would have been happy for me to call it quits at any time. She certainly never let the acting get in the way of my schoolwork or my friendships (although I was never a child who had lots of friends anyway).

From the beginning, my family has not only supported my dream of acting, but they've also kept me grounded along the way. They've always made sure I've stayed humble—never letting my ego soar out of control, no matter how well my career might be going, and never allowing me to feel crushed by the devastating lows that are almost an inevitable part of being an actor.

Of course, I've seen other parents driven by mo-

tives of their own. I grew up with kids who were literally supporting their families with their acting paycheck. Pretty sad. If that's why a kid is acting—if it's the parents' dream and not the child's—it's not going to work. In my own childhood, I loved every minute of auditioning and acting. But it can be a pretty terrible life when it's not the life you want.

So how do I respond when parents approach me and ask, "How can I get my kid into acting?" When parents seek my advice, I tell them, "If your child really wants to give it a shot, go ahead and see if she likes it. But if she doesn't, you've got to follow her lead and let her back off. If she starts to complain about not getting to see her friends or if she's falling behind in her schoolwork, then it's time to reevaluate."

Bitten by the Acting Bug

It's almost a joke, but it's true: No matter what your age, if there's anything else in the world besides acting that you could see yourself doing, perhaps you should consider doing it, or at least having it at the ready as a safety net. Breaking into the acting business is *very* difficult, and the chances of making a living at it are so slim (the city of L.A. wouldn't have any waiters were it not for all of the out-of-work actors!). On the other hand, if acting is in your blood (like it is in mine), and you just can't do anything else, then I encourage you to chase your dream. I completely understand when young people (and adults) tell me that acting is something they *have* to do.

Of course, the acting business can knock the wind out of you without any warning at all. Sometimes, you leave an audition convinced that you did a great job, only to learn that you didn't get the part because they wanted a red-headed kid instead of a blonde, or they were looking for someone taller or shorter than you. They might have been seeking an actor with freck-les, or someone without

(Author's personal collection)

them. It's also possible that your acting performance just didn't impress them, and if that's the case, brace yourself. Casting directors can be brutally honest. They might tell your agent or manager everything they didn't like about your audition, with the hope that it will help you do better next time. Maybe so, but it can be tough to hear criticism, particularly when you're a kid. If you're making acting a ca-reer, however, you have to be able to hear the neg-ative comments, and find something constructive in them.

Believe me, I've weathered my share of audition disappointments. Of course, I've also been very fortunate to land some great parts (think Sami Brady!). But during those times when I'd crash and burn at an audition, it was nice to have someone nearby to help lift my spirits. Enter my mom. She was always great, even when someone else got the

part. Not long ago, she told me that when I was a kid, she'd be so disappointed for me, but all she ever said was, "Honey, they don't know what they're missing out on." She'd find a way to make me feel good about myself.

I know that 98 times out of 100, even the most talented actors are rejected for roles. But if you have a passion for acting, you learn to persevere, confident that successes are on the horizon. You learn to accept the disappointments because they're part of the business. If you beat yourself up over them, it's harder than ever to bounce back. I've gotten down on myself from time to time when I *really* wanted a part, felt I was absolutely perfect for it—but just didn't get it. I give myself a day or so to be truly bummed about it, but then I try to move on. There will be another audition. There will be another wonderful part. And I can hardly wait to give it my best shot next time.

Of course, particularly when I was younger, there was something else I had going for me in terms of self-preservation. As I've mentioned, I loved auditioning, as though it really didn't matter whether or not I got the part. I loved meeting new people. I loved getting all dressed up. Of course, it also didn't hurt that I'd occasionally get to leave school early for an audition. And I absolutely enjoyed spending time with my mom. There's a lot of "waiting around" at auditions before your name is called, and although I'd usually go over my lines a few times, my mom and I used to spend much more time just chatting and playing word games to occupy ourselves. Some of my best memories are playing Hangman or other games with my mom.

What was my favorite game? My mom or I would start making up a story, and then we'd take turns

jumping in and creating the next sentence of the story line. One time, however, when I was about nine years old, I was sipping on a milkshake as we played the game. Big mistake. At one point, the story got so absolutely funny that laughter got the better of me. What happened next? I accidentally spit up my milkshake all over my clothes. What a mess!

Rather than panicking, my mom and I took action. Get this: We splattered the rest of the milkshake all over my outfit, hoping it would look like it was part of the attire! It's not as crazy as it sounds—the part was for a tomboyish little girl, so I'd worn overalls with splattered paint on them. The chocolate ice cream fit right into the look! Even so, it was a wardrobe department's worst nightmare! Never let it be said that we didn't know how to impress a casting director!

Even during moments like this, I rarely felt any stress associated with the auditioning experience, although some of the other kids clearly were dealing with the pressure (especially those whose moms insisted that they "don't talk to the other kids; just practice your lines!"). I enjoyed performing for the adults I was auditioning for, making them smile and, if I was lucky, even making them laugh. Most of my memories are positive. I don't ever remember reflecting back on the day and saying, "Well, that was another job I didn't get!" I looked at it more like, "I had so much fun today."

Again, I have my parents to thank for the emotionally smooth ride during much of my acting career. Few things irritated or stressed me out, even when I was juggling a heavy schedule at school along with the life of a working actress. From an early age, my mom and dad taught me that when

there are challenges in front of me, I should not look at them as titanic in size and virtually insurmountable, but rather should break them down into smaller goals that can be achieved, one at a time. If you look only at the big picture, it may overwhelm you. But if you take it apart and confront it a step at a time, you can beat it, and not let it defeat you.

Life on the Stage and Screen

As valuable as commercials were in my own development as an actress, my appearances on TV shows, in motion pictures and on the stage may have been even more important learning experiences. In 1985, I got my first real acting job in a TV show. It was an episode of *St. Elsewhere*, titled "Santa Claus is Dead." In the show, Santa collapses at a children's party and is rushed to St. Elsewhere (where else?). It was a touching story, and I played a character named Chrissy, one of several children who arrive at the hospital, clamoring to find out about Santa's well-being as the doctors work to keep him alive. It was a small part, but I did have a few lines (although nothing was more challenging than "Where's Santa Claus?"). But, hey, I was only five years old, and it was a good stepping stone in an acting career.

I had bigger parts on other television shows, and at times the episodes dealt with very sensitive and important issues. You probably remember *Webster*, the TV series starring Emmanuel Lewis, Alex Karras, and Susan Clark (like me, Emmanuel started his career doing commercials, including some national spots for Burger King). In January 1985, when I

was eight years old, in an episode called "The Uh-Oh Feeling," I played a student (named Beth) in Webster's classroom who was being molested by a substitute teacher. Webster overhears a conversation in which the teacher asks me to stay after class.

Beth tells the teacher, "I don't like it when you touch me there."

The teacher responds, "Just don't tell anybody. You'll start to like it."

It was pretty chilling and ahead of its time. It still makes me feel a little creepy just thinking about how terrible that can be for a little kid. It was the first time that a situation comedy—or just about any other TV show, for that matter—had confronted the issue of child molestation.

The program had an enormous impact. Near the end of the episode, a teacher tells the children, "If anything makes you uncomfortable, tell the principal or another adult you trust." After the show aired, kids in all parts of the country came forward and, for the first time, told what had happened to them. That's the power of television. Looking back, I'm so proud that I was part of that show.

By the way, I recently ran into Steve Sunshine, the executive producer and head writer of *Webster*. He is a producer for a daily entertainment show, and he remembers that episode of *Webster* well. He told me how proud he still is of that story and the impact it had. Nineteen years later, it's still rewarding to hear such nice things from your boss!

Along the way, I also performed in two equity-waiver plays in the Los Angeles area. I had known that I wanted to be an actress since I was a little child, and so I went on auditions for everything. My mom thought, "Why not try theater, too?"—after all, my acting classes often took on the format

of performing in front of a dozen or so other child actors, which gave me a sense of what performing before a live audience was like.

At the age of six, I was cast in *The Wedding Band*. I played the part of the daughter in a very poor family who was building a porch onto their house. I had only a couple lines in the play; I remember one line, said in a very bratty voice, was: "My new tennis porch!" (don't ask me why, it's been so long I've forgotten the storyline!). It was a line that has taken on a life of its own in my real family; my dad and brothers still sometimes tease me—whenever they think I'm being bratty, I hear: "My new tennis porch!"

At age ten, I performed in another play, *The Traveling Lady,* by Horton Foote (one of America's leading dramatists). I enjoyed doing the play so much, although there was one embarrassing incident that happened after a few months of that show's run. At one point in the play, the actress who played my mom called my character's name, which was my cue to come onstage. But one night, I was backstage in my dressing room not paying attention, and I missed my cue—really missed it! My onstage mom called my name again and again for about forty-five seconds, and I was nowhere to be seen. It must have been an unbearable amount of time for her to be standing there, alone on the stage, waiting for her distracted cast-mate to appear.

Finally and mercifully, I did hear her, and I raced onto the stage. We continued the scene, rather awkwardly as I recall, and then the script called for us to exit down the theater aisle and through the audience. When we reached the lobby, I got such a tongue-lashing from her (which I certainly deserved!). She leaned into my face, shook her fin-

ger at me, and said, "Don't you ever miss a cue
again! I know you were goofing off backstage.
From now on, you better pay attention!"

Well, I almost started to cry. But I did get the
message: Acting is serious business, and you better
take your commitment to heart because everyone
else in the cast is depending on you and your performance.

Despite moments like that, both of those childhood plays were so much fun and were such great
experiences. Perhaps more important, they were
pivotal in contributing to my growth as an actress,
even at such a young age. More than ever, they
convinced me that acting was something I wanted
to keep doing.

I also learned that live theater is completely different than acting before the TV cameras. Even
though you're saying the same lines in a play, performance after performance, something completely
different can happen every night, and it often has
to do with the audience. When you go to the theater, remember that you're part of the experience,
not just a witness to it. The actors are definitely affected by you, whether you're laughing, crying,
feeling tense, or having the time of your life. It can
be such an exciting experience for the actors.

Staying Centered

There are all kinds of perks that come with acting,
and when you're a kid, even the smallest ones seem
pretty spectacular. When I was ten years old, I was
chosen as a regular cast member of a new ABC situation comedy called *Family Man.* It starred Richard

(Author's personal collection)

Backstage on the set of *Family Man*

Libertini and Mimi Kennedy, and I played Mimi's daughter, Rosie. (I was starstruck meeting Richard for the first time—he's in one of my all-time favorite comedies, *All of Me*, with Steve Martin.) In one episode of *Family Man*, the script called for me to get my ears pierced. What a thrill! After all, my mom had established some age boundaries for ear piercing and most other childhood milestones, and I knew not to expect to get my ears pierced until I was twelve. So when I saw the script, was I ever excited! My mom was hesitant, of course, but she finally gave in. I got my ears pierced two years ahead of sched-

(Author's personal collection)

One episode of the show was about my character getting an embarrassing haircut and being teased at school. My mom was able to talk the producers into a wash-out perm. Equally embarrassing, but not quite as long-lasting.

ule (although the pain associated with the procedure certainly got my attention!). *Family Man* didn't last long—it was canceled after only seven episodes—but at least I had a few pairs of earrings to show for it.

My mom occasionally bent on other issues, but she held her ground on many more. She was a Stage Mom in the best possible sense; she guarded me and looked after me without being intimidated by anyone, and she always spoke up if she thought a

script crossed the line. Remember, my mom insisted
that I have as normal a childhood as possible, and
in an era when kids were being cast in horror movies
like *Poltergeist*, she kept me away from auditions for
those kinds of films.

I remember one motion picture, *The Price of Life*,
which I appeared in at age twelve. It had a futuris-
tic plot in which I played a rebellious girl named
Alice, who had a tough attitude and made the wrong
turn at every point in life. The script called for me
to smoke and curse, which definitely didn't find a
warm place in my mother's heart. In particular,
she is very antismoking, and when it came to a
twelve-year-old—particularly her own twelve-year-
old daughter—smoking in a movie was simply out
of the question.

My mom dug in her heels with the director of
the movie. She was determined to reach some kind
of compromise that would keep a lit cigarette out
of my mouth—and she ultimately succeeded. They
finally agreed that I would be allowed to hold the
cigarette and pretend to smoke it. But I never really took a puff.

It was just one of several incidents where my
mother intervened, speaking on my behalf, usually
without me even knowing about it. She insisted
that I always show up on the set prepared, take the
job seriously, and know my lines. But she protected
me from the tough negotiations that sometimes
went on behind the scenes. She wanted me to enjoy
the acting experience as much as possible without
stressing out about some of the details and the fine
print.

My mom also did something else that was very
important: As I continued to act and was cast in
better and better parts, she made sure that I stayed

(Author's personal collection)

On location with the cast of *A Brand New Life*

humble. As I mentioned earlier, Hollywood is renowned for egos soaring out of control, but my parents wouldn't stand for it. In 1989, a year after *The Price of Life*, I landed a role in a new NBC situation comedy called *A Brand New Life*.

In the show, Don Murray portrayed a millionaire father of three who marries a blue-collar waitress (played by Barbara Eden) with three children of her own (no, we weren't the Brady Bunch, despite the obvious similarities). Don's character raised his children in a permissive, free-spirited household, and Barbara's family grew up in a much more conservative environment. Much of the series' conflict grew out of the attempts to merge the families (the original name of the show was *Blended Family*, although that title never got out of the starting gate).

I played Barbara's daughter, and Jenny Garth (pre-*Beverly Hills 90210*) was cast as one of my siblings.

One day backstage on *A Brand New Life*, a hairdresser was brushing my hair, and when I felt she was tugging on it too hard, I raised my voice and complained to her. Bad move.

Later, the hairdresser took my mom aside, and said, "You may want to talk to your daughter and tell her to get her act together. My job is to make her look good. If she's going to go anywhere in this business, she needs to treat everyone here with respect."

Ouch. That really pressed my mom's buttons, and she wasn't happy with me at all (and understandably so).

"Look, Ali," she told me, "you aren't entitled to a 'star attitude' here. You aren't going to be a 'star brat'—you're my daughter, you're a normal kid, and you're very lucky to be working here. So start treating people with respect, or you're not going to be here for long."

True story.

My mom was right. And I'll never forget it. Let's face it: At age twelve, it's a rather make-believe life to be on television, have people tell you how special you are, and pamper you endlessly by tending to your hair and makeup. If you're not careful, it really can go to your head. But I was lucky to have parents who would bring me down a notch or two if necessary, and make sure I kept things in perspective. It was an important lesson, and as I matured, I've never allowed myself to think I'm somehow better or different than other people just because of the type of work I do—because I know I'm not.

Nowadays, my husband, Dave, also helps me stay grounded. He's not only a wonderful guy, but

it's such a relief to spend so much time with someone *not* in show business (Dave's career is in law
enforcement). He's not starstruck. He's not particularly impressed with what's going on in Hollywood.
Our life together really is separate from my job,
and I've learned that it's important for me to avoid
immersing myself in show business twenty-four
hours a day. As much as I love the entertainment
industry, I also know it's good for me to go home
at night and enjoy time with my husband, play with
the dogs, and lead a completely normal, nonshow-
business life.

You Gotta Have Friends

Both before and during *Days*, I've had the opportunity to work with some wonderful people both in
front of and behind the camera, and I've learned
so much from them. In 1991, I appeared in *The End
of Innocence*, a feature film in which Dyan Cannon
not only starred, but served as director and screen-
writer. It was a movie about the challenges of growing up female, and I played Dyan's character,
Stephanie, as a preteenager (the late Rebecca
Schaeffer was cast as the same character at a little
older age). Dyan is not only a talented actress in
her own right, but she was a wonderful director to
work with—never pushing me in ways that would
raise my anxiety levels off the charts, but still challenging me at every turn. She'd say things like, "I
know you can do this. You're the best. That's why I
hired you, Ali." When she'd talk to me like that,
I'd think, "I *can* do this." With her support, I did.
    I landed a number of other roles in my pre-*Days*

career, including guesting on TV shows like *Simon & Simon*, *Tales from the Darkside*, and *I Married Dora*. *Tales from the Darkside* was such a dark show, similar to *The Twilight Zone*. In the episode I was in, my character would say "goodbye" to people and then they would die. A pretty creepy script. I remember my mom talking to the schoolteacher on the set about all the special effects that would be required to fulfill the writer's vision. One scene required me to stand in the set while the crew filled the room with smoke. My mom was really concerned about me inhaling all that smoke, as was the on-set school teacher (who was also a social worker and was responsible to help protect minors). Fortunately, this particular production company was very responsible and didn't question the teacher's authority. A special kind of smoke was used that isn't damaging to the lungs, and the camera angles were changed to minimize the smoke that was required. The scene was still powerful, and the show was a success.

Since joining *Days*, one of my most memorable guest appearances, and one that fans often ask me about, was my appearance on *Friends* in 2000, in which I portrayed an award-winning, diva actress on *Days of Our Lives* (of all soaps!).

On the set of this successful prime time series, I could see that the cast and crew were so dedicated to creating the best possible show. Similar to *Days*, *Friends* has a confident cast and crew who had created a routine that was professional yet comfortable and easygoing. The atmosphere at *Friends* is different than that of a first-year sitcom that's just getting started and trying to prove itself. On the new shows, life can be hectic and even a bit chaotic as the cast and writers try to prove their worth to

the network. It can be a high-tension, high-wire act with a lot of jobs on the line. However, on *Friends,* there was no tension—just a great time.

On the show, my character was a bit of a bitch, but really fun to play! I had a scene with Jennifer Aniston and Matt LeBlanc. During my first day on the set, we rehearsed the entire script. It was the first time I had met Jennifer, and she asked me, "Do you work with my dad?" (Her father, John Aniston, has been on *Days* for many years.) I told her, "Yes, in fact, we play bitter enemies. He's tried to kill me several times on the show!" Both of us laughed until we got back to the serious business of rehearsing.

On Friday of that week, we rehearsed the show again until the director and producers were completely happy with everything and ready to put the show on tape. The actual taping took place on Friday night.

Friends is taped before a live audience, a setting that was mostly new and enjoyable for me, but also the source of anxiety. After all, you're not only trying to be funny, but with an audience, you know right away whether you've succeeded. As an actor, you definitely feel a powerful energy from the audience, and since they're on your side, it's an energy that can drive you to perform even better. At the same time, even though I had been on *Days* for many years, it was a little jarring when I realized that a live audience would be out there, watching my every move. It had been so long since I had performed in front of an audience, and I did have a brief moment of freaking out a little, thinking, "Oh, oh, I'm not prepared for this!"

I remember standing backstage with Matt LeBlanc, waiting to make our entrance, and I half-

jokingly whispered to him, "My gosh, what do I do differently here? Got any advice?"

Matt was so nice. "You'll be fine," he said. "It's just the same as what you've always done. Just wait for the laugh."

A *Days* Debut

Now for some *Days* trivia: Do you remember what character I played before Sami on *Days*? At the age of six, I played a character named Adrienne Johnson Kiriakis as a child, portraying her in a flashback scene when she was abused by her father. The adult Adrienne was played by Judi Evans for about five years (she later moved on to *Another World*, and as is only possible on soaps, she's now *back* on *Days* playing an entirely different character, Bonnie). When Adrienne reflected back on what had happened to her as a young girl, I played her in those childhood flashback scenes. Judi and I had scenes together just recently and I reminded her of how we'd worked together before. She had no idea that little girl was me!

Judi (Bonnie) told me when she played Paulina on *Another World* she was a *Days* fan, and that Sami was one of her favorite characters! I was so flattered—but it was definitely a "mutual admiration society"; I told her that when she came back to the show, I had to remind myself that her real name was Judi—in fact, "Adrienne" (her first *Days* character) kept popping into my head!

My *Days* debut as a young Adrienne was very exciting, even though it lasted just two days. At the time, *Days* was being shot at the Sunset-Gower

Studios in Hollywood, several miles from where we tape the show today. I auditioned for the part along with a roomful of other kids, and when I was fortunate enough to get the job, one of my older cousins became more excited about it than I was (geez, I was only six!). She was a huge fan of *Days*, and so as a family favor, I got members of the cast (none of whom I had heard of at the time) to sign my script for her.

When I gave my cousin the heavily autographed script, she almost died! I gotta admit, she absolutely loved it!

Chapter
4

Although I've been an actress for almost as long as I can remember, my life is probably really not much different than yours. In fact, my motivation for writing this book is to relate some of my growing-up and life experiences to my fans while also describing some of my most interesting moments as an actress in Hollywood, particularly on *Days of Our Lives*. By telling my story, I hope you may be able to better understand issues that are relevant in your own life: finding friendships in a world where too many people don't seem to care . . . coping with peer pressures when they're taking you down paths that aren't in your best interest . . . surviving in a culture that worships thinness . . . finding balance in day-to-day living when you're being pulled in a thousand different directions . . . and discovering your inner self by examining your core beliefs and values.

Yes, I've grown up and still live in the public eye,

and it's not always fun. Because of the work that actors do, all of us come under the scrutiny of the media. But despite that higher visibility, I've still had to overcome the same problems and make the same adjustments that virtually every girl and every young woman has had to do. Adolescence and young adulthood do have a way of making life interesting—at times, truly amazing; at other times, downright depressing—but perhaps my reflections on my own experiences can help you find your own way through both the good and the rocky times as you discover where you fit into the world.

Making Friends Count

No matter what your age, your gender, or your place in life, I think we can agree on the following: There are few pleasures greater than spending time with friends. If you make friends easily, you're very lucky. Not everyone is so fortunate. You might

(Author's personal collection)

even find yourself taking them for granted—but that's certainly not something that I've ever done.

I went to the same school for thirteen years—a small college preparatory school in a suburb of Los Angeles. It was very academically oriented, and I spent a lot of time cracking the books. Add to that the many hours occupied by my acting career—including auditions after school, and the making of commercials, TV shows, and motion pictures—and perhaps I didn't have as much time to make friends as some of my peers did. Even so, judging by my social life at and away from school, I was never going to be Prom Queen. Far from it.

Here's the bottom line: I always felt that a lot of my classmates didn't like me. And I never really understood why. In elementary school, I didn't have lots of friends, and that isolation only eased up a little in the middle-school and high-school years. I remember being shunned by most of the girls at school, and as best I could tell, the boys weren't particularly interested, either. I was rarely invited to parties, and I spent a lot of Saturday nights at home with my family. I certainly wasn't a very good athlete (that's an understatement!), and at recess and in gym class, I was always the last kid picked for the kickball team.

You can imagine how painful that was. I'm sure a lot of you know exactly what I'm talking about or know someone who does. Like a lot of kids who often feel that they're on the outside looking in, I would have done just about anything so classmates would like me. But I was shy and had trouble fitting in and making friends. That's what happens to some kids, and for no apparent reason. I was one of them.

It can really hurt.

I remember one girl in high school—I'll call her Lucy (I'm changing her name to protect the . . . well, whatever). She was something of a "ringleader," and she tormented me throughout high school. She seemed passionate about making my life as miserable as possible. Not long ago, in an interview in *Soap Opera Digest,* I was asked if there was one person in high school who I'd like to "get back at" by "rubbing her nose" in my show-business success. Well, guess who came to mind? For all the pain she caused me, Lucy's name was flashing like a neon sign in my mind. But during the interview, I bit my tongue and thought better of naming names. I did mention that there was someone who had picked on me in high school. But I said that I had moved on, and hoped she was happy, wherever she was. Enough said.

There were some other girls who used me for target practice as well. Even when I tried to be cool, it usually seemed to backfire. I remember clearly one incident when I was in the seventh grade. The captains of the soccer squads in P.E. class were selecting their team members, and (of course) I was absolutely terrible in soccer. After everyone else had been picked, I was the last one left, standing alone in all my embarrassment. Well, lucky me, the captain (her name will be "Kim") who "got stuck" with me didn't hide how angry she was that I had ended up on her team. She apparently felt it was just fine to humiliate me, simply because I wasn't very good. I'll never forget how mean she was during our games. When I wasn't playing to her level of satisfaction (which was most of the time), she didn't even try to hide how much she resented having me on her team. Let's just say girls can be very mean at that age.

I remember talking to some classmates after school that afternoon. I really wanted to be their friend, and perhaps as a way of trying to fit in and lash out, I complained bitterly about Kim. "She's so mean!" I said. "What's her problem? This isn't the Olympic Games!" My rant continued on and on. "Why does she have to be like that? She's such a bitch!"

As I spoke, I could see that the girls I was talking to began looking over my shoulder as if someone had walked up behind me. I turned, and was face to face with Kim.

She had heard everything.

It was like a bad movie. A very bad movie. I was absolutely speechless. I wanted to die. I don't think I have ever felt so bad.

I cried all the way home, and when I told my mom what had happened, she was upset, too, *at me.* She insisted that I call Kim and apologize.

No, not that! That was the last thing I wanted to do. Just the thought of dialing Kim's phone number made me shake. But I somehow mustered the courage. I called her at home. It was one of the hardest things I've ever done.

"You hurt my feelings," I told her. "That's why I said some very mean things about you, which was wrong. I'm really, really sorry."

As you might guess, there were some awkward moments during that conversation. But Kim did accept my apology. In fact, she was quite nice about it. No, we didn't become friends. But after that phone call, at least I wasn't embarrassed to see her at school. I also realized something important: My conscience won't let me belittle or put down people. (I'll leave that kind of behavior to Sami for now!)

Boys to Men

Now what about boys? Well, I didn't have a boy-friend in high school, if that's what you want to know. I was a little overweight—not by much, but enough to make me feel self-conscious and cut my self-esteem down to size. By the time I was starting to even think about dating a boy, I was so consumed with anxiety about not feeling pretty, it was almost inconceivable to me that boys might find me attractive.

Did I ever go out in high school? Well, yes. But here's the truth: The boy was more of a friend than a boyfriend (if you get my drift). As sad as it sounds, I actually kissed a boy on TV (on *I Married Dora)* before I kissed one in real life; I think I was a sophomore in high school before my first real kiss.

In that particular episode of *I Married Dora,* my character was the "best friend" of one of the regulars on the show. A 12-year-old boy. I was the "tomboy" who had hit puberty and was becoming a girl. At the end of the episode, my character was supposed to just lean over and plant one on the boy. I remember the director going over the scene with us again and again in rehearsal. He could see how embarrassed we both were, and since this show was taped before a studio audience, he didn't want us to get messed up and forget the scene. The whole thing went off without a hitch—it was a re-ally cute scene. Of course, how many kids invite their grandparents to witness their "first kiss"? Yup—my grandparents were sitting in the front row of the studio audience!!!

Actually, the best relationships I had with boys in high school were with a couple of guys who would

jokingly steal my backpack, ask to borrow a pen, and tease me in good-natured ways. They made me feel good because they actually talked to me, which most kids in the school didn't. It never occurred to me until I was an adult that they might have actually been attracted to me, and if I had shown the least bit of interest in them, one or both might have asked me out. But I never did anything to encourage them. I just didn't get it! Yet all those uncomfortable and embarrassing moments of my childhood have been an invaluable part of my portrayal of Sami. When my mom sees Sami's dark side on *Days,* she often teases me with lines like, "Remind me never to make you angry!" On soaps, the storylines can be so farfetched that it's often hard to "relate" as an actress to what your character is going through. I have to "replace" the storyline situation with something similar in my real life that creates the same type of feeling. And every personal struggle I've ever experienced is fair game when I face a challenging scene. So, in a very real way, I owe all those kids who tortured me in school a big "thank you"!

There were some benefits of having only a few friends, male or female, in school. Here's one: I never went to the parties where the peer pressure to take drugs and alcohol was pretty intense. I spent most of those years in something of a haze of my own making—attending class, doing homework, going to auditions, and working on *Days*—but not much else. I didn't even know that the kids in my school drank and took drugs until I was a senior! I was so naïve and felt like a real outsider.

In a lot of ways, the experiences I had on *Days* and with other acting jobs were more "normal" than my experiences in real life. Remember that

on one TV sitcom, I got my ears pierced at 10 years
old, an age when my mom never would have let me
do it in real life. I had my first kiss on TV. The same
with my first dance. The first time I made love (or
at least acted like I was making love!) was as Sami
on *Days*. When you think about it, it's actually pretty
amusing that many of my coming-of-age moments
happened first on TV.

So if drugs and drinking weren't part of my real
life, what kind of "adolescent rebellion" did I go
through? Well, don't laugh: *TV Guide* once wrote
about a transgression in my younger days when,
along with some other girls, I ran up my parents'
credit line at the local grocery store. Not exactly a
capital offense! Of course, it didn't make my parents particularly happy, but it didn't bring the FBI
to my doorstep, either.

Breaking Out

Here's the irony: I was actually very good at making friends everywhere else but at school. Go figure! I had good friends in all of my afterschool
activities, particularly horseback riding. Maybe because they had no preconceived notions of me, I
was able to be myself, which they seemed to like. I
really connected with some of them. We'd go to
horse shows. We'd have sleepovers. Normal stuff. I
also made friends on the job, whether I was making commercials or on the set of *Days of Our Lives*.

But at school, it was different. Sometimes, I
came home at the end of the day crying hysterically because (in my mind) no one liked me or ever
would. Even after I started playing Sami on *Days*, I

still struggled with my self-esteem, and felt pretty disconnected at school. On those rare occasions when kids would talk to me, I wondered if it was only because I was on TV.

So how did I overcome this lack of friends and the insecurities that accompanied it? As I grew older and felt more comfortable living in my own skin, I became more accepting of myself. As that happened, more people began to like me.

At the time, I was convinced that I was the only one who felt so lonely. But here's what I didn't know: *Most* kids feel the same way at one time or another. In fact, the most unlikely people at my high school believed they were just as friendless as I was. A few years after I graduated, I ran into a girl who I was certain was the reason they invented the word "popularity." No kidding, everyone seemed to like her. But here's what she told me: She cried every day after school because she was convinced that she had no friends. I couldn't believe it. Of course, she was wrong. A lot of kids liked her, and I would have loved to have been her friend.

Who knows? Maybe that was the case with me, too. And maybe with you as well.

Even many of the popular kids—the ones who always seem to be busy on weekends—are insecure. In fact, that may be why they sometimes behave the way they do. Maybe they're often mean because it makes them feel superior and better than anyone else (boy, are they wrong!). As a teenager, of course, it doesn't make you feel any better or any less lonely if you know your tormenter is just as unsure of herself as you are. But that's probably the case.

In a sense, acting was an escape for me from some unhappy and insecure times in my real life.

The characters that I played on TV (at least until I got the part of Sami) were pretty normal—much more normal than my own real life appeared to be. Acting let me get away from the classroom and the kids I didn't feel comfortable around. It gave me the chance to pretend to lead a grownup life, and I was definitely a different person on the set than I was at school. There was something about school that brought out the shyest and most insecure parts of me. But with acting, there's no place for shyness and modesty. You have to be bold and confident and believe in yourself.

My little brother handled things much better than I did. Ryan is a classically trained and extremely talented musician. Since he was five years old, my mom would insist that he practice for an hour a day even if his friends were over at our house. His buddies would watch TV or play Nintendo until the hour was up. The amazing thing is that he was a very popular kid, maybe in part because he stood up for himself. His friends were listening to rock and rap while he was falling in love with classical music. He listened to the music he wanted to listen to, whether or not it was popular among his peers, and he really didn't seem to be concerned whether they liked him more or less because of it. In the process, he was so popular. His friends even went to his classical music concerts. I was envious of him and his strength to be the person he truly was. I was impressed—and, of course, wondered why I hadn't inherited the same friendship gene that he did.

Looking back, I wish I had been more courageous in school. I wish I had been more adventurous and had more experiences. I wish I had gone on more group dates. Instead of trying to fit in with students who apparently didn't want me as part of

their group, I should have been even more aggressive in looking for activities (like horseback riding) where I could meet people and make friends. I know high school kids who worked for charities after school or on weekends. Some made lifelong friends with other volunteers at Head Start programs. I missed out on a lot because I was so shy and so insecure.

Yet I've gained this wisdom over the years: The key is to have good friends, true friends, even if you don't have very many of them. (Of course, this is what my mom always told me when I was crying after school; I didn't believe her then, but, as usual, parents know what they're talking about.) It may be enough to have just one close girlfriend you can relate to and talk to, and with whom you have things in common. You don't need busloads of friends, especially those who spend too much of their time gossiping about others and doing their share of backstabbing. You also don't need to compromise your values in an attempt to fit in, or say nasty things just to "belong."

Stay true to yourself and who you really are at your inner core. You'll be proud you took a stand and stuck to your values.

Who Am I?

As important as a few good friends can be, I've also made an effort to get a better sense of the person *I* really am. Particularly in an industry like show business, where so much of an individual's supposed "worth" is based on superficial things—e.g., their beauty, not their brains . . . their thinness, not

the kind of person they are inside—it's important to recognize the trivialness of it all and not be overly influenced by it. Sure, it sounds like a cliché, but as I identify and make peace with my inner self, I've become a much happier person and deal more effectively with the problems in my life—from relationship issues to job conflicts to health concerns. As I've recognized what's really important—and what's not—I'm making better and more genuine life decisions.

Now, don't get me wrong: My career is very important to me, and so I've learned to accept (and sometimes even embrace) most aspects of show business—the good, the bad, and the ugly. But as much as I love acting, it's only one part of my life. I've learned not to take every disappointment to heart, because in this business, there can be a lot of them. I don't let the setbacks overshadow all the good things in my life, including those that have nothing to do with the television industry. I have a happy home life. I spend as much time as possible with my family and friends. I ride horses. I ski. I've taken up golf. I've learned to play racquetball and basketball. And I never stop reading.

Finding your place in the world—and discovering the activities that make you a more well-rounded, more complete person—is a lifelong journey. Along the way, take advantage of every opportunity to bring quality to your day-to-day life.

By the way, I don't think you're ever too young (or too old!) to start this process. I remember when I was applying to colleges and was initially amazed that the Ivy League schools and other prestigious colleges were looking for students who were not only academic superstars, with a 4.0 GPA or better. They also wanted their incoming freshmen

to have accumulated a lengthy list of extracurricular activities—sports, clubs, school plays, and musical performance. They wanted young people who had done charity work and made other important contributions to their community. Get the picture? In short, these colleges were seeking people who were well-rounded, with broad interests, even if they didn't excel in every one of them.

I think there's something to be learned from these college-admission criteria. No matter what your stage of life, open your eyes to everything the world has to offer. You might discover new interests along the way—some serious, some recreational, and some that may become lifelong pursuits.

I really enjoy basketball, for example. I play a little—I'll talk about my participation in Jim Reynolds' Charity Basketball Games a little later—but I'm also a huge fan of the sport, attend both L.A. Lakers and Clippers games, and I'm in a "fantasy basketball league" with several of my *Days* co-stars.

Be Flexible

Each week, I get many e-mails and letters from fans seeking my advice—not only about making it as an actress, but also about achieving virtually every other goal in their lives. I tell them how I've realized many of my own dreams—by focusing on the prize, working hard, making sacrifices—and being flexible. Yes, I've learned that unforeseen events can often derail the best-laid plans, at least temporarily; whether you're an actress, a stockbroker, a stay-at-home mom, or a professional athlete, there will still be inevitable and unexpected twists and turns

that can throw you offtrack. But if you're ready and willing to roll with the punches, I think you'll emerge as a stronger person.

For most of my life, I had always assumed that I'd go to college. In fact, the issue was never *whether* I'd go to college, but rather *what* college I'd choose. But then at sixteen, my life took an unexpected turn. I got this wonderful role on *Days of Our Lives*, and it changed everything and forced me to re-think my future. As I prepared to graduate from high school, I realized that college just wasn't in the cards, at least not at the time. All those college applications I filled out were really for naught. It just wasn't practical to think I could be both a full-time student and a full-time actress. There are only twenty-four hours in a day.

Yet I remember how difficult it was to let go of my dream of college, or more accurately, to put it on hold. I know what you're thinking—"What, are you crazy? Dreaming of *college* when you've got a job like *that*?!!?!" Of course, I'm proud of what I've achieved as an actress. But at the same time, my parents have always emphasized the importance of an education. I grew up with a strong belief that a degree would be one of the most important tools I could give myself. That way, no matter what happened with my acting, I'd have something to "fall back on." So while I'm certainly happy with my good fortune to spend more than ten fantastic years on *Days*, it was still hard to let go of what I had planned for my life for so long.

By the way, for a time, I actually did try to do both—show business and higher education. I actually began taking a few evening classes at UCLA. The executive producer of *Days* told me, "If you can find a way to make it work, give college a shot

and we'll try to help you out with the schedule."
And he did. The show's producers helped in every
way they could. But it was still impossible to find
time for everything.

In my second quarter at UCLA, my economics
professor provided the coup de grace to my college career. One day after class, he told me, "Look,
if you're ever late for class, don't bother to show
up at all!" He couldn't have been more direct. At
that point, I realized that I just couldn't commit myself to college right then. Sometime in the future,
maybe—but not then.

I still keep my mind active. As I mentioned, I
read all the time, and read all kinds of things—
from magazines (*Vanity Fair, Entertainment Weekly,
The New Yorker*) to every type of book imaginable,
including romance novels, the classics (Jane Austen,
Victor Hugo) and "chick-lit" (a la *Bridget Jones' Diary*).
I frequently check out what's on the best-seller list,
and I'm an easy mark for attractive displays at bookstores. I encourage others to read, too, and enjoy
the challenge of taking someone who doesn't like
reading and finding a book for him that he can't
put down.

I was very fortunate that my own love of reading
was nurtured as a kid. My aunt and uncle live in
Connecticut, and growing up, I would visit them
and my cousin every summer. As a preteenager, I
began going to a small bookstore in their community, which was (and still is) owned by a wonderful
woman named Diane, who would always recommend fabulous books for me to read. Each year,
she'd ask me about the types of books I liked and
what I'd been reading lately. She'd almost inter-

view me about my reading interests. I'd leave her store with more than a dozen books that she "assigned" me to read in the next 12 months—some were light reading (fun but well-written), and others were serious fiction. I always read all of them, and when I returned the following summer, I'd give her a report on which books I liked and which I didn't.

I've been back to Diane's Books every year, and always leave with a new stack of reading. There's no bookstore like Diane's where I live, where the staff is so knowledgeable about books and that hasn't been suffocated by the warehouse bookstores.

Let me also tell you about my book group. We're all in the entertainment industry (Ari Zuker of *Days* is part of the group). Whenever all of us finish the book we've chosen to read, we meet, talk about it, and select the next book. Everyone comes with suggestions, and our new choice tends to fit into a different category than our last book—if we just finished reading a heavy or a sad story (*The Lovely Bones*, for example), we might shift to a Jane Green novel next time that's more fun and lighthearted. Sometimes we meet at one of our homes; other times, we go out to dinner and discuss the book.

I also keep current on what's going on in the world, and get most of my news on the Internet. But at least right now, college isn't right for me. And I'm at peace with that decision.

The moral to the story? You can never predict how your life is going to unfold. I've made some tough choices, but they're choices I can live with, and I've made them with as much thought and wisdom as possible.

A Memorable Afternoon

After I had joined the cast of *Days,* most of the kids in my high-school classes knew about my acting career, and some seemed fascinated by it. Although I still wasn't winning any popularity contests at school, they'd sometimes ask me what it was like being on TV or what some of the other actors on the soap were like.

In my initial days on the show, my character Sami was being portrayed as a loving little sister and a "good girl"—before her eventual fall from grace. In one early episode, I had a scene with Carrie (played by Christie Clark), Sami's older sister, where she was teaching me how to kiss a boy. Christie began kissing her hand, while showing me how to kiss my own hand so I'd be ready for the "real thing" once a boy finally entered my life. In some ways, it was a hilarious scene—but also rather embarrassing. I remember that Christie and I felt pretty stupid shooting the scene. But our embarrassment on the set was only beginning!

Three weeks after that episode was shot, I was in my history class at school, and the teacher brought out a TV and a VCR to show us a video on World War II. Well, the videotape malfunctioned, and the teacher announced that he'd walk over to the school library to get a different video. "I'll be back in five or ten minutes," he told us.

As soon as he left the classroom, one student boldly stood up and announced, "Hey, *Days of Our Lives* is on TV right now. Let's watch Ali!"

Oh, no. But I thought, "What are the odds that I'll be on today, right?"

Everyone cheered—everyone but me. They turned on the TV, and switched channels until they found *Days*. Within about a minute, I was on the screen. And guess what episode was airing that day? With the entire class watching, there I was, kissing my hand with as much passion as my fifteen-year-old character could muster.

So embarrassing!

While the whole class roared with laughter, I put my head in my hands, absolutely mortified. The class's hysterics continued in waves for several minutes. I wanted to disappear.

It sounds like a scene out of a sitcom, doesn't it? I wish it had been.

Chapter

5

Are you one of those people who turns on the TV set every afternoon, asking yourself, "What in the world will Sami Brady do today?"

If there's one thing you can say about Sami, she's certainly unpredictable. And let me tell you, it seems that everyone has an opinion about her. Whether you love her or hate her, you have plenty of company among the millions of *Days of Our Lives* viewers.

Can you believe some of the things Sami has done over the last ten-plus years? Her behavior is sometimes so outrageous that it's taken me a long time to get used to playing a character who provokes so much audience venom, and yet at the same time so much sympathy for the messes she gets herself into. Poor Sami. Sure, you have to admire her spunk and her commitment to what she believes in (whatever that may be at the moment!), and even her need for support and yearning to be

loved. But let's admit it, there are also times when you simply want to wring her neck—as tightly as possible.

When I first joined the show in 1993, I just wasn't prepared for how crazy my character would become, and how she would evolve in so many ways—from how she behaved to how she dressed. How good is your own memory about the teenage Sami? Do you remember those Gap long-sleeved tees and vests I

(Lesley Bohm)

wore, day after day, on the show (a rather monotonous fashion statement, don't ya' think?)? And don't forget Sami's very, very long blonde hair down to the waistline that (mercifully) is a bit shorter these days (down to the middle of the back). Bryan Dattilo (who plays Lucas) teases me constantly about how I used to bee-bop around like Jan Brady, with my hair bouncing back and forth.

By the way, whenever I've cut or colored my hair, I've always consulted with the producers of *Days* in advance. A few years ago, I wanted to do something different, and decided to dye my hair red (yes, red!) just for fun. I asked the producers, and got their OK; they even said they'd write it into the script. One of them told me, "Sami's the kind of girl who'd do anything—you can count on her to throw you a curveball!" In fact, they've encouraged me to try different styles and colors with my hair, figuring that these kinds of changes will be right in sync with Sami's unpredictable character.

Looking Back

As you might know, Sami was named after her aunt, Samantha Evans (the twin sister of her mom, Marlena). If you're a longtime fan of the show, you're aware that Sami is a kindred spirit of the woman whose name she shares; Samantha was a wannabe actress who was a ruthless hell-raiser in her own right, driven by jealousy and addicted to pills. Here's just one example of her behavior: Taking sibling rivalry to a new level, Samantha stole Marlena's blank prescription pads (and checkbook) and drugged her sister. Then, while impersonating

Marlena, she got her sister committed to Bayview Sanitarium and a series of shock treatments. (By the way, Deidre Hall's real twin sister, Andrea, played Samantha; after a few years on the show, Andrea's character was murdered by the Salem Strangler, a serial killer who preyed on women in the town— but that's a whole other story!)

As you can see, Sami Brady—as the namesake of Samantha Evans—had quite a reputation to live up to. And, of course, Sami hasn't let us down! Early on, *Soap Opera Digest* described her as a "trouble-maker in training." Sami may have started out with girl-next-door goodness, but she has used her own brand of insanity to create plenty of chaos in Salem, again and again. She has fought her way through bulimia, been raped, and given birth to a baby out of wedlock. She has schemed to win the attention of one guy after another, shot one of them, and used drugs to lure another into bed. The list goes on and on.

If you're like me and find Sami absolutely fasci-nating, much of the credit should go to the writers of *Days*, who created and carefully crafted Sami's character from the start. Sami has had a background and a history that has helped explain the reasons and the motivation for her behavior, including how and why she evolved into the irresistible vil-lain that she quickly became. Jim Reilly, who is back as our head writer, created the "adult Sami," based on everything that has happened to her in the past.

Along the way, I've never tired of getting into Sami's skin and seeing what makes her tick. In fact, as each new script has arrived, just reading about her antics has kept me pretty entertained! Face it, you've probably never been bored watching Sami, either.

A Little Days History

From the start, it was *Days'* unique stories and characters that attracted viewers and kept them hooked. There were some incredible and truly mind-boggling story lines that preceded Sami's emergence on the show, and paved the way for the character that I'd eventually play. Of course, there are plenty of soap operas on daytime TV that you might consider as competition for *Days of Our Lives*. But from its beginnings in 1965, *Days* was a cutting-edge soap that took risks and went in directions where others feared to tread. Unlike most soaps, which were set in big cities, *Days* called the rural Midwest its home, and America's heartland has never been the same.

Open the television history books, and you'll find that some critics singled out *Days* for assuming the lead in taking afternoon TV into the sexual revolution. According to *Time* magazine, it was the "most daring drama" on daytime television. There were story lines that dealt with sex in ways that might have left some viewers uncomfortable and squirming—but still kept them coming back for more. No exceptions. So many of the episodes were surprising, upsetting, and titillating, and people have watched by the millions. Executive producer Ken Corday once said that you're only as good as your last episode, and *Days* has always kept viewers coming back.

Over the years, there were enough affairs on *Days* to keep most marriage counselors and divorce lawyers busy for a lifetime. There also were characters who fell in love with siblings, and mothers who dated their daughters' lovers. There were murders and manslaughters, pregnancies and malignan-

cies, blackmail and black sheep. There were characters obsessed with greed and possessed by the devil. Some were poisoned, others merely buried alive. Yep, Salem is not a safe place to live!

Sami Finds a Home

Once Sami surfaced in that dark overcoat in 1993—supposedly after a *very* long visit with her grandparents in Colorado—there's one thing for sure: It has always been a challenge bringing her to life amid everything else that transpires in Salem. But it's a challenge that I've enjoyed and certainly tried not to let overwhelm me.

Particularly in my first few days on the set in 1993, I remember feeling absolutely astounded at times, thinking, "My God, I'm on *Days of Our Lives*! I don't believe it!" It really was a dream come true, particularly for a sixteen-year-old who loved the show long before I auditioned for it. At the same time, there was no time to be a kid. I realized that this was serious stuff. I needed to be professional, arrive on time, know my lines, and deliver them convincingly. I needed to hold my own with the amazing cast of the show. I had a pretty good work ethic before joining *Days*, but by necessity it became a way of life in no time. I was never one of those actors who was full of herself and had attitude (Thanks to my mom!), but if I had been, I realized that no one at *Days* would have ever put up with it.

In those first few weeks and months, when a scene was particularly challenging or difficult, I did sometimes ask myself, "How am I going to do this? How am I going to make it work?" Fortunately, as I've al-

ready mentioned, there were other actors on the set who I could turn to when I needed a bit of advice. Whether the script called for something subtle or something over the top, I knew that people like Deidre Hall (Marlena), Wayne Northrop (ex-Roman), and Drake Hogestyn (John) were among those who would always offer guidance if I asked for it. Making a TV show is incredibly demanding on everyone, and as actors we rely on each other to help elevate our performances to the level that the scene requires.

Another factor has been at play almost since day one, and this probably won't surprise you: Particularly after Sami's transformation from being sweet and innocent to wicked and nasty, I've made an effort not to let her craziness affect me once the camera is shut off and the lights are dimmed. Fans often ask whether Sami's evil ways seep into my soul and actually surface in my real life from time to time. Luckily (particularly for my family and friends!), I've always been able to separate fantasy and reality. I've sometimes told reporters that Sami allows me to get any unkind thoughts out of my system. But, really, it's not something that I've ever worried about. I don't get very melodramatic on my own time, and as I hope my husband Dave would tell you, I'm usually pretty relaxed and even-tempered. You could say that I leave Sami on the set and never let her pull the strings in my personal life.

The Bulimia Story

I've already told you how Sami was introduced to America. But the first major and meaningful story

line that involved my character focused on the subject of bulimia. Apparently, the writers of *Days* already had the idea of dealing with bulimia on the show before I was even cast for the part—and what a timely subject! Bulimia—the bingeing-and-purging syndrome that creates such chaos in the lives of so many girls and young women—is almost an epidemic in America.

Of course, as I'll write about in great detail later in the book, I've gone through periods in my life where I've been absolutely obsessed with and fixated on my weight. When the number on the scale wasn't where I thought it should be (when was it *ever* where I thought it should be?), I would absolutely freak out. It was pretty sad, but at times my happiness (or lack of it) revolved solely around my weight. It became a dominating issue in my life.

To be honest, in my more despondent moments of struggling with the scale, I thought seriously about vomiting as a way to win the battle of the bulge. More than once, I remember sitting in the bathroom at home and trying to make myself throw up. Not a pretty image, is it? But my body wouldn't let me vomit. I'd stick my fingers down my throat, but nothing would happen. I don't know—probably a mental block of some kind, my brain's self-defense mechanism, but whatever the reason, it just didn't work. Thank goodness!

But over the years, I've known a number of girls who turned bulimia into a way of life. Some vomited after meals. Others took laxatives. I suppose they thought it worked for them, at least for a while. But I also know it must have taken a terrible toll on their health. Some bulimic girls become so ill that they can't keep any food in their stomach, even when they want to. As soon as their body senses

food, they become nauseous, and vomiting becomes almost automatic. It's shocking, but that's what this culture does to so many girls who are absolutely desperate to have the "perfect body."

The producers of *Days* were really quite remarkable in the way they handled my part in the bulimia story line. On the show, the teenage Sami began bingeing and purging because of the difficulties she was going through in her life. At the time, I don't know whether the producers were aware of my own struggles with weight, but they certainly made sure that I was comfortable portraying a bulimic. At the time, newspapers and magazines were filled with articles about Tracy Gold, the actress on the ABC sitcom *Growing Pains*, who had gone public in 1992 about her personal struggle with self-induced starvation (anorexia nervosa) beginning at age twelve. So at *Days* and probably a lot of other shows, everyone was more sensitive than usual about the dieting obsessions and the devastating eating disorders that can occur with young actresses. They wanted to make sure that in playing a bulimic, I didn't become so immersed in my character that I lapsed into an eating disorder in real life. True story.

The producers of *Days* talked with me and my parents about the bulimic story line to be certain that we were okay with it. As it turned out, my character struggled with bulimia for most of my first summer on the show. At the time, Sami was coping with some absolutely mind-boggling stresses in her life. She dearly loved her mother and father (played by Deidre and Wayne). But things changed instantly when she saw her mom, Marlena, cheating on her father by having sex with John Black in the conference room at a publishing party. Sami

absolutely melted down. She just couldn't handle it.

Then, to complicate matters (as if that were necessary!), Marlena learned she was pregnant. But things got even worse: She wasn't sure who the father was! Was it John (her lover)? Or Roman (her husband)?

Are you following this? Welcome to the crazy world of Salem!

Until that time, Sami was innocent and naïve, and believed that her parents were perfect. Of course, every kid eventually comes to the realization that her mom and dad, like all human beings, have flaws. But for the moment, Sami absolutely lost it. She became worried sick about her adored father and how he would react to the news that he might not be the father of Marlena's baby. What angst for such an insecure teenager!

As the saga played out, Sami tried to protect her father by doctoring the baby's blood-test results in the hospital computer. As a result, a very relieved Marlena believed that Roman, in fact, had fathered the baby.

Through it all, Sami continued to find herself right in the middle of this mess. And what was her way of surviving this emotional train wreck? She never told anyone that she had seen her mother and John having sex. To soothe her own pain and sorrow, she gorged on food and then vomited what she had eaten, day after day, week after week.

In Sami's mind, her family had driven her to find solace in an eating disorder, and Sami's pain was portrayed very powerfully on the show. And judging by the fan letters I received, this storyline really hit home with the viewers.

To understand this problem better, I talked with several psychotherapists at a treatment facility for eating disorders in L.A., and consulted with some private therapists as well. Looking back, I believe that we depicted bulimia in a very sensitive and accurate way, and it was definitely challenging to play.

During and immediately after the airing of the bulimia episodes, I got plenty of mail from girls who were living with anorexia and bulimia. Many of those letters were absolutely amazing. Girls poured out their hearts with very personal and moving accounts of struggling for years with eating disorders. I'm sure they cried plenty of tears when they wrote them. I shed some just reading them. They were pretty intense. In letter after letter, young women described becoming ensnared in the grip of an eating disorder, and how they had lost control of their lives. Of course, I didn't feel qualified to advise these viewers, but I was able to refer them to reputable resources for more information and for treatment, and was as understanding and sympathetic as possible in my letters to them.

Over the years, thanks to Sami and the writers of *Days*, I have felt extremely lucky to have been involved in episodes like these that have confronted very important issues in the lives of our viewers, and really touched people's lives. One of the most moving fan letters I've ever received was from a teenage viewer who described how she had followed my suggestion and gotten help. She wrote that she knew she might have to struggle with her eating disorder for the rest of her life. But her self-esteem was improving, and she felt she was finally on the right track and making progress on the road

to recovery. Those kinds of letters make me realize that we're doing something important on *Days*, and I'm so proud to be part of it.

The Marlena-John-Roman-Sami story line continued for quite a while. Marlena's new baby, Belle (who, of course, was also Sami's sister), became ill, and when she needed to have blood drawn, Sami became petrified that through the baby's blood typing, her parents would discover that Belle was really John's daughter, not Roman's. So what was Sami's solution? Naturally, she pushed the envelope as far as it would stretch. She decided to kidnap the baby and sell her on the black market. That was Sami's way of keeping her parents' lives from being "ruined."

Leave it to Sami and her convoluted thinking to come up with a strategy this bizarre! It set the stage for the kind of behavior that my character would exhibit in the years ahead. The kidnapping was the first time that Sami crossed the line and committed a serious crime (if you don't count switching Belle's paternity test results because, after all, her heart was in the right place)—but, of course, it wasn't a major transgression to her. In Sami's mind, the kidnapping was something noble, trying to protect her father and preserve her parents' marriage. To her, the abduction of her baby sister was a way of rescuing everyone around her.

If you don't remember how the story line ultimately evolved (and for all you fans who have started watching since then), let me indulge you in a brief refresher course: Sami freaked out when a buyer for the baby seemed kind of sketchy, so she decided to move to Florida with Belle. Though she was only sixteen years old, Sami decided that the best course of action was to raise the infant herself. But

before that scenario could ever play out, the truth finally emerged, indicating that Belle was really John's daughter. And, of course, these facts surfaced in the most shocking way possible. Just consider this: Marlena had learned the truth about the baby's real father, and shortly thereafter, she was surrounded by family members at Belle's baptism ceremony—and the secret came out right then and there! Stefano had threatened to blackmail her, and she felt she had no choice but to announce to the entire gathering that she had had an affair with someone else. It was unbelievable. Roman was absolutely devastated. Before long, he figured out that John was Belle's real father, and that all of Sami's emotional and eating problems were related to this long and bizarre turn of events. Roman left Salem, and he and Marlena divorced.

Are you following along? You practically need a road map and name tags to keep everything and everyone straight, don't you? Don't even think of trying to do a Salem Family Tree.

A Little Advice

A final interesting note: I know that viewers really relate to Sami, and they never run short of advice for her. As this kidnapping saga unfolded on TV screens across the country, mail poured in from viewers who were horrified by Sami's behavior. In Los Angeles, several people stopped me on the street and said things like, "Give the baby back! What are you doing? Return the baby."

They were so angry at Sami!

Some of my favorite letters were from fans who

took the time to recount and explain the entire story line to me. One of them wrote, "Dear Alison: You need to give Belle back to Marlena immediately because the baby is very sick, and you're only sixteen years old and can't take proper care of her. Please, Alison, do it for Belle."

I respond to all my fan mail, and there's a part of me that feels like answering letters like the one above by saying, "It's only a television show!!" But I think better of it, and I'm just so grateful that viewers are so loyal and so involved that they sometimes don't seem to differentiate TV from real life!

Here's what I think about Sami and her relationship with her fans: Even if many viewers don't want to admit it, Sami does the kinds of things that they always wanted to do to their boyfriends or family members but just couldn't, because in real life people can't behave that way. That's what I love about Sami. She puts herself out there and does these unbelievably insane things. Yet as crazy as it seems, her behavior comes from a real place. It's a product of her insecurities and her love for her family. So even when she's not very likeable, fans keep coming back for more.

Good for them—and for me!

Chapter

6

If you can say anything about the fans of *Days of Our Lives*, it's that they're loyal. Many arrange and rearrange their schedules just to make sure they're near a TV when the show airs. Others set their VCRs before they leave for work or school in the morning. If they miss the show they can now surf the Internet for detailed descriptions of the day's events—the show's agonies and the ecstasies, the affairs and the afflictions, the tenderness and the torment, the passion and the persecution.

Just a typical day in Salem.

Remember the statistics that I cited in Chapter 1: In an average week, about six million Americans watch *Days of Our Lives*. That makes it one of the most popular soaps on television. Among college-age women, *Days* has ranked only behind *ER* and *Friends* as the most videotaped program in the United States. How cool is that?

Of course, producing an hour-long show five days

a week is an immense undertaking. That works out to 265 episodes a year! There are no lengthy breaks. No summer hiatus. Barely a moment to catch your breath. Compare that to most prime-time shows, which produce about 22 episodes per season. One-hour primetime dramas spend seven to ten days on each episode. Sitcoms take five days to do a half-hour show. But in daytime, we can't air reruns, so we are under constant pressure to produce one new hour of television every day! But it all gets done, and we're so proud of the finished product—and the credit should go not only to our dedicated group of wonderful actors, but also to the many talented, behind-the-scenes men and women: the producers, the directors, the writers, the crew, the makeup artists, the hair stylists . . . the list goes on and on. All of us work very hard. All of us want nothing more than to produce a finished product that fans love and that keeps them coming back for more.

That's the bottom line.

A Day in the Life

When fans tell me that they love watching *Days*, they also often ask how the show is actually put together. With five hours of new programs per week, some wonder if we just about live and sleep on the set. "When do you ever go home?" they ask. "When do you have time to think about anything else?"

Good questions.

Let me tell you, I'm very grateful for the professionalism of both our cast and crew. The set is as energetic and as animated as Grand Central Station, with a nonstop rush of adrenaline that lasts from

sunup to exhaustion (I've heard it referred to as "barely controlled chaos"!). People are racing in all directions . . . the production staff, directors, writers, set designers, cameramen, stagehands, electricians, prop crew, wardrobe personnel, makeup artists, hair stylists, audio technicians, even the security guards. All of us know our respective roles in the process. All of us approach our responsibilities seriously and thoughtfully. When unforeseen problems arise, they're resolved quickly because we have no other choice. The show has to stay on schedule. Falling behind just isn't an option.

There's really no *typical* day on the set of *Days.* In Chapter 2, I briefly sketched out what the daily schedule was like when I started on the show in 1993. These days, I usually have early calls that require me to arrive at the expansive NBC lot in Burbank between 6:45 and 7:30 in the morning (the alarm clock jars me awake all too early on those days—it hurts just writing about it!). By the time the cameras roll, the cast looks beautiful (or handsome, depending), but at 6:45, some are a little disheveled, others shuffling quietly to their dressing rooms, eyes still half-shut, brains just getting in gear (that's me!). There's rarely the opportunity to "sleep in" on workdays, although occasionally I'm not called to the set until 1 P.M. or so (hooray!).

No matter what the arrival time, the actors may gulp down a cup or two of Starbucks coffee to help us greet the day. Then we have our hair and makeup done and begin working with the director to "dry block" our scenes, which (as I've written) means becoming familiar with the marks already laid down, indicating where we'll be standing, and when and where we'll be moving. (A one-hour script will have hundreds of camera shots, so there's a lot for the

directors and the actors to remember; many of us make notes on the script and review them before the actual filming starts.) If an actor has questions about a scene, the director (or sometimes the stage manager) will help you sort them out. Then it's off to wardrobe, getting yourself dressed—and then making yourself comfortable (studying lines) in your dressing room until it's time to shoot your scenes.

If there's an extended period of time to kill in the dressing room—and there are definitely days where you have a *lot* of free time on your hands—I answer fan mail, or use my laptop computer to respond to e-mails or chat with fans on the Internet. It's so much fun to communicate with my fans this way! I'm always dying to know what they're think-

From an early age, I loved curling up with a good book.

(Author's personal collection)

ing about the show and about Sami.

I also usually have a book with me in my dressing room to help pass the time. Or I'll watch TV. Or knit. Or I'll call friends and bother them while they're trying to get work done. Or I'll just hang out with the other actors, sometimes running through our lines together.

Some actors take a catnap. Others get a little exercise (can't sweat too much or the wardrobe and makeup departments will kill you!). Or they'll grab a late breakfast or an early lunch on the studio lot (I'll talk later about the super-low-calorie meals that so many actors seem addicted to!). There are a thousand ways to pass the time, but I try not to allow my mind to stray too far from the scenes that I'll be taping sometime that day.

Practice Makes Perfect?

Now, what about rehearsals? Well, if you're an actor who feels the need for a lot of rehearsing, maybe soaps aren't for you. Remember, there's an hour show to be taped *every day!* So because of the time pressures, extensive rehearsals (or run-throughs) are something of a luxury. We might run through a scene once—at most, twice—before shooting, often a dress rehearsal where everyone is in complete makeup and wardrobe. And you better know your lines right out of the box, because there's just no time or tolerance for someone to be stumbling through their dialogue after they've arrived on the set and shooting begins. Thinking back to when I started on the show, the limited rehearsal time was a little nerve-wracking at first, and it was really an

eye-opener to be thrown into the fire with seasoned actors. Even though I always knew my lines, I'm sure my comfort level would have risen considerably if we had more time for rehearsing. But that's when I really benefited the most from advice from Deidre. It's amazing how fast I got the hang of things, thanks in large part to the support of the veteran cast members, as well as the wonderfully understanding producers and directors. I owe them a huge thank you.

These days, we might get a script a week before we shoot it, but don't kid yourself that this gives us a generous window of time to become familiar with it. Depending on how busy we are shooting previous scripts, and how much camera time we have on those days, I may not get a chance to look at the new script until the day before we tape it. To add to the pressure-cooker atmosphere, episodes aren't necessarily taped in order, so to keep the story flowing accurately in your own mind, you need to stay focused to make sure your own character is always reacting appropriately within the context of the story line, even if the filming itself is rather fragmented.

Fortunately, I can learn my lines pretty quickly. I've developed an amazing short-term memory. But there's a catch: Don't ask me about the script we shot a week or two ago; those lines have disappeared somewhere within the creases of my brain, probably never to resurface! (I sometimes joke that I wish I had had this same great short-term memory when I was in school; I could have learned just about anything for a test in nothing flat!—just as long as the exam was sometime within the next twenty-four hours or so!)

Can You Do It in One Take?

Because we're working on such a tight, unforgiving schedule with *Days*, there's also not much room for error once the "ON AIR" sign is lit and the cameras are rolling. The goal is pretty simple: Wrap up each scene in just one take (although sometimes it takes two or three). We're moving at such breakneck speeds that, at times, mistakes are made—maybe the lighting isn't quite right in the first take, so the scene is reshot. Or perhaps an actor stumbles over a line—never me of course. (Just kidding! They have a "blooper reel" at every Anniversary party, and I blush every year dreading how many of my stumbles, both verbal and physical, end up on that tape!) Inevitably, things happen that impede the race to the finish line, but you can't let too many of those glitches get in the way and interrupt the flow. It really is a high-stress atmosphere, driven by the need to get it right and get it finished. And here's the good news: We usually do.

By the way, there's really neither the time nor the inclination for much ad libbing on the show. The scripts are so carefully crafted and story line-specific that you really can't mess with them. Of course, there are occasional exceptions to the rule: Particularly in the early days when I was playing a troubled adolescent, the writers were receptive to my suggestions when the script contained teenage slang. After all, "teenspeak" seems to change almost daily, and what's cool today can be so uncool tomorrow. So I'd sometimes tell the writers, "I really don't think kids talk that way." After a while, they actually relied on me to add the "whatevers" and

the "likes" where it was appropriate. (Like, totally!!) Other times, they'd write a scene where Sami was using an expression or an idiom, and I'd have absolutely no idea what it meant! Before long, they told me, "Ali, if you're completely in the dark about this piece of dialog, then a sixteen-year-old wouldn't be saying it. What would you say instead?"

Of course, Sami is in a league of her own. She has rarely met a wicked thought or act that she didn't embrace, so she's prone to saying some pretty outrageous and embarrassing things on the show. At times, upon reading the script, my initial reaction is, "C'mon, she's not so dumb or so evil that she's going to say something like that!" Or is she? One time my executive producer said, "Ali, I'm really happy that you've identified so completely with your character and taken her side. But she's a villain! The reality is, this is the way she'd talk and behave. Don't you see it?"

He was right. I should have saved my breath! The script stayed untouched.

The heart of the matter is that while we may reshape a few lines of dialogue here and there, it's rarely anything major. Obviously, neither I nor any of the other actors have the freedom to change the character's logic or the direction of the story line (as in, "Well, if you really want to know, my preference is that my character doesn't die on the operating table and disappear from the show altogether!"). But if you have trouble saying a particular line the way it's written—if it just doesn't roll off your tongue like it should—you can do a little fine-tuning without ruffling any feathers or sinking the ship.

With *Days* being an ensemble show, the writers work hard to make sure every word is perfect and

every actor gets his or her share of scenes and lines. As a result, sometimes you work five days a week; other times, just a couple. You never know what to expect until you check the schedule and then adjust your personal life accordingly. Some weeks, the pace gets accelerated into fast forward, and we'll tape six episodes in five days, building in a little breathing room so we can take a couple weeks off around Christmas, for example. But other weeks, the pace is a bit slower.

So like everyone else on the show, I've learned to be flexible. You might have to adjust to last-minute script changes during the day. Or portions of particular scenes might be designated as "tentative cuts," which means they could be preempted at the time of taping without altering the story line itself. As an actor, you have to be so familiar and comfortable with the script and the scene that, at the drop of a clapboard, you can adjust to instantaneous cuts and never miss a beat. Ain't that a challenge!

As each day of shooting is laid out, you may have five scenes spread throughout the day. But if all your scenes are scheduled for morning shoots, you might be finished by 10 A.M. and be on your way home by midmorning. (I know, days like that are awesome!) On most days, though, you better be psyched up and ready for the long haul. You'll stay on the set until you're done, which might mean a "wrap" at 4 in the afternoon, 7 in the evening, or past midnight. It can be pretty grueling sometimes, and you have to pace yourself through the day (sorry, no yawning allowed during the late-night shoots—the director sometimes has to remind us, "It's a party scene . . . wake up!"). Then you have to get as much rest as you can that night in antici-

pation of a new (and full) day starting early the following morning!

I'll never forget one day, we were shooting a big
party scene—those always take longer because the
more cast members in a scene, the longer it takes
to shoot. Anyway, my call time was 6:15 A.M. because they had so many people to get ready in time
for the tape to roll at 9 A.M. We didn't finish those
scenes until 2 A.M. the following morning(!), and
my call time for the next day was 6:45 A.M. I thought
about my half-hour commute to and from work,
and went to my makeup artist at the time, and said,
"Nina, please call me and wake me up when you're
ready for me," and I slept in my dressing room that
night! By the end of the second day, I ended up
going two full days without going outside once. It
was kind of weird. At one point I even asked, "What's
the weather like out there?"

Who said showbiz was all glamour and glitz?!

A Heartbeat Away from Death

Despite the hard work, the payoff comes in fabulous letters from fans, who tell us how much they
love the show and how important it is in their own
lives. They'll often describe their favorite Sami
story lines and ask me about mine. In this and several subsequent chapters, I'll tell you about some
of my favorite *Days* scenes and story lines, and some
behind-the-scenes experiences with them. (If you're
caught up on your *Days* history, feel free to skip
ahead to Chapter 7, or bear with me as I describe
the details of several of the more intriguing plot-

lines. . . . Grab a pen and paper if you need to take notes!)

When I think of my own favorites, the reason they rank so high is often because they were particularly challenging for me. They pushed me as an actress, motivating me to achieve new heights and reach a new level of performance.

With that in mind, do you remember the death row story line in 1999 where Sami was on the brink of execution? And I mean *falling off* the brink!

Of course, Sami's no angel (trust me on this one!). But she also may not strike you as a hardened criminal whose photo belongs on a Post Office bulletin board. In this particular story line, however, she did end up convicted of murder and sentenced to death. Her downfall began with an ugly custody fight with Lucas (played by Bryan Dattilo), the father of her child. But, of course, there was a lot more going on in Sami's life as well, including her obsession with Austin and her lifetime chase after him. As if that weren't enough, enter Franco Kelly (played by Victor Alfieri). Sami was at a particularly vulnerable place in her life, and Franco decided to exploit it. He saw Sami as his ticket to a green card that would allow him to stay in the country and avoid a contract on his life by a Mafia family in Italy, and he promised to help Sami drive a wedge between Austin and Carrie. (Stay with me here . . .) He also started to seduce Sami, and she began to fall madly in love with him. Before long, and to save his own skin, Franco proposed marriage—and (leave it to Sami!) she jumped at the offer. Sami was clueless, and she convinced herself that with Franco, she could finally end her preoccupation with Austin. So she answered "yes" to

Franco faster than you cay say "You've got to be
kidding, Sami!"

*Let me digress a moment and tell you about one of the
more unforgettable moments in this Franco storyline. At
one point, when Sami thought that Franco was cheating
on her, she struck him on the head and knocked him out
in the Titan building complex, then stripped him of his
shirt, wrote "DOG" in red lipstick, and pushed him out
onto a window washer's platform. When Franco regained
consciousness, he began begging for Sami's forgiveness
from the sky-high platform. With Sami peering out at
him from a window, he desperately tried to sweet-talk his
way back into her good graces, hoping to convince her
that he had actually been loyal to her. At one point, he
pulled Sami's head forward to kiss her—and accidentally banged her (aka" my") forehead into a post on the
window.*

Ouch!

*My head practically bounced off the window pane,
and the cracking noise must have nearly shattered an
eardrum or two of the sound man! It was another klutzy
Sami moment—and I can tell you that there have been
quite a few over the years. We had to reshoot that scene
with stars still spinning around my head!*

Before the passion could be cooled down a bit
on Sami's love affair with Franco (and before the
forehead bruises could completely heal), events
began spinning out of control. Other Salemites
had a much clearer vision of Franco's real motives,
and at one point, as Kate was on the brink of ex-
posing him to the INS, Franco started to attack
her, and Lucas grabbed a gun and killed Franco.

What a mess!

As you've probably guessed—(this is *Days of Our
Lives*, after all)—the story didn't end there . . . not
by a long shot. Austin had confronted Sami on her

wedding day with proof that Franco had been cheating on her. Enraged, Sami had stormed off to confront Franco, screaming "I'm going to kill him!" But she was too late! She walked in and saw Franco's dead body, and fainted . . . and that gave Kate an absolutely malicious brainstorm. She hurriedly wiped the murder weapon to remove Lucas's fingerprints, and placed the gun right in Sami's hand.

As some of you may remember, when Sami woke up she didn't remember a thing about what had happened. But there was the murder weapon cradled in her hand, and Franco was lying dead next to her. Could she really have killed him?

Almost immediately, the wheels of "justice" began turning, and Sami was the prime target. In all her insecurity, Sami wondered if she might have actually pulled the trigger and murdered her fiancé ("Maybe I really did do it," she said). But she just didn't know. She couldn't remember.

In seemingly no time, Sami was indicted and went on trial. But her memory gradually began to return, and during a Christmas Eve church service, she started having flashbacks and memories of seeing Franco upon his demise, and she finally pieced it all together. She vividly recalled walking in and seeing Franco already dead on the floor. In the middle of the church service, she suddenly yelled out, "I didn't do it!!" It was her Christmas miracle.

Maybe Sami had realized that she was innocent, but no one believed her. After all, she had lied so many times about so many other things. So why would anyone believe her now?

Waiting for the verdict, Sami was a wreck. High anxiety. Tight throat. They really wouldn't convict her, would they?

When the jury finally cast its votes, Sami was

convicted of murdering Franco, her fiancé. Her sentence: Death by lethal injection.

Sami, stunned and distraught, was transported to death row and waited for the inevitable. But she also decided that she wasn't about to die without a fight—and not a run-of-the-mill fight at that. Crushed when Lucas married someone else (it was Nicole) to get custody of their son, Sami's scheming shifted into overdrive. She pretended to collapse from an anxiety attack and was rushed to the hospital. Then, in typical Sami style, she poisoned the guard assigned to watch her (not fatally) and escaped from the hospital. In no time at all, she had snatched her son Will and crossed the border into Canada, along with perhaps the only person who believed she was innocent—Austin.

Still paying attention? If your brain is overloading, please feel free to take a break and regroup!

Okay—so, Roman tracked down Sami in Canada, and convinced (well, forced) her to return to Salem and fight to clear her name. She finally agreed, but as soon as she was back in custody, the district attorney persuaded the court to have her executed immediately. (Yeah, *thanks*, Dad!)

The story continued to build (it took more than a year for the entire saga to be presented on *Days*). Audiences across America were tied in knots and became glued to their TV sets. VCRs were working overtime. Would Sami somehow escape her ominous fate? Or would she finally die (and in the process, exile me to the Hollywood unemployment line!)?

As the clock ticked, Sami's demise seemed like a dead certainty (no pun intended!). But as her despair deepened, events continued to unfold in an even more bizarre fashion. Kate became worried

when Franco's friend threatened to reveal incriminating information, and she panicked. Kate's solution: She gave the hapless friend an injection of saline, and he lapsed into a coma.

Sami's crunch time finally arrived. Just before the stroke of midnight, she was led to the death chamber, and was strapped down with her arms stretched out to her sides in a Christ-like pose. She was in tears, hysterical, anticipating the worst.

But wait a minute.

Before I tell you how it all ended, let me tell you about how challenging it was to play Sami as her execution approached. There were schmaltzy but very demanding scenes where Sami said a tearful goodbye to her son and the rest of her family. What agony! All the while, as Sami stared death in the face, she finally realized how selfishly she had behaved for so many years, and how her anger and bitterness had created upheaval in the lives of so many of the people around her. With death looming, she and her mother, Marlena, finally reconciled. After so many years of being go-for-the-jugular enemies, Marlena cradled Sami in her arms within the prison walls. Sami suddenly seemed so fragile. Marlena sang her a lullaby. Both of them wept. Both were able to forgive the other and forgive themselves. And Sami grew up a little—but perhaps too late.

I'll never forget those scenes with Deidre. They were high-stakes, highly emotional scenes, beautifully written and wonderfully directed, and Deidre was absolutely amazing. I had to draw from deep within to reach the emotional intensity that the script called for, and I'm so proud of those episodes and how moving they were for millions of viewers.

To make the execution scene itself even more challeng-

*ing, here's something that most people don't know: I'm
very claustrophobic in real life, and being in that make-
believe death chamber, strapped down on the execution
table and pleading for freedom, it was actually* extremely
traumatic—*both for me and for Sami! Yes, I knew that
these events weren't happening in real life, but let me tell
you, there were moments where I absolutely experienced
every ounce of terror that Sami was feeling. I felt truly*

**Sami in happier times with mom,
Marlena, and her twin, Eric.**

*threatened. I was petrified. Real tears streamed down my
face as the fatal drugs were injected into my veins.*

*As a side note, while I lay on the execution table, film-
ing this incredibly dramatic scene, the crew took a five-
minute break. Shooting temporarily stopped, and the director
asked if I would mind just staying there, strapped down,
until filming resumed. Well, claustrophobic or not, I agreed
because it was so much work for the prop department to
strap me back in. But it was traumatic to lie there with
my arms and legs restrained, unable to move at all (not
even to scratch an itch!). Bobby Bateman, one of the prop
guys, brought me a glass of water with a straw, and held
it while I took a sip. Then, sure enough, about that time
my nose started to itch. Can you imagine what it's like to
have to ask someone to scratch your nose?*

Well, if you're a true Sami fan and just can't get
your fill of her wild and weird world, you probably
remember the end to the execution story. Just as
Sami was given the lethal injection, Lucas burst
into the room (he had decided to give himself up
to save Sami, and spent the whole episode trying
to get there in time to stop the execution), and he
confessed that he had murdered Franco. At that
moment, the governor placed an urgent call and
the execution was halted. Sami was saved—or was
she? The deadly poisons were already moving
through her veins. In an instant, she slipped into
cardiac arrest. She was rushed to the hospital and
nearly died. That's right, *nearly.*

Of course, Sami did survive (both my agent and
I are forever grateful!). She had a memorable reunion with Austin, and her obsession with him was
resuscitated at about the same time that she was.
Not long thereafter, she bumped into the Salem
district attorney who had prosecuted her for the
murder, who told her, "I'm really sorry about the

whole execution thing; would you like to go out sometime?" Or words to that effect.

Can you believe it?!

Well, dear readers, that was my own near-death experience. While I could tell you that Sami and everyone else lived happily ever after, I think you know better. C'mon, this is Sami we're talking about!

Chapter 7

Almost from the beginning, I learned just how important *Days of Our Lives* is to millions of Americans. And maybe their devotion to the show isn't that surprising.

Just think of it this way: *Days* comes into your home for an hour a day, five days a week. If you're a loyal viewer, my fellow actors and I probably spend more time with you than anyone but your closest family members and friends. So like part of the family, when our characters have one of those "I-can't-believe-she-did-that" moments—saying something that you find absolutely crazy, or acting in ways that border on the absurd—you'll probably let us know.

Fans usually write very positive letters, but I also get some correspondence from viewers who tell me quite bluntly how unhappy they are with the way my character behaves. "How could you do that?!" they ask. "What were you thinking?!" (The thing is,

I'm not the master of Sami's fate—I'll leave that to *Days'* writers.) Fans write detailed letters that describe how they handled situations in their own lives, and seem baffled that Sami could have managed the same circumstances so poorly. In the process, they sometimes reveal secrets about their personal lives that they may have never shared with anyone else (except perhaps a psychiatrist here and there, and maybe Dr. Phil!). On occasion, they even ask me for advice on how to regain custody of a child after a divorce, or how to make peace with their mom. They see Sami on TV every day, and if they don't have anyone else in their life who they can trust, they sometimes turn to me.

The same goes for our hairstyles and our clothing on the show. If our physical appearance sends chills down their spine, we might hear from them about those issues. No problem! I love to hear what you're thinking. Through letters and e-mails (and in the very active *Days* online message boards), fans often try to set us straight, and I'm so happy that viewers feel comfortable letting us know what's on their mind, whether their comments are positive or negative. My favorites are the fans who pick apart each moment in a scene, analyzing and overanalyzing every expression, trying to figure out what the character was thinking and/or feeling. It only shows that *Days* means a lot to them; they feel a certain ownership of the show, and they want to be "part of the action." These fans just can't get their fill, and they're very opinionated about how they want the story lines to unfold and the characters to behave. And I think that's awesome!

Can't Get Enough of Days!

At times, I'm actually amazed when fans tell me how dedicated they are to the show. Nothing, it seems, gets in the way of their watching *Days* and following their favorite story lines. If you think the Postal Service is committed to delivering the mail through rain, sleet, and snow, *Days'* fans go the same extra mile to make sure they don't miss even one line of dialogue or a single misdeed or sinful act. Some take later or extra long lunch breaks at work to make sure that they're in the employee lounge when the *Days* hourglass appears on the screen. They'll interrupt a shopping spree and rush to a row of televisions at an electronics or department store. They'll watch in their cars on a TV plugged into their cigarette lighter. They'll spend hours trying to make sense of the owner's manual for their VCR, just to make certain that they properly record the show each day.

Some college students tell me that they select their courses each semester with *Days* in mind, making sure that their classes don't conflict with their soap viewing. When I was at Harvard University a few years ago touring the campus, *Days* was playing on the television in a dormitory lunchroom, and sure enough, there was a large group of students perched around the TV set. (Even at Harvard, studying for finals can wait if Sami's getting herself in trouble!)

When a major news event preempts *Days*, watch out! My advice for the network's switchboard operators is to fasten their seat belts! They've been bombarded with angry phone calls from fans who

(Lesley Bohm)

Getting ready for one of my first photo shoots

can't seem to live without their daily fix of the romantic adventures of Bo and Hope, the passionate drama of Marlena and John, or the greedy-on-the-outside-but-secretly-dreaming-of-true-love-on-the-inside Nicole Walker. Sure, the news bulletins may be important to the news desk, but fans seem to prefer reading about the floods, fires, and wars in the morning paper rather than having them take over afternoon television. Legend has it that back in 1973, when the show was preempted by live coverage of the Watergate hearings in Congress, many fans went absolutely ballistic, particularly when the episodes aired revealing the fate of one of the Hortons, Mickey (played by John Clarke), after he had suffered a massive heart attack. Mickey was in real trouble. He was in critical condition and close to flatlining. He was rushed into the operating room for emergency bypass surgery, and his life teetered in the balance. Fans across the country were holding their breath and saying a prayer.

But what did viewers see as they awaited Mickey's fate? How about the latest testimony about the Watergate scandal? So many *Days* fans were seething. After all, they could find out about Nixon on the evening news. But they needed to know about Mickey *now!*

Fan Feedback

I'm so grateful for our fans and so moved by their commitment to the show. I love it when they recognize me on the street, and approach me for an autograph or just to say "hi." I don't mind sharing a few moments with them because that's part of my

job. So I try to be as generous with my time as possible. Also, I secretly like each opportunity to show fans that in "real life" I'm not at all like Sami.

Sometimes the circumstances of these encounters can be pretty funny. Fans may see me on the sidewalks of L.A., and they're just not prepared for bumping into a TV actress. They don't want to let me get away, but they don't know quite what to say, either. They need a few seconds just to sort out their thoughts so they can say what's on their mind. But in the meantime, they may stammer for a few seconds, or become just totally speechless! It always brings a smile to my face.

I really think it's so cool when people just want to tell me that they like Sami—or even that they *don't* like her—and that they're having so much fun watching the show. But before I have you believing that *all* of my encounters with fans are absolutely wonderful, let me set the record straight. Sometimes, they're *not* interested in singing our praises. Fans have cornered me in restaurants or clothing boutiques, and have really let me have it when they've been so inclined. They might blurt out something like, "I watch *Days* all the time and I *hate* you so much!" Geez! ☹

On occasion, I'm really startled by a comment like that. But after the initial shock, I realize that they're talking about Sami—(at least I hope they are!!)—and they're just taking me along for the ride!

I've gotta admit that there have been some incredibly awkward situations from time to time—but in retrospect, they're usually pretty funny. Imagine being in a public restroom at a restaurant, and fans recognizing you and wanting an autograph? Picture coming out of a bathroom stall, and finding some-

one standing there, waiting for you, pen and paper in hand, and dying to get your autograph. Face it: That's pretty uncomfortable!

At times, fans seem to forget that I'm a normal person just like them, and that I have a life and have feelings. At the same time, I understand that fans sometimes get excited when they meet an actor who they see on TV every day, and with very rare exceptions, they aren't being intentionally inconsiderate.

I've also got to thank my husband, Dave. He is so patient when we're together in public and fans approach me. He knows it's part of being an actress, and he's very supportive. It never seems to bother him—well, almost never. I remember once when a fan was particularly rude (probably unwittingly) and Dave became really irked. It was a few years ago when we were dating, and Dave and I were at a restaurant, waiting to be seated. We were having an "intimate moment," standing no more than a foot apart from one another. There was plenty of eye contact and electricity between the two of us.

Then out of nowhere, a fan appeared. She literally stepped right between Dave and me, with her back to Dave, as if he didn't exist! Not only did she start talking to me as if Dave weren't there, but she called me a "bitch" and in a raised voice, proclaimed, "I just *hate* you!" Now, I realized almost immediately that she was just joking, telling me how she felt about Sami. But she was a bit impolite, don't you think? Not to mention that Dave took a little longer to realize it wasn't his girlfriend this woman was attacking, but rather a *character* on TV. It took Dave a while to get used to that kind of attention, but these days he's an old hand at dealing with

fans. In fact, now he helps ease a fan's embarrassment and sets them at ease by offering up a pen for an autograph or suggesting that he take a photo of us together.

On other occasions, I've been out in public and really rushed, trying to get to a meeting or a doctor's appointment. In those cases, I always feel uncomfortable having to tell people, "I'd love to talk, but I really have to go." A few years ago, I remember being in such a huge hurry that I didn't even take the time to explain to a fan that I couldn't talk with her. I just headed for my car to dash to my appointment. Way to go, Ali!! Afterward, I felt just terrible. The fan seemed *so* disappointed! What would it have cost me to give her a smile and a very quick explanation of the appointment I had to get to? I really beat myself up about that one. As much as possible, I really make an effort now to give fans the time they deserve. If I only have five minutes, I'll explain why I'm in a rush, I'll take a moment to sign an autograph or take a picture, do my best to make it a positive experience for them, and then run along (in some cases, literally *run* along!).

I think I owe it to my fans to go the extra mile for them. With very rare exceptions, they've always been absolutely wonderful to me. More than 99 percent of the mail I get is from fans of *Days* who are totally supportive, and just want to reach out and tell me how they feel about the show and about Sami. I participated in an online chat not long ago, and more than 500,000 Sami-Fans logged on and took part. More than 25,000 unique new visitors access the Alison Sweeney website each week (for the uninitiated, check out *www.alisonsweeney.com*). I will never, *ever* take that fan interest and support for granted. ☺

But fans do get caught up in the story lines, and sometimes they just have to get things off their chest. Earlier in the book, I told you the story of the woman who approached me on the street during the episodes in which Sami had kidnapped her baby sister—and she swung her purse at me and yelled, "Give the baby back!" That's how emotionally involved people are in the show. To some of them, there doesn't seem to be a line between fantasy and reality.

By the way, when people stop me on the street, and tell me that they're big fans of *Days*, I often tell them that *I'm* a big fan of the show, too. I really am! When they describe what they love about the show, I often find myself nodding my head and thinking, "Me, too! I feel exactly the way you do!" I sometimes freak out, too, when I read the upcoming scripts and find out what kinds of predicaments the characters are getting caught up in next. It's as exciting for me as it is for you!

Celebrating *Days'* Fans

I think I can say the following not only for myself, but on behalf of every other actor on *Days*: You and all our other fans are so important to us, and we think it's important to *show* it, not just say it. That's why we hold an absolutely awesome Fan Weekend for *Days'* aficionados in Los Angeles each spring—usually in May or June—and about 600 fans each year can't wait to participate. There's a lot of chatter, a lot of laughter, a lot of hugs, and a lot of fun for both the cast and the fans. It's such a blast just hanging out with our loyal audience, in what

turns into a very, very long party! I hope you'll
come to one of these fan events sometime, and if
you do, you'll not only be able to meet and talk
with us, but you're liable to see us sing and dance
for you, too! ☺

What can you expect? Well, in the last few years,
the cast has gotten together and put on a live show
for the fans, displaying talents that you never see
on the TV show itself. In 2003, we put on a performance to remember—Kevin and Patrika's "Last
Blast"—in which all of us donned our dancing shoes
and entertained the crowd (and without even one
sprained ankle to show for it!). In earlier years, we
staged our own version of *Moulin Rouge*, which was
the brainstorm of Patrika Darbo (ex-Nancy) and
Kevin Spirtas (ex-Craig). In those shows, some of
us sang, some of us danced, and some did both
(those of us who aren't particularly stellar in either
category gave it our best shot, and sure had plenty
of fun doing it!). I remember how Ari Zuker (Nicole)
and I—and a few other brave *Days'* actresses—
sweated and strained for weeks (it seemed like
months!) to perfect two challenging dance numbers for *Moulin Rouge*. OK, as much as I love to
dance, maybe I was in a little over my head, but we
had such a spectacular time! The costumes were
great, and Ari and I loved playing dress-up and
dancing to those wonderful songs from *Moulin
Rouge.*

What else do we do on Fan Weekends? There is
an Official Breakfast for both the fans and the cast,
some great raffles, a lot of Q & A sessions, and plenty
of autograph signing and photo taking. In 2003, I
took part in Lauren Koslow (Kate Roberts) and
Josh Taylor's (ex-Roman Brady) Fan Breakfast, and
I think everyone could see how much Lauren and I

enjoy each other's company, which might come as a surprise because, on-screen, there's certainly no love lost between our characters, who always seem to have their daggers drawn whenever they're in the same story line. We joked with each other about hating the other's character, and shared with the audience how much we actually enjoy our fight scenes together. Lauren and I get along so well personally and professionally, and trust each other enough to really put our all into the catfights. We feel as though that's the key to the success of our vicious knock-down-drag-out confrontations: our friendship. Makes sense in a weird way, right?

We usually close out the Fan Weekends with a Jim Reynolds' (ex–Abe Carver) Charity Basketball Game. Sometimes members of the *Days* cast have played against one another, or we've competed against actors from other soaps. Other times, our team has played a local high school team (usually leading to a pretty ugly loss on our part—no surprise there!).

Now, I can be ridiculously competitive on the basketball court (although let me put Shaq's mind at ease—you have nothing to worry about!). In 2003, I ended up with an unsightly bruise on my arm from a little too much physical contact on the court, and a couple years before that, I sprained my ankle in the final minutes of the game—and it hurt so much. The ankle swelled up to the size of a baseball—no, make that a softball!—and for the next few days back at work, I had to limp around on the set. It was such a pathetic sight! As I explained (in good fun) on my website in the aftermath of that "carnage," in which a bunch of us ended up falling over one another, there was plenty of debate over who was to blame for that pile of actors

stacked on top of one another at center court! Justin (Melvey, ex-Colin) insisted upon his innocence (yeah, right!), but there were witnesses who claimed that he got a little carried away playing rugby rather than basketball. I think Frank Parker (Grandpa Shawn), who ended up somewhere in the pile, and I bore the brunt of the melee.

I'm pretty "smiled out" by the end of the Fan Weekend. The fans are so incredible; many fly in from across the country (and in some cases the world!). We have such a blast! We'll continue to have these weekend events for as long as our loyal viewers want them, and let me tell you, there's not the slightest sign of any waning interest. (See you there next spring!)

Throughout the year, the cast of *Days* participates in other extracurricular endeavors as well, all of them aimed at meeting and entertaining our fans. I remember a trip to South Carolina not long ago where the *Days* cast got to meet with fans and play a softball game. As I said, I'm competitive and want to win, but I hadn't picked up a bat since the seventh grade. I tried honing my "skills" by taking some last-minute batting practice before the game started, but here's the truth: It really didn't help much. Yes, I actually hit the ball during the game, but the New York Yankees didn't come calling afterward! At least we won the game! (There I go, showing my competitive side again!)

Almost the whole cast participates in these special events throughout the year. From charity walka-thons to mall-signings . . . we travel throughout the country signing autographs and meeting fans from all over. The guys (hunks) have the busiest personal appearance schedule—sometimes they

are out of town every weekend doing events. We all have gotten pretty familiar with the airports around the U.S. from all the traveling we do. But the whole experience just reinforces how unique the relationship is between our characters and the fans. And I like to think that Sami has certainly struck a chord with the *Days* audience. After all, when fans vote you an Emmy Award for Favorite Villain, which happened to me in 2002, you know that your character really is stirring up the passions of viewers and leaving some of them seething. Fans have told me that they've actually used their TV sets for target practice, throwing any object within reach at the screen during my scenes—or firing off an obscene word or two when Sami has really infuriated them ("bitch" seems to be a particular favorite among Sami haters!!).

The chat boards can be just as amazing. When I check out the *Days* bulletin boards on America Online, for example, some fans really let loose on Sami (or as some of them call her, "Scami"). I guess they figure they're completely anonymous when they're online, and they don't hold anything back! They have their say and can be pretty cruel, that's for sure (I'm not joking about that!). But again, I realize that they're just letting off steam about my character, not about me—and I know Sami can be pretty irritating at times. So I try not to take it personally.

Because of the kind of person that Sami is—creating her own style of mayhem in Salem, year after year—I'm not surprised at the good-natured venom. (In a way, it shows that I'm doing my job well!) Sometimes, when I'm rehearsing or taping a scene in which Sami is being particularly bitchy, I'm some-

times thinking, "Man, Sami's going to get viewers screaming at their TV screens today!" It makes playing her all the more fun!

An International Following

While it's on my mind, here's something else you may find interesting about *Days* fans. I've found that when I travel overseas, the interest in *Days* seems to tag along with me. The show is an international phenomenon, not confined just to the United States.

During the Christmas holidays in 2002, James Reynolds (ex-James Carver), Matt Cedeno (ex-Brandon Walker), and I took part in a USO tour overseas, just months before the start of the war in Iraq. We flew from Kennedy Airport in New York to Madrid, and then traveled farther into Europe to spend time with the troops stationed in the Mediterranean before they shipped out to the Persian Gulf. It was an amazing experience. We stayed on a military base and slept in officers' quarters (not fancy, but not bad!). It was so cool to hang out with the soldiers and sign autographs for them—and I was so proud of every one of them. We spent Christmas Day with them, and we even served them Christmas dinner. They were so appreciative—and they were also so young! I was twenty-six years old at the time, and I was older than most of them. We're so lucky to have these men and women who serve our country, and I made sure they knew how grateful Americans are for what they're doing for us.

Jim and I went on a USO tour again in 2003,

with Kyle Brandt (Philip) and Eric Winter (Rex). You'll have to read about it on my website. . . . Oh, and I've got tons of photos from both tours posted on my site as well.

In traveling to other parts of the world, I've learned just how universal the appeal of the show has become. Of course, *Days* is watched by millions of people in the United States each day, and it is taped in Burbank, California, at NBC Studios. But eyes around the world watch our show, with a little help from subtitles or voice dubbing. *Days* has fans in all parts of the globe, from Paris to Rome, from Melbourne to Montreal to Jamaica. It really is quite amazing, and we have huge ratings in some of these countries. In fact, I've been recognized in the most unlikely places!

Here's a funny example. In October 2002, Dave and I vacationed in Europe. It was a great trip, and we started with five days in Paris. It was the first time we had been to Paris and some of the sights just took our breath away. We spent almost an entire day in Versailles, where the gardens and the palace are truly stunning. We went to the Louvre and visited Notre Dame.

I haven't mentioned the Eiffel Tower yet because I've saved the best 'til last! It is so amazing to see it in person—even more magnificent than I had imagined—and when we went to the top of the Tower, the view was absolutely spectacular (What tourist could pass that up!). We even ate dinner in the Eiffel Tower.

Now the reason for this story: Dave and I were waiting in line to take the elevator up the Tower. The line was very long, and it snaked back and forth so you saw the same people again and again as you gradually moved closer to the elevator. And

one by one, people started to recognize me (I wasn't wearing much makeup that day, and I would have preferred to have remained totally anonymous—it always seems to happen that way, Murphy's law or something). A couple of German tourists recognized me first. Then people from Singapore. And Frenchmen. And several Americans. Well, all of them had their cameras with them because they were visiting one of the most popular tourist attractions in the world—and a lot of them wanted their picture taken with me. That was fine with me, of course—although things did take a rather unusual twist. As the line wound back and forth, and I kept seeing the same tourists again and again, even those people who didn't have a clue who I was began asking to take a picture with me. (None of them asked, "Who are you again?" but they might have been thinking it!) They figured they'd take a picture with a celebrity—even if they had no idea how or why I might be well known. It was a little embarrassing—but pretty funny!

Now, one piece of advice: If you're going to be traveling to Paris, I don't recommend that you spend a lot of time in your hotel room, switching the television dial, looking for *Days of Our Lives*. (Even though I love *Days*, I have to acknowledge that there might be more exciting things to do if you ever get to Paris!!) But if TV happens to be your thing, you'll definitely be able to watch the show there. I did some press interviews with French magazines, so I spent a lot of time thinking and talking about *Days*. I found out that it comes on at 8:30 in the morning—and it airs without commercials. The last day we were in Paris, I watched the show in our hotel room, and there all of us were— *speaking French* (thanks to the art of dubbing). It

was actually hilarious. (I even taped it on my camcorder for posterity!) In the episode I saw, there was a scene at Johnny Rocket's with Sami, Austin, Roman, and Carrie, talking in voices that weren't ours, and in a language that none of us spoke. To add to the entertainment value of the experience, French television doesn't air the most recent *Days* episodes—I saw a three-year-old show that day. Actors no longer on *Days* were in the episode. And we all looked *so* young!! Totally weird!

Chapter

8

Back to show memories: 1993–2002: Sami and Austin. Austin and Sami. Lives intertwined, for seemingly forever.

Almost from the beginning of my life on *Days*, Sami was obsessed with Austin Reed. He was her true love. She wanted desperately to have a life with him. She dreamed and schemed and was determined to have him for her own.

So who was this guy Austin? And why was Sami so preoccupied with him?

I think answers to questions like these will help you understand Sami a little better and will certainly show you the kind of character I've been playing for all these years. You can find so much of what makes Sami tick in the enduring relationship (or obsession) she has had with this one man. So let's spend a few pages unraveling the Sami–Austin relationship, and learn something about Sami in the process, including the challenges I've encoun-

tered and the fun I've had playing her for more
than ten years.

The Austin Saga Begins

If you're a longtime *Days* fan, you know that Austin
(played first by Patrick Muldoon, then by Austin
Peck) came from a difficult background—a divorced
family and an abusive father who was hooked on
drugs. Somehow, Austin emerged carrying very little emotional baggage (at least it seemed that way)
when he showed up in Salem in 1992, about a year
before Sami returned to town. Over the ensuing
years, their lives became entangled in one intriguing plot line after another.

*(OK, here we go again—more story lines. If you're al-
ready up to speed on everything you'd ever want to know
about Austin and Sami, just fast forward to Chapter 9
and spare yourself the smallest details.)*

Early on, from the time she was only fifteen,
Sami fantasized about being a part of Austin's life.
It became a fixation. It became her obsession. But
almost from the start, there was a major obstacle in
her way, coming from someone who also had the
last name "Brady." Sami's sister, Carrie, had fallen
in love with Austin, and in fact, Carrie and Austin
planned to be married.

The thing is, Sami started out trying to encourage the two to be together. See, Carrie was horri-
bly scarred when a loan shark tried to throw acid
on Austin—it hit Carrie instead. She was so insecure about her scar that she tried to break up with
Austin. Sami did everything she could think of to
get her sister back into Austin's arms—I know what

you're thinking: "*Sami?* Trying to *help?*" But, yes . . . it's true! And it worked, Carrie and Austin eventually reunited, and Sami was happy for them, though she never got over her teenage crush.

So when did it all go bad, you ask? Well, this creepy guy Alan came on the scene. He was obsessed with Carrie, and tried to kidnap and rape her on several occasions. When Austin rescued Carrie from Alan's clutches, he turned his evil attentions on Sami as a consolation prize. With no man to rescue her, Sami became a victim of Alan's obsession, and was date-raped by him. (I'll write more about this in the next chapter.)

Skipping ahead a little, Lucas finally discovered the truth about what had taken place and helped Sami tell her family what had happened to help her. Carrie was determined that Sami seek justice, even though Sami was violently opposed to airing the whole story in public. Carrie promised Sami that justice would be served and Alan would go to jail. But that's not what happened. Just as Sami had feared, Alan got off, and the end result was Sami's name (and photos) splashed on the front page of the tabloids. Humiliated, Sami held her half-sister responsible for not keeping her promise— forcing her into the spotlight and embarrassing her. That was the beginning of the end of Sami and Carrie's sisterly bond.

Don't you love how I'm telling the story lines as if these are real people? In some ways, Sami, Lucas, Austin, and Carrie are like real people to me—I don't know, maybe like in an alternate universe or something! I've been a part of Salem for so long now that sometimes I forget how outrageous some of this stuff can sound to other people. (Maybe I should talk to Dr. Phil!)

Sorry for digressing. Now back to our story:

With Austin committed to Carrie, most sisters would have backed away. But did Sami? After the Alan experience, Sami decided Carrie wasn't "good enough" for Austin and decided to pursue him herself. As you know, Sami's on her own planet when it comes to dealing with love.

Maybe you remember that both Sami and Austin lived in the same apartment building on Guilford Street (I didn't know Sami lived on Guilford Street. I had to look it up!) and—forever scheming—she used every opportunity to win his attention. When her air conditioner broke down, she convinced Austin to fix it. When her plumbing needed repairs, Austin got the call. She'd call him to claim that Alan was after her again. You get the picture, she stopped at nothing.

But Austin wasn't a fool. He figured out what Sami was up to. Yet that didn't stop Sami's conniving—of course not. Her devious actions only got more creative. Sami certainly wasn't about to allow Austin to spend too much time in someone else's arms, particularly her sister's. And anyway, she simply wasn't very fond of Carrie . . . Okay, she detested her! Blood just hasn't run too deep in the Brady family, and the battle over Austin was enough to drive Sami toward behaviors that bordered on the bizarre. She wanted Austin all to herself, and she'd do whatever it took. It was all so crazy.

The Chase After Austin

Here's one thing all of us have learned during the years that I've played Sami: When she sets her mind to something, she won't let anything stand in her

way. She even slipped a drug into Austin's drink at the Cheatin' Heart, and then tricked him into having sex with her at her apartment. Poor Sami, she was actually convinced that after sleeping with her once, Austin would fall in love with her. Well, that didn't happen. Just to show you how complicated things got, a heavily drugged Austin thought he was actually making love with Carrie instead (Sami even doused herself in Carrie's perfume to help lure him into bed!). Once Austin realized what had actually happened, he ran back to Carrie, and made Sami promise never to tell her sister that they had made love.

Well, Sami was devastated by this turn of events. No one was better at self-pity than Sami, and feeling that her world was collapsing around her, she fled Salem.

As for Lucas, he and Sami went way back (to 1993, to be exact), and had a rather auspicious beginning when, at a rock concert, Sami and Carrie stumbled upon Lucas getting out of bed with a rock star named Cherish. Later, Sami ran into him when he was dressed in full military-school uniform, appearing as preppy as it was possible to look. But Sami had his number from the start; she remembered him very vividly from their encounter at the rock concert.

Lucas and Sami became close friends (he also happened to be Austin's half-brother), and initially Sami saw him as a way to make Austin jealous. As great comrades, Lucas and Sami often schemed together. In fact, they worked together to break up Carrie and Austin—Lucas wanted Carrie, and Sami wanted Austin. Perfect, right? Wrong! Lucas (in his full military uniform) agreed to take Sami to a local dance, where she knew that Austin would see them

together. In her own clueless imagination, she pictured him becoming furious, and demanding to have Sami for his own.

A side note: Bryan (Lucas) took me to a real school dance—which I'll discuss in more detail later.

Back to the story: In the aftermath of Sami's sexual liaison with Austin, Lucas did more than soothe her emotional pain and help her in her scheme to win the attention of Austin. While Lucas and Sami were plotting together, he had become a true friend and confidant of Sami's, and—you guessed it—Lucas and Sami ended up sleeping with one another. (That sure took her mind off Austin, at least for the moment!) Here's how it happened:

Sami had tried to seduce Austin before resorting to the "drugged drink" routine. When he turned her down flat, she began to beat herself up over it, telling herself that she wasn't pretty enough and that no one loved her. To console herself, she headed for a bar (at the tender age of seventeen), was turned down when she tried to order a drink, and then became the target of some heckling (and a spilled beer on her shirt), courtesy of a group of unruly guys at the bar. Sami was becoming frightened when Lucas unexpectedly appeared and came to her rescue, escorting her from the bar.

Poor Sami.

She and Lucas ended up at the Titan Photo Lab, where she put on Carrie's bowling shirt since hers was drenched with beer. And then Sami proceeded to cry a river—with Lucas as her audience—telling him how no one's ever going to love her. Lucas began to console her, saying, "I love you; you're my best friend." Well, in the ensuing minutes, they became *very* friendly—and ended up

making love. It really wasn't a romantic thing (believe it or not)—it was more a show of friendship and demonstrating how close they were.

Well, guess who walked in on them? Austin showed up, saw Sami's blonde hair and a shirt with Carrie's name on it, and assumed that Carrie and Lucas had slept together. He was mistaken, of course, but the confusion of identities couldn't have made Sami any happier! Sami became immediately revitalized, convincing herself that Austin would leave Carrie and (of course) want to be with Sami. Now, she had a chance with Austin—or at least that's what she thought. So she put the drug in his drink, fully expecting him to fall madly in love with her after realizing they'd made love.

You can almost imagine what happened next, right? Sami had become pregnant. But who was the father of the baby? Lucas? Or Austin?

Sami convinced herself that Austin had impregnated her—and she was absolutely thrilled. Still, the question lingered in Salem: Could it be Lucas's baby instead?

I'll discuss Sami's incredible pregnancy in a moment, but suffice it to say that she was quite content believing that Austin was her baby's father, and never sought any tests to prove it one way or the other. Even after the baby was born, she lived with the belief (or was it a fantasy?) that her beloved son Will was Austin's.

Now, I know what you're asking: If you didn't follow *Days* when these episodes aired, you're probably wondering whether—in the insane world of Sami—was Austin the actual father of her baby? Well, not really! Sami's world began to turn upside down when Will was two years old, and he and his stroller accidentally ended up in the river. Carrie

leaped into the water and saved his life, and he ended up in the hospital (don't most kids in Salem spend time hospitalized with a serious illness or trauma?). While he was in the hospital, Sami saw the results of routine blood tests conducted on Will, and was stunned by the results. She realized that Austin was not Will's father—Lucas was.

Well, Sami was determined to perpetuate the lie. She promised herself that no one else would ever learn who the father of her child was. No one would ever know that Austin was not the real father. Absolutely no one.

In the true tradition of soaps, however, the truth did come out on the day of Sami's wedding to Austin, no less (I'll get to that story later). Anyway, when Lucas finally learned that his night of love-making with Sami had produced a baby, he became furious. (Carrie gave her a solid right hook across the jaw—that's still a fan-favorite moment!—and I'll write more about that unforgettable punch later.) After all, Lucas was upset not only because he had been deprived of enjoying the first two years of his son's life, but also because Will believed that Austin was his dad. And Sami had used Austin's love for Will to drive a wedge between Austin and Carrie.

Lucas became almost crazed with anger. He couldn't contain his contempt for Sami. He became just the latest in a long string of Salemites whom Sami had manipulated and antagonized.

The 11-Month Pregnancy

Okay, let me tell you, I am exhausted from trying to keep that whole story straight in my head. And

I'll admit I had to look up more than a few incidents to include all those details. But let's step back for a moment and talk about Sami's pregnancy. When we taped that story line, it turned into one of the more challenging periods of my time on *Days*. I was only 19 years old, and let me tell you, portraying a pregnant woman was unlike anything I've ever done in front of the cameras.

Let's put this into context: I do plan to have children myself some day, and I really look forward to the experience of carrying a child for nine months. Of course, on *Days* I wasn't really pregnant—I was just playing a pregnant woman on TV. So to look the part, the wardrobe department created a padded undergarment for me to wear. A *heavily* padded undergarment. It was *very* uncomfortable . . . both physically and in other ways, too.

As I've mentioned—and will discuss in much more detail later in the book—I've struggled with my own weight at various times in my life, including while I've been on *Days*. And with body image in mind, I've got to admit that it was *definitely* horrifying to see myself in the mirror with a big, padded belly. Of course, I knew that it really wasn't my own stomach that was getting bigger. But as they added more padding every few weeks, it didn't do much for my weight-conscious ego.

Every few weeks, I'd go to the wardrobe department and find that an extra pad had been added to the undergarment. Just what I needed! There were moments, particularly as I'd really become completely immersed in my character and the pregnancy, I sometimes would actually get frightened (as in: "I can't believe this is happening to me"). By the end of the "pregnancy," all I needed was a fake white beard and a red outfit, and I could have

worked as a department store Santa Claus during my off-hours! I was absolutely huge! (If you're a mom, I really don't have to explain this to you, do I?)

By the way, did I mention that I may have also set a record by having the first 11-month-long pregnancy on television (or probably anywhere else, for that matter)? That's right—11 months! The actual taping of these *Days* episodes extended over an 11-month period—more than a pregnancy would last in real life, of course. But fans of the show never complained about the time discrepancy—either they were so caught up in the story line that they didn't notice, or they were so intrigued with Sami's pregnancy that they didn't want it to end. And at times it seemed like it never would!

As you can imagine, when Sami finally gave birth, she was ready for the baby to arrive (or at least I was!). But nothing is easy in Sami's life, and those delivery scenes were pretty challenging. Sami ended up being all alone in her parents' old house, in her old bedroom, when she went into labor. The phones weren't plugged in, so she couldn't reach anyone or call for help. So there she was, terribly frightened as she went through several cycles of agonizing labor pains.

Fortunately, Sami was finally discovered by Austin, and was rushed to the hospital. But her ordeal continued (and how well I still remember it!). She endured a full two episodes of additional labor in the hospital, with no end in sight. Finally, and mercifully, her obstetrician interceded and decided that an emergency C-section needed to be performed.

Amazing, isn't it? It was *so soap* to go through four episodes of absolutely agonizing labor and then have a C-section.

By the way, these "labor" scenes are always difficult to shoot. For one thing, as a 19-year-old actress, I had absolutely NO idea what real labor felt like for a woman. All I had to base my performance on was movies I'd seen. There was a makeup artist standing just offstage, ready to spritz me with water to make me "sweaty" . . . and then I was practically hyperventilating with all the heavy breathing and screaming I was doing. At the end of those days of shooting, I was exhausted and definitely wary of the whole process. Dave and I certainly want to have children some day, but hopefully my real-life experience won't be anywhere as strenuous as Sami's!

Austin at the Altar

The unusual relationship among Sami, Austin, Lucas, and Carrie just kept getting more entangled. And all the while, the role of Sami continued to be so much fun to play. Each time I'd pick up a new script, I'd be on the edge of my seat, wondering what kind of quicksand she and the others would be sinking into next. And along the way, it was such a blast to be in so many scenes with such great actors and good friends—Christie Clark (Carrie), Bryan Dattilo (Lucas), and of course Austin Peck (Austin).

Let me give you an example of how the lives of these four characters were so often intertwined. As I mentioned, Lucas had taken a liking to Carrie, and at one point he started doing some plotting of his own. He told Sami that if she would just lose a little weight, and pursue Austin more aggressively,

she could drive a wedge between Carrie and Austin—clearing a path for Lucas to win Carrie's attention. (Just what I needed—someone to tell me to go on a diet! Give me a break!)

The thought of chasing after and snaring Austin sounded wonderful to Sami, of course. But as always, things didn't go according to plan—at least not the plan that Sami had in mind. In fact, before the plot could play out, Carrie and Austin decided to get married—and Sami was absolutely beside herself. The wedding was all set for St. Luke's Roman Catholic Church—the same church where Marlena and Roman had been married a decade earlier.

If you were watching in 1995, you might remember Carrie and Austin walking down the aisle in their gorgeous, elegant wedding. The weddings on *Days* really are something to behold. (They draw a huge viewership, and they're fun for the actors, too.) The best part is, you never know if a wedding in Salem is actually going to take place—more often than not some terrible event takes place to stop the proceedings. This one, of course, was no exception. Sami had run away from home days after sleeping with Austin (and Lucas). Lucas found her barely surviving in Seattle (of all places) and brought her back to Salem just in time to have her appear at her sister's wedding. But seeing Austin marrying her next of kin was more than she could bear. So she took action, as only Sami could!

Compliments of Sami, one small unexpected glitch arose during the Carrie–Austin nuptials. Never one to refrain from creating bedlam in other people's lives, Sami chose the ceremony itself to make an announcement guaranteed to ruin even the best-laid wedding-day plans: She faked a fainting

spell (a common soap pregnancy syndrome!) and
when she "came to" she told the gathering that the
groom (aka Austin) was the father of her baby!
That's right—it happened right there during the
ceremony, before the vows could be completed.

Well, it wasn't true, of course. Austin was *not* the
baby's father. But who can be bothered with facts
at a time like this! That wedding day would definitely be something to remember.

Sami at Her Worst

Sami's manipulations were barely beginning. Without spending the better part of this book recount-
ing every last detail (I think I've done enough
recapping already), suffice it to say that the scripts
sure kept me busy with one Sami psychodrama
after another. Sami worked hard to persuade Austin
that he really was Will's father. Then all of their
lives took a bizarre twist when the baby was kidnapped by Sami's neighbor and ended up in Europe.
Ever the schemer, Sami convinced Austin that the
best way to get the child home was for Sami and
Austin to go through a marriage ceremony. So in
Paris, Sami and Austin actually tied the knot (although if Austin had known the truth at the time,
he might have decided that the knot would fit better on a noose around Sami's conniving neck!).
Sami, of course, was ecstatic with this turn of events,
and when Austin agreed to marry her, she finally
felt she could claim the trophy that she had sought
since she first set eyes on him. But as for Austin, he
was much more inclined to consider his marriage

to Sami as one of convenience, simply for the sake of Will and his safe return home. He didn't show much interest in consummating his marriage with Sami on their wedding night, and much to her chagrin, the marriage was eventually annulled.

Meanwhile, Carrie and Austin ultimately did get married, but somehow we knew that their legal union wouldn't last forever, nor would Sami ever accept a life without Austin. That's just not Sami's style. When I saw the next few scripts, I realized how correct I was. Marriage license or not, Sami was determined to destroy the Carrie–Austin bond, and I braced myself to play Sami as she had never been seen before.

The scriptwriters sure didn't disappoint. Sami started by getting a hotel room next to Carrie and Austin's honeymoon suite, and in behavior that might have qualified her for a job with the CIA, she spied on them having sex. At one point, she even concealed herself under their bed (could it get any kinkier?!).

Shall I continue? There were several false starts that could have brought Sami and Austin back together, perhaps for good. (Wait—is anything "for good" in Salem?) However, there were always unexpected, last-minute speed bumps that arose in Sami's path that disrupted any fantasies that she had for a lifelong relationship with Austin. As recently as 2002, Sami was once again on the brink of marrying Austin, this time in Las Vegas. She had finally won the man of her dreams, the man she had been chasing for years—or at least that's what she thought. But just before the couple was about to recite their wedding vows, Austin overheard Sami talking to Lucas, and describing all of her deceit

and lies to win Austin's heart. My line (or actually Sami's) was, "Austin's never going to find out the truth. He believed me then and he'll believe me now!"

Well, Sami, not exactly. Austin was stunned by Sami's unwitting confession, and their wedding plans dissolved instantly. The next step was an easy one for Austin: He stood her up at the altar, furious over her dishonesty and ignoring her desperate pleas for forgiveness. There were two episodes where a heartbroken Sami fruitlessly begged Austin to take her back, pleading, "I don't regret what I did because I did it for love. I did it because I love you."

That girl is really something, isn't she? Austin turned a deaf ear, rode out of town, and left Sami to bake alone in the Las Vegas sun. The best part of it for those viewers who find watching Sami as appealing as the sound of fingernails on a chalkboard is that she always does it to herself. It's such beautiful justice that her own words did her in, silencing her smugness, at least for a while.

Sibling Rivalry to the Max

As you've already surmised, Carrie and Sami were like oil and water. It's hard to think of two sisters who had more contempt for one another (and so different than the relationship I had with my two real-life brothers). Christie Clark (who played Carrie) and I are actually friends in real life—when I first started on the show, she was like an older sister who took care of me—but you'd never know it by

our bitter on-screen relationship and an occasional slap, smack, or slug here and there.

Of course, Sami has been involved in many other feuds along the way, including her long-time battle with Kate (played by Lauren Koslow), who more than once tried to expose Sami for her many schemes—although most of the time, Sami was able to tap-dance her way out of it, somehow turning the tables to make Kate look bad for saying the things she did. *(My personal take is that Kate and Sami have always been similar types of people. So that means that they'll either be best friends or they'll hate each other. In this case, Salem wasn't big enough for both of them, and their nonstop feud was almost inevitable.)*

But back to that memorable *Days* scene when Sami's scheming for Austin became more than Carrie could stand, and she unloaded on Sami with a slap heard 'round the world—or at least 'round TV sets in every part of the world! The truth can be told that Christie and I rehearsed that slap sequence a number of times, and she was never supposed to make contact with my cheek. During the rehearsal, we moved at what is called "half speed," showing the cameramen what was going to happen so they'd be able to follow the action. In true Hollywood fashion, Christie was supposed to swing, miss my face by at least two or three inches, and I was supposed to stumble backward like Muhammad Ali had just landed a right jab on my chin (fortunately, thanks to camera angles and good acting, you don't have to actually strike someone to make it look like the real thing). Well, everything went fine in rehearsals—but with the camera rolling and the bright lights turned on, it was a different story. We had never practiced the scene standing on our

marks (I realized afterwards), and when it really counted, Christie was closer to me than she had been during our practice sessions. So when she swung, my face got in the way of her hand's trajectory.

Christie's hand planted a hard slap right onto my cheek. I certainly wasn't expecting to be hit, and it literally spun me around. I lost my balance and tumbled over. On the way to the floor, my head banged into a nearby piano. I may have used a four-letter word or two on my way down. (If I did, I plead "temporary insanity"!)

Now, in the script, I was supposed to be knocked out cold by Carrie's slap. Well, for a few moments there, I wondered whether method acting had come to *Days*, and whether I was really about to lose consciousness!

Of course, it wasn't intentional (Right, Christie?). While I'm at it, I must tell you that Bryan (my dear, sweet, supportive friend) thought it was hysterical that I was cursing like a sailor. He literally ran off the set holding his hand over his mouth so that I wouldn't hear him laughing at me! I have managed to forgive him for his treacherous behavior, and now I definitely have a sense of humor about the whole thing. But the camera guys still tease me about it.

Before the piano stopped resonating, production called a "five." Once I regrouped, we reshot the scene, and this time it went according to plan (for which I'm eternally grateful!). Take two was the one that audiences saw when the show aired. In the meantime, if you ever need a sparring partner, Christie might be a perfect choice!

Driving Sami up the Wall

I know that over the years, Sami has deserved her share of slaps (as well as a clenched fist or two on occasion). But perhaps nothing can compare to the pounding she took from Austin—or to be more accurate, from Austin's car. Now, playing Sami, I'm used to portraying a character who lives life on the edge. I've been called on to do a lot of crazy things in Sami-land, but when they told me that I'd be hit by a car driven by Austin—or, more accurately, hit by his car *twice!*—it did get my attention.

Poor Sami really was hit by Austin's car and slammed into a wall. It happened on New Year's Eve, not long after Sami had decided to take Austin's car and he had reported it stolen. She finally returned it to the police station, where Austin retrieved it. But as he drove away, the car accidentally shifted into reverse and struck Sami, propelling her into the wall—more than once! (I can only imagine what Sami's New Year's resolution was at that moment—perhaps just to live to see January 2nd!)

Now, by this point, fans were very familiar with (and perhaps sick of) Sami and her insane shenanigans, and probably some of them would have loved to have seen Austin's car screeching at about 90 miles per hour or more right at me. In fact, you won't believe some of the letters I received after that episode. One of my "fans" wrote, "Too bad he didn't hit you a third time!" (Ah, the warm feelings that Sami stirs in our viewers!)

Sami did survive her run-in with Austin's car, but

just barely. She underwent emergency surgery at Salem University Hospital, had a near-death experience that would give anyone the shivers, and finally awoke from her coma, thanks in part to a guilt-ridden Austin sitting for hours by her bedside. When she awoke, she was suffering from amnesia and temporary paralysis below the waist.

Let me tell you, lying in that hospital bed playing a critically injured Sami was a real challenge. Every day, I was fitted with bandages around my head, a collar around my neck, needles in my arm, IV drips overhead and an oxygen tube helping me breathe. For weeks, my most stylish attire was a hospital gown!

It wasn't exactly how you picture glamorous soaps!

During this time, as Sami struggled with amnesia, she convinced Austin to marry her for the sake of Will, who she believed to be their son (at least at the moment). But when her memory returned, and she realized that Austin hadn't fathered her baby after all, she decided to fake that she still had amnesia—and we were on our way toward another of *Days'* famous wedding days.

Plans for that Sami-Austin wedding actually moved forward, right up to the day of the ceremony. But just moments before their marriage was to become official and with Sami dressed in an absolutely gorgeous wedding gown, Carrie burst into the chapel to halt the proceedings and deliver a literal knockout punch to Sami's wedding plans—and to her cheek![3] Carrie and Eric (Sami's twin) had unearthed the information that Lucas, not Austin, was really

---

3. No actresses were injured in the shooting of this scene.

Will's father. As you can guess, after Carrie's slap the wedding plans instantly dissolved.

As I've written, Lucas was furious about being deceived. When he learned that he, not Austin, was the father, he made a decision that would create absolute chaos in Sami's life: He fought for the custody of little Will. I'm sure the lawyers on both sides—and their bank accounts—couldn't have been happier with all the legal maneuvering!

Up on the Roof

If you need any more examples of Sami's manipulating mind, let me take you back in time to one of my favorite Sami schemes, designed to drive Carrie and Austin apart. It unfolded when the couple was already having trouble in their relationship, largely because of Sami's conniving (there's a surprise!). At one point, Carrie and Austin arranged to meet on their apartment building roof at exactly midnight on New Year's Eve. They decided that if one of them didn't show up, they'd know that their relationship was over.

Well, in a bit of skillful eavesdropping, Sami overheard them making their plan, and she immediately devised a sinister plot: She snuck into Austin's apartment, and changed his clocks so he would show up on the roof an hour after midnight—long after Carrie had come and gone. And that's exactly what happened. Carrie arrived on the roof at midnight, found herself alone, and returned to her room brokenhearted over the apparent end of her relationship with Austin. Sami came by to "console" her sister, although in no time, Lucas burst

into the apartment, obviously drunk. Within minutes, he passed out and the girls put him in Carrie's bed.

That's when Sami's wild conniving took over. She slipped a sleeping pill into her sister's glass of New Year's champagne, and when Carrie collapsed, she dragged her into bed next to Lucas. Before long, Austin arrived at Carrie's apartment, and Sami made sure that he saw Lucas and Carrie in bed together. Austin was stunned. In his mind, not only did Carrie not show up on the roof at midnight, but she had decided to sleep with Lucas instead! That caused plenty of agony between Carrie and Austin until they figured out what Sami had done.

It is so much fun doing scenes like that—putting drugs in people's drinks and dragging Christie Clark across the floor to the bed. These just aren't things that happen in real life (thank goodness!).

Other Men, Other Mayhem

Even though Austin was the man who Sami obsessed over for years, there have been other men in her life, which has given me the chance to do plenty of romantic scenes with other cast members of *Days*. How about Brandon Walker (played by Matt Cedeno) for example? In one story line back in 2000, Brandon and Sami schemed to infiltrate the mob that hung out at a local strip club, all as part of a greater (and elaborate) plan that would ruin Lucas's credibility and give Sami sole custody of Will. Brandon came up with the idea that he'd play a pimp, and Sami would dress up as a hooker in order to penetrate the circle of gangsters. To

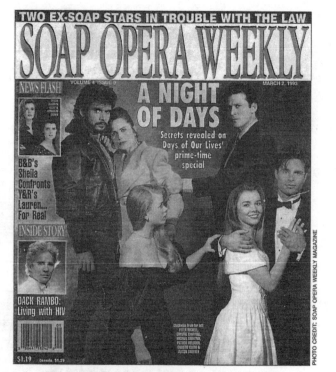

This is my first *Soap* magazine cover shoot ever.
I have to laugh, thinking back on how my parents
were horrified by how revealing my dress was!

Shooting "Alan the rapist" was my first big story on *Days*. What an entrance.

Austin Peck took over the role of "Austin" in 1995.
Christie and I both thought he was such a hunk!

FAMILY TREES FOR ALL THE SHOWS!

FEBRUARY 13, 1996

SOAP OPERA DIGEST

SHOCKING DAYS AHEAD

- **Watch Out For Billie!**
- **John & Marlena...**
- **Sami Gets Her Man**

$2.69

07

0 14014 18207 2

WEDDING PREVIEW

WHO WILL SAY "I DO"

Here's the classic Sami cover line – Sami spent nine
years chasing after Austin!

Bryan, Christie and I worked
together for almost nine years.
Austin was there for almost seven.
It's amazing how time flies, huh?

Why ③ Stars Really Left

JUNE 4, 1996

SOAP OPERA DIGEST

VCR ALERT: Can't-Miss Episodes!

DAYS OF OUR LIVES
Watch Out, Sami...
You're About To Get Caught!

$2.69

Soaps' Worst Boyfriends

I never spent a lot of time at photo shoots—Sami was either smirking or unhappy!

Yup—Sami pulling the strings. Can you believe that "lion's mane" of hair? All I can say is it was the '90s!

A huge part of Sami's character are her insecurities. I've always been able to hide mine in my character

As Sami continued to wreak havoc in Salem, I grew up and started showing a more mature side of myself and my character.

Sami's big breakthrough. Her time on death row really turned Sami into a woman. Sami's execution was one of the most challenging stories I've had to play on *Days*.

You'll notice in this photo I have very little
makeup on. I really wanted Sami to seem
as young and "innocent" as possible.
Though soaps are famous for actresses
always looking glamorous, I wanted to have
as little makeup as I could through all these
scenes. The makeup department was thrilled
that I wanted to stay "real"!

I laughed when I first saw the cover line. "Size Matters" could be misinterpreted, but once reading the article, fans saw that I was very openly discussing my weight loss and how difficult it is to struggle with diet.

Woman's World was the perfect opportunity to spread my message to more fans. I feel so strongly about promoting a healthy mental image for women, and I was glad to have this opportunity.

SPECIAL EDITION $1.99

soap OPERA digest
THE TRUE INSIDER GUIDE

MAY 21, 2002

THE Diet ISSUE

- Before And After Photos
- Secrets To Dressing "Thin"
- How Actresses Drop Pregnancy Pounds
- Plus-Size Star: Live A Little!

Talk Of Return For GH's Vanessa Marcil!

PLUS! EMMY SPECIAL!

DAYS's Alison Sweeney Cried When Fans Called Her Fat. LOOK AT HER NOW!

Display Until 5/24/02
$1.99 Canada $1.99

21 >

8 75470 08185 9

Soap Opera Digest has always been a big supporter, and I was thrilled to be offered the chance to talk about my weight loss and what the fan reaction had been like.

Austin always used to tickle me when we were doing really serious poses at photo shoots. It's funny to me how "serious" we all look here since I know we were laughing between each shot.

Matt Cedeno and I had such fun working together. He is such a great guy, a talented actor and let's face it– a total hottie!

I posed for *L.A. Brides* during my engagement to Dave. It was so much fun trying on all different types of wedding gowns to help me figure out which one I wanted in real life.

This is the first "Lumi" cover! Bryan and I did a really fun set-up at the shoot where we got to spray water hoses at each other. We had so much fun soaking each other!

Fired DAYS Star Returns!

www.soapoperadigest.com

soap OPERA digest

NOVEMBER 18, 2003

Lucas & Sami: The Moment DAYS Fans Have Been Waiting For

Watch This!
A Week Full Of Surprises

GH: Carly Wakes Up A Changed Woman

ONE LIFE'S Gabrielle: "I cried buckets."

$3.50 Canada $4.50

Judi and I got to hang out and chat during this photo shoot. Since it was a "Diet" issue, I'm sure you can imagine what the topics were...dieting, eating, exercising, etc. We swapped our weight-issue stories.

MARLENA'S DEADLY MISTAKE!

www.soapoperadigest.com

soap OPERA digest

SPECIAL PRICE $1.99 CANADA $2.99

MARCH 2, 2004

DAYS

How 3 Stars Dropped Over 110 Lbs (And How You Can Do It, Too!)

DAYS' Judi Evans

"I was too embarrassed to go to the gym."

DAYS' Alison Sweeney

Y&R's "Tricky Story"

ONE LIFE'S Catherine Hickland

$1.99 Canada $2.99

her credit, Sami wasn't too keen on the idea, but after finally agreeing to go along with it, she tried out some pretty outrageous outfits in Brandon's apartment—with him as an audience of one—to get just the right woman-of-the-night look (after all, what does the well-dressed Salem streetwalker wear these days?). Before long, Brandon and Sami were dancing together, and the heat in the apartment got well past the boiling point. Before long, he planted a passionate kiss on Sami's lips (wow!), and she was completely swept away. There was an intense attraction between these two. For weeks, fans wondered whether Sami would abandon her feelings for Austin and give in to her desires for Brandon.

But I don't have to tell you that relationships are never simple in Salem (thank goodness, or people might stop watching!). Sami and Brandon continued to draw closer together, and as their attraction became more passionate, Lucas and Kate developed a scheme of their own against Sami, with Kate determined to drive Sami haywire. While they were all in Italy, Kate convinced Lucas to lace Sami's salad with a mind-altering herb while Sami was having dinner with Brandon at Moroni's restaurant. Lucas succeeded in tainting the salad, but there was much more of the hallucinogen than anyone realized. Before long, Sami had slipped into a frightening drug-induced state. She began convulsing. She was having difficulty breathing. She had some terrifying hallucinations and flashbacks, not to mention a seizure or two.

Well, as you've guessed by now, Sami pulled through. The incident was just one more time when she extricated herself from the jaws of death. But who would want it any other way? After all, without

Sami around, there would be one fewer person to create chaos in Salem, and no one wants that, right?

The good news is that the perils of Sami keep *Days'* fans glued to their TV screens to find out what's going to happen next. If you've been one of those loyal viewers, year after year, the high ratings sure have made the producers and network happy! So thanks!

(Author's personal collection)

(Author's personal collection)

My brothers are so important to me. Through all our childhood pranks and endless teasing, we've always been there for each other. Every year my dad gathers us up, and we take family photos for Christmas cards and stuff. Here are two of those photos.

Chapter 9

As I've written, *Days of Our Lives* often deals with topical issues in very realistic ways. That was certainly the case when the story line concentrated on the subject of rape, which is one of the worst of all possible nightmares for girls and women. Just the thought of it is terrifying. But early in my career on *Days of Our Lives*, when I was barely 16 years old, I had to live through a rape through my character, Sami. It is as close as I ever want to come to the real thing.

In the scene, I was assaulted by the character Alan (played by Paul Kersey, a really nice guy in real life!). He had originally targeted Carrie, but Austin (who was then Carrie's boyfriend) intervened before Alan could do any damage. So he turned his attention to Sami, whom he had actually dated as a way to get closer to Carrie. (I know I told you part of this story in the previous chapter, so bear with me as I give you more details.)

The plot thickens. Sami was cooking dinner for Alan at his apartment. But the evening unraveled for Sami very quickly. Before long, Alan had duped her into posing for some suggestive photographs. Then before she knew what was happening, he suddenly and unexpectedly became physical with her. She clearly said "no," but he held her down on his sofa and raped her. The story line was that Alan was so outraged over being rejected by Carrie that he turned his fury on Sami, and he showed no mercy. Yes, it was only acting, but for me it was a very scary experience.

As you can imagine, the rape scene was very physical and very violent, and I really had no frame of reference on what to expect. As the cameras rolled, Paul held me down on the sofa, gripping my wrists with one of his hands and holding my arms over my head. The director had instructed me to fight back while Paul was sitting on my stomach, kissing me, and ripping my blouse with his free hand. Believe me, I fought that guy with everything I had. I could feel Sami's terror with every fiber of my being. I resisted. I kicked. I bucked. I screamed. I tried to get free of his grip in any way I could, using literally every ounce of strength that I had. But I couldn't get him off. I couldn't budge him at all.

The sad truth is that if Paul had wanted to, he could have held me there all day, and there was nothing I could have done. I was completely at his mercy. Yes, all along I knew that we were acting, but as I became swept up in the panic that Sami was feeling, it was shocking to realize just how helpless I was. In an actual rape, the terror must be multiplied a million times!

When the director finally yelled "Cut," Paul

climbed off of me and I was so relieved to be free of his control. There was a short break in the shooting at that point, and everyone must have sensed just how difficult it had been for me. One of the cameramen tried to lighten the mood by saying "We'll get him for you, Ali! Just let me at 'em!" It made me feel instantly better to be reminded that it was only a scene, and that I was surrounded by friends. But I still sat there stunned for quite a while. During the five-minute break, I remained by myself on the set, just trying to collect my thoughts. I had so closely identified with what Sami was going through that I felt completely traumatized by the experience. I felt violated. I felt assaulted. It was so scary, especially since I was sixteen years old. Those feelings of terror lingered, long after the scene had been shot.

Here's something else that I found quite remarkable: That experience really affected how I thought of men for a while. I became very careful (and I still am) about being alone with men whom I don't completely trust. The whole thing was pretty creepy!

In that *Days* story line, Sami didn't tell anyone what had happened in the immediate aftermath of the rape. But Lucas eventually discovered the provocative photos of Sami in Alan's wallet, and she finally divulged that he had raped her. What an upheaval in Salem! Before long, Carrie had convinced Sami to bring charges against Alan, and a very traumatized Sami testified against him. But there just wasn't enough evidence to convict him. To make matters worse for Sami, a tabloid published the alluring photos of her! She was publicly humiliated, and in her despair, she tried to retreat from the public eye.

What happened next? Well, Alan remained furi-

ous at Sami. He pursued her with more sinister motives in mind. At one point, face to face, he threatened her with a gun and there was a violent scuffle. Sami somehow gained control of the weapon—and in the chaos of the moment, she shot him. The bullet struck Alan in a rather sensitive area—well, let's just say that after the shooting, it would have been very difficult for Alan to enjoy an active sex life. The Salem tabloid that had attacked Sami during the trial came up with a memorable headline after the shooting: "Sami Brady Bobbittizes Alan Harris."

Ah, sweet revenge!

All You Need Is Love

As difficult as the rape scene was for me, I'm fortunate in that I've had many more on-screen scenes that have been completely romantic! (Nice transition, huh?!) I've been in plenty of love scenes on *Days*, but they do take some getting used to. Some have definitely been embarrassing, particularly when I was younger. But you do what you have to do (or as the cliché goes, "It's a tough job, but somebody's gotta do it!"). Love scenes are always easier when they're with an actor who makes it easy for you. But no matter what the circumstances, it's part of the job, and you do eventually get the hang of it. I'm an actress, and whether the script calls for a love scene or one that involves a rape, you do what the writers and director ask for.

For the love scenes—well, imagine what those rehearsals are like! Actually, I've always made an effort to keep the rehearsals as relaxed and lighthearted as possible, having a little fun with the other

- -

actors and crew members and making sure no one is feeling tense or uptight (particularly me!). It's such a balancing act: You try to stay relaxed, and stay emotionally in character, but at the same time there are so many things to be aware of. Once the cameras are rolling, there's definitely no playing around. Love scenes are similar to dance scenes—both are carefully choreographed! And the cast and crew are all involved. Since the woman is often wearing something skimpy, both the cameramen and the actress have to be aware of not showing *too* much! The actors have to follow very specific direction about where to kiss and what angle to position their bodies, and the cameras have to be in the right spot at the right moment to get the perfect angle on each movement. There's a job to do, and it couldn't get done without the complete professionalism of the crewmembers and the cast. (Now in revealing all this inside information, I hope I haven't ruined for you the romance of the next love scene you watch. We want you to forget about all the hard work that went into it, and enjoy the story!!!)

As you might guess, the same is true with highly dramatic, highly emotional scenes. During rehearsals, the cast and the crew remain pretty serious, giving the actors room to reach the emotional peak called for in the scene. It can get pretty tense. At times, you really can hear a pin drop!

Then, once the actual taping begins, the mood is absolutely dead serious. Sure, there are occasional funny moments where an actor flubs a line or a slap actually hits the intended target when it was supposed to miss by a few inches (I'll never let Christie forget that one! . . . Just kidding!). As you might imagine, we sometimes crack one another

up because of something that happens unexpectedly. But in general, everyone's pretty thoughtful,
making sure the scene turns out perfectly.

Here's one lighter incident that comes to mind:
Miriam Parrish was playing Jamie Caldwell, and we
had a scene together where we were outside a
women's rest room and overheard a bulimic woman
vomiting behind the door. Our task was to *pretend*
that we were actually hearing and reacting to the
unsettling sounds of a woman throwing up, although the actual noises associated with the vomiting were going to be dubbed in later. But suddenly,
coming over the loudspeaker, there was a very loud,
graphic, and realistic soundtrack of someone vomiting, followed by a toilet flushing. Miriam and I
looked at one another. The sound effects had caught
both of us by surprise. It was only seconds until we
could no longer keep a straight face. We really tried!
But sure enough, our composure didn't last, and
we laughed uncontrollably. We had absolutely lost
it!

Take two!

Some actors on *Days* are more prone than others to break up laughing when something strikes
them funny, but in general, we try to keep the in-
terruptions and distractions to a minimum. With
our tight schedule, we just don't have the time.
Not long after I joined the show, there was a little
"Brady family dance" that we'd do whenever we
completed a scene in just one take. I think Deidre
and Wayne came up with it, and it caught on. One
time, it even appeared on the show in an ice skat-
ing scene, with all of us dancing around the pond
as if the Bradys had taken leave of our senses. It became our way of saying, "Yes! We did it the first
time!"

Of course, everyone blows a line from time to time, and while it might be amusing enough to make it onto Dick Clark's "bloopers" show now and then, stumbling over your dialogue time after time is not the way to win friends and influence people (particularly if those people are your fellow actors or directors!). With the time crunch we're usually under, those retakes can test everyone's patience. After you mess up four or five times, you might be laughing nervously, but the people around you may be ready to punch you out! The crew is probably dying to take a break, and you're working on take six! Get the picture?

All in the Family

Whether we're taping difficult scenes like the rape episode, or doing scenes that are much more routine, one of the great things about working on *Days of Our Lives* is having the support of so many wonderful fellow actors. You hear so much about jealousies and back-stabbing in Hollywood, and I'm sure some of that goes on. It must be such a drag. Fortunately, I've never seen it on the set of *Days*. In fact, some of my closest friends are the actors who, like me, call *Days* their home.

I've always felt that our cast and crew are part of a big family (sure, it sounds corny, but it's really true!). You can't help but feel close to people you work with for so many long hours and share such enjoyable—and at times stressful and challenging—experiences. During scenes that are particularly demanding, it's amazing how supportive everyone is, helping you work through it and reach your po-

tential as an actor. All of us want *Days* to continue
as the excellent show that it is, and so we want
everyone on the soap to succeed. It's not unusual to
complete a difficult scene, and have fellow actors
come up to you and say, "I saw that scene you did;
you were *so* good in it!" Imagine how great that
makes you feel! Yes, all of us (by necessity) are preoccupied with our own story lines, and we don't
have a lot of time just to "hang out" with cast members that we don't work with a lot. But when we do
get a chance to watch each other, we're the first to
give each other a high five! It really is a wonderful
environment to work in!

I think this closeness is very important, and we're
so lucky to have such tight relationships that have
allowed the show to grow with so little envy and re-
sentment. We've all heard rumors about actors on

(Author's personal collection)

**A bunch of us girls at the *Days of Our Lives*
anniversary party**

other shows who sometimes think or say, "Why does she get more camera time than I do?" But *Days* is different. It's a true ensemble show where everyone gets his or her time to shine. And we work too hard, and have too strong a commitment to *Days*, to let pettiness get in the way of producing the best possible show.

Who are my closest friends on *Days*? They're really the actors who I work with repeatedly on one story line after another. Take Arianne Zuker, for example. On the show, Ari plays Nicole, who is Sami's bitter rival. It seems that Nicole and Sami are always screaming at one another and raking each other over the coals. It's simply their modus operandi. But off camera, it's really a different story. Ari is absolutely great and one of my closest friends! The on-camera battles and bitchiness are purely acting. In fact, Ari and I have plenty of fun playing enemies on the show, really getting a kick out of the bad blood between our characters, and finding ways to make our on-screen relationship as wicked as possible! But I wish you could see us rehearsing in one another's dressing rooms. We often crack each other up, finding ourselves in stitches over the venomous dialogue coming from our lips; once we're on the set, however, we put on our game faces, and get through the scenes with as much animosity and hatred as we can muster.

Ari is just one of my close friends on the show, and I don't have the space to write about each of them. But let me tell you, because *Days* is a soap, cast members often leave the show and then return—and it's so great when a true friend comes back. Bryan Dattilo played Lucas for many years— he and I started on the show at about the same time, but his character disappeared from *Days* (it

happens all the time on soaps!) for a short time, only to return in 2002. Over the years, Bryan and I have had so many fun scenes together, whether we're being affectionate or we're at each other's throats. He and I have had our share of very physical scenes—we're either fighting (Sami has choked Lucas on several occasions), or I'm passed out and he's saving my life (My hero!). We've been together on camera so many times over the years that sometimes a word or a line will remind us of something funny that's happened in the past, and we'll both break up laughing. It's been so much fun to work with him again.

By the way, Bryan is not only a close friend, but also one of the funniest people I've ever known. At various times, he's played pranks on me—from placing Vaseline on my dressing room doorknob, to putting gel in my telephone. (It's OK, Bryan, I forgive you!.. . . Boys will be boys!) And of course, I got him back!

Before I forget, I have to mention that one of the most enjoyable experiences I've had on the show is working with the boys who have played Sami's son, Will. As you may know, when Sami gave birth to her baby, the infant was played by twin boys, Shawn and Taylor Carpenter, starting when they were just six weeks old. Over the years, I had a wonderful relationship with them, both in front of and behind the cameras. They are such sweet and special children, and it was so great watching them grow up. They were always a blast to work with, and quite amazingly, even at a very young age they seemed to know when to be quiet and when to let loose. They somehow knew when the cameras were rolling and when they needed to be silent. As they became older and they had lines to speak, it

was sometimes hard to get them to talk because they were so used to being still and quiet. But everything changed as soon as they walked off the set; they became totally normal kids—running, shouting, playing games with us, and jumping all over Austin Peck as if he were a jungle gym. Like I said, boys will be boys!

In particular, I remember a scene I had with Shawn when the twins were just infants. The script called for me to become really emotional, crying hysterically, and speaking a long, tear-stained monologue while standing over him in his crib. Well, Shawn looked up and saw me crying, just as the script called for. But my tears really upset him, and *he* started crying and screaming, too. The two of us were quite a sight, each of us sobbing and bawling, as if trying to upstage one another!

Shawn, of course, had been used to seeing me laughing and joking, and certainly didn't understand that I was only acting or pretending. Through my tears, I could see how frightened he was, and as the cameras continued to run, I instinctively reached down, picked him up and tried to comfort him. All the while, I continued speaking my lines, but tried to make them sound a little less painful so the baby would calm down. It actually made for a very powerful scene. As Sami, I was putting my child's needs first, dealing sensitively with his emotions, no matter what I was going through.

I recall one particularly memorable episode not long after Lucas discovered that he was Will's real dad. In this scene, Lucas leaped to the head of the class when it came to clumsiness. In the script, he *dropped* Will while roughhousing with him—specifically, while playing "airplane" with his son. (Don't worry, no babies were harmed in the filming of

this episode!) On the show, Sami became furious, convinced that the lump on Will's head occurred when Lucas struck the boy in a drunken stupor. Sami, ever the protective mom, was so angry that she was determined to press charges.

No matter how evil or sinister Sami's behavior has been at times, she has always absolutely adored her son. When it comes to being a mom, she's the real deal! Even Sami has redeeming qualities!

Eventually, Shawn and Taylor fell victim to the "rapid aging syndrome," where *Days*' producers decided to replace the boys (at about age six) with a ten-year-old (the role of Will is now played by the adorable Christopher Gerse). It happens a lot in soap operas, where characters become several years older literally overnight. Once you agree to watch a soap opera, you agree to suspend rational thinking from time to time. (It happened to Sami, by the way, when the actress who played her before me—Christina Wagoner—left the show in 1992 at the age of nine, and I took over the role the following year when I was sixteen years old!). While they were on the show, Shawn and Taylor were wonderful to work with, and it was sad to see them leave.

A Little "Sibling" Support

Let me close this chapter talking about two other very important characters on *Days of Our Lives*. As you know, while I have two wonderful brothers in real life, I'm the only daughter in the family. But I've had two "sisters" on *Days*—Carrie and Belle— and I have felt very close to both of them. Of

course, when you're talking about Christie Clark (who played Carrie for many years), our characters were at each other's throats for most of our time on the show together. But off camera, Christie definitely fulfilled the role of a surrogate sister. We spent a lot of time teasing and joking with one another about the amazing messes our characters got themselves into. In real life, however, I turned to Christie for advice on many occasions. I felt like I could tell her anything, and she definitely shared some of her own life experiences with me as well. (Thanks, Christie!)

And then there's Kirsten Storms, who plays my little sister, Belle. We have a great and supportive relationship, and like any sibling, she asks for my advice from time to time about matters both on and off the small screen. I remember the time she had planned to cook dinner for her real-life boyfriend, and she asked for my help. Together, we came up with a menu—Kirsten told me what they liked to eat, we developed the recipes and all the ingredients, and I gave her advice on everything from chopping vegetables to sautéing. It was so cool to have her ask me, and it was so much fun to help.

That's what friends (and "sisters") are for.

We're so lucky to enjoy this kind of camaraderie on the show, and it has always been that way. Just ask Frances Reid, who has been a mainstay on the show from the beginning. She was in the very first episode of *Days* (although as she points out, another actress played Alice Horton in the pilot for the show). Frances is such a wonderful woman and a talented actress, and I've been so fortunate to have worked with her for so many years.

From the beginning, when I was just a teenager,

several of the show's actors took me under their wing and became like older brothers to me. They looked out for me, always asking if I had any questions or concerns, and wanted to make sure I was enjoying the experience of being part of the large ensemble cast. Actors like Drake Hogestyn and Josh Taylor (ex-Roman) in particular played a very fatherly role. Drake, for example, who plays John Black, has always been so thoughtful and sincere in his interest in my experiences on *Days* and in my life in general. Drake is such a great dad in real life—he talks about his daughters and son all the time—and his caring and compassion sure come through in his work on the show. When Drake and I have scenes together, he has this wonderful paternal way about him, and while Sami is often being ruthless and bitchy, I end up thinking, "What a great dad! I can't believe I'm so mean to him!"

Even I cringe once in a while at some of the meaner and more evil things that Sami says, especially to John and Marlena. Of course, at the same time that I'm thinking, "I can't say that—it's so mean!", Melissa Reeves or Deidre Hall may tell me, "What do you mean, you don't want to say that line—I wish I had lines like that." They may relish the opportunity to be mean once in a while, whereas I'm mean all the time! Ah, the life of Sami!

Chapter
10

These are lean times in Hollywood.

No, I'm not referring to the scarcity of jobs that actors are up against, which relegate too many of my peers into unemployment lines or into gotta-pay-the-bills jobs as waitresses or temp secretaries. Instead, I'm thinking of a different kind of "lean times"—namely, the super-skinny actresses who are more razor-thin than ever these days, and are dying to be even leaner (in some cases, almost *literally* dying!). You know who I'm talking about—those actresses who nearly seem to disappear when they turn sideways, and whose daily caloric intake seems to be their answer to the question, "How low can you go?" Some of them look so fragile that an unexpected gust of wind just might take them for the ride of their lives!

Okay, maybe I'm exaggerating a little—but not by much. So many actresses are convinced that

their career success depends on much more than their acting talents. The party line is that they better stay as skinny as possible for as long as possible because there are hundreds, perhaps thousands, of reed-thin actresses eager to take their place. As a result, the obsession with thinness has become rampant throughout every part of the entertainment industry. True story.

Striving to be Hollywood-thin has been practically an obsession with me since I hit puberty. And as an actress who loves my job on *Days of Our Lives* and hopes to continue acting for many more years, I can't ignore what casting agents are looking for—and it seems that for most roles, they're hungering for the slimmest, most svelte actresses they can find. People say that the television camera makes you look ten pounds heavier, so the actresses who appear almost gaunt and skeletal often win the attention of Hollywood decision-makers at the expense of those who have a more wholesome, healthy look. If you see an actress who appears thin on TV, imagine what she looks like face-to-face!

As tragic as it sounds, the industry standards support the passion of some actresses to become anorexic or bulimic because the camera's eye will make them look "normal," not underweight. So they torture their bodies and souls, all so they can do what they love, which is acting.

In this chapter and the three that follow, I'll give you my point of view on show business's preoccupation with weight, and how I've finally dealt with it in a positive way in my own life.

Thin Is In

What effect does Hollywood's weight obsession have on actresses like me? It's so easy to get caught up in the "thin-is-in" ethos, which is why so many of my colleagues are totally preoccupied with the number on the scale and do whatever they have to do to keep it from moving in an upward direction. They eat like birds (anorexic birds at that!). They routinely skip meals. Some of them take laxatives. They've turned near-starvation into an art form.

Before I go any further, I will say that there are a number of women I know who are thin naturally. My friend and costar, Ari (Nicole), is a perfect example of a beautiful, super-model-type figure, and she doesn't have to work at it at all. I know what you're thinking—I hate her, too! ☺ But seriously, even though she has genetics on her side, she makes an effort to be healthy, to work out, and to take care of herself. In fact, she has to work to keep weight *on*! My point is, there is a body type that is naturally thin—and I'm not talking about those women. I'm talking instead about the women who fight their figures throughout their whole careers, and in some cases take that fight to extremes.

Growing up in the entertainment industry, I've known actresses who vomit after almost every meal. For some of the thinnest-of-the-thin actresses, it's as much a part of their routine as brushing their teeth and putting on makeup—they seem to feel that they can't afford to backslide, can't afford to gain even a single pound or two. Physical appearance is everything. More than once, I've walked into a rest room at a Hollywood studio or at a

restaurant with a show business clientele and heard
an actress in the bathroom stall, throwing up her
lunch. Yuck! Almost everyone in the industry pre-
tends that nothing is wrong. But they've got to be
kidding. I've known actresses who seem like they're
about to collapse because they're so malnourished
(I really mean that!). If she's a teenage actress,
someone in the production company may whisper
something to her mom—but even parents are
often in denial. Too often, moms in particular are
part of the problem, encouraging their actress-
daughters to count calories and watch their weight
until it becomes pathological. It is so frightening!

Can you think of any other business or industry
in the world that leads girls and women into this
kind of self-destructive behavior? Well, okay, I mean
besides ballet and gymnastics?

How disturbing do the stories get? Just picture
this. Not long ago, a photographer told me about
a day-long fashion shoot he had just done with a
well-known supermodel who had set new standards
for thinness (just take a look at the models in any
issue of *Vogue* or *Harper's Bazaar*, and you'll know
what I mean). During the shoot, there was plenty
of food available for the photographer, his assistants,
the makeup artists, the agent, the manager—and
the model. But while everyone else was eating generous portions and going back for seconds, the
model didn't touch *any* of the catered food. Probably
obsessed with maintaining her figure, she had
brought her own lunch—a sunflower seed! That's
right. *One* sunflower seed. While others on the set
couldn't resist the generous spread of food during
breaks and during the lunch hour, she could have
carried her meal for the day in a thimble!

Later, the photographer told me, "It's hard to believe, but the only thing she ate during the entire six hours was the sunflower seed! That's it. During the course of the day, she fainted three times under the bright lights. She was starving herself. It was unbelievable."

Is that scary or what?!

There are a lot of stories just like that. A few of them may be urban legends, but most are real. Girls and young women in Hollywood are willing to literally torture themselves and their bodies—surviving on juice, a few grapes, or a cracker or two for the day—just so they'll measure up (or is it measure down?) with the "right look" to help them hold on to their jobs and keep the casting agents on their side.

I've spoken with some wardrobe stylists—those men and women who fit actresses with clothing for photo shoots, parties, and awards shows—and in their most honest moments, they admit that they may be part of the problem. Here's how it works: These very talented stylists receive free clothes from various designers for celebrities to wear at events, and these free clothes are the sample sizes that models wear down the fashion runways (you know the type of body I'm talking about—think of the wafer-thin figures of Elle MacPherson, Kate Moss, and Naomi Campbell). So now these actresses are *not* being fitted to their own size, but they're trying to squeeze into a dress originally worn by a Twiggy-like model—and the actress (who may be a size 2) might get scolded because she's too heavy for the dress! Even if nothing is said, it's so embarrassing to try on a dress in front of people and have it not fit. Just think about how you

feel when you're in the changing room by yourself, and now give yourself an audience!

Of course, I've worked in this culture of thinness most of my life, and it's a business where "anatomy is destiny." In just about any soap opera, or any other TV show or commercial for that matter, the dress size of the average actress is 0 or 2. These are *very* slim women! And most of them believe that if their waist is not thin enough or their body frame is not trim enough, they might lose the part they're dreaming about to a thinner-than-thou actress with the figure of Lara Flynn Boyle or the next Calista Flockhart look-alike. The press even pointed out that the female stars of long-running shows like *Friends* weighed conspicuously less during the last season that the show was on the air than the first; even the biggest stars feel pressure to downsize their bodies, no matter how spectacular they looked in their "before" photos. That's the sad shape of things in Hollywood these days.

Over the years, magazines like *People* have run stories about the almost obscene thinness among actresses in Hollywood. More recently, I've also read articles about the supposed current trend toward "healthier-looking" actresses—those who don't quite fall into the emaciated category—but the articles have used actresses like Charlize Theron as the prototype of these "normal-looking" stars. No offense to *People* or any other magazine, but in my mind, actresses like Charlize are absolutely gorgeous but also pretty darn thin. When I read articles that point to these actresses as examples of a healthier body shape in show business, my heart sinks and I find myself thinking, "If she's 'normal,' what does that make me?"

The Good Folks at Days

Before I go any further, let me make a very important point. In the midst of all of Hollywood's weight obsession, I've been spared much of this insanity, and I have the producers of *Days of Our Lives* to thank for that. Even though I've never been obese, I've also never won any awards as the thinnest actress in Hollywood. I just don't have the body type that's *ever* going to fit the mold of the "average" Hollywood actress. That's just never going to be me!

But I've been so lucky that my weight has *never* been an issue with the producers of *Days*. At times in the past, I weighed fifteen to thirty pounds more than I do today. But they never pressured me to shed some of that excess weight. They never even commented on it. The press did and mean-spirited fans did, but the producers never touched the subject. They didn't slip copies of diets under my dressing room door. They didn't send me out on forced marches to burn a few calories. From the beginning until today, my weight just hasn't been an issue with them (thank you, Ken!).

When I joined the cast of *Days*, I was a few pounds overweight but still a perfect fit for the vision the producers and writers had for Sami Brady. They said that I was a good actress, and that was what was important to them. That's why they hired me. They were bold enough to select me to play Sami, even though producers of other shows might have found me unsuitable because at the time, I weighed a little more than they would have liked. But at *Days*, my weight has always been irrelevant.

I remember one day several years ago, when I was struggling with my weight and feeling pretty bad about myself, I asked one of the executive producers if he thought I should do something about it. I wanted to know if he would have preferred that I live at a health club when I wasn't working, and whittle away at my weight. I was even considering liposuction. There was definitely a part of me that was embarrassed by being overweight, and I figured if he read me the riot act, maybe I'd finally do something about it.

Well, he couldn't have been more supportive. "Ali," he said, "I think you're beautiful, and I want you to do whatever's best for you. Your boyfriend thinks you're beautiful, doesn't he?" (This was before Dave and I got married.)

"Yes, he does."

"Then don't worry about it. You look great. And we're very happy that our show depicts beauty in all of its variety. Men don't like skeletons."

He paused for a moment, and then added, "You know, even dogs like meat on their bones."

How 'bout that! Let me tell you, that was so awesome to hear. As it turned out, I did lose some weight in the months after that conversation, but I was doing it from a place of love and support, and in the pursuit of healthy eating, not starvation. It was so much easier that way. Trust me, I'm so lucky to work for such wonderful and supportive people.

In 1997, there was an article about me in *TV Guide* proclaiming that I was "breaking all the rules." Michael Logan, the writer of that article, said that my "appeal is both surprising and encouraging," considering that one might have expected the

show's producers to have hired a "reed-thin sex-pot" to play the high-profile role of Sami. The article quoted *Days* head writer James Reilly as saying that my looks were an asset. "The audience identifies with Alison's young cherubic innocence," Jim was quoted as saying. "She's real, not like the anorexic, androgynous types you see in the magazines. She proves normal can be very interesting."

How cool is that?! Normal *and* interesting!

Yet even though the *Days* producers have been absolutely wonderful, I know they're the exception to the rule in Hollywood. They're in the minority on the issue of weight. Here's the cruel and ongoing reality: Most producers, directors, and casting agents usually don't hire actresses who are overweight. When I have time to audition for guest starring roles, such as on movies-of-the-week, I'd better be as lean and mean as possible if I want a shot at the role. If I (or any other actress) arrive at an audition even just five pounds heavier than what the casting director is looking for, hasta la vista, baby! There's always the pressure to be thinner. It's a constant. I wonder if it's ever going to change.

Not only do a few extra pounds reduce my chances of getting a part, but at times, casting agents have been pretty blunt in letting me know. More than once, they've told me (through my manager, or in earlier years, my mom), "Ali, can I give you a bit of advice? You should really think about losing ten or fifteen pounds." (Amazingly, they thought they were being kind and helpful! Can you believe it?!) About a year before I got the part on *Days*, when I auditioned for a role on *Beverly Hills 90210*, the casting directors politely informed me that I

didn't have "the right body" for their show (by the way, after receiving that news, I comforted myself by eating—how's that for irony?!).

Of course, this Hollywood reality drives me crazy! At times, it really weighs on me (sorry—bad pun!). OK, we can agree that size and shape do matter on a show like *Baywatch*, where both men and women are parading around in a very limited amount of clothing, and their great bodies on the beach are key to the show's appeal. The same goes for an audition I went to not long ago, where the story line itself focused on the way in which weight affected the relationship between two sisters—one of whom was very thin, and the other who was heavier; obviously, the size of the actresses mattered when those roles were cast. But these are the exceptions. The plot lines of most shows don't revolve around bathing suit models who splash provocatively into the Pacific to save drowning swimmers! With most TV programs and motion pictures, it shouldn't matter whether you're ten or fifteen pounds over- or underweight. Romantic comedies, for example, would still work whether actresses weigh 105 or 140. (Remember *My Big Fat Greek Wedding*?) But, of course, don't bother arguing that case in Hollywood these days. You're wasting your breath.

The Skinny on Being Skinny

What's the logic behind the television industry's obsession with thinness? After all, there are probably many more women across America who could relate to an actress who looks real, whether she's normal-sized or even pleasantly plump—that is,

someone who looks a lot more like *they* do than the actresses they usually see on TV. Take a look back through recorded history, and you'll discover that shapely and somewhat overweight women were considered beautiful (just walk through an art museum and you'll see what I mean!). So let's get real, Hollywood!

But here's the way the argument goes in show business: In most TV shows and motion pictures, there is an underlying romantic story line and a happy-ever-after ending, and most viewers *don't* want to see someone who looks like them in these story lines—they want to see a fantasy of how they'd *like* life to be, including women with perfect bodies rather than more ordinary figures. (Also, don't forget about the men: Most male viewers would rather see an actress who looks like she belongs in a Victoria Secret's ad, not one who's going to Jenny Craig!)

Maybe there's some truth to that. Where are the actresses who look like average American women? Where are the models who look like real people? (Cindy Crawford, commenting on the makeup, lights, and airbrushing that are part of the modeling industry, once said that in real life, "Even I don't look like Cindy Crawford!") Sure, there are a few plump actresses on TV and in the movies, but not many (I love Camryn Manheim, don't you?— Her book, which put it right out there, was titled, *Wake Up, I'm Fat!*). I'm not so sure that the ultimate fantasy for most viewers is an actress who is bone-thin and skeletal, particularly when American women come in so many body shapes and sizes (we accept differences in hair color and eye color, but weight seems to be a completely different matter!).

One of the real ironies about weight and women

in show business is that even though most casting directors I've worked with are women, they appear to be as hard or harder on actresses and their size than their male counterparts—and I just don't get it! I don't know how an entire industry can choose one body type (a very thin one) and presume that it pleases every viewer and every fan. In fact, I know it doesn't. Why can't they open their minds and choose actresses from across the spectrum— all sizes, all shapes? And anyway, I've always thought "variety is the spice of life"! Why not try casting lots of different body types for different TV shows— give people options! If they did, I think shows would attract even wider audiences than they already do.

While we're on the subject of diversity, don't get me started on the issue of aging actresses, either. Actors like Sean Connery and Harrison Ford can play leading roles for forty years, and people still love them. (I know I love them!) But youthfulness is a much bigger issue for actresses. It's such a shame that actresses like Meryl Streep and Diane Keaton sometimes have to fight for roles or create their own, despite their enormous talent. None of us stays young forever, but that doesn't make us any less interesting or talented as we grow older. We're not like gymnasts—we don't peak at eighteen!

I don't know whether things will ever change. But unless and until they do, I'd love to have you eavesdrop on some of the conversations I've had with groups of Hollywood actresses. Diet mania is not their only preoccupation, but sometimes it sure seems that way. If there's one thing actresses are good at (other than their acting ability, I hope) it's finding and exchanging diet plans with one another. When they're together, that is often Topic

Number 1. So for years, I was never without a weight-loss program to replace the one that had just failed. Actresses always tell each other stories about taking one kind of weight-loss pill or another. They're sharing information on the latest exercise fad out there. Now it's even mainstream—at least in L.A., there is always talk about the newest diet fad, whether it's Dr. Atkins, Dr. Phil, the New Hollywood Diet, or whatever. At the other extreme, there are actresses I've met who keep their unusual eating (or, more accurately, noneating) behaviors to themselves, never telling a soul that they're on a near-starvation diet, or that they're bingeing and purging. Some of them can throw up on cue. They exercise well past the point of exhaustion. But they often keep it all hidden. It's their deep, dark secret. But guess what? Nearly everyone around them knows what's happening, particularly when their behavior becomes a little erratic. If you think it's easy to get caught up in the dieting hysteria among your own friends, just imagine what it's like in an industry where your looks are often just about the only thing that matters.

At times, I've become caught up in this rather sick preoccupation of Hollywood. A few years ago, I knew I had hit rock bottom when I actually found myself in an absolutely bizarre conversation. Another actress and I were discussing a new "diet plan" we had heard about: No, it didn't involve cutting calories or exercising more. It required dining on worms! (No, this isn't my *Fear Factor* story—that comes later.) According to the guidelines for this particular diet scheme, once these special tapeworms are in your stomach, they make themselves at home and munch away at the morsels of real food that you eat. In the process, they sup-

posedly keep you from gaining weight! We had heard that we could eat as much as we wanted and still lose tons of weight, thanks to those hungry little worms! Luckily, the way you get them out is so gross and potentially dangerous that we were quickly turned off by the whole idea.

Sounds absolutely insane, doesn't it? And, I agree, it really is outrageous! But I have to admit that for a few brief moments, it seemed to us like something worth trying! What were we thinking?! Fortunately, we never pursued it, and my palate will be forever grateful! But when it actually sounded appealing, even for just a minute or two, I knew we were in real trouble. The sheer lunacy of the pressure to be thin can put such crazy thoughts in your head!

Chapter 11

In this chapter, let me tell you more about my own journey in the battle of the bulge. As I mentioned in the last chapter, the folks at *Days of Our Lives* have never made an issue of my weight. But that doesn't mean that I've been able to ignore it, either. I've been in show business almost all of my life, and since I've been a teenager, I've been very aware of the matter of weight and its importance in Hollywood (and throughout the entire society, for that matter). As I moved through puberty, and once my adolescent growth spurts were pretty much over, I became so busy with school and acting that I began getting less exercise than I should have. I gained a few pounds, although I know I was never really fat. But like millions of other adolescent girls, I became very self-conscious about every additional pound on the scale, particularly at this sensitive time of life where you start thinking about boys and going on dates. I also began to recognize that I couldn't eat

like I did when I was ten years old; it doesn't work
that way (unless, of course, you have a few friendly
worms hard at work in your stomach!).

For a time, I tried a vegetarian diet, and it seemed
like a healthy way to eat. But it sure didn't do
much for my figure. True, I didn't eat meat, but I
had pasta three or four times a week! That many
carbs kept me wearing dress sizes much larger
than I would have preferred. In fact, it really didn't
seem to matter what kind of diet I adopted; at
times, my weight would dip a few pounds, but I always gained it back. It seemed like a losing battle,
and at times I became an absolute wreck! I just
wanted to give up.

But then *Days of Our Lives* became part of my
life. At age sixteen, I joined the show, which lifted
an enormous burden from my shoulders, and let
me put much less focus on the scale—or at least
that's the way it should have been.

However, I've always found myself surrounded
by incredibly thin actresses—and I do mean *incredibly thin*—not only on *Days* but among every other
group of actresses I hung out with. As I described
in Chapter 10, many, many actresses are totally absorbed with their weight, minute by minute. They
feel inadequate and have their spirits absolutely
crushed if they gain just a pound or two, convinced that they're fat.

When you're working with people who are so
weight-conscious, it's almost inevitable that some
of their obsessions rub off on you. Yes, there were
(and sometimes still are) times that I wanted to be
just like them. I might wake up in the morning,
feel hunger pangs, have breakfast, and then become so angry with myself because I had eaten!

When women in size 0 dresses would tell me very nonchalantly that they'd throw up after eating, I thought, "Maybe something's wrong with me—why am I being so moral and health-conscious about this whole thing? What's wrong with doing whatever it takes to become underweight and undersized?" I even thought at one point that a personal "weakness" was preventing me from being able to throw up my meals.

Fortunately, those thoughts didn't linger. And here's the bottom line: I know my body type and body structure, and no matter how little I eat or how much I work out, I'm never going to become the thinnest of the thin, or close to it. For better or worse, that's just not me.

OK, I will admit to the following: There was a time when I wished I had the willpower to become anorexic. I have to admit, I remember days when I felt so desperate that I tried to make myself throw up after a meal. What on earth possessed me to try it? As I wrote in Chapter 5, I remember going into the bathroom and closing the door. I sat down next to the toilet, and stuck my fingers down my throat. But nothing happened. Yes, I gagged, but I couldn't throw up. How did I feel afterward? Both disappointment and relief at the same time. Looking back, maybe someone was watching out for me—if I had been able to successfully vomit, I might have kept doing it. It could have become a way of life and spiraled way out of control. I know plenty of girls and women who have slipped into that trap. Fortunately, I found a way of growing up rather than throwing up, and I embraced a much healthier attitude about eating and body weight. But at times, it sure hasn't been easy.

Crash Diets and Other Disasters

If you're like me, you may have tried *everything* to lose weight, believing it would make you feel better about yourself. In my case, even when people would say to me, "I'd kill to have your body, Ali," I'd sometimes be thinking, "You've got to be kidding! Maybe you'd kill for Britney Spears' body—but mine?!"

Now, of course, I've matured a lot, and I'm not the maniacal dieter I used to be. I'm no longer one of those people who never met a diet she didn't like. Yet thinking back, if I had kept copies of every diet and diet book that I ever tried, they could fill up my entire garage (OK, that's an exaggeration, but not by much!). Over the years, I've gone on dozens of crash and crazy diets—none of which worked over the long term, and some of which chipped away at my overall health. I consumed low-calorie frozen entrees. I cut out snacks. I ate more fat. I ate less fat. I tried starving myself (quite literally), and then after a few days would binge on bowls of ice cream. I became one of the sweating masses crowding into trendy health clubs in Los Angeles. I exercised with several different personal trainers.

I get exhausted just thinking about all of this!

Perhaps the only approach I *didn't* try was one of those meal-replacement shake diets. You probably know the routine—drink shakes two times a day, and then have a dinner of chicken breast and vegetables, or something similar to it. I knew someone who was very overweight and actually lost eighty pounds drinking shakes. But the day he cut out the shakes and started introducing normal eating to his life again, he gained all the weight back—

and more. It turned into a real nightmare for him.
I knew I didn't want that to happen to me. I also
knew that you can't just drink shakes for the rest of
your life.

I continued to try a lot of other approaches,
though. For a while, I ate custom-made meals, prepared by a nutritionist and delivered to my door. It
seemed worth the effort. Well, let me tell you, the
food was *so* bland (I still have this need for some
salt in my diet, and there didn't seem to be *any* in
this program!). The rules were very strict (I was
supposed to eat particular foods in specific amounts
at designated times of the day—and I became overwhelmed just trying to keep track of everything). I
stuck with it for a month but just wasn't losing
weight—or at least not as fast as I wanted to. At the
same time, going to a restaurant was out of the
question. My frustration finally boiled over. I lost
my cool, canceled the delivered meals, considered
myself a failure (again)—and then looked for the
next diet to try!

Get the picture? If there was a diet out there I
didn't try, it was only because I had placed my
hope for the moment in something else. All the
while—all through my teens and early twenties—
my career on *Days* continued to go great. But for
much of the time, I really couldn't enjoy it because
I felt terrible about myself—all because of the
number on the scale. For so long, I never lost any
weight—certainly not in the long term—and I
knew that I wasn't doing my body any good, either.
The only thing that ever got thinner and frailer
was my self-esteem. At times, I could talk as good a
game as anyone, but during the worst times, I didn't
like myself. If my weight rose, I allowed those extra
pounds to undercut my self-respect and self-

confidence. In short, I was making myself miserable.

Crazy, huh?

From Bad to Worse

In the past, there have been many moments when I was so tired of struggling with my weight and so frustrated with Hollywood's vision of perfection that I was at the breaking point! I felt like throwing up my hands and throwing in the towel on show business. That's how deep my despair had gotten. Of course, for my entire life, acting has been my dream. It's what I love. It's what I'm good at. But I admit that sometimes the "weight thing" really got to me.

More than once my self-loathing overheated, and I would absolutely lose it. At the mall, I might try on a cute outfit and feel that it looked absolutely terrible on me, or that it just didn't fit the way I thought it should. Or I would peruse pictures taken of me at a photo shoot, and when I appeared heavy in my own eyes, my unhappiness and misery would boil over. I'd curse myself for not having willpower. I'd have a full-blown meltdown. You get the point, right? It could be pretty ugly.

I remember a few incidents that I'm almost embarrassed to tell you about. Several times, I stormed into my kitchen, sobbing uncontrollably, and cleaned nearly everything out of my refrigerator and cupboards. The sugar-rich soft drinks went first . . . then the Haagen-Dazs bars . . . the lemonade mix . . . the sugary cereals. I tossed every "unhealthy" or high-calorie food within reach into a large trash bag, or

even worse, I'd occasionally fling it against the wall
and watch it land in a heap on the floor (Yes, I was
a cleaning lady's worst nightmare!). Eventually, once
the trash bag was filled to overflowing, I'd drag it
out to the garbage bin, with tears rolling down my
cheeks. Can you imagine whajt that scene was like?
Definitely a pitiful sight. When it was all over, after
calming down a bit, I'd go to the market and fill
up my shopping cart with items from the health-
food aisle—there was nothing with sugar, and certainly nothing that tasted good—and I'd start the
next diet, but I'd do it from a very negative, very
unhappy place. Inevitably, of course, I'd fail on that
one, too, usually ending up by going out and having the dessert that I had been craving for weeks.

This agonizing cycle repeated itself, again and
again.

The Fans Weigh In

In the midst of all this craziness, I used to get my
share of fan letters from *Days'* viewers who said
they had noticed that I had gained five or ten
pounds and were determined to tell me what I
should be doing about it. Most of them tried to be
helpful. Some tucked a diet and a few recipes into
the envelope. On occasion, however, their comments
were pretty surprising. A few actually came right
out and told me how "fat and ugly" I was! (Give me
a break!) Or that I'd "look better if you'd just stop
eating!" One letter writer said, "You fat cow, leave
Austin alone!" (Can you believe somebody would
sit down and take the time to write out and actually mail something like that?!) If that wasn't enough,

one "fan" threw in a comment that I was "a terrible actress," too. No one ever included a Weight Watchers gift certificate along with their letter, but there sure have been some nasty messages over the years.

Fortunately, most of my fan mail is *very* positive. People write and ask all kinds of questions about the show. They love (or they hate) Sami. They describe in great detail what Sami should have done in certain story lines on the show. Or they'll ask me what some of the other cast members are really like. If the subject gets around to weight, most of the comments are very supportive. I weigh less today than I did in my earlier years on the show, and when fans write letters, attend *Days* events, or stop me in shopping malls, a common opening line—and it's a positive one—is, "Ali, you've lost so much weight!" I want to thank every one of you who has supported me that way. But even though only a small minority of the letters and statements are critical, they sure do get your attention! Particularly when I was younger, and would read some of the mean-spirited things people would occasionally write in chat rooms, for example, it really hurt, and sometimes it would even make me cry! When you're fighting your own internal demons, it's hard to have someone egg you on or attack you that way—it's just not helpful or comforting. If I took them seriously, they could ruin my whole day— or more! (By the way, I remember when Bryan Dattilo and some of my other costars showed me some of their "hate mail," and I realized it wasn't just me that fans picked on now and then.) I finally understood the following: You just can't please everyone all the time—particularly when some viewers already don't like you because you're playing a villain!

These days, people still occasionally come up to me on the street and say something like, "I'm so glad you stopped eating so much; you didn't look all that great before!"—and they mean it! Or they'll say, "Ali, you look so much better than you used to!" I actually think most people are trying to be complimentary, so that's the way I take it. What's the point of driving yourself crazy over it?

I've also been strengthened by comments from fans who have described their own battles with weight. Of course, I've known all along that I've never been alone in this struggle, sharing it not only with my acting peers, but also with millions of girls and women everywhere. When I read the statistics that about *fifty million Americans* are by definition overweight or obese, it's very alarming. Too many Americans are ballooning to perilous proportions, which can undermine their self-esteem, trigger depression, and ruin their physical health. Yet my own mail brings the statistics down to a personal level: So many people are so concerned with the way they look, and they're constantly dieting or at least thinking about it.

It seems that so many issues in women's lives—whether it's relationships with men, insecurities about their appearance, even cattiness toward other women—frequently lead back to weight. As girls and women tell me in their letters, the scale is a powerful force that has a grip on how they feel about themselves and relate to the world around them. That's the way our culture seems to work. Like the actresses I described earlier, ever so many overweight people are trying to become thin, and skinny people are trying to become even skinnier. From my own experience, I know it starts in adolescence or even earlier (a Harris poll showed that

one-third of girls ages ten to twelve described themselves as overweight!). In high school, some girls are already taking diet pills and exercising to the point of collapse. And the fashions of the day—including the low-riding jeans and the tight, truncated tank tops—certainly don't help, do they? They reveal tummies that (unless you're one of the chosen few) require hours of sweating and straining in the gym to look "just right."

As you can tell, I have moments of absolute frustration when it comes to the topic of weight. In fact, one of my motivations for writing about this issue grew out of a trip I made to a pizza parlor a few years ago, accompanied by a friend and his younger sister who was eight years old at the time. This young girl sat at a table with six other eight-year-olds, and I remember one of them saying, "We can't eat any bread because it's too fattening!" That's a pretty startling statement, particularly considering that all of these kids were rail-thin! I recall thinking, "There's something terribly wrong here."

I decided that because of my high visibility as an actress, maybe I could help bring some sensibility to this issue. I knew I didn't want to write a diet book, but more than anything else, this section of the book is intended to raise my readers' awareness. That's what you'll find in the pages that follow.

Chapter 12

After years of waging war on my own body, I have a much more positive perspective on diets and weight—and, yes, even on life in general. I've gone through several generations of diets to get to where I am today. But finally, I'm at a place where I want to be. I've been able to stay at a weight that I'm happy with, and most of the stress surrounding eating is gone. I'm going to tell you more about my own journey, but *not* because I want you to start eating like I do (as a matter of fact, I really don't follow a formal diet plan anymore, and perhaps there's no need for you to do so, either). But you might find my own path interesting and even inspiring. Again, this is *not* a diet book with an eating plan that I'm recommending. One thing I'm sure of is that no diet program is right for everyone; what I've learned is that each person is going to have to find the diet or health plan that fits him or her best.

Although I had been preoccupied with my weight for years, my journey toward a much healthier lifestyle actually began in 1998. I had been on *Days of Our Lives* for about five years, and although my career couldn't have been going any better, my battle with the scale was sometimes an absolute disaster.

For me, the change began one afternoon when I paid a visit to Dr. Jay, my dentist (I've changed his name to protect his privacy). I was there for a routine cleaning and examination. But as Dr. Jay peered into my mouth, a startled expression came over his face.

"Ali, I see a cavity." It wasn't the news I wanted to hear, but it wasn't the end of the world, either.

Then Dr. Jay added, "What's with all this sugar you've been eating?"

Sugar?! I had no idea what he was talking about. I tried to keep my cool, and I pleaded my case.

"Jay, I really do eat a healthy diet," I said. "I don't eat very much sugar or anything else that's bad for me. And I brush all the time."

Dr. Jay raised a skeptical eyebrow.

"Ali, your teeth aren't lying to me. You have a cavity. You're eating sugar. Now, tell me what you eat."

I was really getting annoyed. Growing up, I was lucky that my mom didn't believe in keeping a lot of sugar-laden snacks or sugar-rich cereals around the house; fruit was our primary snack. But I have to admit: When my mom wasn't looking, my brothers and I would sneak sugary cereals into the house and hide them. (Sorry, Mom!) So I did develop an appetite for sugar, although my mom certainly had nothing to do with it. And I guess those cravings never really waned as I entered adulthood.

I started to answer Dr. Jay's question.

"OK, I drink one or two Cokes a day."

"Oh, really. Ali, that's *all* sugar. What else?"

Geez, he was getting a little confrontational, and maybe I was becoming a bit defensive.

"I love pasta, so I eat it quite often," I told him. "Maybe three times a week."

"Pasta, huh? Ali, no wonder you're a little puffy."

Puffy!! I had heard a lot of words to describe my excess pounds, but never "puffy!"

I continued to list other foods that I ate regularly. But as I mentioned each of them, one after another, I gradually began to feel this sinking sensation. "Oh, no," I thought to myself. "Maybe my diet isn't so healthy after all."

That was the truth. I wasn't coming close to a sugar-free diet. I ate desserts much too often. I loved breakfast cereals that were "honey flavored." I ate bread, showing little restraint whenever it was on the table.

You get the drift. I felt a little stunned and pretty embarrassed.

Dr. Jay finally said, "Ali, let me tell you how I live my life."

He sat down and began to describe how he had eaten for years. In supermarkets, he spent most of his time in the outer aisles, filling his shopping cart with foods like fresh fruits and vegetables (so it certainly wasn't an Atkins-type program). For breakfast, he had a very low carbohydrate cereal. Later in the day, he ate modest amounts of high-quality, high-protein meats (so it sure wasn't an Ornish-like plan); for a typical lunch, he ate a salad with slices of chicken breast in it. Throughout the day, he kept his intake of carbohydrates well under control. No baked potatoes. No side orders of rice or pasta.

"What about the four basic food groups?" I asked him.

"Forget about them!" he said emphatically. "My approach keeps me fit and healthy. I think the food groups are obsolete."

"And what about losing weight? That's what I'm really interested in."

"You might lose some weight on this type of program," he said. "But you should be less interested in weight loss and more interested in being healthy. If you adopt a healthy diet, the weight will take care of itself."

Despite all the diets I had been on, much of what Dr. Jay was saying made sense. He wasn't talking about a fanatical program that leaves your stomach growling from daybreak 'til bedtime. He wasn't feeding himself only fruit before noon, or gorging on rice after 6 P.M. He wasn't gulping down a cupboard-full of meal-replacement drinks. He wasn't weighing his food or keeping track of every last calorie.

Dr. Jay also talked about following a program for life. That's right—a *lifetime* commitment! (That sure took my breath away for a few moments; I was much more accustomed to going on a crash diet, following it hard-core for three or four weeks, and then being done with it and going back to my old way of eating!) Dr. Jay's approach was so different than the crazy diets I'd been on for so many years.

"Ali, the way you've been eating is not how you should treat your body," Dr. Jay told me. "Maybe my approach isn't right for you. But find a plan that works for you, and stick with it for the long term."

I have to admit, Dr. Jay was a walking advertisement for his own program. He was trim and fit, and

he told me about female patients who had been over-weight, had started eating like he does, and looked fantastic. One of them, he said, had been more than twenty pounds overweight and a year after adopting the program, she posed for *Playboy*! Now that's what I call a transformation! As he told me her story, there was a part of me thinking, "Sign me up—I'll do it!" But more than anything, he sent me out into the world with something to think about.

"Is there a book I can read that describes your diet?" I asked.

"No, the books out there are too intense in terms of playing havoc with your blood sugar. So you can take a few tips from me, but experiment a little, too. Create a program that's right for your own body. You can do it."

Time for a Change

I drove home (with a numb jaw!) thinking about Dr. Jay's advice. Was he right? . . . Could he have found something that might work for me, too? . . . Or could it at least point me in the right direction? Could I create my own way of eating that would put me on a healthier path and keep me there?

Yes, Dr. Jay was truly inspiring. But, let's get real, Ali—I had failed on every other diet I had ever tried. So why would this one be any different?

Later that day, I told Dave (then my boyfriend, now my husband) about my conversation with Dr. Jay. I complained about my weight (as usual). I lamented that I had never found a diet that worked. You should have heard me—it was a classic case of whining! Dave let me ramble on for a few minutes;

(Author's personal collection)

**Enjoying the sunny
Mexican beach
with Dave**

it certainly wasn't the first time that I had griped to
him about my weight, and it was a real pity party
this time! But after I had my say, he jumped in with
a different reaction than I had been used to hearing. In fact, he gave me some food for thought (no
pun intended!) and offered a suggestion.

"Ali, I've told you so many times that I love you
no matter what you weigh. I think you're absolutely
beautiful just the way you are." So far, so good.
"But, Ali, you complain about your weight *all the
time!* You're a go-getter in every other aspect of
your life, but not this one. You go after your dreams
and what you want in life, but not when it comes to
your weight. Why is that?"

Before I could answer, Dave continued. "Decide what you want to do, take action, and stop complaining about it. Don't gripe all the time but do nothing about it!"

Wow.

That was tough for me to hear. In essence, Dave was saying, "Put up or shut up!"

I was silent for a few seconds. I realized that Dave was right. I had always gone after everything I wanted in life—except a thinner body. I had a mental block against committing to any dietary program. No wonder I hadn't succeeded.

There was an awkward pause.

"You're right, Dave," I finally told him.

For the rest of the day—and the rest of the week, for that matter—I did a lot of thinking. I came face-to-face with the reality of how I had approached dieting for years. I admitted to myself that I had been in denial about so many things, from the effect of drinking two or three sugar-laden Cokes a day to the bread that I enjoyed with so many meals. (It's amazing how you can con yourself into believing that your diet is approaching perfection when it's lacking in so many areas.) I realized that if I could apply the same hard work and the same commitment—and show the same resilience—that I did for everything else, maybe I could finally succeed in losing weight. As the days passed, I really began to believe it.

A New Life

Knowing how to eat is 200 percent of the battle. And it's not an exaggeration to say that I embarked

on an entirely new way of life. Seriously! Beginning
in February 1999, I adopted some of what Dr. Jay
had told me, and I changed other components of
his eating plan—sometimes choosing different
foods and doing some other fine-tuning along the
way. But one thing was certain: I became hard-core
about cutting sugar (my big weakness) out of my
diet. Com-pletely.

Today, I keep an eye on the amount of carbohydrates I eat, but there are no hard-and-fast rules
that (in the past) always ended up being broken.
The days of trying to eat zero carbs and zero sugar
are gone. In fact, I'm very flexible and relaxed—
no rigid rules and no concrete eating plan, but
rather some general directions that I'm taking. No
crazy diets because you can't live on shakes or
pineapple all your life—and they'll throw your metabolism into a tailspin! No fad foods because
you'll get sick of them in no time! And I certainly
don't count calories (yuck!) or keep a daily food
diary. If I tried to stick to some strict, unbending
rules, I know I couldn't follow them for a lifetime,
and I'd make myself miserable.

Once I changed my primary goal from being
superthin to being superhealthy—and once I
stopped bashing myself and hating myself because
of what the scale said—I lost a lot of weight. That's
really what happened.

As I write these words, it's been over four years
now, and I'm not looking back. I've lost close to
thirty pounds from my peak weight—yes, thirty
pounds!—and thank goodness, I've been able to
maintain that weight loss (although it's always a
challenge to stay there!).

Initially, as those pounds came off, I remember

Dave telling me that my blue jeans were hanging on me. "You look like a gangster," he teased me. "You need to buy a new pair."

He was right, and I went shopping for jeans at The Gap, and bought a few pair with a better fit (size 8, if I remember correctly). But then I lost another eight or nine pounds, and even the new jeans were literally around my hips! Dave took one look and said, "Ali, haven't you had time to get those new jeans?"

"I did! These *are* my new jeans."

So I went shopping again, and brought home size 4. It was crazy—I was living every dieter's dream of being forced to buy a new wardrobe! As the pounds came off, I felt so much better about myself. I felt healthier, too. It was so inspiring and so motivating. And when the size 4's started to fit a little loose on me—well, I knew I was doing something right.

The Fans React

When I lost all that weight, people took notice. I remember Corina Duran, one of our makeup artists at *Days*, teasing me when I showed up one day wearing a baggy denim jail shirt. (Sami was on Death Row, remember?) She exclaimed, "Ali, how dare you hide your stomach under that big shirt! You look great—you have to show it off!"

So the next day, I arrived on the set with a fitted button-down top that I had tied at my waist. And what was Corina's reaction? She looked at me and said, "Now, you're just showing off!"

(Theo & Juliet Photography/Zelf-Fridlizius)

After slimming down

Positive comments like that—and the weight that I had successfully lost—were motivating. My strengthened willpower came from my new look and those glances in the mirror that had me saying, "Geez, I have to go shopping and buy smaller-sized clothes!"

Meanwhile, viewers of *Days* noticed the change, too, and I was deluged with hundreds of letters and e-mails, with fans asking how I had slimmed down. Here's what one fan wrote:

> *Alison, I envy your determination and inner strength to become healthy and live a healthier life. That determination is something I've had trouble hanging on to. All my life, I've been referred to as the 'chunky one.' Even my family doctor would poke fun at my weight sometimes (which REALLY got my spirits down).*
>
> *Even though no one ever called me 'fat' (at least not to my face), I have always seen myself as fat. The fact that I'm 22 years old, and still can't shed what my parents politely call my 'baby fat,' is pretty discouraging. I have tried almost every diet out there, and haven't found one with lasting results once you stop the plan.*
>
> *I was floored (and jealous and envious) one day when I was watching Days of Our Lives, and you walked out in this flattering dress, and I realized just how much weight you have actually lost and how fit you looked. I've been curious about your dieting plan ever since.*
>
> *I enthusiastically agree with the natural and healthy path you've chosen to assist you in your weight loss and your quest to be healthier. I feel confident that the same path will work for me and a lot of other health-challenged people out there. I*

would greatly appreciate any feedback or advice
you might have for me.

Linda

When I make public appearances at *Days'* events, some fans want to talk about my weight and not much else (even if my eating habits are no longer my own obsession, someone somewhere seems obsessed with them!). When magazines have run articles about how I lost fifteen or twenty or twenty-five pounds, or *Entertainment Tonight* and *E! Entertainment* have documented my dieting efforts, readers have certainly responded, and I've received sacks of letters about it. Most of it has been very positive. There have been plenty of letters from people who told me that they've been motivated by my own success. Many have cheered me on. Or they've

(Author's personal collection)

Posing on the red carpet!

thanked me for publicly acknowledging that the battle to lose weight isn't an easy one. They've described their own struggles, their own successes and their own failures:

Hello Alison—I read your article in Soap Opera Digest *regarding sugar. As an experiment, I decided to give up granulated sugar. Not only did I lose 27 pounds, but I also lost any desire to ever eat sugar again. I went from a size 12–14 to a svelte size 6 (now I'm quoting my husband!). I found that I also crave more protein than carbohydrates and my energy level has soared. So THANK YOU for the interview which inspired me to follow in your footsteps.*

Gail

Hi. I have been a Days *fan for many years, and my daughter Brit started watching with me last year. She took a liking to you immediately. Any time I buy* Soap Opera Digest, *we look for articles about you.*

When we began to notice your weight loss, Brit thought you were losing like other actresses who had become way too skinny. Then we read an article about you talking about your weight loss. When Brit read what you said about being responsible and how you did it for yourself and only you, she was very impressed.

As we read more articles, and learned that you weren't obsessive about your weight, she began to have double doubts about what her friends had to say about weight and how they were so preoccupied with it. She started to realize that you were happy with yourself no matter what. She very rarely mentions her weight anymore, and the credit goes to you.

I just want to thank you for being such an inspiration. Good luck to you in your career, and I hope all your dreams come true.

                                                    Molly

Chapter

13

These days, the way I eat is constantly a work in progress. It's certainly different today than my diet of four years ago, or even four months ago. My own diet plan (I think of it more as a "lifestyle") is constantly changing, forever evolving, always fluid. I don't think of myself as dieting, but rather as eating right for myself.

I've managed to gain some insights with age (I'm all of twenty-six as I write these words!), and I've recognized that feeling great is definitely more important to me than achieving ultrathinness. Sure, I still have bad days when perhaps I overdo it. But if something doesn't seem to be working for a while, I'm not married to it—sometimes I make changes and try new foods and approaches, meal by meal. It makes the process much more interesting.

As I already mentioned, I've never had the intention of turning this into a diet book and recommending a specific program that I think you

and everyone else should adopt. I know better than to think that I have the expertise to counsel you on the diet that's best for you. I'm not a nutritionist, and I don't know what appeals to your palate, nor am I a doctor who understands what's optimal for your own body and well-being. You certainly know best what might work for you, and what it may take for you to stick with it for the long term. If you want to try the latest diet fad, go ahead, but don't allow yourself to be brought down if it doesn't work. More than anything, I want to encourage you to eat a healthy diet, and the rest will probably fall into place.

Now, please don't misunderstand me: I don't approach my eating lackadaisically. I do carefully consider what goes onto my plate every single meal. But it's not an obsession. I try to use good judgment, making sure my meals support my goals, while never being fanatical about it or latching on to gimmicks. Whenever I've tried to follow a strict program, I've ended up eventually cheating, and then feeling angry and resentful that I had tried the diet in the first place.

In this chapter, let me tell you about a few of my own approaches that I've used in recent times when planning my meals and snacks. They may make sense to you—or maybe they won't. But perhaps if you take a little of what I do, and borrow some other dietary strategies from friends, family members, or other books, you might find yourself creating your own plan that's the perfect fit. Remember, this is how *I* often eat, but I don't pretend to have the answers for you. If you want to try some of my lifestyle changes, great—but you might find other ideas that work much better for you:

- I shop completely differently than I once did. It fact, a trip to the supermarket can turn into something of an adventure these days. Years ago, Dr. Jay told me to read food labels more carefully, and I was surprised at just how much information is there. Just an example or two: Breakfast cereals can differ considerably in the amount of sugar they have (some cereals not only list sugar as a major ingredient, but corn syrup and honey aren't far behind!). One brand of wheat bread that I used to buy has corn syrup as its second ingredient!

- I eat breakfast every day. Not only is it important for me to start off the morning right, but on the *Days* set, you never know when you're going to get a break to eat—you can be on stage for hours and never have a moment to grab a bite, and you better be ready to perform the most demanding scenes at 9 or 10 or 11 A.M., if that's what the schedule calls for! For breakfast, I often have Puffed Wheat these days. Or I'll prepare an egg omelet, making it interesting by adding chives and basil from my garden, and perhaps a little cilantro or cheese. Or I'll eat an egg sandwich made with one slice of whole wheat bread, a little cheese, and turkey bacon. And by the way, if there's a particular brand of breakfast cereal that I don't eat very often—but I'm just dying to have it— I will! I'm not going to be driven crazy by my diet, and I'm not going to let it keep me from enjoying life!

- For lunch, a typical meal might be an open-faced tuna salad sandwich, prepared on a piece of bread. Or I might make a salad with plenty of

lettuce, other vegetables, and chicken breast. I'll often chop up and toss all kinds of things into the salad bowl—apples, chives, turkey bacon, shredded turkey, or a little cheese. I try to add a healthy carb like a yam or brown rice at lunch to help me get through the rest of the day.

- For dinner, I usually have some protein—perhaps a modest serving of meat, chicken, or fish (salmon is one of my favorites!). I minimize the carbs I have in the evening, which reduces the likelihood of my blood sugar levels going haywire. In the evenings, I'm also likely to avoid all carb foods like corn, potatoes, pasta, rice, and bread, but I'll have some vegetables like broccoli or green beans. Variety is key, and I don't overrely on any single food or food group—or deprive myself completely of anything, either.

- In general, no matter what meal we're talking about, I lean a little more toward protein than carbohydrates when thinking about what to eat; when I do, fat storage becomes less of a problem for me. Protein also seems to curb my appetite better than other types of food. So I eat modest portions of high-quality, high-protein fish and chicken. And if I have a pasta salad for lunch one day, I make a mental note to take it easy on the carbs the next day. Sensible, but not fanatical.

- I eat plenty of fresh produce. I realize that I need some fruits and vegetables since, without enough complex carbohydrates, I may be playing havoc with my blood sugar levels. I might have an orange in the morning, for example, which doesn't have the high concen-

tration of sugar as a glass of orange juice (I remember reading that juice provides the equivalent of the sugar in eight oranges, but an actual piece of fruit has a much more modest amount of sugar, and tends to fill me up). In the supermarket, my shopping cart may have vegetables like bell peppers in it (I love their flavor, texture, and color). And I'm always trying new foods to cook with—I used leeks in my omelet the other day . . . delicious!

- I spend a lot of time in my dressing room at NBC, waiting to be called to the *Days* set. While it might be tempting to take advantage of the candy and bagels available for the cast and crew, I rarely let that temptation get to me anymore. Sure, the crew works very hard, they're on their feet all day, and they want something substantial for lunch or dinner, so the show's producers make sure they're well fed. But as an alternative, I rely on my own healthy snacks, often stopping at the deli on the way to the studio for some cold cuts (like turkey pastrami or smoked turkey). When I get hungry, I'll raid the refrigerator in my dressing room, roll up some turkey, often using iceberg lettuce as my "bread," and perhaps make it a little more interesting with some Muenster cheese and avocado. Or I might have a healthy snack of celery with a little peanut butter or seasoning salt.

- There are some foods that I eat less often (as far as I'm concerned, no food is taboo, but there are some that I try not to do to excess). Pizza isn't something I overdo. I've reduced the amount of starchy foods I eat. I've cut down on bread and other heavy foods. The same with

refined sugar; at one point early in the process, I eliminated sugar from my diet completely— cold turkey—tossing out the Cokes in my refrigerator (I even gave up my beloved Diet Cokes for a while!), and replacing them with iced tea (with a little fruit water, but no other sweetener). After drinking two or three sugar-saturated soft drinks a day for years, I found that in just a couple weeks, I lost the compulsion to reach for something sweet. I put my sweet tooth to rest. These days, I drink a Diet Coke from time to time, but not in excess. Some people, however, can't stop consuming sugar on a dime, particularly when you're talking about something they've been eating all their life; maybe you need to wean yourself gradually from sugar-laden foods, which is fine. Do whatever works best for you. But, let me tell you, after a while your sugar cravings *will* subside. That's why I even cut out the Nutra-Sweet, too. You have to get your taste buds off the sugar cravings! So if you really cut all sugar and sugar substitutes, eventually sugary sodas and the related stuff aren't particularly appealing.

- I've dramatically reduced my dependence on coffee. For much of my life, I was so hooked on caffeine that I used to salivate just driving by a Starbucks (you're right—that's a bit of an exaggeration!). But once I weaned myself from coffee and switched instead to iced tea or Ice Blended, I could barely stand the smell or the taste of coffee anymore. The acidity of the bean almost made me ill. As for caffeine, I try to keep the lid on the number of caffeine-spiked

diet sodas I consume, which required a real change in mindset. There was a time when my closest friends would give me cases of Diet Cokes as birthday presents! I remember once getting a Coca-Cola lap blanket as a gift. But I now rely on much healthier drinks (although the lap blanket has survived my decision to rid the house of most soft-drink reminders!).

- Now, let me be honest: I still love desserts, and I eat them from time to time. But I don't have them—and certainly don't feel I need them—every day. I remember times when I've been on vacation, and I ended up at some restaurant, and rationalized it this way: "Hey, I'm on vacation—and when am I ever going to come back to this restaurant? So I'll splurge and enjoy myself." Nothing's wrong with that—but I also know that if I have a few cookies four or five nights in a row (which I very rarely do!), I better get back on track once I get home. I also try to choose desserts that I really enjoy (candy bars aren't my thing, so when I'm selecting desserts, I make sure it's something I truly love!). Not long ago, when *US Weekly* did an interview with me and featured my weight loss, I wasn't the least bit hesitant to tell them that I had recently joined some girlfriends for a big dinner at Emeril's in Las Vegas. Why not?! It's all a matter of give and take, appreciating the good things that make life enjoyable, while never losing sight of the overall goal of maintaining my weight at a certain level.

- My advice to my friends (and maybe it will make sense to you as well) is that if you absolutely crave something—let's say a slice of cheesecake,

for example—you might as well have the cheese-cake (a small slice, of course!) and be done with it, rather than feeling deprived and obsessing about it. In my own case, I won't go through life completely avoiding chocolate cake; and if my mom (who is a wonderful baker!) makes a special dessert (like blueberry pie!), I'm the first in line.

I've known people who are just dying to eat a cookie, but have convinced themselves that they shouldn't—so instead they'll have a slice of bread, and when that doesn't satisfy them, they'll end up eating an entire bag of baby carrots with peanut butter (I know this from personal experience!) and maybe a soda or two. Before all is said and done, they've eaten eight or nine different food items in lieu of the cookie—but then they'll probably end up eating the cookie anyway! My philosophy: If you're feeling deprived, you're going to fall off the wagon at some point. So keep the portions of desserts relatively small, give yourself a little latitude, and *enjoy life*!

- I carry a water bottle with me nearly all the time. Water helps control my appetite, so I drink it all day long. If you're accustomed to eating and snacking throughout the day, water will help quench your appetite and keep you from reaching for food as often.

- I used to eat when I was bored or anxious, and there are plenty of tedious times at the studio when you're waiting (and waiting and waiting) to be called to the set for rehearsals or to shoot your scenes. In the past, there were times when I'd pace my dressing room, wondering what I could eat. When that would

happen, I'd often break the tedium by walking to the vending machines, and buy a bag of potato chips, a candy bar, or a soda—just because I was bored, not because my stomach was growling! It became a huge problem for me—and it threatened to make *me* huge as well! So I've worked hard on eating only when I'm hungry. I've found other ways to cut the stress and shatter the boredom that used to lead me to food. I always keep my mind occupied—by answering fan mail or e-mail, for example, or surfing the net. I listen to classical music, sometimes with the lights dimmed and a burning candle nearby (I grew up in a household where my mom played classical violin, and the kids always played one instrument or another). Also, I occupy my time by talking with fellow actors or doing all kinds of absolutely crazy things— I actually taught myself to juggle, if you can believe that!

Even though these are general guidelines that I've often used, let me stress again that my diet is fluid and constantly changing. I've gone through phases where I feel like eating carrots and not much of anything else. Or there have been times when the sight of a hamburger almost turns my stomach, and I can't go near it. I've become very good at "going with the flow," and adapting to whatever works at the moment. If this sounds like a comfortable approach, maybe a rigid diet isn't for you, either. At the same time, I know that I'm in a "rest-of-my-life" situation—I'll never go back to eating (or overeating) the way I used to. It's given me a real sense of "diet liberation."

What About Portion Size?

I realized a while ago that we don't need as much food to sustain us as we often consume. It's just like sleep . . . your body may need only five or six hours a night, but people who are accustomed to getting seven or eight hours feel deprived if they sleep less. So my own portion sizes rarely get out of control—I'm very careful not to overdo it. (Listen up! This is a real key to my success with weight management!)

Our society is obsessed with supersized portions, apparently as a way to "get more for our money" at restaurants. But our bodies don't require that much fuel. Our pasta bowls don't need to be filled to overflowing. We aren't supposed to make every meal a Thanksgiving feast, 365 days a year. I simply don't eat as much as I used to, and because my stomach and my appetite have shrunk with time, I really don't miss overindulging.

At the same time, however, as I've already written, I won't deprive myself, either. If I really feel like eating pasta, I'll have it—but I don't need a Herculean-sized bowl of pasta to feel satisfied. I'm content just having a side-dish-sized portion and not getting carried away—I simply don't need a second or third helping, and I feel quite satisfied without them.

When eating in restaurants, I don't let myself get so caught up in social conversation that I eat unconsciously. Let me tell you what works for me in restaurants: I often order both an appetizer and an entrée, allowing myself to indulge in as many different tastes as possible. So I may order an appetizer such as capreza (sliced tomatoes, Mozzarella

cheese, fresh basil); it's a completely different taste than the chicken and the vegetables that I may have for an entrée. Or I'll have a salad for an appetizer, and then salmon and broccoli as the main dish. I'll leave some of each on my plate, and take the leftovers home for the following day. It's a great way to dine. And when I eat this way, I'm not hungry when I leave the restaurant—but I'm not stuffed, either.

I also don't obsess over what I'm eating; when I was completely preoccupied with the food I put on my plate, I remember having internal debates with myself over whether or not I should take another bite. I'd feel terrible about myself if I ate more than I had planned. What a horrible way to live! If I ate something that wasn't part of my "perfect" program, it chipped away at my self-esteem. For me, that was the hardest part of being on a formal diet—every time I slipped, I'd beat myself up over it, convinced that something was wrong with me. Today, however, balance is what I'm seeking and I usually find it. Gradually, I began to see beyond the scale and started to trust my gut instincts about who I really am, what's really important, and how much I should eat.

What's Cooking?

Now, what about time in the kitchen? Well, I'm no Emeril or Julia Child. I don't ever expect to be, either, and I guess I'm a latecomer to the art of creating culinary masterpieces.

When I was nineteen years old, I got my first apartment and my introduction to dabbling in my

own kitchen. As comfortable as I had been living
with my parents, I was feeling a little crowded at
home and decided to become Ms. Independent!
Most of my friends had already gone off to college
and were living in dorm rooms, and my parents
thought it was fine for me to get out on my own. So
I bought a bed, a beautiful Laura Ashley comforter,
and some wicker furniture, and I borrowed a coffee table from my parents' house. And, of course,
then I had to deal with the kitchen.

Well, some of my earliest efforts—even the sim-
plest ones—were an absolute disaster! Let me tell
you about the time I ruined a bag of microwave
popcorn! Now really, how hard can it be to pop
some popcorn? Yet, apparently it required far more
talent than I could muster at that moment. As I recall, the instructions on the bag called for setting
the microwave oven at two minutes. But that wasn't
good enough for me. I made the executive decision that two minutes just didn't seem right. So I
set it at five minutes, and let her rip!

Well, before I knew it, the bag of popcorn had
actually exploded! And then it burst into flames!
Can you believe it—I started a fire in my own microwave oven! Quite clever, don't you think?!

Fortunately, I'm happy to report that my culinary talents have taken a turn for the better. In
fact, I've actually become pretty good at a growing
number of dishes. But I've also learned a few
lessons—for example, you really have to pay attention! I remember one evening when I was pre-
paring spaghetti with a really yummy mushroom
cream sauce that my mom had made. Well, it's
really not very complicated to make spaghetti, right?
Yet I somehow turned the cooking experience into
a wild event that soon resembled an E-ticket ride at

Disneyland. Here's what happened: I put the spaghetti in a pot, and when the water started boiling, I turned the flame down a bit. So far, so good. But then I went into the living room and began watching *Seinfeld*. Big mistake! Thirty minutes later when the show was finally over, I returned to the kitchen— and was greeted by a torrent of water that might have posed a challenge for a seasoned river rafter! What a mess! The lesson: Don't let yourself become distracted (even by *Seinfeld*!) when there's something cooking on the stove!

As you can tell, I started from literally nowhere, ruined quite a few meals (and caused a flash flood or two), but today, I *love* being in the kitchen—and I'm getting better all the time! I learned a lot by watching the Food Channel, and chefs like Emeril Lagasse convinced me that cooking was something that I could do. He makes it sound so easy, doesn't he? And he makes it fun, too, which is a great way to approach just about everything in life. Many of my meal and dessert creations aren't half bad. (I can also proudly proclaim that I make a pretty mean—and fire-free—microwave popcorn these days, too!) When I eat at restaurants and give instructions to waiters on how I'd like my meal prepared, I often get a rather boring and tasteless dish. But in my own kitchen, I've become creative with spices and herbs, including some from my own herb garden. I love to experiment and try new dishes. I have a great time being inventive— for example, making a chicken dish by sautéing it lightly for flavor (showing some restraint with the oil), then baking it, and finally bringing on the herbs, starting with garlic and rosemary. Take my word for it, the taste can be pretty amazing! Or if I'm in the mood for a Mexican-themed dinner, I

might simmer the chicken, mix in some cilantro, and then use it in a stew (rather than serving it with tortillas).

I sometimes adapt recipes from magazines like *Bon Appetit* and *Gourmet* so they're more to my liking. Or I'll actually combine two recipes—for example, a pasta dish plus a tomato chicken sauce. I'll take the sauce and make it thicker by adding artichoke hearts and broccoli. (I call it my "chicken sink stew," because I'll add any and every vegetable that's in my refrigerator and turn the sauce into a chunky delight! Then I'll prepare the pasta, too (for my husband Dave), although I'll often eat only the stew myself.

I've also enjoyed a bonus that comes with cooking: When I prepare a meal, I'm not as hungry once I sit down at the dining room table. (Does that happen to you?) Maybe I've spent so much time smelling the food in the kitchen that it starts filling me up—at least it seems that way. Cooking is a great stress reliever for me, too, because it keeps my mind focused on following the recipe, measuring ingredients, and so on. It almost becomes something like a meditation. Whatever the explanation, I don't eat as much when I cook, compared to when someone else does the work in the kitchen.

Even though I don't overindulge in treats like cookies, I love baking them for Dave—and so I won't be tempted to overindulge myself, I might put nuts in them (that's because I hate nuts!). I'm not even tempted when I've "doctored" the cookies that way (although I must admit that peanut butter cookies sure can whet my appetite!).

Dave is great when it comes to my cooking. He has inspired me to become very adventurous in

the kitchen, and usually likes whatever I whip up (at least that's what he tells me). Of course, he and I also love eating together, and—here's the best part—he often cleans up the kitchen afterward. He says that since I've worked so hard to prepare the meal, the least he can do is wash the dishes. What a sweetheart!

A Little Perspective

As you can tell, I've done a lot of thinking about food, diets, and weight in the last few years. I see so many of my fellow actresses torture themselves over what they should and shouldn't eat. But I've had the luck of making some very good girlfriends in the biz who have helped me keep my head on straight about the whole issue. Although I'm still very aware of my diet, I have a much healthier perspective these days.

Here's the bottom line: If I really need to starve myself to be an actress in Hollywood, I'll find another line of work. I could always go behind the cameras as a director (that's a long-range goal of mine), or maybe as a producer. Or I could go back to college and pursue a completely different career. Of course, acting is still my first love. I'm so happy in front of the cameras. But let's be clear about this: I'm not going to make myself miserable and send myself into an emotional tailspin trying to rise to some impossible ideal! As much as I love acting, I could do something else.

With each passing day, I think I'm strengthening the healthy attitude I now have about food,

diets, and the person I see in the mirror. But it hasn't happened overnight. It's taken a long, long time to get to this point. Because of the industry I work in, it's always going to be important for me to be conscious of what I weigh; Hollywood is absolutely obsessed with how people look, and as long as I'm a working actress, I can never lose sight of that. But fortunately, many of my close friends—inside and outside of show business—have a levelheaded point of view about diets and weight. Although we hear the message that "you can't be too thin"—the truth is, you definitely can! Everyone knows that eating disorders can be hazardous to your health: damaging vital organs, impairing the thyroid gland, and even causing cardiac arrest and death. Thousands of people, most of them young women, die each year as a direct result of anorexia or bulimia. Why would someone risk her life just to impress a casting director or producer? It's absolutely insane!

Even so, I know so many actresses who have suspended good judgment and continue to be caught up in self-starvation. They only seem to have their sights focused on the short-term goal, which is staying thin and getting and keeping their acting jobs. I see it all the time.

But I won't let this way of life grab ahold of me like it once did. I can't allow it to take me over and affect how I feel about myself. I really have learned to accept and love myself, whether I'm ten pounds heavier or ten pounds lighter than I was a month or two earlier. Yes, I know I'm never going to be pencil-thin—but I do want to be as healthy as possible. So I try to eat right because it's a way to stay healthy, not because I'm driven to fit the mold of the actress-with-the-perfect-body. Once I shifted

my focus away from the scale and more toward leading a fulfilling, healthy life, my excess weight started to disappear.

It took me years to change my thinking to get to this place, and I have a much happier and wiser perspective about weight than I once did.

These days, I don't weigh myself. Ever. While I guess I have a general sense of what the number on the scale would be, it means much less to me than how my clothes look on me when I gaze into the mirror. If I look good in a favorite dress (I wear a size 2 or 4 today), that's all the motivation I need. I can see the payoff that comes with maintaining a healthy and comfortable weight. I'm also honest with myself—if the clothes are getting a little snug, it's time to back away from the cookie jar!

Sometimes, fans write me letters that say something like, "How can I get my daughter to lose weight like you did?" Well, just like I decided not to include a formal diet in this book, I decided not to give fans anything more than just some general information about what I did that finally worked for me. In the same way, you should find your own path. Someday, if I have a Ph.D. after my name or training as a registered dietitian, then maybe I'll get more specific. But for now, all I can really do is tell you about the success I've had, and suggest that everyone figure it out for herself. Find a way of eating that you can live with, and then stick with it. I hope you reach your weight-loss goals. But more than anything, I want you to be happy with yourself, no matter what your size. It really shouldn't matter what you weigh; if you don't look like the models on the cover of *Cosmo*, you can't spend your life feeling miserable about it.

Fans also sometimes ask for my thoughts about dietary supplements, which I've used on occasion (you may have seen me in TV commercials and print ads for a supplemental product not long ago). I've used supplements to maintain the weight loss I've already achieved, and to kick-start my workouts for bathing-suit scenes, and so forth. If you're like me, you've probably discovered that while losing weight is always a challenge, it's even more difficult to keep it off. And because of my unpredictable work schedule—where many hours can go by without time to eat, and where the buffet table near the set is always a temptation—I've sometimes used supplements as a safety net, helping me control my appetite, particularly when I have weak moments. Some supplements can speed up metabolism, making workouts more effective, and they can also make you thirsty, so you end up drinking lots of water (which is good for appetite control). But let me make this clear: I've *never* overused or overrelied on these supplements, and I refuse to let myself become dependent on them. I know that some people have had problems with certain supplements (although not the one I've helped promote) when they've overdone it, using them day after day (often several times a day), frequently at very high doses. When I've used supplements, it's only in moderation and with common sense as a guide. As with so many things, it's all about moderation.

As I tell my story in this book, I think I do have an important message to communicate—in particular to teenage girls and young women. As you mature and find where you fit into the world, don't let Hollywood dictate the way you need to look or how you feel about yourself if you don't have the

"perfect body." You don't need to be a size 0 to pursue your dreams. The world isn't going to come to an end if you don't fit the stereotype of whatever happens to be the "right look" at the moment. Just be yourself, and your friends and family will love and appreciate you for it.

Chapter 14

Are you a couch potato?

Sound appealing?

There are times when the thought of living a sedentary lifestyle seems pretty attractive. Imagine curling up on the sofa in front of the fireplace and getting lost in a good novel all afternoon, barely moving hour after hour—and there's a time and a place for that! But it's the exception, not the rule.

I know better than to get too comfortable being lazy. Not only for my physical health, but also for my psychological well-being, I need to keep active.

Since some of this book has discussed weight and dieting, I can't neglect the importance of incorporating physical activity into an overall weight loss and fitness program. But as with my approach to dieting in this book, I'm not going to recommend a specific exercise plan that *you* should be following. That's not my purpose here. How-ever, I will spend a few pages telling you what *I* do—what

works for me . . . what keeps me in shape . . . what helps maintain my weight at a comfortable level. The foods I put on my plate, of course, are very important to keeping my weight where I want it. But exercise is just as essential to my lifestyle. It burns calories. It makes me feel better. It gives me more energy to keep pace with my hectic schedule.

It's like that billboard I've seen at malls lately. It says in big letters, "The Miracle Diet Pill," with a picture of a pill below it. But in black letters, one side of the pill says "diet" and the other side says "exercise." That really is the only way to get and stay fit—eating right, and exercise, exercise, exercise!

The Value of Exercise

For as long as I can remember, I've known the importance of exercise. For starters, as someone who once kept one eye on the scale, I can tell you that losing weight is much more difficult unless you're staying active and burning calories. Trust me, that's a no-brainer. However, bear in mind that when you exercise, you just might find yourself also gaining muscle mass, which will slow the speed of your weight loss. That's often what has happened with me when I work out. Yes, exercise keeps me healthy and fit, and it does help produce the loss of unwanted pounds over time. But it may not translate into an immediate lightning strike of weight loss when you expect it to.

Nevertheless, don't underestimate the ability of your workouts to contribute to your overall weight

management. In fact, just spend a little time traveling through Europe, and you'll see firsthand the value of physical activity. The United States has many more overweight people than France and most other European countries do, and you can't blame all of it on genetics. Yes, I'm sure there are some dietary factors at play: The French are much less reliant than Americans on high-fat fast food, and when they do eat rich cheeses, they keep the portions small—just enough to fit on a cracker or two! They eat slower, and they eat less. But perhaps most important, *they walk constantly*. The French aren't as reliant on automobiles as we are, and they wear out a lot more shoes than tires. Yes, New Yorkers walk a lot, but in most other American cities, people are hooked on their cars. No wonder obesity isn't as big a problem in Europe as it is here.

Making Fitness a Priority

Although I've always known that exercise is good for me, it was really driven home by Dr. Jay, my dentist, who I wrote about in Chapter 12. (Remember, he was the one who described me as "puffy," which I guess was better than calling me "fat"—but not by much!) I followed Dr. Jay's way of eating as closely as I could, but mostly he convinced me to reevaluate the way I was leading my life. And for Dr. Jay, exercise has been just as important as eating right. "You need to work out to be healthy," he told me.

Of course, I knew Dr. Jay was right, and for most of my life, I have been physically active. All I had to

do was think back to my childhood, when, like most kids, I never stopped moving. Most children are outside playing from morning 'til night, and they're burning calories all the while. When you're that age and that active, having a Haagen-Dazs ice cream cone during the day is really not going to matter. But once life became much busier in adolescence and adulthood, I found that I needed to make fitness a priority or I'd never find time for it.

These days, I have to schedule my workouts just as I do every other appointment in the day. It needs to be as important as any other event or meeting. Listen, I block out time for doctor's appointments or meetings with my agent, right? So why not do the same for my workout? And on those days when I'm just not in the mood for physical activity, it's harder to feel lazy when I've already blocked out the 4 o'clock hour to get moving!

Now, let's put things in perspective: I've never been a person who wakes up in the morning and says, "I can hardly wait to get on the treadmill today!" For so many years, I just wasn't dedicated to my workouts. For a while, it became a real chore for me to get myself out the door to walk through the neighborhood or head for the gym. I'd force myself to do it at least two or three times a week, but my motivation sometimes waned if I didn't see much change in my weight (which was often the case because I was building up muscle mass). When that happened, I'd often throw in the towel for a month or two. I'd just take off my sneakers and store them in the closet for a while.

But since my heart-to-heart talk with Dr. Jay, physical fitness has become a way of life. For me, my workouts not only helped me lose weight, but even more important, they sure have helped *main-*

tain my current weight. They also make a huge difference in the way I feel.

How often do I exercise now? I don't feel the need to make it a six- or seven-day-a-week habit. But if I'm not lacing up my gym shoes three or four times a week, I've definitely fallen short of my goal. In fact, I've gotten to the point where I often actually crave those workouts—not only enjoying the activity itself, but also the adrenaline rush afterward. You've probably heard about the "runner's high"—that sense of exhilaration that can last long after you've wiped away the perspiration and showered. Exercise releases brain chemicals called *endorphins* that are known to produce a feeling of well-being. When you challenge your body—even if you're tired after the workout—the positive aftereffects are truly amazing!

I also don't overdo it when I work out (what would be the point of that?). I certainly don't have to push myself to the brink of exhaustion to get something out of it, nor does my workout have to be complicated. When I get my adrenaline flowing and my muscles working to the max (or close to it), that's all it takes—and this comes from someone who often hated exercising in the past! Recently, I saw a news story about a study involving two workout groups; it found that the women who worked out for less time but more intensely didn't lose any more weight than women who did a lower stress workout for a longer period of time. So walking uphill on the treadmill for forty-five minutes is right up my alley (so to speak).

Some people describe themselves as being "addicted" to exercise (how cool is that!). I might not go that far, but my workouts are the best means I've found for relieving the stresses and anxieties

of the day. No matter what mood I've been in before my workout, I *always* feel better after a spirited game of basketball or a brisk walk in the park. I've also found that exercise tends to dampen my appetite and strengthen my resolve to stick with my eating plan (let's get real—after exercising for thirty minutes, you may not want to spoil the benefits you've achieved by splurging on a dessert that isn't part of the diet you're following). Exercise also elevates your calorie-burning metabolism not only during your workout, but also in the minutes and hours afterward. And as I've already mentioned, a good workout should give you much more energy during the day than if you had chosen to skip your exercise session.

How Much? How Often?

Over the years, I've tried tons of workout programs, sometimes even using a personal trainer who has helped me create an exercise plan and learn to use the equipment at the gym. And here's what I've found: What works best for me is to vary my exercise routines from one session to the next, with no rigid routines that have to be followed—or else!

Maybe I'll walk on the treadmill one day, use my stationery bike during the next workout, and walk my dog the following one (Dave and I have three dogs—Paco, Consuela, and Frieda). Then I might take a cardio-workout class at the gym on the fourth exercise day of the week. Sports can be fun, so I may play volleyball on the beach with friends, or test my skills in a touch football or basketball game

for a change of pace (hmm, still no pro contracts being offered!). Dave and I also play racquetball as often as twice a week for two hours at a time (yes, this can really be exhausting!). I love skiing, too—in fact, my favorite travel destinations can be narrowed down to anyplace with a ski slope!

I also spent two years learning to kickbox (how 'bout that!). I started kickboxing when Patrick Muldoon told me about a kickboxing gym that he had been going to in Santa Monica. I figured it was something I had to try, and I stuck with it for a couple years and got a lot out of it. But eventually, it became impractical to keep it up; the commute to the gym just got to be too taxing, and I looked for ways to exercise closer to home. Before long, I started going to a boxing gym just ten minutes from home. Austin Peck told me about it, and I took one-on-one classes there. I actually put on the gloves and sparred in the ring with a trainer! Can't you just picture me?! I wasn't quite ferocious enough to strike fear into the hearts of Muhammad Ali and George Foreman, but it sure was great fun and wonderful exercise.

By varying my workouts as much as possible, it keeps them from becoming repetitive and routine. And whether I'm in the mood to be alone or with other people, to be indoors or outdoors, there's always a form of exercise I can do.

I'm certainly not a jock, but I realize that I don't have to be. I love to take long walks, and let me tell you, almost *everybody* can walk (even you, even me!). It doesn't matter how young or how old you are, whether you're overweight and out of shape or have the finely tuned body of an Olympic athlete. You don't need expensive clothing or costly shoes to walk, either, nor do you need to join a

gym. An hour-long brisk walk (moving at about three to four miles per hour) burns 300 to 400 calories, which can really add up, day after day. And here's what you'll find: Once you've been walking for a while, it gets easier. You'll be able to walk farther as you get in better shape.

Well, now that I've given you an idea of my favorite types of workouts, here's some additional food for thought: Formal exercise isn't always necessary. *Any* kind of movement helps; even cleaning the kitchen (ugh!) or gardening burns calories and adds to your overall fitness, a little at a time.

(Author's personal collection)

Taking a ride with Ghost

But that's not all. Stairs are everywhere, and if you walk up a flight or two instead of taking the elevator, it all counts. Park farther away from the mall entrance next time! It all contributes to your overall fitness. In my own case, I love gardening, and the calories it burns do accumulate. Swing dancing is another one of my passions, and it's a fabulous form of exercise.

When I'm ranking my preferences for physical activity, I've told you about nearly all of them, with one exception: Let's not forget the ponies! I've been horseback riding since I was a little girl, and when you're really working with your horse, whether it's a mare or a stallion, it's a great form of exercise and an awesome experience! When I was a kid, I took horseback-riding lessons almost every other day (I was so allergic to horses that I had to take allergy medicine just to get through the lessons— but that's how much I loved horses!). Today, I'm lucky to have my own horse, Apparition (with the nickname Ghost!).

For all the years of great experiences riding and competing, I will never forget the most embarrassing moments. One time, on a very (and I do mean *very*) hot day in Los Angeles, I was at a local horse show. I was wearing the usual competitive riding attire—long britches, long-sleeved shirt, wool coat— they weren't exactly perfect duds for a 100-degree afternoon. To make the situation worse, I wasn't drinking as much water as I should have. Well, you can guess what happened: In the middle of the course, all by myself in the ring and with all eyes on me, I began feeling weak, dizzy, and then very faint. Before I knew it, I had toppled off my horse and hit the ground with an ungraceful thud. Ouch! What I remember most about the incident was my

mom and my trainer Nancy bringing me Gatorade and then helping me back onto the horse. The saying is completely true—you have to "get back on the horse" right away; otherwise you never will. I got onto his back again, jumped the jump, and learned a good lesson about myself. I may be afraid—but I won't let it stop me! Afterwards, I took off my coat and poured water on my head. Then I felt OK. But I was SO embarrassed!

Getting Motivated

OK, we all agree that exercise is important, whether we're doing it to lose weight or just to stay healthy. But as I mentioned at the beginning of this chapter, sometimes the couch looks awfully inviting. Motivating myself to get moving is still occasionally a challenge, and judging from some of the letters I get, many of my fans have the same problem—how to get inspired to put on the walking shoes and get going. One letter writer described it this way:

> *Dear Alison—I was an active child and teenager involved in many sports, and many of the same activities you enjoy. But as an adult, I've always had trouble finding the motivation to start a diet and exercise program because the results aren't always noticeable right away. Once I start to see some positive results, I can get motivated and get going, and I don't always need that extra outside push when it comes to exercising.*
>
> *How did you get in such good cardiovascular shape, and did you do any strength training along with your workout? And who did you turn*

> *to for support when you found yourself having a
> tough day or not wanting to exercise (other than
> your husband)? Was getting started ever a problem
> for you? How did you get yourself motivated in the
> beginning and stay motivated throughout? I
> would greatly appreciate any feedback or advice
> you might have for me. I look forward to watching
> your continuing quest for optimum health.*
> *Sincerely, Kimberly*

There are times when in only an instant, I can
weave out of thin air an excuse for not exercising!
Maybe I didn't sleep well the night before, and I'm
so tired. Or perhaps it's too hot outside (or too
cold or too rainy). Or maybe I have to get up early
the next morning to catch a flight. But when your
choice of an exercise is convenient and just seconds away, it makes it harder to procrastinate, and
much tougher to delay or dawdle. Unless I'm truly
sick or injured, it's so much easier to stick with a
workout program when it's readily available.

One of the best aspects of walking is that it's so
convenient. It's harder to make excuses to stay on
the couch when walking is on the agenda. Yes, there
are days when I just don't feel like getting into the
car and driving to the gym; it turns exercise into a
bigger production than I'm prepared for. But to
get ready for a walk through my neighborhood, all
I need to do is put on my walking shoes and step
out the door. Could it get any easier?

Sure, I still have days when I'd just rather not exercise. But here's something that I've found: I love
to read, and I'll often get caught up in a book for
hours. So rather than just reading while sitting in a
comfortable chair, I'll slip on a pair of sweats and

climb onto the exercise bicycle with my book, usually for thirty minutes at a stretch. I can read just as well when my feet are pedaling, and before I know it, I've finished twenty-five or fifty pages and have barely been aware that I've worked out (except for the beads of perspiration that have dripped onto the book!). The time goes by so fast!

Here's an additional component of this entire issue of motivation, and it has to do with your partner (Husband? Wife? Friend? You fill in the blank). While I know that my workouts help me maintain my weight where I want it, my husband Dave has *never* had a problem with weight. He has a very high metabolism that always seems to be in fourth gear. He can eat anything he wants and exercise as much or as little as he has time for, and he's not going to gain a pound. (As I've told him, "If we could bottle what's inside your body, we'd be multi-billionaires!") If I let it, it would drive me crazy knowing how easily Dave maintains his weight and how I always need to stay vigilant. But I've got to admit, Dave *does* work hard at staying healthy, and he motivates me to keep going. We exercise together whenever possible. Sometimes we'll take long walks on the beach or just through the neighborhood. It's a great way for us to spend time together.

If you enjoy walking like we do, change your route every day—it's a great way to become reacquainted with sections of your neighborhood that you might not have seen for a while, and you'll enjoy the change in scenery. (By the way, I know where Dave's enthusiasm for exercise comes from: His parents walk almost every day, keeping a steady pace both up and down the hills near their home. They're very inspirational!)

Staying Fit! Staying Slim!

There are plenty of other calorie-burning and fitness strategies that take almost no time, but go a long way toward keeping you fit. Here are just a few that are easy to fit into the day's activities, some of which I've already mentioned:

- When you're shopping—whether at the supermarket or the mall—park your car at the far end of the parking lot and walk the equivalent of a block or two to get to the store entrance.
- When you're visiting an office building, use the stairs rather than the elevator (if you need to go up more than just a couple floors, get off the elevator two or three floors before your stop and take the stairs the rest of the way).
- Take advantage of every opportunity to walk— for example, when you need to pick up some milk at the convenience store, walk instead of drive. You can also walk while you talk, using a cordless phone or a cell phone when calling friends. Two of my coworkers, Bryan Dattilo (Lucas) and Peter Reckell (Bo), often bicycle into work from their homes. Talk about getting your cardio in! It keeps them both incredibly fit!
- When you're looking for something to do on a weekend afternoon, take a family hike through the nearby mountains instead of taking in a movie.

You get the point, right? With a little creative thinking, you can work exercise into your days without any real strain.

Defining Health and Fitness

Before I close this chapter, let me make another very important point. I probably define health and fitness a little broader than many other people. Health and fitness mean more than just exercising regularly and keeping my body in shape and well-toned, as important as that is. It means more than working out or choosing my diet carefully. To feel truly healthy, both physically and psychologically, I'm committed to being as happy and content as possible in every aspect of my life. That means pursuing a career that brings me fulfillment. It means caring about others and making time for friends, even if it's just a group of us hanging out and talking late into the night. It means minimizing the stress that I know can take a toll on my body—making sleep difficult, and over time leading to illness and depression.

It means being more accepting of myself, with all my strengths and all my weaknesses. It means setting goals and working hard to achieve them. It means being willing to change as my life evolves. It means trying to make every year better than the last one . . . and not beating myself up when I indulge once in a while! ☺

Chapter 15

(Author's personal collection)

We took this shot in front of the plane. Dave and I fly all over the place with our plane for mini-vacations. In fact, we often take our puppies with us.

I'm always fascinated by some of the questions that viewers of *Days of Our Lives* ask me in their fan mail—or, for that matter, what reporters ask in interviews for newspapers or the soap magazines. Of course, I understand the curiosity of fans about what goes on at *Days*; in fact, that's one of the reasons I wrote this book. For most *Days* fans, missing even a single episode would be unimaginable. For them, watching *Days* is a serious commitment—it's something they can't seem to live without. They never miss the show, and if they're at work or out-of-town on weekday afternoons, their VCR is pre-set and ready for action.

Judging by my mail, fans want to know just as much about me and the show's other actors as about the heartaches and happiness that our characters

Riding a moped around Tahiti with Dave on our honeymoon

are experiencing. Where did we meet our real-life spouse (or boyfriend), and if we're single, who are we dating? Who are our friends, both on and off the set? Where do we like to shop? What lipstick was I wearing in that scene on Tuesday in Salem Place? What do we do for fun? What advice do we have for their own romantic problems?

Because we're invited into America's living rooms five days a week, many fans feel that we're part of their family, and that they know almost everything about us, or at least want to. They're never hesitant to ask questions or offer advice. It's really quite a unique relationship.

In this chapter and the next one, let me describe all you've ever wanted to know about Alison Sweeney that I haven't written about thus far—well, maybe not *all!* And don't worry—if there are questions I

haven't answered in this book, I'll keep reading and answering your fan mail. And if these pages spark any new questions, drop me a line and I'll do my best to fill in the blanks.

My Home Life

I'm amazed at how much fans know about my life with my husband, Dave. While I'm used to having the spotlight shine on me, Dave's the kind of guy who is quite content staying out of the public eye, and as I've mentioned, he works in a profession (law enforcement) that has nothing to do with show business. So while he's not particularly eager for attention, he's married to me and so he knows that some of it comes with the territory. We can't go out in a public place and expect that we'll always be able to enjoy a quiet dinner without a fan approaching from another table and asking for an autograph or a photo. Neither of us minds it—a *Days* viewer may appear and just want to spend a few moments with us. For the most part, however, Dave and I lead a very normal, very private life. (Let's face it, after acting in a soap opera all day, where the story lines and our characters' behavior can border on the unusual—including the predictable hell-raising of Sami—I need the calmness and stability that Dave brings to my life.)

When did I meet Dave? Well, we've known each other for as long as either of us can remember— literally! My mother and Dave's father worked together for many years; both of them are violinists whose talents you've probably heard on many motion picture soundtracks. Our families have always

(Lesley Bohm)

Unlike Sami, I've been very lucky in love.

been friendly, and so I knew Dave when we were growing up. In fact, when I was about ten years old, I had quite a crush on him, although I'm sure he didn't know it; he was older (about fourteen years old at the time) and, of course, he couldn't be bothered with a kid like me when he was meeting girls his own age. Before long, Dave went to college; we lost contact for a while, but we saw each other again at a party at his parents' house in 1997—he was twenty-four at the time, and I was

about to turn twenty-one. There was definitely a
lot of chemistry there—and if you're wondering,
there still is!!!—and I just couldn't take my eyes off
of him. Before that night ended, I invited him to
my twenty-first birthday party. One thing led to another . . . and here we are, living happily ever after!

Once we were a couple, things happened very
quickly. We have so much in common, and there
was never a question in my mind that he was Mr.
Right (I know that sounds pretty cheesy, but it's
absolutely true!).

After dating for several months, Dave gave me a
big-time clue of what the future might hold. "Someday," he said, "I'm going to ask you to marry me,
and we're going to spend the rest of our lives together." Wow! That was so amazing! That's not
something that you'd expect to hear from most
guys. But early on, he was already thinking about
making a commitment. Well, guess what: I was already feeling the same way!

I'll never forget my first Valentine's Day with
Dave. It was sooo romantic! Now, Dave doesn't
particularly enjoy musical theater, but it's never
been a secret that I absolutely love it! (Hey, remember our *Moulin Rouge* productions at Fan
Weekends?!). So (leave it to Dave!) he planned a
Valentine's evening for us at the theater, which
meant so much to me (I knew it wouldn't have
been *his* first choice of an ideal night on the town).
We also had a *very* romantic dinner in downtown
L.A., not far from the theater in an incredible high-
rise restaurant with a spectacular view of the entire
city. It was an absolutely wonderful evening (Dave,
I still remember that Valentine's Day—it was so
special!).

By the way, now that Dave and I are married, Valentine's Day may be even more important to us. Once you're married, it's less about trying to impress the other person and more about taking the time to have some special moments together; it's a wonderful occasion for spoiling your significant other, setting aside some time for romance and cuddling, and keeping the fires burning (if you get my drift!). Because our respective schedules can be so hectic, we often end up celebrating Valentine's Day sometime in the vicinity of February 14th when both of us have free time, but often missing the exact day. Both of us also have a knack for finding humorous, sweet cards for one another, and we usually exchange small personal gifts. But the most important part is that we've set aside a night to be together.

Well, I've already given you examples of how romantic Dave can be. But I haven't described the night he proposed marriage. That's a night I'll *never* forget! We went to Catalina Island—26 miles off the coast of Los Angeles—for a quick getaway. Nothing seemed particularly out of the ordinary— Dave appeared easygoing and low-key when the weekend began. But then it all changed. At his suggestion, we took a stroll along the boardwalk by the ocean and exchanged small talk for a few minutes. But once we reached a secluded spot on the sand, the mood changed (did it ever!). I looked over and Dave had knelt down on one knee. Oh my God, I almost died! Before I could catch my breath or say a word, he proposed to me on the spot. I was *so* shocked—and so happy! Fortunately, my part in this monumental and memorable event was pretty small: All I really had to say was "yes"—

(Author's personal collection)

One of Sami's many wedding styles . . . she should write a book!

Dave took care of everything else! Now, *that* was definitely one of the most romantic moments of my life!

Although Dave and I didn't get married right away, it seemed like the planning was upon us before long—and let me tell you, making all the arrangements can be very involved and time-consuming! I knew that this was the one and only time I'd ever get married, and I wanted everything to be just right. But I didn't realize that there are so many things to organize, to plan for and keep track of, and it's so easy to overlook some of the tiny details if you're not careful.

At first, I wanted Dave to help me plan everything—but that didn't last long! Yes, we both picked out the location, agreeing on an outdoor wedding near the ocean; we reached those kinds of really big decisions together. But he finally admitted to me that he would prefer to let me do all the "girly" stuff that he didn't have much interest in, which was just fine. I continued to ask his opinion on a lot of things—but I called a lot of the shots myself (with the help of my mom!), and I just hoped Dave would agree with them (which he usually did). Even when my mom and I differed on some of the details, we'd sit back and say, "Let's think about what each of us has in mind, and we'll come back and work it out so everyone's happy!" And we always did!

Everybody had told me in advance that when I went shopping for my wedding dress, I'd know it when I saw it (although I had my doubts about that). On *Days of Our Lives*, I had already worn three wedding gowns on the show, and so I wasn't sure that I was going to have this magical feeling when I finally chose the one for my own wedding. I spent a lot of time visiting different shops and trying on plenty of styles. I listened to everyone's opinions. Luckily, my best friend Carrie was there with me— and more than looking at each dress, she'd look at my face, and she could tell right away if the dress was "the one" or not. Once I had found the dress that I eventually chose, guess what? The first time I tried it on, I knew immediately that this was the one . . . this was the perfect dress for me. I was certain it was right, and I never had any second thoughts.

Dave and I were married in July 2000, and before the big day, *Entertainment Tonight*'s producers contacted me about sending a camera crew to tape

(Robert Sebree)

the event for airing on their show. Well, as I've mentioned, Dave doesn't seek the limelight, but he said OK about the TV coverage, although he did add, "Just don't make me talk a lot!" I know he liked the idea of having professional cameramen cover the wedding from beginning to end (we were promised a copy!), and they sure did a great job—there were shots of me getting ready (with the curling iron working overtime!), images of me walking down the aisle with my father, the vows themselves, the exchange of rings, and the reception afterward, including our first dance. And, of course, there were glimpses of the cast of *Days* congratulating us, and partying into the night.

(Robert Sebree)

Dave's dad and my mom performed a duet during our wedding ceremony. Here we are applauding their beautiful performance.

Of the *Days* cast, Bryan Dattilo, Arianne Zucker, Jensen Ackles, Matt Cedeno, and Josh Taylor were able to attend. I have such a great photo of all us toasting with champagne. And my dad was so cute— he mentioned my *"Days* Dad" in his Father-of-the-

Bride speech. What a day, and thanks to *Entertainment Tonight*, we have a great wedding video, and of course, some wonderful memories. It also meant a lot to me that my fans got to share in our special day when it aired on *ET*!

If you're a young woman thinking about or actually planning your wedding, here's my advice: Never lose sight of the fact that this will be one of the most memorable days of your life. So don't let yourself stress out too much over it. On *Days of Our Lives*, I've taken part in many on-screen weddings that were wrecked by one unbelievable disaster or another—but I just knew that my own wedding was going to be great, and that any minor glitches sure weren't going to spoil the party. Nothing was more important than enjoying the day. And we sure did!

A few months after Dave and I were married, two of my best friends on *Days*—Ari Zuker and Julianne Morris—and I joked with Ken Corday (our executive producer) at a Christmas lunch that we were all going to walk into his office on the same day and announce that all of us were pregnant! Now, wouldn't that have turned his life upside down?!

Friendships and Relationships

When you think of Sami Brady, it's hard to imagine anyone who is more adept at ruining relationships, including her own (OK, maybe there are a few other characters on *Days* who could give her a run for her money from time to time!). Nevertheless, despite Sami's sinister side, fans still often write to me for advice, figuring that I probably bring more

sanity and common sense to these issues than Sami
might.

One subject they ask a lot about is friendships,
although I'm not sure I'm a real authority on the
topic. When I joined the cast of *Days*, I was in my
teens, and even though everyone was very nice to
me, I saw my fellow actors as "work friends"—not
to be confused with "personal friends." I frequently
kept to myself on the studio lot, often doing homework in my dressing room. But I eventually realized
that these cast members were very special people,
and I became much more comfortable around
them. I started hanging out with people like Julianne
and Ari, and today, some of the *Days* cast members
are among my best friends. Those friendships were
there right in front of me the entire time; I just
didn't realize it. Overall, I learned it is more important to have a handful of great friendships than
a plethora of mediocre ones. I work to make time
for my girlfriends and my husband, and they are
all rewarding and meaningful relationships.

But while friendships are a common theme in
my fan mail, there's a much more pressing issue that
girls and young women often ask about—how can
they get guys interested in them? Or how can they
keep boys from hurting them? Or how far should
they go? Or what's the best way to break up or
make up with boyfriends? These letters come mostly
from teenage girls who somehow think that I hold
all the keys to successful dating. (Little do they
know. . . .)

When those letters arrive, however, I do answer
them, and sometimes give some general advice. (I'm
no Dr. Laura, but I do have an opinion about almost everything!) Thinking back to high school,
those teenage years can be such a challenge—just

trying to make good friends, much less having and keeping a boyfriend. In my own case, I was terribly shy and insecure, consumed with the belief that I was overweight and very average looking. When it came to school dances and parties, I certainly wasn't part of the popular crowd, and to me, my life seemed pretty uneventful and uninteresting compared to theirs. I wanted to have more friends than I did.

So I struggled with friendships for such a long time. Having a boyfriend almost seemed out of the realm of possibility—at least that's the way I viewed it. Looking back, I wish I had been a little more assertive with boys. I sometimes tell teenage girls not to be afraid to make the first phone call or the first move with boys. I had such a lack of confidence during adolescence that it never crossed my mind that boys might actually like me. Only years later did I realize that, yes, maybe some of those cute boys in school did give me a second glance from time to time.

> *Dear Ali—I know you'll be married soon so you have experience with relationships. People say I'm pretty nice, but my problem is that guys always hurt me. I've been crushing on a guy from work for a long time. He knows how much I care for him because we're friends. And we dated a lot last summer. But then he started pulling away. Tonight someone made an innocent comment about him having a girlfriend. I felt like I had been punched. So my questions are, "How do you get guys to stay interested in you? How do you know when someone really cares about you or if they're just using you?" This person is someone who knows so much about me. And I always be-*

lieved he cared. He's not just a "talker." Still, why couldn't he tell me the truth?

I know you probably don't get many letters like this one. So I'm sorry. I shouldn't dump my problems on you. I just look up to you and would appreciate any thoughts and advice.

Love, Kelly

When I answer mail like this, I may include comments from the vantage point of someone in her mid-twenties with at least some life experience. More than anything, I tell fans that no matter what their age or circumstances, be true to yourself when it comes to boys and men (and everything else in life, for that matter). I know that's sometimes so hard to do. But step one: I encourage girls to work on building their self-confidence and on liking the person they are.

Too often, of course, we don't make the best decisions when it comes to boys and men. One colleague of mine had a boyfriend who's an actor, and many of her waking hours were devoted to keeping him happy. She had suffered from anorexia in the past, and amid the stress of this relationship, found herself slipping back into eating behaviors that bordered on self-starvation. She tried desperately to compete with the models he dated when he wasn't going out with her. She wanted his attention so badly that she was literally willing to put her own health on the line. All for the "love" of a man.

Another friend had a boyfriend who didn't treat her well at all. In fact, he beat her up, and did it more than once. (How disgusting is that?!) But here's the ironic part: Not only is she beautiful,

outgoing, and funny, she is also one of the strongest and most assertive young women I've ever met—except when relating to her boyfriend. She finally found the strength to untangle herself from that relationship, but when she told me and the rest of our friends about the abuse she had taken, we were so upset that we were ready to kick his ass ourselves! She did eventually learn to stand up for herself, and she has created very healthy relationships for herself since then. (It's like that Christina Aguilera song, "Thanks for making me a fighter!")

I've also known young women who have gone through one imperfect relationship after another

(Author's personal collection)

Future prom king
and queen?

and have become so desperate for marriage that they're willing to settle for something less than what they really want. One of my girlfriends comes immediately to mind. All she wants is to meet the right guy, get married, and raise a family with him. At one point, she tried to convince the rest of us that the man she was dating at the time was perfect for her. Yes, he was very good-looking. Yes, he was definitely in love with her. But there was a "minor" problem: She wasn't in love with him. Even though she really tried to *make* herself love him, it just didn't work. Yet she still drove herself (and at times the rest of us) crazy trying to convince everyone that she could somehow make their relationship work. That's how much she wanted a family, the house in the suburbs and the picket fence.

The dating world really is a jungle at times, isn't it? Maybe I'm lucky that before Dave and I began dating, I really didn't go out that much. I guess you could say that the dating scene wasn't my thing— okay, to be more accurate, I was really picky!! I didn't go out just to be going out. I just didn't enjoy spending a lot of time with someone I wasn't sure I wanted to be with. Yes, there was a group of friends of both sexes who I hung out with a lot—we'd socialize as a group, play volleyball at the beach, or organize a tag football game. I went on individual dates from time to time, but looking back, I was *ultra*selective and not willing to put up with the craziness of dating if it wasn't for real. (No regrets!) In fact, Dave was the first and only man I ever had a serious, long-term relationship with—and I knew right away that he was the person I wanted to spend the rest of my life with!

For most of my life, my best friends have been actors, but I always had trouble seeing myself dat-

ing one. But here's a bit of trivia: If you want to go all the way back to high school, Bryan Dattilo was my date for the prom, and it may have been particularly memorable because a waiter recognized us from our work on *Days!* It was the first "fan experience" for both me and Bryan, and when you're not used to getting that kind of attention, it makes an impression!

A Word About Sex

Well, I know what you're thinking. With all this talk about men, boys, dating, and marriage, what about sex? As with most of these interpersonal issues, I'm not an expert, although you'd think I was, judging by the number of letters I get on the subject.

Here's what I do know: Many young girls are dressing more provocatively these days and seem to be having sex earlier than ever. While sex can be a wonderful and deeply fulfilling experience, it's also something that can undermine your self-esteem if it's not with the right person at the right time. As I sometimes tell teenagers, no matter what your friends are doing, and no matter how much pressure you're feeling, you should always feel free to say no. It's okay to wait if that's what you really want to do. There may be a lot of reasons to have sex, but if you decide to become intimate because you think it will help you keep your boyfriend or because it will help you fit in with one clique or another, that usually doesn't work.

When I was in high school, our teacher in human sexuality class quoted a study that described the ultimate fantasy that girls have for their first time.

Having the right make-up artist and hairdresser are key—I am very lucky to be friends with such talented artists!

Here's what it involved: The love of their life, romantic candles, and a bearskin rug. (Sound familiar?) But according to the study, 90 percent of the girls surveyed never get close to that dream. So I tell girls not to be held hostage by their (or his) hormones, and to use good judgment. Be true to yourself, and don't put yourself in situations that are difficult to get out of. (One recent study found that one in ten girls reported being raped or physically abused on dates.)

The bottom line: Sex is wonderful but it's also pretty serious business (no kidding!). Move at your own pace. Go slowly if that's what feels comfortable. Your time will come. And remember, it's your body. It's your life.

Fashion Statements

As an actress, I have to do photo shoots from time to time, and they can be a fun part of the job. It's a great chance to play dress-up, wearing a lot of different clothes that are provided for you. The costume designers and wardrobe stylists usually bring in a ton of dresses and outfits to choose from—although the stylists I work with on *Days* know pretty well the kinds of clothes I like, and those that I wouldn't wear in a million years.

I've always found these photo shoots to be so liberating. Once I'm in front of the photographer, and he's snapping one roll of 35mm film after another in rapid-fire fashion, it's a time when I can be absolutely uninhibited. I can strike sexy poses. I can make faces. I can act absolutely crazy. What a blast!

At the same time, however, photo shoots can be hard work. You're frequently striking poses and positions that are incredibly uncomfortable and awkward. ("Straighten your arm, okay, balance on your right elbow, now suck in that tummy, arch your neck . . . now look relaxed!!!") I once did a photo shoot in the Pacific Ocean, wearing a mermaid costume; it might have been L.A., but the water temperature was in the mid-50s, and I was so cold and miserable that I'd whimper in between each click of the camera.

On *Days*, we can choose the clothes we wear, but both the wardrobe department and the actors do have to pay very close attention, and here's why. When there's an ongoing story line, I may have to wear the same dress every day for three weeks if that's what the script and the scenes call for; if the story lines are being shot out of order, it can get pretty complicated. There's also the small matter of trying to match the same hairstyle from one day's shooting to the next to maintain story continuity. God bless our makeup staff and hair stylists, who always seem to pull off the impossible.

As if you couldn't guess, I dress very differently than Sami in real life (it's another instance in which Sami and I are very different). When I'm trying on clothes for Sami—to see which ones I'm comfortable wearing and that fit well—I'm judging them as Sami, not as Ali. Clearly, Sami has her own style of dress that's much more revealing and sexier than my own. I'm much more often found in jeans or sweat pants, and Abercrombie & Fitch is one of my favorite clothing stores. But Sami's much more into fashion than I am.

At the same time, whether or not you're an actor, all of us want to look our best. Fashion fads come

and go at supersonic speeds, and sometimes it seems that you can walk out of a mall with a shopping bag filled with new clothes, but by the time you get a chance to wear them, they could be painfully out of style. When I look back at the wardrobe I wore when I started on *Days*, I want to flinch and even laugh out loud. I wore a lot of preppy clothes—khaki pants, polo shirts, penny loafers. You get the picture. Even though the early 1990s weren't that long ago, now the fashions that were so popular then look like they belong in the Smithsonian Institution. Internet message boards are filled with critiques of every outfit that an actress wears, and most of them aren't particularly flattering.

What Are You Wearing?

As I've mentioned, in the stampede to be stylish, so many of today's teenage girls and young women are hooked on eye-catching, seductive, and sexually driven designer clothes. The fashion industry and the pop celebrities of the moment are selling themselves with provocative clothing that certainly gets them noticed—and for better or worse, they are often the trendsetters for girls who may be too young to dress in these same titillating styles. In this grow-up-fast culture, the fashion industry is marketing sex appeal, and many girls (some as young as ten years old and occasionally even younger) act like their world would end if they couldn't wear a Britney Spears look-alike outfit. But sometimes I ask myself, "What happened to their childhood?" I was wearing OshKosh B'Gosh clothing at age nine, and I certainly wasn't concerned about being trendy or

sexy. But today, I swear that Lolita has nothing on some of these kids!

I tell adolescent girls and young women that it's silly to get sucked into a trend, particularly if it makes you cringe a little when you look in the mirror. We all have different body types, and what looks great on Christina Aguilera may be a bit embarrassing on most of us. Don't let Christina or Britney be the sole influence on how you should look in order to fit in. There are ways to be trendy without degrading yourself, and you don't have to reveal as much skin as some of today's superstars do.

Kids often don't realize that they're already beautiful and don't need to go overboard. As for the moms of these young girls, they sometimes tell me, "There's nothing I can do about it—she just wants to wear those Britney-type outfits!" Maybe a preteenager does want to dress that way, but moms can wield more influence than they think, especially since they're probably footing the bill for those overly revealing clothes!

From time to time, some girls actually write to complain that they just don't feel comfortable in the fashions of the day. I remind them that when it comes to fashion trends, the pendulum will swing the other way before long. Back when Madonna was the rage, my friends and I wore bangs (sprayed and teased to the max), rubber bracelets up to our elbows, and so much blue mascara that we actually looked a little scary. Now, I make sure that the old photos of me in that attire are buried deeply in my closet where no one can locate them. Not even me!

If you're a teenage girl, find a style that makes you look good and feel confident. Forget about

what the current generation of Madonnas or other
MTV icons are wearing at the moment, and choose
clothes that are appropriate for your body type.
It's so easy to get swept up by peer pressure and
the clothing craze of the hour, but stick to the fashions that make you feel comfortable. Find clothes
that show *you* off—not the clothes! You might even
ask your mom to help choose your clothing, providing another set of eyes for what looks best on
you. (How's that for sounding square!)

Let me make one other "fashion statement": I
know there are certain kinds of clothes from head
to toe that I look good in, and there are others
that don't belong on or anywhere near my body!
That even goes for shoes. Because I'm not particularly tall, I'm an ideal candidate to wear high heels.
But I hate them! Sometimes I wish they didn't exist!
Yes, I wear them when I have to, but that's not very
often—I'm just not going to ruin my feet and my
back just to fit the image of what someone else
considers to be stylish.

My alternative: As I write these words, I'm wearing a particular pair of sneakers that have been my
shoes-of-choice for months. Sneakers all winter, flip-
flops all summer—that's my official dress code. You
almost have to force me to try something different. But I've learned through hard-earned self-
acceptance that even with those well-worn and
tattered sneakers, I can still look pretty good, feel
comfortable with myself, and spare my feet the unnecessary agony.

When push comes to shove, I'd choose to dress
casually seven days a week if I could. I'm a jeans and
T-shirt kind of gal, and if you spot me in a restaurant
or at a mall, that's probably what I'll be wearing!

Chapter
16

Show business has been my life seemingly forever. But I wouldn't have it any other way. It's so fulfilling. It's so much fun. I truly believe that acting is what I was meant to do, and I'm so lucky to have had the opportunity to be part of the *Days of Our Lives* cast for so many years.

I remember telling a reporter not long ago that I find myself in something of a funny position. In some ways, I feel like a veteran on the show, and just in terms of the length of time I've been on *Days*, I am one of the "old guard." On the other hand, I'm still only 26 years old (as these words are written). At times, as younger and younger cast members have been added, I've thought, "I'm not the teenager, I'm not the new kid on the block anymore." It's been almost like going through a midlife crisis at the age of 26! Yet as each actor joins the show, I've often been able to help them learn

the ropes when necessary, just the way Deidre Hall and some of the others did when I started playing Sami. As I've already acknowledged, Deidre taught me so much, sometimes just by letting me watch her be the true professional she always is, but also by generously giving me instruction when I needed it about some of the basics—camera angles, lighting, hitting your marks, and saying your lines with confidence. I guess at some point, these younger actors will be there to help the next generation of *Days* stars.

Is Show Business in Your Future?

You've heard it before: When selecting a career, you couldn't choose one any tougher than show business. Yet as I mentioned in Chapter 3, parents often ask me whether this is a business that makes sense for their children, and young men and women ask whether they should chase their dreams of an acting career.

I know that I've been more fortunate than most actors—and I'm *so* grateful for the success that I've had. So many of my peers have had their dreams shattered and their spirits crushed by an industry that often seems to treat its talent like yesterday's newspaper. It's not fair, but that's the way it works. Of course, many people are drawn to Hollywood, attracted by the glamour, the celebrity, and the major paychecks they read about. But no matter how successful an actor has been, he or she is always aware that there are a hundred fresh new faces waiting in the wings, eagerly hoping to take the

place of those already there. It can be a ruthless business, and even when careers get off the ground, they are often extinguished long before the actor is ready for it to end.

Jack Lemmon once described his career as "a one-in-a-million shot that worked." Sometimes, the odds seem as imposing as Lemmon suggested. Even so, there are a great many exciting and rewarding aspects to this life. I can't imagine being happier doing anything else. Even if I were still struggling to get my first acting jobs, I don't think I'd have any regrets. Actors have to act. I knew as a child that I wanted to tell stories on the stage or in front of the cameras. So I followed that passion, as so many others do—even when the jobs seem scarce and even when our spirits and morale are challenged.

Are you thinking of giving acting a shot? If you believe in yourself and believe in your talent, and if you feel you have what it takes to make it in this business, I encourage you to go for it. Whether you're seeking your first acting job or already have a growing list of credits, work at developing your craft at every opportunity. That's what I do. Even though I've been a working actress most of my life, there's still so much I want to learn. There are so many good acting teachers and college drama programs that there's no excuse for actors to be untrained. There's no justification for coming to the set or the stage unprepared. There is no reason to do your scenes on the fly, particularly if you want to have longevity in this career. Remember, this is a business, and you need to be ready when opportunities present themselves.

Sharpening Your Skills

Even though I'm able to refine my acting talents five days a week on *Days of Our Lives,* I still take acting lessons whenever I can squeeze them into my schedule. I've been doing that since I was a kid, when my brothers (Sten and Ryan) and I took just about every type of class or private lesson imaginable at one time or another. In my case, there were acting and commercial classes, not to mention piano, voice, ballet, tap, jazz, tennis, gymnastics, and trampoline lessons. I studied the violin for eight years and practiced hours every day. (That's a serious commitment!) I still have so much appreciation for classical music—I remember doing homework to Mozart during much of my childhood—although I did eventually give up music lessons when there weren't enough hours in the day to do it justice.

I'm a firm believer that acting classes are not only a chance to practice and nurture your craft, but it's also valuable to have a skilled acting teacher or coach observing and guiding you. When you're like me—acting consistently, day after day—it would be very easy to get into bad habits. Nothing can take the place of someone with expertise watching what you do, offering constructive criticism, and guiding you on improving your performance. For me, one of the most exciting parts of acting is learning something new, developing my art, and gaining insights into the character I'm playing. And a good acting coach—one with an excellent track record—can analyze my performance, tell me what he or she sees, and help me take my acting to the next level so I'm not just "phoning it in," day after day.

I've always heard that "acting is reacting," and with that in mind, you need to develop the skill to *really listen* to what the other characters on the stage are saying, even though you're familiar with the script from top to bottom. Yes, you know their next line and you certainly know yours—but once the cameras are rolling, you have to make it look as though you've never heard it before. With the help of an acting coach, I've become much better at staying in the moment with my character, keeping her fresh, and avoiding the trap of unconsciously becoming lazy and overrelying on what I've done in the past. There's nothing worse than an actor who resorts to shortcuts or puts the performance on autopilot. If you're not careful, your character can become stale, and audiences sure notice.

My favorite classes are improvisational classes. Improv is such a fun technique—think *Whose Line Is It Anyway?* and you have an idea of how we spend a three-hour class. Whether you want to write, direct, or just become more comfortable speaking in public, improv is a great way to refine your skills and talents. I was even a member of the Los Angeles Theatresports Troupe for a few years, and I still keep in touch with them, still hoping to be able to perform from time to time. If you ever want to be highly entertained some night, go see an improv group—there are tons of sites that can guide you to local theaters. Enjoy!

To stay razor-sharp, I've enrolled in other classes—for example, one-on-one acting classes, group classes, and auditioning classes. I even still take dance classes now and then. OK, without a doubt, I know I'm *never* going to dance professionally, but I feel I can improve and get better at just about anything

if I set my mind to it—and there are actually some acting benefits from my pursuit of dance. Let me tell you, I've made progress in every dance class, and as that has happened, I now have more control over my body and I'm more aware than ever of my posture, where my hands are, where I carry tension, and how my body movements project on camera. That has translated into improvement in my overall acting. There's always something to learn, and I'm always up for a challenge.

If you're an actor—whether you're just starting out or are already enjoying success—search for the learning environment that's best for you. It might be private coaching, or it could involve joining a group class. Whatever you choose, it can be an invaluable learning experience, and one that makes you a better actor. Do what it takes to move ahead—and stay optimistic.

If you don't already have an agent, you'll need one, so ask your actor friends for recommendations. A personal referral will help protect you from the Hollywood sharks—you know, the ones whose scams seem to be featured regularly on *20/20*. Be careful—con artists exist by the hundreds, preying on young people who are naïve about the business and don't really know what to expect and who to trust. About the only thing these pseudoagents are good at is taking your money and making it all sound reasonable. Be careful!

Once you start going on auditions, remember that your mission is to sell yourself. So be positive. Be enthusiastic. Become the actor they want to hire.

At the same time, acknowledge that some disappointments are almost inevitable. You might get rejected a dozen (or maybe a hundred) times for

every acting job you get. Be prepared. Develop some thick skin. Become as resilient as possible if you're going to be in this business to stay.

If the Disappointments Mount . . .

I sometimes advise young actors that it's a good idea to have a fallback position. Listen, you should pursue your acting career with all the enthusiasm and positive energy you can muster, but sad to say, the bolt of lightning spelled F-A-M-E and S-U-C-C-E-S-S doesn't strike everyone. I encourage young people who want to be actors to go to college so they'll have the option to pursue another career if the acting life proves elusive. College is not only a great place to take acting classes, but it presents wonderful opportunities to meet other students and professors you can network with for the rest of your life. There's plenty to learn in college, and a lot of connections you can make during your four years on campus.

As I described in Chapter 4, I had planned to attend college and visited a number of campuses while I was in high school, trying to decide which university would be the best fit. But the opportunity to continue working on *Days of Our Lives* was just too good to pass up, and I decided to put my college dreams on hold. It was a very difficult decision—one of the hardest of my life—particularly because my family (especially my father) is so strongly committed to the value of an education. My dad was also concerned about how I would support myself if my acting career hit a tripwire or two. He felt

that an education is something you can always fall
back on (not to mention recognizing the importance of acquiring knowledge and challenging
yourself each and every day). I love studying and
reading about many topics, so someday I know I'll
find the time to put in my four years at a university! Stay tuned . . .

My dad was certainly right about one thing—actually, he's been right about most things! (Thanks,
Papa! ☺) He knew that the majority of actors don't
have those Jack Lemmon-like careers that span a
lifetime. When you think about it, so many actors
have been on hit TV shows, but once the show has
run its course, they're never heard from again.
Success in one TV series or one motion picture
doesn't guarantee that another acting job is right
around the corner. Actresses in particular seem to
be swimming upstream in a profession where youth
is a huge asset. As I wrote in Chapter 10, there is a
window of opportunity for most actresses, and if
you don't catch the wave in your "prime" (before
the Attack of the Gray Hair and Wrinkles!), your
time as an actress might just pass you by. It's almost
like being a competitive swimmer—age can be an
enemy, and if you haven't won your share of ribbons by your midteens, the people who count may
no longer take you seriously. (So unfair!)

A Little Diversification!

As I've suggested, I'm always up for a challenge!
Sure, acting is my first love, but I also enjoy a little
variety and have never been one to back away from

a show-business dare. If someone tells me I can't do something—well, those are fightin' words! In fact, I've tried some things on television that I once couldn't have imagined myself doing. Here's an example or two: How about eating worms on national TV? Or balancing on a narrow ledge on the 36th floor of a Los Angeles office building?

Well, I can thank *Fear Factor* for providing some of my most death-defying moments on television. Unlike the execution chamber scene on *Days of Our Lives*, or the scenes where Sami was fighting for her life after being struck by a car driven by Austin, the *Fear Factor* segments were for real. They were *really* for real! One slip on that high-rise building, and the only thing between me and a close-up view of the street-level concrete would have been the strength of the safety harnesses.

How did my appearance on *Fear Factor* come about? I met the producer of the show at an NBC party, and I told him how much I loved the show and how grossed out I was watching a recent episode. He must have appreciated my attitude, and sure enough, he invited me to be on an upcoming celebrity episode of the show.

Actually, before *Fear Factor*, you may have seen me on a few game shows, most notably *The Weakest Link*. If you saw that program back in March 2002, you'll remember it as a Battle of the Soaps—some of us from *Days of Our Lives* competed with cast members from *Passions*—all of us playing for our favorite charities. And it was so much fun!! From *Days*, I was joined by Matt Cedeno (ex-Brandon), Jim Reynolds (ex-Abe), and Jason Cook (Shawn). And it really went down to the wire. I fought my way into the final round and ended up playing

against Jim. And let me tell you, I got pretty concerned near the end. The championship was decided on my final question, which was: "What does the 'T' in 'ROTC' stand for?"

Oh, please! I had absolutely no idea!

I took a few seconds to collect my thoughts, and must have raced through a dozen or more words that started with "T". Still no clue. The only word that made any sense was "Training." So what the heck—I took a deep breath and gave it a try!

Amazing! It was the right answer! All of my friends and Dave back in the green room must have been working overtime sending mental-telepathy messages my way for me to get that one right!

James was so nice about it—he was genuinely happy for me. I was so excited to be able to send a big check to the charity I was playing for—the California Highway Patrol 11-99 Foundation. I won $68,500 for the foundation, and every penny went to these wonderful CHP widows and children who can certainly use the help.

Facing Down Fear

When I appeared on the celebrity edition of *Fear Factor,* I played again for the CHP families—and brought home another $10,000 for them. The other celebrities on the show—my rivals—were Stephen Baldwin, Kevin Richardson (of the Backstreet Boys), Ali Landry (*Spy TV*), Kelly Packard (*Baywatch*), and Alan Thicke. It was a wild ride for all of us—so outrageous . . . so thrilling . . . so terrifying. It's the

kind of show where your heart could end up in your throat if you're not careful.

Now, if you remember the opening moments of each *Fear Factor,* there's an announcement that the stunts were designed and supervised by professionals, and because of their danger, they shouldn't be attempted *by anyone at any time.* A standard disclaimer, I assume, but with at least one of those stunts in mind, maybe I should have taken those words to heart. I absolutely came unglued at one point—but I'll get to that in a moment.

So many people have asked me about *Fear Factor* (and still do!) that I'll spend a few pages telling you all about it. If you saw the show, you may remember my opening comments, which were something like, "I don't think my fans are going to be surprised to see me on the show, because my character Sami Brady on *Days of Our Lives* is a villain. She has drugged people, poisoned people, pushed people around, and tried to choke people to death! I've done everything on the show, so now I'm going to give it a shot in real life!"

How's that for an opening?!

Well, I'm pretty competitive. In fact, I made a comment that the women on daytime television sometimes have a reputation for being divas, but I was going to break that stereotype for good and show how tough we really are! But the other celebrities on *Fear Factor* were just as confident—or in the case of Stephen Baldwin, downright cocky (sorry, Stephen, but it's true!). In an off-the-cuff, macho monologue, Stephen proclaimed, "Here's the deal. I don't even have to compete right now because I've already won! Seriously, I might as well go take a nap, because I'm the winner."

Stunt #1

I was absolutely determined to win the Triple Crown on the show, and my confidence level couldn't have been any higher when we began at the foot of a Los Angeles skyscraper and peered up to its stratospheric, nosebleed-level heights. Joe Rogan, the host, explained that we were about to embark on a *Spiderman*-like stunt, climbing out of a thirty-sixth-floor window and inching our way around the outside of the building, tiptoeing on a narrow, one-inch-wide window sill and using overhead handholds along the way. We had three minutes to grab as many yellow flags as possible and transfer them one at a time from the starting point to the finish line. The four contestants who transferred the most flags in three minutes would advance to the next round. In other words, two of us would be heading home very soon.

When it was my turn and I got up to the thirty-sixth floor, I remember looking at the street below and thinking, "My God, it's so far down there," but also telling myself that I could do it. It was pretty intense. It was so challenging. The wind was blowing hard, too, which sure didn't help. But I truly believed that I could polish this one off with no problem. Once I was all hooked up, I stayed determined and resolute. I was completely focused on the task at hand.

Do you remember what happened? I maneuvered on my tiptoes during my entire time on that ledge. It was tough—real tough. After grabbing and delivering the second flag in less time than Kelly did, and giving a thumb's up to the cameraman because I knew I'd done enough to stay in the game, I suddenly lost my grip and careened into

the L.A. sky. Fortunately the safety harness didn't forsake me. I dangled and bounced against the window panes on the lower floors until the crew could pull me in. It actually felt pretty cool hanging in midair, and I was so confident in the safety measures that I didn't freak when I took the plunge.

That entire experience was so amazing, so exciting, so frightening—all at the same time. I remember Kelly saying that the stunt had been so intense that her arms felt just like Jell-O. I know exactly what she meant. More than anything, my calves were killing me, as if they were on fire! Ali Landry admitted that she had said a little prayer before she stepped out onto the ledge, with the street a distant 36 floors below! But this was *Fear Factor*, and none of us expected to be able to coast through it. Kelly and Alan were eliminated and went home after that first round. When I asked Joe who in the world came up with the ideas for these insane stunts, he said, "They have a whole team of freaks!" That sums it up.

By the way, Stephen continued to talk trash throughout that first stunt, and in fact he bet all of us $100 that he would get four flags—but he didn't come close to four (he quit after only two!!). So here's my message to Stephen: "I'm still waiting for my $100, Stephen! You know where to reach me!"

Stunt #2

We moved on to the second stunt, which I'll never forget, and I do mean *never!* It still gives me the creeps just thinking about it. One by one, each of us had to lie down in a Plexiglas "coffin," which the

Fear Factor crew had divided into three sections. From the knees down, thousands of nightcrawlers were poured onto us. Then the middle section was filled with one hundred red and white snakes. And finally (get ready for this!) our head and face were bathed in 3,000 huge Madagascar cockroaches— crawling, hissing cockroaches that were as terrifying as anything I've ever seen (or had crawling all over my face!). The game called for each of us to find and grab the white snakes swarming over our midsection, and put ten of them into a nearby bin as quickly as possible.

Well, I went first (lucky me!). Before I climbed into the box, Joe must have sensed that I was already becoming rattled, and he asked if I was OK. With my voice quivering, I said, "Of course not! You lie down in this empty thing, and then they put these f—ing bugs on your head!"

I wasn't acting. Man, I was *really* scared. Absolutely petrified.

I put on a pair of goggles, and as I stepped into the box, I was already very upset, even before the stopwatch started ticking. Stephen began singing "La Cucaracha" as all the little critters were poured on top of me (Stephen really is *crazy!*). I was wearing a pair of shorts, and I screamed and shrieked as the worms were emptied onto my legs. ("Oh, God, eeahh!") Then the snakes. Then the cockroaches. The roaches were beyond disgusting, crawling all over the place (and all over my face). I've never seen so many hyperactive bugs in my life! I was dying to get started—actually, I was just dying!— and wanted to get this miserable experience over with as quickly as possible.

"Hurry up!" I shouted. "Hurry up!"

At long last, the timer was started, and I frantically

tried to find the white snakes while also slapping the crawling cockroaches away from my mouth and nose. The hissing of the roaches was so scary, and I was starting to lose it. Shouting. Shaking. Panicking. I was a real mess. With those cockroaches all over me, I had definitely met my personal "fear factor."

Finally, I got ten snakes off my midsection and into the bin. My time: 1:54.

At that moment, however, I really didn't care what my time was. I just wanted to escape from that "coffin." *Really* quickly. I began screaming for help in getting me out of the box, but I had to wait until all the snakes and other creatures were removed. So there I was for a few more seconds, with only the cockroaches to keep me company! I began pleading, "Get me out of here! Get me out! NOW!" My shouts were ear-splitting.

Ali Landry was holding my hand and telling me, "Just breathe!" Joe was trying to calm me down, too, saying "Nothing bad is happening to you. It just feels gross. You're fine!"

"Please hurry!" I shouted. "I'm about to seriously FREAK OUT!! Get me out of here!!"

My motor was really racing. Finally, all the snakes were removed and I flew out of the coffin; I could have made the Olympic high jumping team with that leap. I mean, I was so close to totally flipping out. Once I was on solid ground, I hopped in the air a few times, trying to slap any remaining creatures off of me.

That was so petrifying. It took me a few minutes to regain even a bit of composure. I mean it, I was coming out of my skin.

Ali Landry held my hand, and said, "I've never seen anybody freak out like that in my life!" Trying to catch my breath, I remained pretty flustered and

shaken for a while, and mumbled, "Those cockroaches are the most disgusting thing I have ever felt crawling all over my face. Oh, my God! . . . You think you have an idea of how creepy it's going to be—it's maybe 150 times worse!"

Joe seemed stunned by my reaction. "This is the most freaked out I've ever seen anyone on the show." Maybe he was right.

Frankly, I could barely watch the others going through the same stunt. I began to get anxious all over again just seeing the crew pour the bugs and the snakes on Ali. She admitted later that she was afraid of snakes, and she ended up with a scratch on her nose from the cockroaches. But through it all, she stayed pretty calm. Tears came to my eyes while I watched her grab the snakes, one by one, and toss them into the bin. I backed into a corner, crossed my arms over my chest, and tried to keep it together. I admit it, I was bonkers by that point.

Unfortunately for me, all of the other players got their ten snakes into the bin faster than I did. Stephen's time was something like one minute flat! I was crushed by finishing last. I just figured that I had done my best but would be on my way home—and after that experience, I thought maybe it was time!

But then Joe made me an offer. "Ali, since we're playing for charity, if you eat one of these roaches, you can go into the finals." He also promised me that if I ate a roach, he would, too!

Oh, no. Was he kidding? On the one hand, I was excited by the chance to move on to the next round. But I could still hear the roaches hissing. And I started to freak out all over again. I told Joe, "Dude"—(I say "dude" a lot; I'm a Valley girl!)— "Dude, I can't believe you offered me this!"

As I collected my thoughts, I made him a counter-offer. I proposed eating a worm instead of a cockroach. (I have my dad to thank for my negotiating skills!) Joe and I finally settled on me eating three worms—and Joe still eating the cockroach.

"I can't believe I'm doing this," I said. "This is so wrong!" I remember wondering if eating the worms would be bad for my health. I also didn't want to throw up on national television!

The others were egging me on ("This is for your charity, Ali"). So I bounced the worms from one hand to the other for a few moments, then covered my nose and popped the worms in, one by one. Yes, three very wiggly worms. Three very slimy worms.

This is the question I always get—"What did the worms taste like?" Oh, God, they were disgusting! I chewed them as quickly as possible, feeling their nasty, sour juice squirting into my mouth (sorry if that was a little graphic, but it's true!!). I leaped into the air with disgust. I coughed. I gagged. I desperately wanted to put this horrible experience behind me.

Finally, it was done. But it took me a while to recover from that one. A long while. I don't know what I would have done if Joe hadn't agreed to the "three-worm deal" instead of the cockroach. Meanwhile, as he had promised, Joe did eat one of the cockroaches, with each noisy crunch echoing off the walls. He looked like he might lose his lunch, but he got through it. I'm not sure I would have!

Meanwhile, Stephen Baldwin saw me go through all of this, and was stunned by what he had witnessed. Later, here's what he said, word for word:

"This show is totally insane! Alison Sweeney is whacked! Sweeney's the one I'm worried about now.

*If you can freak like that, come back and eat three
worms, anything's possible! That was one of the sexiest things I saw in my life!"*

I guess that was a compliment. With Stephen,
you never know.

By the way, after the cameras were turned off, I
chucked up whatever was in my stomach, including the worms. I didn't want to have nightmares,
wondering what was crawling through my stomach
that night!

Stunt #3

By comparison, the third and final stunt was a
breeze. We had to enter a steel cage, which was then
padlocked and lowered into a large tank of cold
water. Our challenge: Grab a ring of keys, find the
right key to unlock the cage, throw open the door
and swim to the surface and to a nearby buoy.
Stephen went first, and he was pretty awesome. He
completed the stunt in an incredible twenty-four
seconds. He was moving so fast and so frantically
that he cracked his head on the cage and was
bleeding from the forehead when he came to the
surface of the water. But twenty-four seconds—that
would be tough to beat. Yet I still felt confident.

Kevin Richardson fumbled and groped with the
keys and lost his chance of winning (his time: forty-
three seconds). Ali Landry was next, and seemed to
panic once she was underwater and the keys didn't
work right away. After a few moments, she jettisoned
herself through the cage's emergency exit and was dis-
qualified (while the safety divers came to her rescue).

Then it was my turn. I stepped into the cage, gave the thumbs up, and was lowered into the tank. I began working quickly. After just a few seconds, I had opened the lock. With still a little time to spare, I swam furiously to the surface, but made a fatal error: I hadn't thought about where the buoy was when I came out of the cage. I burst through the surface of the water, but had no idea which way to swim. After a few more precious seconds passed, I finally splashed my way to the buoy. My time: twenty-nine seconds—five more seconds than Stephen. He won $50,000 for his charity; I won $10,000 for mine.

After all was said and done, Stephen was still shaking his head. Going into the last stunt, he remained steadfast that I was the only one he was worried about. "If you can bug out, recover, come back, eat three worms, that's hard core! Alison, I think you're terrific. I think you're a rock-solid righteous chick!" Then he added, "Win or lose, this kid is what it's all about!"

That was nice of Stephen to say. But, Stephen, you still owe me $100, buddy!!

Looking back, I'm so proud of getting through all three stunts (especially the second one!). I can't say I loved *every* minute of it (think worms and cockroaches!). But I'd do it again if they asked me to! My time spent bonding with the cockroaches was later repeated on *Fear Factor*'s "Best Of" show, featured as one of the program's most outrageous moments! The executive producer of *Fear Factor*, Matt Kunitz, put it this way: "Alison Sweeney is one of my all-time favorite *Fear Factor* contestants. Even though she was horrified and gave us one of our most outrageous 'fear' moments, she finished the stunt and proved that fear was not a factor for her!"

Chapter 17

Show business is in my blood. I'm sure you've figured that out by now. Even though I've been an actress almost all of my life, I hope that in terms of the length of my career, I'm barely out of the starting blocks, and that this is only the beginning.

Since I've been on *Days of Our Lives*, I've received more awards than I ever could have imagined. As I write these words, I've won the *Soap Opera Digest* Award four times, as well as the Breakout Performer of the Year Award from *Soap Opera Weekly*, and the Best Bad Girl Award from *Inside Soap* (the Australian magazine). My head is still spinning from the twenty-ninth Annual Daytime Emmy Awards in 2002, where the fans themselves voted me an Emmy as America's Favorite Villain. (For all of you who cast your votes for me on the Internet, I'm still saying "thank you"!)

Those awards sure mean a lot to me—just being

(JPI Studios, Inc.)

With the cast of *Days* at the TV Guide Awards

nominated is such an honor—but with my schedule and the demands on my time often so unpredictable, I've sometimes made those awards programs a little more tense and exciting than they need to be. I'll never forget my first *Soap Opera Digest* Awards show, where my older brother Sten was my date. We were running so late (my fault, not his!), and when we finally arrived, the ushers rushed us in, right at the moment my award was announced! I had barely sat down when my name was called as the winner, and I had to get right back up and accept my award. I was a little out of breath and a bit frazzled when I reached the stage, but fortunately my acceptance speech was coherent and resembled the English language for the most part, and I somehow remembered to

thank everyone who I wanted to thank. Everything worked out, but what a close call! By the way, I'd like to be able to tell you that I learned my lesson that year, and that ever since I've been punctual for the annual show—but that would be a lie! I've been late to every *Soap Opera Digest* Award show when I've been a nominee—yes, every one of them—and I'm sure I've raised the blood pressure of the show's producers as the clock ticked and they wondered where in the heck Alison Sweeney was—again! When I've been only a presenter on the show, the pressure's been off, and I've always breezed in with time to spare, ready to hit my mark. But as a nominee, the award show "curse" seems to take me over, and being a late arrival has become something of a way of life. Go figure . . .

Fortunately, critics don't write reviews about showing up late to awards shows, and in fact, I've been lucky to have gotten some fabulous reviews over the years for my acting, although I'm the first to give much of the credit to my talented fellow actors on *Days.* I remember when I read a critique in *Soap Opera Digest* that said, "Sweeney holds her own with the best of them on *Days of Our Lives,* including powerhouse Deidre Hall." Of course, I'm enormously flattered by comments like that. But I know that so much of the praise should go to Deidre and the rest of the cast of *Days,* who have supported me and helped me develop as an actress for more than a decade.

Even more important than the critics, however, are the fans. They're the ones who keep me inspired, who show up at events at NBC or at shopping malls and ask for autographs or for a few moments just to say hello. In June 2003, I took part

in a wild and long weekend in Nashville where fourteen of us from *Days of Our Lives* and *Passions* attended the Country Music Association Fan Fair, where we mingled with fans for the weekend, attended parties (including a crazy one at the Wild Horse), and signed autographs until well past the time when writers' cramp set in. I must have had way too much fun, because after I got back to Los Angeles I couldn't talk for *four days*! Coincidentally, Sami had a throat injury at the same time on the show, too, so the fans never heard my raw vocal cords.

Sami is so much fun for me to play. In some ways, she's a young woman who never really grew up fully. From the first day I began playing her, one of her driving motivations has been to have her parents (Roman and Marlena) be together again. She has always wanted—and always lacked—the love and security of a family unit. She has seen the woman she has become, and blames the shortcomings she sees in herself on the absence of a happy, healthy home life. She is very complex and always a very interesting character to play.

With each passing year, I've become more comfortable playing Sami, and I've brought more of myself into my character. Subtleties in my own personality and characteristics get incorporated into Sami. I often interject my sense of humor and facial expressions into Sami when it's appropriate. I've always been an animated talker, but when I play Sami, I sometimes go over the top with the way that Sami reacts to the world around her (after all, she is an over-the-top character, isn't she?). And by the way, there's much less Sami in Ali than the other way around (thank goodness!). She's a char-

acter who laughs and cries, who loves and hates to the extreme, which is what makes her so interesting.

As for the fans, they continue to feel empathy for Sami one moment, and despise her the next. And it's totally understandable, based on her behavior. She often does the right thing, and she certainly cares about her son. She's also very insecure, and a lot of people can relate to that. Viewers sometimes tell me that they see something of themselves in her. But Sami is also so spiteful and malicious at times that you can't help but hate the hell-raising side of her. When her evil nature surfaces, I know she drives fans absolutely mad! But even after she's been embarrassed and humiliated—and sometimes it gets *really* bad—Sami always picks herself up, dusts herself off, and gets on with life. And that's pretty admirable.

Here's one letter I received not long ago:

> *I love to act, and I would love to get a spot on a soap opera. And who knows, maybe I could end up playing the bitch! I can't wait to see the next show and see what scheme Sami is cooking up next! I love you as an actress; you add that extra special spice to the show. Keep doing what you're doing because you're awesome at it!*
>
> *Your loyal fan,*
> *Heather*

An Unexpected Visitor

As I mentioned earlier, I can get a little star-struck, too. But probably nothing compared to a very mem-

orable recent moment on the *Days* set, when I had a completely unexpected "celebrity sighting." It occurred one afternoon just before Thanksgiving in 2003. We were dry blocking, and Steve Wyman (our co-executive producer) was directing the show that day. I was off-stage at that moment, waiting to make my entrance, when I glanced to my right—and couldn't believe my eyes. Shaquille O'Neal was stepping out of the shadows, and walking in my general direction.

Well, I'm a huge basketball fan—and as it turned out, Shaq is a big *Days* fan. He was on the NBC lot to appear on the *Tonight Show*, and while waiting for his taping to start, he wandered over to the *Days* set. When I caught sight of him, I was absolutely astounded. It's not every day you bump into a 7-foot-1, 340-pound basketball superstar! I rushed over to him and introduced myself while desperately trying to keep my cool. He was so friendly, and as we found out, his wife watches *Days* all the time, and that's how Shaq got introduced to the show.

I wanted to stay and talk with Shaq, but I had to get back to work, darn it. But let me tell you, I was so overwhelmed for a few moments. Other *Days* cast members told me that I was blushing, and I began fanning myself with my script to try to regain my composure.

During the dry blocking, I kept glancing over as Shaq was being given a mini-tour of the set. I tried to pay attention to my work but it was hard. Then I saw that other cast members were getting their photo taken with him, and—well, this was an opportunity I couldn't pass up. I finally said to Steve, "Can I *please* go take a picture with Shaq?"

Steve must have thought I was crazy, but he said, "Sure, go ahead."

That photo with Shaq is one of my all-time favorites. He had his arm around my shoulder, and it just about enveloped my entire upper body. He is so huge!!

The Road to the Future

As I look ahead, I have all kinds of goals for myself. Playing Sami for so many years has been unbelievable. Even though I've been portraying the same character for so long, Sami has changed and grown in a million different ways—and yet she's still the same person at heart (and sometimes that heart is pretty sinister!). But as Sami has evolved, it has given me a chance to develop as an actress as well.

Of course, playing Sami is *never* boring, thanks to escapades like kidnappings, tampering with paternity tests, drugging her older sister's fiancé, trying to sell her baby sister on the black market, and facing her own execution on Death Row. It certainly doesn't remind you of the Waltons, does it?

I'm used to the pace of performing in a one-hour soap every day, but it can still be a challenge. There are thirty pages of dialogue to read and learn each day (I still occasionally have nightmares about forgetting all my lines!). There are early calls that leave no room for sleeping in or idling away the morning hours (6:45 A.M. tomorrow morning as I write this!), and there's certainly no time or tolerance for feeling full of yourself, self-centered, or big-headed. Fortunately, I've always had a strong work ethic, and that keeps me focused on what

needs to be done, day after day, one show after another.

Because *Days* continues to keep me so busy, it's hard for me to find much time for other acting jobs, like guest-starring roles on situation comedies or TV movies of the week. When I was a kid, I went to a lot of auditions and I just loved it (in prekindergarten I jabbered so much—telling random stories whenever I spoke in class—that my teacher finally told my mom, "You know, your daughter talks so much; why don't you take her on auditions and let her make some money from all that chatter?!").

Today, I try to make auditions from time to time, but I work so much on *Days,* I often don't feel it's the best use of my down time to spend three hours at an audition, particularly the so-called "cattle calls" where a hundred actresses may be chasing the same role.

Yes, I do have breaks in the *Days* taping schedule now and then, but they don't occur with the kind of regularity that makes it possible to do much advance planning. It's hard enough to arrange a doctor's appointment, much less prepare for an audition! I've come to terms with the fact that if I'm not going to get to most auditions, that's okay. I'm not going to let myself stress out over it because scheduling conflicts make it impossible for me to be there, or because I've gotten stuck in an L.A. traffic jam that means I'll never make it on time. If it's something beyond my control, it's not worth freaking out over it.

As you can see, I'm working on keeping my life and my psyche in balance. Yes, I still have many, many days when I'm extremely busy at NBC. But I'm also doing better at becoming grounded, and

finding time not only for work but also for family and friends. I've found that when I put too much emphasis on one part of my life—or when I exaggerate the importance of one event over another—it does nothing for my well-being, either physically or emotionally.

As I've told you throughout this book, very early in life I was unusually lucky to discover the career I wanted to pursue. I dreamed of being an actress from the age of four, and I always believed that I would succeed. But while I seemed to have my act together in front of the camera, I was brimming with insecurities inside. I've had to find out who I am and what makes me happy. My life experiences have provided me with insights and the confidence to strive even harder toward my goals.

Not long ago, I showed up for an audition. I read my lines and thought I did pretty well. But apparently the director didn't agree. Another actress got the part—and what did I get from the director? Nothing but a nasty comment or two. Yes, I was bummed out on the drive home. But then I made a conscious decision not to dwell on it and let it ruin my evening. I shook it off and went out to a movie with Dave. I refused to let one person's negative opinion undermine my usually positive frame of mind. It's not worth it, whether it lasts an hour, a day, or much longer. I'm not going to give it more importance than it deserves—not when I have much more significant people and things to take care of in my life, whether it's having a quiet dinner with my husband, or simply enjoying happiness wherever it appears.

For the long term, I'd not only like to build upon my skills as an actress, but (as I mentioned earlier) I also hope to direct someday. Yes, I know what

you're thinking: Doesn't *every* actor in Hollywood want to direct? But this is a path that I'm determined to pursue in the future. There have been times when I've felt that there must be some dark comedies out there waiting for me to direct (that's where my own sense of humor lies!).

I've actually been traveling along the learning curve toward becoming a director for years now. On the set of *Days*, I'm constantly watching our own directors at work and I've taken volumes of mental notes. When opportunities present themselves, I've asked our directors one question after another, and I've learned so much about the creative process from them. They have such enormous talent and so much responsibility, and I've taken every chance to learn from them. And they've been so generous with their time and their expertise.

Fan Feedback

If you haven't already done so, I hope you'll begin spending time on my website: *www.alisonsweeney.com* (at last count, there are about 26,000 unique new visitors to my website each week, and I hope you'll join them). It's a great way to stay in touch and keep up to date on recent happenings in my life and my upcoming personal appearances. One of my favorite parts of being an actress on an afternoon TV show is hearing from and communicating with fans who always seem to have an opinion about what Sami's been up to. I hope you'll drop me a letter or an e-mail from time to time and let me know your ideas about some of the issues I've discussed in this book, as well as what you think about Sami's

latest escapades. I read every letter and answer as many of them as possible.

I'd also like to hear about your own life, your own goals, and how you're working to turn them into reality. I hope this book has inspired you to follow your desires and your heart, and to make the most of the years ahead. I certainly don't claim to be an authority or to have the answer for every question. But as I've spoken to and received letters from so many fans, I realize that there are a thousand ways to make the journey and pursue your dreams, whether your goals are to have a fantastic career, build meaningful relationships, manage your weight, improve your fitness, or simply to find happiness in the world.

Over time, I'm achieving more happiness and more peace of mind. No, I don't have a perfect life. But I've discovered a way of living that works for me. I've come to accept and love myself, no matter what the achievements and setbacks in my career may be . . . no matter how many friends I have . . . no matter what problems I may be facing . . . no matter how much I weigh. The number on the scale, for example, certainly doesn't change who I am; I don't take it personally anymore.

I encourage you to find your own path to happiness and fulfillment. As much as possible, live more in rhythm with the person who you really are and want to become. Listen to your heart and your inner voice, and strive for a life that you find rewarding and meaningful.

In the role of Sami Brady, I did break the mold and the stereotype of what a daytime TV character should be like. I didn't necessarily have to be the nicest, the thinnest, the most secure, or the most popular person in the world for fans to like me.

If it suits you, I'd like to see you break the mold, too. Remember, you can be happy and healthy, even if you don't fit the stereotype of perfection (which *none* of us really does). You don't need to be perfect to have a successful life. You just need to be yourself.

Thank you again to my many fans who have supported me through my life.

Stick around—the plan is for it to keep getting better.

Afterward

Soap 101

There are tons of rumors about *Days of Our Lives* on the Internet and just about everywhere else. For instance, I always find it so entertaining when fans come up with crazy theories and assumptions each time actors leave the show. Were they fired? Or did they leave by choice? Did they have major disagreements with the producers? Did the writers find them difficult to work with? Was money an issue?

There is a lot of fan curiosity about every aspect of the show. In this Afterword, let me address some of the issues that fans most often ask about. Throughout this book, I've already described much of what goes on behind the scenes and on the set. But let me spend a few more pages describing the exciting life and hectic pace of being an actor on *Days*.

When an actor joins a soap, the standard contract is for three years, and the first contract is broken into thirteen-week cycles. This means that while the actor commits to the producer for three years, the producer reserves the right to fire the actor every thirteen weeks (in subsequent contracts, the 13-week cycles may be replaced by twenty-six-week periods). In the contract, the actor is also guaranteed a minimum number of episodes that he'll appear in during every 13-week cycle, and the actor gets paid in full, even for episodes that were promised but never materialized. If the producer decides to terminate the actor's contract at the end of a thirteen-week cycle, the actor has to be notified six weeks before his or her tenure on the show ends.

I've been fortunate to be on *Days* since I was sixteen years old—more than a decade now. And as I've mentioned earlier in the book, we have a very cohesive, tightly knit cast, with none of the cutthroat atmosphere you hear about on other shows. There's no competition for so-called "front-burner" vs. "back-burner" story lines because the writers constantly cycle all the characters so each of us has our moments to be front and center with one story line or another. You have to be patient, but everyone's opportunity comes up with regularity.

The *Days* actors aren't on the set every day—only on those days where our characters are in the episode being taped. So we sometimes find ourselves with two to three days off a week, but with little advance notice. We may get our schedules two weeks (or sometimes less) ahead of time, so trying to schedule a dentist's appointment or a long weekend getaway is often a fly-by-the-seat-of-our-pants experience.

The producers are contractually obligated to give each actor two weeks of vacation a year, but they're not necessarily the two weeks you want, and most certainly not two weeks in a row. You better ask way in advance if there's a particular week you want to travel to a family reunion or wedding, for example. With advance notice, the scripts can be shaped to work around your absence. Or the producers may pre-tape your scenes so your character never misses an episode and the audience never knows you're gone.

The show goes on hiatus two weeks a year at Christmas. Everyone gets those two weeks off. To make that possible, we tape ten extra episodes a year—usually six episodes in a five-day period, or sometimes we work Saturdays to create a back-log of extra shows so we can spend the two weeks at Christmas with our families.

Before the actors see the scripts, of course, the writers have spent a lot of time creating and fine-tuning every word. Our head writer—Jim Reilly—as well as the outline writers and the dialogue writers all take their turns sharpening each script before it ends up in the actors' laps.

At *Days*, our writers are very receptive to input from the actors, and not just when we feel that our character would say a particular line a little differently. At times, the dialogue writer may not have a comprehensive picture of our character's history or a total recall of what may have happened to our character on an episode he or she didn't work on.

I remember one episode revolving around one of Sami's "non-weddings" to Austin, and I had a huge two-page monologue to memorize, where Sami pleads with Austin not to tell her family about the terrible things she had done that made Austin want

to break up with her before reaching the altar. In
the script, Sami recaps the difficult life she has led
in a plea for sympathy from Austin, and in hopes
that he and her family would not judge her too
harshly.

I memorized this entire two-page monologue
(not to mention the rest of the episode, which had
plenty of Sami dialogue), and when I arrived on
the set on Monday to shoot the scene, Drake
Hogestyn told me, "I'm sorry, Ali, this script is all
wrong—you can't say some of these lines because
that's not what happened. This isn't what took
place in Sami's childhood on the show."

Well, I wasn't on *Days* when my character was a
little kid, and there had been some very complicated story lines that were there before my time.
Drake was around for those early episodes, and so
he made a lot of suggestions for revisions.

We were so grateful that Drake had caught these
errors. But after spending the entire weekend memorizing my monologue, I had about ten minutes to
change gears and memorize the hurriedly revised
script! To make my task even more difficult, I was
just memorizing words, and had no visual context
to put them in. In general, to help me learn my
lines, I can usually call on *Days* scenes that I remember from the past, and I can use them to assist me
in committing the new lines to memory. But this
new task was a real challenge. Eventually, it was
mission accomplished, but it wasn't easy!

At times, mistakes do slip by everyone—except
the fans, that is. One year at Christmas, Sami had a
line where she said, "I hate egg nog!" Well, in a scene
the following year, I carried some egg nog and
poured it into a glass in the background of a scene.
And leave it to our fans! I got a letter from a viewer

who remembered that Sami hated egg nog! I guess our fans are our ultimate fact-checkers.

I know that I'll never lose sight of the fans and how important they are to the success of the show. Yes, we often work very hard and very long hours. But none of us has anything to complain about. It's a great job, and it's so wonderful being part of the lives of our millions of viewers five days a week. I'm a very lucky person—and I know it.

Kensington Profiles:
The Rich and Famous

Love, Betrayal and Forbidden Passion Are Now Available... At Your Local Bookstore!

Are you looking for more titles by

NORA ROBERTS

Don't miss this chance to order additional stories by
one of Silhouette's favorite authors:

Silhouette Intimate Moments®

#07397	+SUZANNA'S SURRENDER	$3.29	☐
#07433	UNFINISHED BUSINESS	$3.39	☐

Silhouette Special Edition®

#09685	+FOR THE LOVE OF LILAH	$3.29	☐
#09768	*CAPTIVATED	$3.39	☐
#09774	*ENTRANCED	$3.39	☐
#09810	§FALLING FOR RACHEL	$3.39	☐

Silhouette® Books

#48232	†DANCE TO THE PIPER	$2.95	☐
#48238	NORA ROBERTS 2-IN-1	$4.50	☐

Nora Roberts Language of Love

#51001	IRISH THOROUGHBRED	$3.59	☐

+The Calhoun Women
*The Donovan Legacy miniseries
§Those Wild Ukrainians miniseries
†The O'Hurleys miniseries
(limited quantities available on certain titles)

TOTAL AMOUNT	$
POSTAGE & HANDLING	$
($1.00 for one book, 50¢ for each additional)	
APPLICABLE TAXES**	$ _____
TOTAL PAYABLE	$ _____
(check or money order—please do not send cash)	

To order, complete this form and send it, along with a check or money order
for the total above, payable to Silhouette Books, to: *In the U.S.*: 3010 Walden
Avenue, P.O. Box 9077, Buffalo, NY 14269-9077; *In Canada*: P.O. Box 636,
Fort Erie, Ontario, L2A 5X3.

Name: _____

Address: _____ City: _____

State/Prov.: _____ Zip/Postal Code: _____

**New York residents remit applicable sales taxes.
Canadian residents remit applicable GST and provincial taxes.

NRBACK1

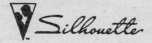